THE COLLECTED LETTERS OF THOMAS AND JANE WELSH CARLYLE

Oil portrait of Thomas Carlyle by John Linnell, 1843. National Gallery of Scotland.

THE COLLECTED LETTERS OF THOMAS AND JANE WELSH CARLYLE

DUKE-EDINBURGH EDITION

EDITORS

CLYDE DE L. RYALS

Duke University

KENNETH J. FIELDING

University of Edinburgh

ASSOCIATE EDITORS

IAN CAMPBELL

University of Edinburgh

AILEEN CHRISTIANSON

University of Edinburgh

HILARY J. SMITH

Duke University

VOLUME 16

January–July 1843

DUKE UNIVERSITY PRESS
DURHAM AND LONDON
1990

Printed in the United States of America
on acid-free paper ∞
LC 71-101132 ISBN 0-8223-0702-2
This publication has been supported by the
National Endowment for the Humanities, a federal
agency which supports the study of such fields as
history, philosophy, literature, and languages.

CONTENTS OF VOLUME 16

ACKNOWLEDGMENTS

The editors wish to express their continued appreciation to individuals and institutions acknowledged previously. In addition, there are some who deserve particular mention. Among these are the National Library of Scotland and Dr. Iain Brown; the Edinburgh University Library and John Howard, Keeper of Special Collections; Carlyle's House, Chelsea, and the National Trust and Colonel Bruce Holford-Walker and Mrs. Geraldine Elwes; and Joe Rees. Since the last set of volumes special thanks are also due to the University of Edinburgh General Council Appeal for its extremely generous support of the project in 1988–89, and to the University of Edinburgh Development Fund, Dr. Diana Henderson and her staff, especially Alistair Lawson. Further acknowledgments will be due on publication of the next set of volumes, but among those who can already be thanked are the Pilgrim Trust; the British Academy; the Carnegie Trust for the Universities of Scotland; the Saltire Society; Emmanuel College, Cambridge; and among individuals Professor Carlisle Moore and Eluned M. Brown. Continued help has also been received, in other ways, from John Hall, new Sub-Librarian of Cambridge University Library, and Timothy Hobbs, Sub-Librarian, Trinity College, Cambridge.

INTRODUCTION

Full as the record of the Carlyles seems, they are unknown in many ways, and the present set of volumes continues to show what a high proportion of their letters is new to readers. The introduction to volumes 13 to 15 reviewed the situation at that stage, when we claimed that as many as 70 percent of their letters had not been completely printed before and that well over half had not been previously published. Of 633 letters in the present set, over 42 percent have never appeared before: 233 by Thomas and 37 by Jane; and of the remainder though 22 percent can be found with some difficulty in various collected volumes, the others have appeared incomplete, so that once more well over half these letters are only now delivered to whatever new readers they will find.

It might possibly be said that they tell a familiar story, with no other advantages than being complete, correctly transcribed, properly dated, explained and chronologically arranged. But this would hardly be true. They are also qualitatively different, affecting our judgment of the writers and their times. The Carlyles have often been seen as typically and conventionally Victorian; but the question arises whether we know either of them well enough for such judgments. Some of their activities are certainly unfamiliar.

As Jane, for example, begins to play a greater part in these years, the emphasis falls differently; more of her letters began to be kept and, as well as having an increasingly prominent role in Carlyle's circle, she developed one of her own. Among many who belonged to it were her feminist Liverpool and Manchester friends, Elizabeth Paulet and Geraldine Jewsbury, with whom she had meant to write a novel after the manner of George Sand; and although Jewsbury was left to finish it alone, she continuously discussed it with Jane, who arranged with Chapman and Hall for the publication of the three-volume *Zoe* in 1845. It is only recently that we have begun to appreciate the extensive influence of Sand on early Victorian fiction and opinion, which with Jane Carlyle was reinforced by her friendships with Mazzini and Godefroy Cavaignac, who knew the French writer personally; but she was also generally alert to advanced ideas from France, Germany and Italy. It would be wrong to overstress her liberality, but we can find similar feelings focused through such friends as Anna Jameson or correspondents such as the novelist Martha Lamont, congratulated by Jane for her protests at male complacency (17:222–23).

This is only one example and it would be easy to illustrate Jane's originality and independence, whether in her personal behavior, moral and religious opinions, or political judgments in which she differed little from her husband. It is less usual to recognize that Carlyle himself was a spokesman for independence and political freedom. Their friendship with the Italian revolutionary Mazzini was chiefly kept up by Jane, but it was Carlyle who took a strikingly outspoken liberal position on the British government's interception of Mazzini's mail. Carlyle's letter to the *Times* (18:72–4) was strongly effective in its support of justice and liberty, and was repeated in private company with a reproof to the arrogant Lady Holland for absurdly believing the slander that Mazzini had "kept a gaming-house": "the proudest person" in their company could not be further above it than Mazzini (18:115–6).

We are reminded that in these years Carlyle was seen as a champion of national independence, and was the friend of many European revolutionaries, German, French, Polish, and Italian. We notice his caring little for the Prussian ambassador ("Alas, Bunsen is not beautiful to me!" [18:295]), but much for Richard Plattnauer, a Prussian political exile, even to the extent of cheerfully welcoming him to their own home after Plattnauer's cautious release from a lunatic asylum. Much of this independence came from Carlyle's Scottishness, his "Covenanting" sympathies, or can be found in his attraction to the seventeenth-century Puritan revolution; and his essential truth and integrity were recognized at this time in *Past and Present* and were to attract even the national and revolutionary leaders of Young Ireland (Gavan Duffy and others) who were to meet him in 1845.

The Scottishness of the Carlyles has had surprisingly little attention, and for the moment can have no more than a momentary reference. But these were the heroic years of the Disruption of the Scottish Church, when more than a third of its ministers were ready to give up their homes and stipends in the cause of independence. To the visiting American Julia Ward Howe it seemed a rather inexplicable "movement tending to disestablishment" (16:184), but to Jane it was a concern for tears (16:275–6), and to Carlyle, as to many of his countrymen—for he cared little for the Church itself—a matter of national pride and independence. He rises to admiration at the "lump of an old woman, half-haveril [idiot] half-genius" who acted in defiance of the great magnate the Duke of Buccleuch by giving for a new church the only unoccupied patch of ground he did not control: " 'I got it from the Lord and I will give it to the Lord';—and there the Free Kirk it seems in spite of Duke and Devil is to be!" (17:102).

Carlyle's published works can speak for themselves, but the letters of this time show the completion and reception of *Past and Present* and the end of his persistent struggle to find the right form for his work on the Cromwellian period; and only by collecting the letters and studying them with his scattered drafts for *Cromwell* has it been possible to see why he found the book so difficult to write. In both *Past and Present* and *Cromwell* he turned from history to fundamental questions of the day: "There is no use in writing of things past," he told Emerson, "unless they can be made in fact things present" (14:229). Nor was his radicalism confined to the rhetoric of the published works. His chosen correspondents were often radical or reformist, such as Samuel Bamford, friends such as Mill, Harriet Martineau, the Wedgwoods, or the younger Charles Buller, or Thomas Ballantyne, the free-trading liberal editor of the *Manchester Guardian*.

Both the Carlyles carried their convictions into practice. His sense of distress among the people runs through his letters, like his recollection in *The French Revolution* of how the voice of the Viennese populace "crying to their Kaiser: Bread! Bread!" had given Glück "the ground-tone of the noblest passage" in his opera *Iphégenie en Aulide* (*Works* 2:194). Early in 1843 such distress seemed less in London than elsewhere, "yet you cannot walk along the streets without seeing fearful symptoms of it. I declare I begin to feel as if I should not hold my peace any longer" (16:6). As best they could, both he and Jane tried to help individuals directly, and both were closely bound to Carlyle's family—shopkeeping, tenant-farming and housepainting in Scotland—who kept them in touch with everyday realities.

Carlyle writes to his emigrant brother Alick, "No abatement . . . yet visible of the *Universal* distress. Rejoice that you are out of it"; for the younger brother and family had felt driven to leave for North America. Most of the letters they exchanged have been published before; but we can now see how the whole Carlyle family was involved, not only giving financial help but in preparation, obtaining expert advice, helping with the actual departure and continued communication which was eventually to lead to a family reunion through the marriage of Carlyle's Scottish niece Mary Aitken to Alick's son Alexander, who went on to live with him at 5 Cheyne Row and edited many volumes of his letters. Nor was it only Alick who experienced emigration: he had been preceded by their elder stepbrother, John, their brother-in-law Robert Hanning, numerous friends, and several more distant relatives. There is, in fact, no other collective contemporary record which so vividly tells what the experience of emigration meant, from the scene of departure among their tearful neighbors (16:214) to Carlyle's imagining (from his brother's description) the family on their new farm, "planting Indian corn, the Father digging holes, and the little ones dropping-in grains" (18:186). It is an aspect, like others, neglected by historians.

These are no more than a few examples of many changes in our conception of the Carlyles and their times which biography has not been able to take into account; and, extensive as the whole archive is, new letters are still being found. The last set of volumes made use for the first time of a large collection of family letters which came from a solicitor's office in Arbroath. The present one begins to draw on the vast correspondence of both Carlyles with the Barings and Ashburtons, to which we have been able to add many letters previously unknown. Later volumes will begin to reveal much more of the remarkable circle which gathered round the Ashburtons.

The introduction to volume 13 briefly mentioned the extent to which texts in various collections of the letters have been bowdlerized or modified for the convenience of both biographers and editors, and this continues to be apparent. In the present volumes we have continued to follow, as exactly as possible, what the Carlyles wrote. As Jane's letters increase in relative extent, her misspellings and other eccentricities begin to be an embarrassment, but only a proportion of them are noted. It is hoped that readers will feel that they can trust the editors and will not be inconvenienced.

One editorial complexity connected with Jane was not explained in the introduction to the first volume. Almost all of her letters are given from her own manuscript, but many of the notes that Carlyle wrote for them are taken from what are referred to in the headnotes as "longhand copies" in the Berg Collection of the New York Public Library (and which in subsequent volumes will be referred to as "copies"). These were from copies of the letters made for Carlyle and bequeathed to Froude, who had agreed to finish Carlyle's undertaking, most of which eventually appeared, mainly as the *Memorials of Jane Welsh Carlyle Prepared for Publication by Thomas Carlyle edited by James Anthony Froude*. In fact, as Alexander Carlyle tells us and newly discovered papers confirm, there were once two such sets of copies, though the second, less-complete one now seems lost. Hence it arises that we have a partial explanation for the survival of some of Carlyle's notes as recorded by Froude even when they are not to be found with the copied letters in the Berg Collection. If this mainly concerns the editorially minded, it raises the hope that there may be still further letters of the Carlyles yet to be found and added to their great record.

K.J.F.

LETTERS TO THE CARLYLES
1843–1844

From	*To*	*Source*	*Date*
Geraldine Jewsbury	JWC	Ireland 145–52	[3 Jan. 1843]
William Graham	TC	NLS 1766.110, 112	7, 9 Jan. 1843
Letitia Macready	JWC	NLS 1891.180	19 Jan. 1843
Frances Wedgwood	JWC	NLS 1891.182	[24 Jan. 1843]
Giuseppe Mazzini	JWC	NLS 1893.98	[mid-Feb. 1843]
A. J. Scott	TC	State Univ. of Iowa	[22 Feb. 1843]
R. W. Emerson	TC	RWEMA	26 Feb. 1843
Lord Monteagle	TC	State Univ. of Iowa	[3 March? 1843]
Anna Maria Hall	JWC	State Univ. of Iowa	6 March 1843
John Davidson	TC	NLS 1766.114	8 March 1843
K. A. Varnhagen von Ense	TC	Yale	12 March 1843
John A. Carlyle	TC	NLS 1775A.268	[17 March 1843]
James Booth	TC	NLS 1773.191	5 April [1843]
Charles Dickens	TC	Hist. Soc. of Pa.	18 April 1843
J. G. Lockhart	TC	A. Lang, *Life and Letters of J. G. Lockhart* (1897) 2:238–9	27 April 1843
R. W. Emerson	TC	Slater, *CEC* 341–4	29 April 1843
R. W. Emerson	TC	Slater, *CEC* 344	30 April 1843
Julia Strachey	TC	NLS 1773.335	7 May [1843]
John A. Carlyle	TC	NLS 1775A.271	11 May 1843
Francis Jeffrey	TC	NLS 1766.116	12 May [1843]
C. K. J. Bunsen	TC	NLS 1766.119	15 May 1843
John A. Carlyle	TC	NLS 1775A.274	19 May [1843]
John A. Carlyle	TC	NLS 1775A.277	23 May [1843]
John A. Carlyle	TC	NLS 1775A.292	[24 or 31 May 1843]
T. S. Spedding	TC	John Spedding	26 May 1843
Charles Buller	[TC?]	Huntington Lib.	5 June [1843?]
John A. Carlyle	TC	NLS 1775A.280	12 June 1843
John Morgan	TC	NLS 1766.122	14 June 1843
John A. Carlyle	TC	NLS 1775A.282	[17 June 1843]
John A. Carlyle	TC	NLS 1775A.284	21 June 1843
John A. Carlyle	TC	NLS 1775A.286	22 June 1843
Alexander Carlyle	TC	NLS 665.55	24 June 1843
D. L. Richardson	TC	NLS 1766.123	24 June 1843
J. G. Lockhart	TC	Lang, *Lockhart* 2:225–26	[June? 1843]
John A. Carlyle	TC	NLS 1775A.287	27 June [1843]
Geraldine Jewsbury	JWC	Ireland 85–88	[27 June? 1843]
John A. Carlyle	TC	NLS 1775A.289	1 July [1843]

From	*To*	*Source*	*Date*
John Sterling	JWC	NLS 602.102	[2 July 1843]
C. K. J. Bunsen	TC	Yale	4 July [1843]
W. E. Forster	TC	NLS 1766.124	7 July 1843
C. K. J. Bunsen	TC	NLS 1766.126	7 July 1843
Betty Braid	JWC	NLS 602.108	10 July 1843
Swynfen Jervis	TC	NLS 602.112	11 July 1843
Jeannie Welsh	JWC	NLS 602.111	[12 or 13 July 1843]
Jane Wilson	TC	NLS 602.113	[ca. 12 July 1843]
Edward FitzGerald	TC	NLS 665.67	[ca. 16 July 1843]
W. M. Thackeray	JWC	NLS 665.49	25 July 184[3 or 6?]
Giuseppe Mazzini	JWC	NLS 1892.56	Mon. [31 July? 1843]
Giuseppe Mazzini	JWC	NLS 1892.63	[early Aug.? 1843]
Frances Wedgwood	JWC	NLS 1892.65	Wed. [9 Aug.? 1843]
W. E. Hickson	TC	NLS 602.127	10 Aug. 1843
R. W. Emerson	TC	Slater, *CEC* 344	15 Aug. 1843
John Leitch	TC	FC	24 Aug. 1843
Charles Redwood	TC	NLS 602.135	28 Aug. 1843
John A. Carlyle	JWC	NLS 602.137	29 Aug. 1843
Amalie Bölte	JWC	NLS 602.138	30 Aug. 1843
Edward FitzGerald	TC	Terhune, *LEF* 1:397–98	[2 Sept. 1843]
Thomas Erskine	TC	NLS 1773.246	[7 Sept. 1843]
Edward FitzGerald	TC	Terhune, *LEF* 1:398–99	9 Sept. 1843
K. A. Varnhagen von Ense	TC	NLS 665.56	16 Sept. 1843
Margaret A. Carlyle	TC	NLS 1763.241	[21? Sept. 1843]
Jean Carlyle Aitken	TC	NLS ACC. 9086.36	6 Oct. 1843
Geraldine Jewsbury	JWC	Ireland 74–77	[17 Oct. 1843]
Henry Cole	TC	NLS 665.57	24 Oct. 1843
R. W. Emerson	TC	RWEMA	30 Oct. 1843
Edward Bulwer-Lytton	TC	H. G. Fiedler, "Friendship of T.C. and V. von Ense" *MLR* 37 (1943):35n	[ca. Nov. 1843]
Thomas Erskine	TC	NLS 1766.127	8 Nov. 1843
Mary E. Lambert	TC	NLS 1892.93	11 Nov. 1843
Henry Sutton	TC	FC	13 Nov. 1843
B. W. Procter	TC	NLS 1766.129	17 Nov. [1843]
Marmaduke Wright	TC	NLS 1766.130	21 Nov. 1843
George Hobson	TC	NLS 1766.132	22 Nov. 1843
Giuseppe Mazzini	JWC	NLS 1892.26	[5 Dec. 1843]
John Sterling	TC	*Life of Sterling, Works* 11:254–6	7 Dec. 1843
Susan Long	[JWC?]	NLS Acc. 8140	21 Dec. 1843
Catherine Macready	JWC	NLS 1892.112	[30 Dec. 1843]
R. W. Emerson	TC	RWEMA	31 Dec. 1843
Edward FitzGerald	TC	FC	3 Jan. 1844
Geraldine Jewsbury	JWC	Ireland 96–101	[9–10 Jan. 1844]
Jean Carlyle Aitken	TC	NLS 1775A.294	14 Jan. 1844

From	*To*	*Source*	*Date*
Janet Carlyle Hanning	TC	NLS 1775A.296	15 Jan. 1844
John Hawkshaw	TC	NLS 1766.134	22 Jan. 1844
John A. Carlyle	TC	NLS 2883.300	[24 or 31 Jan. 1844]
Charles Dickens	JWC	NLS 665.58	27 Jan. 1844
K. A. Varnhagen von Ense	TC	H. G. Fiedler, "Friendship," *MLR* 38 (1943):34–35	4 Feb. 1844
Geraldine Jewsbury	JWC	Ireland 101–8	[11 Feb. 1844]
Geraldine Jewsbury	JWC	Ireland 169–71	[18 Feb. 1844]
Geraldine Jewsbury	JWC	Ireland 112–16	[25 & 26 Feb.? 1844]
Henry Cole	TC	Pierpont Morgan Lib.	28 Feb. 1844
R. W. Emerson	TC	RWEMA	29 Feb. 1844
Geraldine Jewsbury	JWC	Ireland 108–11	2 [1] March 1844
Geraldine Jewsbury	JWC	Ireland 116–19	[3 March 1844]
Margaret A. Carlyle and James Carlyle	TC	NLS 1763.231	15 March 1844
Jean Carlyle Aitken	TC	NLS 1775A.298	17 March 1844
Geraldine Jewsbury	JWC	Ireland 157–60	20 March 1845 [1844]
Edward FitzGerald	TC	Terhune, *LEF* 1:429	20 March 1844
Jean Carlyle Aitken	TC	NLS 1775A.300	25 March 1844
Lady Ashburton	JWC	NLS 1892.183	Friday [April? 1844]
Edward Bulwer-Lytton	TC	NLS 5509.121	[mid-April 1844]
Frances Wedgwood	JWC	NLS 1892.185	Monday [15? April 1844]
Geraldine Jewsbury	JWC	Ireland 120–25	Friday [19 April 1844]
Francis Jeffrey	JWC	NLS 787.86	13 May [1844]
Geraldine Jewsbury	JWC	Ireland 77–81	[26–31 May 1844]
Geraldine Jewsbury	JWC	Ireland 125–27	[2 June 1844]
Geraldine Jewsbury	JWC	Ireland 127–30	[10 June 1844]
Geraldine Jewsbury	JWC	Ireland 130–32	14 June 1844
Giuseppe Mazzini	JWC	NLS 2883.151	[14? June 1844]
R. W. Emerson	JWC	Berg	19 June 1844
Edwin Chadwick	TC	Univ. Col., London	20 June 1844
Geraldine Jewsbury	JWC	Ireland 133–35	[20 June 1844]
Geraldine Jewsbury	JWC	Ireland 135–36	[23 June 1844]
H. F. Cary	TC	NLS 2883.152	24 June 1844
S. Sketchley	JWC	NLS 602.154	[29 June 1844]
Catherine Dickens	JWC	NLS 602.157	1 July 1844
Lady Munro	TC	NLS 1774.45	1 July 1844
Mary Ann [Phoebe] Chorley	JWC	NLS 602.155	[1 July 1844]
Geraldine Jewsbury	JWC	Ireland 137–38	[4? July 1844]
H. F. Cary	TC	NLS Acc. 8140	9 July 1844
Margaret A. Carlyle	TC	NLS 1763.243	[11 July 1844]
Geraldine Jewsbury	JWC	Ireland 139–42	[21 July 1844]
T. S. Spedding	TC	John Spedding	18 July 1844

From	*To*	*Source*	*Date*
Alfred Tennyson	TC	NLS 665.59	7 Aug. [1844]
John Sterling	TC	NLS 1766.136	10 Aug. 1844
Charles Spring Rice	TC	Yale	12 Aug. 1844
Elizabeth Barrett	TC	Yale	14 Aug. 1844
James Baillie	JWC	NLS 1892.252	24 Aug. 1844
Elizabeth Barrett	TC	Yale	[ca. 24 Aug. 1844]
John Sterling	TC	NLS 1766.139	26 Aug. 1844
A. C. Sterling	TC	NLS 1766.145	30 Aug. 1844
R. W. Emerson	TC	RWEMA	1 Sept. 1844
John A. Carlyle	TC	NLS 602.173	11 Sept. 1844
Thomas Erskine	JWC	NLS 602.175	13 Sept. 1844
A. C. Sterling	JWC	NLS 1766.148	28 Sept. 1844
Geraldine Jewsbury	TC	Ireland 142–44	17 [29] Sept. 1844
R. W. Emerson	TC	RWEMA	30 Sept. 1844
Philip Pusey	TC	NLS 665.60	[14 Oct. 1844]
John A. Carlyle	TC	NLS 1775A.304	[7 Nov. 1844]
John A. Carlyle	TC	NLS 1775A.302	8 Nov. [1844]
S. Gambardella	JWC	NLS 1892.280	[22? Dec. 1844]
R. W. Emerson	TC	RWEMA	31 Dec. 1844

KEY TO REFERENCES

Berg. Berg Collection, New York Public Library.

Bliss, *JWC.* Bliss, Trudy, ed. *Jane Welsh Carlyle: A New Selection of Her Letters.* London: Gollancz; New York: Macmillan, 1950.

Bliss, *TC.* Bliss, Trudy, ed. *Thomas Carlyle: Letters to His Wife.* London: Gollancz; Cambridge, Mass.: Harvard Univ. Press, 1953.

Boswell, *Life of Johnson.* Ed. C. B. Tinker and R. W. Chapman. Oxford Standard Authors, rev. edn. London, New York: Oxford Univ. Press, 1953.

A. Carlyle, *CMSB.* Carlyle, Alexander, ed. *Letters of Thomas Carlyle to John Stuart Mill, John Sterling, and Robert Browning.* London: T. Fisher Unwin, 1923.

A. Carlyle, *CS.* Carlyle, Alexander. "Thomas Carlyle and Thomas Spedding." *Cornhill Magazine* 50 (1921):513–37, 742–68.

A. Carlyle, *LL.* Carlyle, Alexander, ed. *The Love Letters of Thomas Carlyle and Jane Welsh.* 2 vols. London and New York: John Lane, 1909.

A. Carlyle, *NL.* Carlyle, Alexander, ed. *New Letters of Thomas Carlyle,* 2 vols. London and New York: John Lane, 1904.

A. Carlyle, *NLM.* Carlyle, Alexander, ed. *New Letters and Memorials of Jane Welsh Carlyle.* 2 vols. London and New York: John Lane, 1903.

Carlyle, *Historical Sketches.* Carlyle, Thomas. *Historical Sketches of Notable Persons and Events in the Reigns of James I and Charles I.* Ed. Alexander Carlyle. London: Chapman and Hall, 1898.

Carlyle, *Reminiscences.* Carlyle, Thomas. *Reminiscences.* Ed. C. E. Norton, intro. Ian Campbell. London: Dent, 1972. Repr. of Everyman text (London: Dent, 1932).

Carlyle, *Works.* Carlyle, Thomas. *Works.* Centenary Edition, 30 vols. London: Chapman and Hall, 1896–99.

Carlyle's House. Illustrated Memorial Volume of the Carlyle's House Purchase Fund Committee, with Catalogue of Carlyle's Books, Manuscripts, Pictures and Furniture Exhibited Therein. London: Carlyle's House Memorial Trust, [1897].

Chambers, *CRC.* Chambers, C. E. S. "Carlyle and Robert Chambers: Unpublished Letters." *Littell's Living Age* 225 (1900):211–16.

Conway, *Carlyle.* Conway, Moncure Daniel. *Thomas Carlyle.* New York: Harper, 1881.

Copeland. Copeland, Charles Townsend. *Letters of Thomas Carlyle to His Youngest Sister*. London: Chapman and Hall; Boston and New York: Houghton Mifflin, 1899.

DL. House, Madeline, Graham Storey, et al., eds. *The Letters of Charles Dickens*. Pilgrim Edition. 6 vols. to present. Oxford: Clarendon Press, 1965–.

Dodds, *LC*. Dodds, James. *Lays of the Covenanters. With a Memoir of the Author by the Rev. James Dodds*. Edinburgh: John Maclaren, 1880.

Duke. Duke Univ. Library.

Dyer. Dyer, Isaac W. *A Bibliography of Thomas Carlyle's Writings and Ana*. Portland, Maine: Southworth Press, 1928.

EUL. Edinburgh Univ. Library.

Espinasse. Espinasse, Francis. *Literary Recollections and Sketches*. London: Hodder and Stoughton, 1893.

Faulkner. Faulkner, Peter. "Carlyle's Letters to Charles Redwood." *The Yearbook of English Studies* 2 (1972):139–80.

FC. John Forster Collection, Victoria and Albert Museum.

Fielding, *FR2*. Fielding, K. J. "Froude's Second Revenge: The Carlyles and the Wedgwoods." *Prose Studies* 4 (1981):301–16.

Fox. *Memories of Old Friends; Being Extracts from the Journals and Letters of Caroline Fox . . . from 1835 to 1871*. Ed. H. N. Pym. London: Smith, Elder, 1882.

Froude, *Carlyle*. Froude, J. A. *Thomas Carlyle: A History of the First Forty Years of His Life, 1795–1835; A History of His Life in London, 1834–1881*. 4 vols. London: Longmans, Green, 1882, 1884.

Froude, *LM*. Froude, J. A., ed. *Letters and Memorials of Jane Welsh Carlyle*. 3 vols. London: Longmans, Green, 1883.

Greville, *Memoirs*. Greville, Charles C. F. *The Greville Memoirs, 1814–1860*. Ed. Lytton Strachey and Roger Fulford. London: Macmillan, 1938.

Hanna. Hanna, William, ed. *Letters of Thomas Erskine of Linlathen*. 2 vols. Edinburgh: David Douglas, 1877.

Hansons, *NE*. Hanson, Lawrence and Elisabeth. *Necessary Evil: The Life of Jane Welsh Carlyle*. London: Constable, 1952.

Harrison. Harrison, Frederic. *Carlyle and the London Library*. London: Chapman and Hall, 1907.

Harrold, *Sartor*. Carlyle, Thomas. *Sartor Resartus*. Ed. Charles F. Harrold. New York: Odyssey Press, 1937.

Howells. Howells, John. "Carlyle's Holidays in Wales." *Red Dragon Magazine* 5 (1884):333–41, 461–69, 553–63.

Huxley, *JWCLF*. Huxley, Leonard, ed. *Jane Welsh Carlyle: Letters to Her Family, 1839–1863*. London: John Murray; New York: Doubleday, Page, 1924.

Huxley, *LJWC*. Huxley, Leonard. "Letters from Jane Welsh Carlyle." *Cornhill Magazine n.s.* 61 (1926):493–510, 622–38.

Ireland. Ireland, Mrs. Alexander, ed. *Selections from the Letters of Geraldine Endsor Jewsbury to Jane Welsh Carlyle*. London and New York: Longmans, Green, 1892.

JWC. Jane Welsh Carlyle.

Kelly, *Scotish Proverbs*. Kelly, James. *A Complete Collection of Scotish Proverbs*. London: W. and J. Innys and J. Osborn, 1721.

Last Words. *Last Words of Thomas Carlyle*. London: Longmans, Green, 1892.

Marrs. Marrs, Edwin W., Jr., ed. *The Letters of Thomas Carlyle to His Brother Alexander, with Related Family Letters*. Cambridge, Mass.: Harvard Univ. Press, 1968.

Mineka. Mineka, Francis E., ed. *The Earlier Letters of John Stuart Mill, 1812–1848*. 2 vols.; *The Later Letters . . . , 1849–1873*. 4 vols. Toronto: Univ. of Toronto Press; London: Routledge and Kegan Paul, 1963, 1972.

MUL. McMaster Univ. Library.

Napier. Napier, Macvey, Jr., ed. *Selection from the Correspondence of the Late Macvey Napier*. London: Macmillan, 1879.

NLS. National Library of Scotland.

Norton, *CE*. Norton, Charles Eliot, ed. *The Correspondence of Thomas Carlyle and Ralph Waldo Emerson, 1834–1872*. 2 vols. London: Chatto and Windus; Boston and New York: Houghton Mifflin, 1894.

Preuss. Preuss, Richard. "Letters from Carlyle to Von Ense." *New Review* 6 (1892):408–29, 593–608.

Reid, *RMM*. Reid, T. Wemyss. *The Life, Letters and Friendships of Richard Monckton Milnes, First Lord Houghton*, 2 vols. London: Cassell, 1890.

Ritchie. Ritchie, David G., ed. *Early Letters of Jane Welsh Carlyle*. London: Swan Sonnenschein, 1889.

Rusk. Rusk, Ralph L., ed. *The Letters of Ralph Waldo Emerson*. 6 vols. New York: Columbia Univ. Press, 1939.

RWEMA. Ralph Waldo Emerson Memorial Association, Harvard Univ.

Sanders, *CBCR*. Sanders, C. R. "The Carlyle-Browning Correspondence and Relationship." *Bulletin of the John Rylands Library* 57 (1974–75): 213–46, 430–62.

Sanders, *CF.* Sanders, C. R. *Carlyle's Friendships and Other Studies.* Durham, N.C.: Duke Univ. Press, 1977.

Shepherd, *Carlyle.* Shepherd, Richard Herne, ed. *Memoirs of the Life and Writings of Thomas Carlyle.* 2 vols. London: W. H. Allen, 1881.

Simpsons. Simpson, Alan, and Mary McQueen Simpson, eds. *I Too Am Here: Selections from the Letters of Jane Welsh Carlyle.* Cambridge and New York: Cambridge Univ. Press, 1977.

Slater, *CEC.* Slater, Joseph, ed. *The Correspondence of Emerson and Carlyle.* New York: Columbia Univ. Press, 1964.

Stirling, *JHS.* Stirling, Amelia E. *James Hutchison Stirling, His Life and Work.* London: T. Fisher Unwin, 1912.

E. Strachey, *LC.* Strachey, Sir Edward. "Some Letters and Conversations of Thomas Carlyle." *Atlantic Monthly* 73 (1894):822–34.

G. Strachey, *CRG.* Strachey, George. "Carlyle and the 'Rose-Goddess.'" *Nineteenth Century* 32 (Sept. 1892):470–86.

G. Strachey, *Rem.* Strachey, George. "Reminiscences of Carlyle with Some Unpublished Letters." *New Review* 9 (July 1893):17–33.

SND. *Scottish National Dictionary.* Ed. William Grant and David D. Murison. 10 vols. Edinburgh: Scottish National Dictionary Association, 1931–76.

Strouse. Norman and Charlotte Strouse Carlyle Collection, Univ. of California, Santa Cruz.

TC. Thomas Carlyle.

Terhune, *LEF.* Terhune, A. McK. and A. B., eds. *The Letters of Edward FitzGerald.* 4 vols. Princeton: Princeton Univ. Press, 1980.

Trinity. Trinity College, Cambridge, Library.

Wilson, *Carlyle.* Wilson, David Alec. *Carlyle.* 6 vols. London: Kegan Paul, Trench, Trubner; New York: E. P. Dutton, 1923–34.

Wilson, *CLW.* Wilson, David Alec. "Carlyle's Unpublished Letters to Miss Wilson." *Nineteenth Century* 89 (1921):802–11, 1017–23.

Wright, *EFL.* Wright, W. A., ed. *Letters and Literary Remains of Edward FitzGerald.* 3 vols. London and New York: Macmillan, 1889.

Yale. Yale Univ. Library.

CHRONOLOGY, 1843–1844

1843

January. TC continues to write *Past and Present,* mainly putting aside his work on Cromwell. John Sterling dangerously ill at Falmouth. Tennyson visits Cheyne Row with Edward Moxon. 16: JWC borrows French novels from the London Library in Erasmus Darwin's name, and (19) attends a Corn Law lecture with Mazzini, their frequent visitor. She also continues to write to Geraldine Jewsbury and Elizabeth Paulet about Jewsbury's feminist novel *Zoe,* and, on TC's suggestion, invites Jewsbury to stay.

February. Thackeray and Edward FitzGerald visit. 6: Geraldine Jewsbury arrives. JWC is godmother to Lydia Jane Macready. Her uncle John Welsh is seriously ill at Liverpool. 22: the first part of *Past and Present,* a "red hot indignant thing" (as TC tells Sterling), is sent to the printer. By the 24th JWC is annoyed at the length of Jewsbury's stay.

March. JWC is pleased to find that Mazzini, Darwin, and Elizabeth Pepoli do not like Jewsbury. TC attends Charles Lyell's lectures on geology (7–31), and finishes *Past and Present* (8). JWC visits the Chinese exhibition; TC hears Wellington speak in the House of Lords (9); he complains about the neighbors' piano playing; and (11) Jewsbury finally leaves. TC arranges American publication of *Past and Present* with Emerson. He sits for his portrait by John Linnell. 19: Jewsbury calls again. 24: Gambardella returns from Liverpool with his portrait of John Welsh; and TC writes about public distress and JWC's private charity. Thackeray and FitzGerald dine with them. 25: JWC sits for her portrait by Gambardella. TC briefly speaks at the first public meeting of John Robertson's Society of Authors. 29: JWC decides to keep her servant Helen Mitchell.

April. 5: TC and JWC attend a party at Edwin Chadwick's. 7: Lord Jeffrey and William Empson call. 11: the printer "finishes" *Past and Present.* 12: Jewsbury, temporarily "a vile creature," visits briefly. To JWC's irritation John Carlyle arrives to stay. 16: John Sterling's mother, Hester, dies, then (18) his wife, Susannah, in childbirth; his father, Edward, looks to JWC for support. 21: copies of *Past and*

Present are sent to reviewers, family, and friends. 29: Alexander Carlyle (later TC's editor) born at Ecclefechan. 30: JWC dines and quarrels with Edward Sterling.

May. TC declines joining the Society of Authors and has been learning Danish and reading Norse sagas. 6: TC and JWC dine with Forster. 10: TC cancels a visit to Naseby with FitzGerald and starts work on "Dr. Francia." John Sterling visits London in mid-May, having decided to move to Ventnor with his children, and gives JWC Tieck's *Vittoria Accorombona.* TC praises Dickens's Association for the Protection of Literature (to protect copyrights) but refuses involvement. JWC searches for a post as governess for Amalie Bölte. 22: JWC meets the "immensely large" and witty Lady Harriet at the Bullers' and is charmed by her, while TC entertains Samuel Gridley and Julia Ward Howe. 24: TC attends a soirée of the Prussian ambassador Bunsen.

June. TC writes "Dr. Francia" and (14) sends Alexander £250 to help him emigrate. JWC is concerned about Mazzini's health and looks for work for two daughters of the destitute Mudie family. Jewsbury is restored to favor for being a regular correspondent, even without replies from JWC. TC continues to help Alexander, who (25) sets sail with his family from Liverpool to New York.

July. TC begins his summer excursion by visiting Julia Strachey at Clifton. 4: JWC visits Greenwich with Edward Sterling and (5) begins supervising alterations and painting at home. TC visits Chepstow, then (6) sails to Cardiff for a holiday with Charles Redwood at Llandough. 14: JWC's 42d birthday; she has a visit from Kitty Phillips (b. Kirkpatrick). 15: Forster pays £50 for "Dr. Francia" for the July *Foreign Quarterly Review.* 16: Arthur Helps and Darwin call. 17: TC visits Dr. Connop Thirlwall, bishop of St. David's, at Carmarthen, passing tollgates destroyed by Rebeccaite rioters. A situation is found in Manchester for Juliet Mudie. 21: TC goes to Liverpool via Gloucester and Worcester, Cromwellian battle sites. Mazzini tells JWC of projected risings in Italy. 24: TC hears Father Mathew speak to thousands at Liverpool; and (26–30) visits North Wales, where he climbs Snowdon with John Carlyle.

August. On TC's return he and John visit the Paulets and Jewsbury at Seaforth House. 3: TC sails for Annan. 5: JWC is deeply impressed by Father Mathew at one of his meetings in London and (8–12) visits the Isle of Wight with Edward Sterling, where she encounters bedbugs, only to find bugs and fleas on returning home. TC stays in Annandale, with his family, until the end of the month, when John returns to

Cheyne Row, and JWC finds Bölte work as a governess for the Bullers' young Theresa Revis.

September. TC leaves Dumfries and visits Grace Welsh's grave on his way to Edinburgh. 2: he calls on Jeffrey and David Laing, then goes to Haddington to visit the Miss Donaldsons; and (3) walks to Dunbar and back to see the battlefield. 5: While staying with the Ferguses at Kirkcaldy, he bruises himself in a fall when riding. 9: he visits Edinburgh where he meets Dr. Samuel Brown and James Dodds at John Gordon's; breakfasts with Jeffrey (10) and returns to Kirkcaldy. 11: he visits Thomas Erskine at Linlathen, Dundee. Letters arrive from Alexander in Canandaigua, N.Y. 15: TC sails from Dundee and returns home to admire JWC's improvements; but (28), disturbed once more by piano-playing, decides that his room must be moved, and work on the house begins again.

October. TC restlessly restarts work on the Cromwellian period, while JWC suffers from dealing with the alterations. American visitors call, sent by Emerson. 30: barrels of supplies arrive from Scotsbrig. 31: TC tells Emerson that his "Book on Cromwell, is impossible," but he "must" write it.

November. 11: Alexander's letter arrives to say that he has "entirely renounced whisky." Mazzini is still unwell. Elizabeth Mudie is dismissed. Henry James, Sr., calls. JWC has flu.

December. TC immersed in Cromwell. Elizabeth Paulet sends JWC caricatures of Jewsbury. 5: TC takes the great decision to burn many of his recent notes about the Cromwellian period and to collect Cromwell's letters and speeches before writing a biography or history. He and John Carlyle arrange to pay their sister Janet £10 each a year. Dickens sends Carlyle his *A Christmas Carol,* and JWC passes it on to John Welsh (23). Charles Redwood sends a Christmas hamper. 26: JWC attends Nina Macready's birthday party at which Forster dances wildly with her and Dickens performs as a conjurer.

1844

January. 1: Mazzini "first foots" JWC. 7: Henry James, Sr., and relatives call. Jewsbury sends the revised *Zoe,* and JWC feels that "the present state of Cromwell is almost more than flesh and blood can bear." Anna Jameson stays a night (26) at Cheyne Row. William Coningham buys a sketch or picture by Raphael for £1,000. JWC's cousin James Baillie calls; Mazzini tells JWC about further Italian risings; TC receives £32 for American sales and sends Emerson $121 for his British sales.

February. 2: TC dines at the Monteagles'. 15: he applies for permission to consult the records of the City of London. Edward Sterling is quieter since reemployed in writing for the *Times;* JWC often drives out in his carriage. She admires the revised *Zoe.* TC questions David Laing, Henry Cole, and Edward FitzGerald about Cromwell. 19–22: William Fraser brings a suit against a former friend for seducing Mrs. Fraser, which he loses; JWC furious with him. 24: JWC takes the MS of *Zoe* to Chapman & Hall and visits Mrs. Fraser.

March. 2: Elizabeth Rigby is greatly impressed by the Carlyles. 3: JWC visits Mrs. Fraser. An Italian rising in Calabria is easily suppressed. 17: JWC calls on Chapman & Hall; *Zoe* is accepted. Alexander and his family leave Alton, N.Y., for Brantford, Canada.

April. 1: TC receives a further £36 from U.S. sales. 4: John Sterling is dangerously ill after breaking a blood vessel. 12: Colin and Helen Mackenzie (who later find TC "a warm-hearted genial friend") call. Both Carlyles visit the Chinese exhibition; JWC dines at Jean Cunningham's with the Mackenzies and sees "General Tom Thumb" with Charlotte Sterling. 21: Jeffrey and Empson call at the same time as Plattnauer; Mrs. Fraser calls; James Baillie writes from a debtors' prison.

May. JWC is concerned about Garnier's insanity. 7: the Carlyles visit H. F. Chorley, where Browning and the Howitts are present. 8: TC notes, "My progress in '*Cromwell*' is frightful"; he meets Edward Everett, U.S. ambassador; and (12) attends a meeting for the Society for Improvement of the Labouring Classes. Amalie Bölte stays at Cheyne Row before going as a governess to Lady Graham. Edward Sterling takes JWC to Euston to say farewell to Jeffrey, who is ill. TC writes to gather Cromwell's letters. 27: Caroline Fox calls and enjoys TC's talk. 30: John Sterling is still dangerously ill.

June. JWC plans a visit to Liverpool. 14: The opening of Mazzini's letters on orders of the home secretary, Sir James Graham, is raised in the Commons; and (18) TC writes to the *Times* about it. 24: JWC goes to Liverpool. 25: TC calls on Mrs. Buller and Bölte (dismissed by Lady Graham) and on Lady Harriet; and (26) sees an exhibition of old masters. He sends JWC *Punch* cartoons of Sir James. 27: JWC visits Hale and Speke Hall with her uncle, and (30) TC visits the Barings at Addiscombe.

July. 1: TC returns to London. 2: another debate in the Commons about Mazzini's letters. 5: Gambardella takes JWC and her cousins on a picnic. 6: TC refuses an invitation to a Burns festival in Ayrshire. JWC goes to Chester and Eaton Hall; and (7) TC visits Addiscombe for the day to enjoy aristocratic company, including Lady Holland's. 8: Though unwell, JWC stays with the Paulets at Seaforth, where she is joined by Jewsbury. 10: TC and Milnes visit the exhibition of cartoons at Westminster Hall. 11: JWC is angry at Jewsbury's jealousy; and (15), when riding, her horse bolts. 15: She meets James Martineau and his wife and (16) returns to Liverpool. 18: Mazzini calls on TC and talks of the Bandiera brothers' capture. 20: JWC cancels a visit to Jewsbury; (21) calls on James Martineau; and (23) returns to London. 25: the Bandiera brothers are executed; the mother of the Welshes' servant Margaret is murdered.

August. 1: TC accepts that Sterling is dying; and (10) Sterling writes his farewells. 11: TC visits Addiscombe; and G. L. Craik, at JWC's request, tracks Plattnauer to a lunatic asylum. Progress on Cromwell is still slow. 20: JWC visits the asylum and (26) collects Plattnauer. Sterling returns their letters and some books. 27: TC sends a farewell letter; but (30) Sterling declines to see him. TC writes "An Election to the Long Parliament."

September. 10: TC stays at the Grange with the Ashburtons and Barings, where he proofreads "An Election." JWC refurbishes the house. TC complains about the dullness of the party except for himself and Lady Harriet. 13: The Grange party goes to Winchester. 18: John Sterling dies, leaving TC and Julius Hare as his literary executors. 19: TC returns to London. 20: Plattnauer leaves for the Continent; Mrs. Paulet calls on George Sand with an introduction by Mazzini arranged by JWC. TC arranges for Henry James, Sr., to return to Emerson his letters to Sterling. Proofs arrive from America for a British edition of Emerson's *Essays, Second Series.*

October. 1: "An Election" appears in *Fraser's,* and TC recommences *Cromwell,* working on the letters and speeches; he asks about international copyright for John Chapman and proofreads some of Emerson's *Essays.* 2: the Paulets call on their return; and (4) JWC goes to town with her. James Carlyle, at Scotsbrig, is looking for a new farm to lease. 10: Tennyson pays an "unforgettable" visit.

November. Anthony Sterling's wife, Charlotte, believes that he is in love with JWC. Harriet Martineau attributes her recovery to mesmerism. James Carlyle is to stay at Scotsbrig after all. Emerson's *Essays* are published with TC's prefatory notice. 12: JWC is worried about Jewsbury, but *Zoe* is being printed. TC teases JWC as a "destroyer of the peace of families," since Bessie Helps is also jealous. Supplies arrive from Scotsbrig.

December. TC's cousin Marion McKinnon has died. 3: TC attends Dickens's reading of *The Chimes* at Forster's. 13: JWC is scathing about Martineau and mesmerism. TC receives a copy of Goethe's death mask from Ary Scheffer. 25: TC gives JWC a cloak; the Ashburtons have sent game, and Redwood a Christmas hamper.

VOLUME 16

January–July 1843

JWC TO JEANNIE WELSH

Sunday night [1 January 1843]

My dearest Babbie

Here we are then in the beginning of a new year! May we do as much of good in it and as little of harm as possible!—for this much we may pray with an assured conscience—for all the rest; it is in Gods hands—where we had best leave it! We know not what more to ask,—what it were good for us to have for the asking!—whether to live or to die—to be well or to be sick—to be at ease in Zion,[1] or to be troubled about many things[2]—all these are transitory conditions, and their joy or their sorrow is transitory—but no joy, no sorrow no anything I suppose is given to us in vain—and the *ultimate issues* lie far beyond our poor human vision stretching away away into eternity—so for my part I ask of heaven only what I have said—that I may live my life wisely thro this new year—not foolishly—not wickedly, and I advise you Babbie of my affections to ask neither more nor less than this same—

John dined here today—as usual[3]—and now Carlyle is *convoying* him home—and I am here alone, and shall sleep the better for having written you, if not a letter at least the beginning of a letter— First as to *the books*—for business should always take precedence of other topics—the books my dear are after all—a *loan!!* "Why do you ask? What could make you suppose I should have meant them as anything else?"[4] Ay what indeed?—the fatal romance of my character could alone have made me suppose such a thing!— And yet there are traditions in the world of men who have laid crowns and kingdoms at the feet of a beautiful woman, never to

JWC-JW, [1 Jan.]. MS: NLS 1891.154 inc. Pbd: Huxley, *JWCLF* 68–69. Dated by the beginning of the new year and the loan of books to Jeannie Welsh in Dec. (see 15:256). Jeannie Welsh, also known as Babbie, da. of JWC's maternal uncle John Welsh (d. 1853); lived with her widowed father and her brothers and sisters at 20 Maryland St., Liverpool.

1. Amos 6:1.
2. Luke 10:41.
3. Dr. John A. Carlyle (1801–79; *DNB*), TC's brother, regularly dined on Sun. at Cheyne Row when in London.
4. Quoting John Carlyle.

TC TO CAROLINE FOX

Chelsea, 5 jan*y*, 1843—

Dear Caroline,

Your Bulletin of yesterday gave us a great alarm.[1] Mr Sterling instantly proceeded to pack portmanteaus, be in readiness for a race to Falmouth;[2] but your Sister's news today,[3] for which a Servant from South-Place was in waiting, have happily stilled all that; and given us, as you may imagine, the welcomest relief. We are now terribly angry at your Patient; now that we are no longer so terribly frightened about him! We trust and hope the danger is now past—till the *next* imprudence, at least![4]

Mrs Sterling is kept in the dark;[5] and yet, as we may suppose, not wholly. She sees, by her Husband's packings, and disconsolate looks, that something is wrong at Falmouth; tho' hitherto she knows not what. This is a twilight more annoying to her than the clear light, as we now have it, would be. I conclude that Mr Sterling will instruct her accurately how it stands, today or tomorrow. She is in her usual state of strength, or a degree beyond it. If we had but tomorrow's post also favourable,—we should then give free scope to our *anger*, casting the terror mostly away!

Many thanks to you for your care of poor Verran.[6] I think, that will be a useful thing; and we are not to neglect such, when they offer themselves among the half or wholly useless things so enormously copious round us.

You are the one, are you not, that sat at my right hand here, in the little parlour down stairs; and called me "Thou," in the clear silver voice, with the bright laughing eyes,—the very eyes seeming to say so

TC-CF, 5 Jan. MS: Strouse. Pbd: Isaac Foot, *Michael Verran . . . and Thomas Carlyle* (1946), 42–43, facsimile opp. 38; quot: Fox 175–76. Caroline Fox (1819–71; *DNB*), quaker diarist; see 12:45.

1. About the health of John Sterling (1806–44; *DNB*), living in Falmouth.
2. Edward Sterling (1773–1847; *DNB*), journalist, John's father; see 8:144. He lived at South Pl., Knightsbridge.
3. Anna Maria Fox (1815?–97), Caroline's sister, also living in Falmouth.
4. While helping the cleaning maids lift a heavy table, Sterling broke a blood vessel and hemorrhaged extensively; see *Life of Sterling, Works* 11:242.
5. Hester Sterling, b. Coningham (d. 1843), John's mother; see 8:130. She had been in ill health herself.
6. Michael Verran (1808–62), who helped save a fellow miner and thereby evoked TC's praise and starting of a small fund for his benefit; see 15:175, 228–29. Caroline Fox recorded in her diary, 19 Nov. 1842, that Verran was saving his money "in order to leave off work and get six months' learning" (Fox 174).

musically, "Thou!"[7] I declare I have a great mind to call you *Thou* also; but must not venture at present.

In haste I subscribe myself / Caroline's Friend

T. Carlyle

TC TO MARGARET A. CARLYLE

Chelsea, Friday, 6 jan*y*, 1843—

My dear Mother,

Jenny sent me a small welcome Note last week;[1] and I have felt ever since as if I were *doubly* in your debt. I am terribly busy; and so many interruptions occur;—but surely I might contrive to find half an hour some day for scribbling half a word of news to my dear good Mother! Well; I decide on doing it today,—today when my whole day's *task*, by one foolish botheration and another, has gone to the winds; and it is now time for my going out without having got *anything* done! I will have it to say at least: I wrote a scrape of a pen to my Mother!—

Jane is taking some medicines of John's, and really finds some benefit, I think,—tho' she has to complain sadly that Jack will *take no hold of her*, but seems almost to forget both that she is a Patient and he a Doctor. He is indeed terribly *loose;* in great *haste;* for most part; and flies round everything, too like a bundle of loose *thrums* [threads],—not at all like a hard *hammer*, to *hit* it well!—— The good Doctor: we saw him yesterday, *incidentally* here, his Patient being out on some excursion;[2] so that Jack could get down to us. He and I walked up far into the Town together; and had talk enough, amid the noisy *glarry* [muddy] streets: he seems as well as I have seen him for many years; a great comfort to us to see here once a week!

My own health keeps good; better than it used to do. I am fast getting ready something for publication too,—tho' it is not *Cromwell* yet; it is something more immediately applicable to the times in hand.[3] I do hope you will see it soon,—tho' it is a terrible business getting a

7. For Caroline Fox's accounts of her visit to Cheyne Row, 28 May and 6 June 1842, see Fox 153–56, 160–64.

TC-MAC, 6 Jan. MS: NLS 521.9. Quot: Froude, *Carlyle* 3:284–85. Margaret Aitken Carlyle (1771–1853), TC's mother.

1. Janet (Jenny) Carlyle Hanning (1813–98), TC's sister. Her husband, Robert (d. 1878; see 6:99), had emigrated to the U.S. and Canada, 1841, and she was staying with her mother.

2. John Carlyle served as personal physician to William Ogilby (usually spelled Ogilvie by TC), who suffered from mental illness.

3. *Past and Present*, to be pbd. in April.

thing wriggled out of the confusions it stands amid, and made ready for presenting to mankind! It is like *building* a dry *brick-house* out of a *quagmire* of clay and glar!— As Tom Garthwaite said of his strained leg, "we must not stop for strained legs, we will *work out the strean* [strain]."[4] Tom did "work out the *strean*": how much more ought I!

We have had hardly any winter here yet; hard[ly][5] a half-dozen days of frost, and never more than two at a time; the weather often warm as in the fine days of Spring. I doubt, it is no good sign of a season; perhaps there will be a cold enough summer to make up for this. However, we ought to be glad of good weather in the meanwhile, and not *anticipate* evil too much.— The distress of the Poor, I apprehend, is less here at present than in almost any other large Town: yet you cannot walk along the streets without seeing frightful symptoms of it. I declare I begin to feel as if I should not hold my peace any longer; as if I should perhaps *open* my mouth, in a way that some of them are not expecting! We shall see, if this Book were once done.

Poor Mrs Sterling continues very weak; not immediately in danger, but Jane thinks her radically all wrong. We had a notice too yesterday that *John* Sterling the son, far away off at Falmouth, had been straining himself with some heavy lift, and had burst a bloodvessel in his lungs, which had as near as possible killed him! He is getting slowly better, we now understand; but is as weak as water.

Poor Isabella does not improve,—nor will she, till she have been *worse*, I suppose.[6] It is a great comfort to me to think of Jenny being with you. *She* lights the fire; that is right. Keep *yourself* snug, my dear Mother; out of the raw winter; *you* have already fronted it long and bravely.—— I hear no news from Jean at Dumfries; none from Alick or anybody.[7] Jamie has a little Note here. Somebody will write to me by and by. My heart's-blessing with you all, writing or not writing. Adieu dear Mother. A *joiner* is in my room working for the last half hour! Your affectionate

T. Carlyle

4. Tom Garthwaite, Ecclefechan tailor; coterie speech.

5. Letters omitted in MS.

6. Isabella Carlyle, b. Calvert (d. 1859), wife of TC's brother James, called Jamie (1807–90), farmer at Scotsbrig. Margaret Carlyle also lived there. In poor health for some time, Isabella was pregnant and seems to have been mentally depressed.

7. TC's sister Jean Carlyle Aitken (1810–88), m. to James Aitken, house painter at Dumfries. TC's brother Alexander Carlyle (1797–1876) lived at Ecclefechan, where he kept a small store; see 1:166.

TC TO JAMES CARLYLE

Chelsea, 6 jany, 1843–

Dear Jamie,

You find here inclosed a Document, which you have to carry over to Postie at Ecclefechan and sign; whereupon Postie will hand you two sovereigns for it. You are to give one of these to Isabella, and the other to Jenny who is now up stairs with my Mother; and say that they are New-Year's Gifts from me, with many brotherly salutations and "good wishes for the season," to both the one and the other. Having done this, your commission for the present is ended; and I will thank you beforehand.— Solely farther, if you have an old Newspaper, you may direct it hither in token that the thing came *safe;* and in that case you can ask of Alick too whether his *two* things were safe; and I will take the Newspaper as a sign in the affirmative from him too. I have little doubt but all goes safe that one hands in that way: but an express word or sign to that effect is also satisfactory. You are all terribly *sweer* [reluctant] to write; therefore I suggest a Newspaper as handier; not by any means as equally good.

But, in truth, my dear Brother, I consider that you might easily do worse than actually set about *learning to write freely,* and have more than once counselled. Suppose, you went up stairs, to the end-room, some day, with a fire lighted (which will dissipate the damp too), and all your men fairly at work out of doors; and then, taking a good roomy sheet of paper, honestly set yourself to fill it for me! It would be productive of several good effects, and no evil one at all! You have only to commit yourself heartily to the business, and *try.* Your rugged Annandale *sense* and *uptake* is altogether right for us; good and sound: you have only to learn *writing it down.* Mind the *periods* and points; the spelling; the dividing at the end of the line by syllables &c;—above all to *try,* and *persevere!*— —

My news are all in the bit of Paper which I write to my Mother; which she will communicate to you. I am very busy; have many *interruptions* which I cannot stave off. My blessings with you dear honest Brother, and farewell!

T. Carlyle

TC-JC, 6 Jan. MS: NLS Acc. 9086. Hitherto unpbd.

TC TO CHAPMAN & HALL

Chelsea, 6 jan*y*, 1843–

Gentlemen,

A Lady of my acquaintance wants a copy of the *French Revolution*[1] to be sent her "without *additional* cost" to the care of "some Bookseller in Worcester," or what were still better, "to Lamb, the Keeper of the Library in Great Malvern": She will pay for it at either of these places; but wants it I think almost *immediately;* and does not expect to have any carriage to pay. I suppose it will be possible for you to manage this,—even tho' the Magazine Monday[2] is over? I send here a cover with the Lady's Address: will you insert in that, so soon as the Book is fairly off, an announcement of the fact, a prediction *where* it will arrive and when;—that is to say, at whose shop in Worcester, if not in Malvern, the Lady can call for her *French Revolution,* and pay for the same.

I do not understand that the Book is to be *bound;* but I am specially charged to be careful and *most* careful that it be "a handsome copy"—as it is intended for a gift! I suppose there is small choice in the "handsomeness"; but you will select the handsom*est,* and at any rate a perfectly clean one.

The only doubt I apprehend is as to your means of *immediate* conveyance; for the Lady seems to be about quitting G*t* Malvern very soon, and coming back to Town.

If the *payment in Wor'stershire* occasion any difficulty, I give you another Address, which will instantly convert that part of the business into a *payment in Town;*—as follows on the other side of the leaf:

"Miss Wilson / 1. Upper Eccleston Street / Belgrave Square."[3]

I hope you perfectly understand this momentous mysterious Transaction, and will accomplish it successfully without delay!—

I remain always / Most truly yours / T. Carlyle

Mssr. Chapman & Hall.

TC-C&H, 6 Jan. MS: Strouse. Hitherto unpbd. Chapman & Hall became TC's publishers, 1842, after the death of James Fraser, 1841.

1. Jane Wilson (1790–1890), London friend of the Carlyles since 1835; see 8:151. Chapman & Hall had pbd. a new issue of the second edn. (1839) of *The French Revolution,* 3 vols. (1842).

2. The first Mon. of the month, the day on which most monthly and quarterly magazines were pbd. and dispatched; see next letter.

3. She lived at no. 2, not 1.

TC TO JANE WILSON

Chelsea, 7 jan*y*, 1843—

Dear Miss Wilson,

Thanks, hearty tho' in the utmost hurry, for your good kind Note of yesterday. How happy for me too, were I on the Malvern Hills, with the green earth under me, the eternal sky over me, and God's Silence round me, that I might consider deeply of many things! Instead of Belial's Tumult,[1] in which one can consider nothing! Ballad-singers, "without food for the last three weeks," bray under my windows; an enchanted young lady drums her hapless piano to no purpose on the other side of the wall,—an emblem to me of a whole world *enchanted;* possessed by Falsities—(*Devils* as they used to be called); following merely one another and the Devil! Truly one had need to be a "man of genius" to do anything considerable here.—

Yesterday I straightway despatched your order to the Booksellers; explaining it, as I hope, to the meanest capacity. On the first Monday of every month, what is called "Magazine Monday," any London Bookseller can with perfect ease do such a feat as you require: but these people of mine, "Chapman and Hall, 188 Strand," have superior facilities for conveyance; and probably can manage directly what you want. I impressed upon them your probably *speedy* return to Town,—which I myself wanted to believe. I sent them a Cover with your Address, in which they were to announce to you what they *had* found it possible to do; and where the Book, if any Book, was to be inquired for in Wor'ster or Malvern. There is little doubt but it will be all right.

John Sterling has alarmed us all by a new hemorrhage,—rupture of a blood-vessel, brought on by most imprudent useless over-working of himself; "lifting of tables," they say, "to save servants trouble"! He lies very weak, but happily thought out of danger for the present; and will have to lie, the Doctor says, for at least a month to come.

Well; I think you had better [come?] back to London now, Belial's tumult tho' it be! My Wife, who is pretty well *for her,* sends you and Mr Wilson many salutations along with me.[2] "May the *worst* of our years be past": that used to be poor Edward Irving's toast.[3] Ulysses

TC-JW, 7 Jan. MS: Whicker Collection, Montana State Univ. Pbd: Wilson, *CLW* 1022–23.

1. One of TC's many terms for London.

2. Her brother, Thomas Wilson (d. 1872), with whom she lived. He had been at Cambridge, 1807–11, where he was listed as of Staffordshire.

3. Edward Irving (1792–1834), the Carlyles' great friend, preacher, and religious leader; see 1:92. For the quotation, see *Reminiscences* 134.

says to his men, "Endure, O friends";[4]—and all Sea-Captains and effectual persons still say, "Bear a hand, be *alive* there!"

I remain, dear Miss Wilson, in hope to see you soon,

Yours ever truly (in endless haste!)
T. Carlyle

TC TO EDWARD MOXON

Chelsea, 7 jan*y*, 1843—

My dear Sir,

Many thanks, far heartier than thanks often are, for the munificent Gift of Books that arrived here yesterday. I think I may say,—considering both the outer body of these ten handsome massive Volumes, and the spirit of sterling enduring Wisdom that lies contained in them,—I never received so valuable a Present of Books before. It happens too that of all these works, known to me from old times, I possess no complete legible copy till now, except of Shakspeare alone.[1] I might long have gone without making the due effort to get them; and now here they all are, to consult, and commune with, when I like! I hold myself, very literally, much *obliged* to you; *bound* by a real service done me, to do you the like, if I ever can.

This Enterprise, of serving all the world by offering them good Books on cheap terms, is one that ought to prosper! Small handy volumes, one page cut into four, would please me better, as I said to you the other night. But these too are right handsome volumes, tho' weighty ones; and all the world ought to be very well content. I bid you, Go on, with more and more success.

Hoping some chance may lead you hither again before long,

I remain, with many thanks,
My dear Sir, / Most truly yours
T. Carlyle

E. Moxon Esq

4. *Iliad* 2:299.

TC-EM, 7 Jan. MS: EUL. Hitherto unpbd. Edward Moxon (1801–58; *DNB*), publisher; see 7:245, 271.

1. For the books sent by Moxon, see JWC to JW, [ca. 12 Jan.].

TC TO DAVID LAING

Chelsea, 7 jan*y*, 1843–

My dear Sir,

Many thanks for the Third Volume of *Baillie,* which arrived here safe the other day.[1] I have read the *Life;* which I find profitable to correction, for illumination, on this hand and on that. It is as clear and complete as a *Life of Baillie* could, at this date of time, be made; I suppose we shall never know more of him than you have contrived to make out.

And now I think you have a right to feel, your long rough task fairly done, that you have accomplished a very genuine piece of service to all men, in thus culling *Baillie's Letters* from the tombs; fairly into visibility, into new centuries of accessible continuance! Here he is, the huge fat monster; a huge *Pactolus,*[2] with copious gold-grains, and continents of mud: we can all sift and separate in him, and fish and wash, for true metal, at discretion. I have yet fallen in with no Book, on those Times, better worth printing. In the name of all readers of English History, I give you thanks.

The *Woodrow Society,* among others, sends its Books into our London Library.[3] They are a very notable Phenomenon, these new fast-spreading Printing-Clubs; and betoken curious results for Paternoster Row,[4] among other things!

I hope the Knox enterprise, tho' difficulties must abound in it, has not been abandoned? No; we want a Knox from you very much![5]—

Believe me always / Yours with thanks and true regards

T. Carlyle

TC-DL, 7 Jan. MS: EUL. Quot: *Scotsman,* 30 May 1932. David Laing (1793–1878; *DNB*), Scottish antiquarian, librarian of the Signet Library, Edinburgh; see 5:397.

1. *The Letters and Journals of Robert Baillie, 1637–1662,* ed. D. Laing, vol. 3 (Edinburgh, 1842); see 13:261. Robert Baillie (1599–1662), presbyterian divine.
2. A small river in Lydia, Asia Minor, famous for its gold, which according to legend was because Midas had bathed in it.
3. The Wodrow Society, founded, Edinburgh, 1841, for the pbn. of the works of early writers of the Church of Scotland; dissolved, 1847, after publishing twelve works; named after the Scottish ecclesiastical historian Robert Wodrow (1679–1734). The London Library, 57 Pall Mall, founded 1840; see vol. 12.
4. A street immediately N of St. Paul's Churchyard, chiefly occupied by booksellers.
5. Laing's edn. of the works of the Scottish divine and reformer John Knox (1505–72), 6 vols. (1846–64).

JWC TO JEANNIE WELSH

[8 January 1843]

Just because, in virtue of his being *the least unlikable* man in the place,[1] I let him dance attendance on my young person, till I came to *need* him—all the same as my slippers, to go to a ball in, or my bonnet to go out to walk. When I finally agreed to marry him, I *cried* excessively and felt excessively shocked—but if I had then said *no* he would have left me—and how could I dispense with what was equivalent to my slippers or bonnet? Oh if I might write my own biography from beginning to end—without reservation or false colouring—it would be an invaluable document for my countrywomen in more than one particular—but "decency forbids"!

Walter was here the night before last—talked of being off this morning.[2]— Do you know I find him far more intelligent and agreeable away from all you young ones— He staid that night till near *twelve* and I was not sleepy!—you may infer from that how miraculously well he must have managed!— And Carlyle too thinks him "*not* at all a bad fellow! *not* at all without sense"—which means in his dialect—what Pepoli in *his* would call "*un angelo di bonta* [an angel of goodness]—and—"PIENO PIENO *d'ingegno* [full full of intelligence]."[3]

I send Helen an autograph of the American Poetess M*rs* Segurney[4]—which does infinite credit to her total want of penetration!—the evening of which she makes such grateful mention—would have been remembered by any one else with feelings of quite another sort—even *I* who do not give much way to remorse, have often had qualms of conscience in thinking about it. Her coming and still more her bringing along with her two geerpoles of the name of "Johnson or Tomson" a

JWC-JW, [8 Jan.]. Addr: 20 Maryland Street / Liverpool. PM: Chelsea, 9 Jan. 1843. MS: NLS 1891.162 inc. Pbd: Huxley, *JWCLF* 76–79.

1. The previous pages are missing and apparently were about TC.

2. Walter Welsh (1799–1879; see 15:210), Jeannie's brother, who had been presented to Auchtertool, Fife, Nov. 1842, but confirmation of whose appointment had been delayed by antipatronage feeling (see JWC to JW, [26 Jan.]); or possibly Walter Macgregor, Jeannie's cousin from Liverpool, who may have visited London more often than her brother.

3. Count Carlo Pepoli (1796–1881), Italian exile in London, m. to the Carlyles' friend Elizabeth, b. Fergus (d. 1862); see 8:194–95.

4. Helen Welsh, Jeannie's sister. Lydia Howard Huntley (Mrs. Charles) Sigourney (1791–1865), American author; see 12:311. She had written to TC, 9 Dec. 1842: "I know not whether I may flatter myself with having left any trace on your remembrance. . . . I have a very deep recollection of a delightful evening spent at Cheyne Row, listening to the conversation of one, whom I had long desired to see: and with my particular regards to her, who contributed to render that visit so agreeable." She also sent TC one of her books.

male and a female[5]—as little Miss Adam would say (did I tell you of her asking me in the presence of Mazzini whether *Gorgon* whom she styled *"one of the graces,"* for my better understanding, "was a male or a female"—?)[6] her coming with this tag-ragery quite spoiled a pleasant party that happened to be here—the Wedgewoods Darwin M*rs* Rich and Julia Smith[7]— We had all set in to be talkative and confidential—when this figure of an over-the-water-Poetess—beplastered with rouge and pomatum—barenecked at an age which had left *certainty* far behind—with long ringlets that never grew where they hung—smelling marvellously of camphor or hartshorn and oil—all glistening in black satin as if she were an apothecaries *puff* for black *sticking-plaster*—and staring her eyes out, to give them animation—stalked in & by the very barber-block-ish look of her reduced us all to silence—which effect was heightened by the pair who followed at her heels—the *male* in an embroidered satin vest—the *female* also in satin with—fancy it in *that* room—and in *that* company!—with *a gold tiara on her head!* These two never spoke a word but sat with their eyes fixed on Carlyle as if they had paid their shillings at the door— M*rs* Segurney also made large eyes at him—and *she* took the liberty of poking at him now and then to make the lion roar—but he was not in the vein—and would not roar finely that night for all she could do— The rest of us meanwhile, feeling ourselves agrieved at being regarded with no more curiosity or politeness than as many domestic cats in comparison of the Lion, repayed them in their own coin— *I never addressed one word to them!* this is a literal fact—of "her who helped to make that evening so pleasant to remembrance"[8]— Faith it is not true that "we reap not where we have not sown"[9]—my harvests are far

5. Apparently in late Feb. 1841. Mrs. Sigourney wrote to TC, 18 Feb. 1841: "I have by no means forgotten your invitation to spend an evening with your wife and yourself. Will you allow me to bring M*r* and M*rs* Jameson, English friends of much intelligence, and who have long been desirous of seeing you?" Geerpoles are thin upright poles upon which a mason might hang his gear.

6. The young Miss Hunter (see 15:207–8) was the da. of JWC's cousin Dr. Adam Hunter (d. 1843), originally of Leeds but now living in Hastings for his health (see 9:232). The Gorgon was one of three sisters of Greek myth whose looks turned men to stone.

7. Hensleigh Wedgwood (1803–91; *DNB*), mathematician and philologist, m. to Frances (Fanny) Wedgwood, b. Mackintosh (1800–89); see 9:106–7. Erasmus Darwin (1804–81), Hensleigh Wedgwood's cousin and Charles Darwin's brother (see 7:290). Mary Rich, b. Mackintosh (1789–1876), the widowed half-sister of Frances Wedgwood, who lived in Woolwich; see 10:35. Julia Smith (1799–1883), friend of both the Carlyles and the Wedgwoods; see 13:84.

8. Paraphrasing Mrs. Sigourney.

9. Cf. Gal. 6:7 and Matt. 25:26.

oftenest of that highly improbable sort— I will send Old Sterling's last note as another instance of this infraction of *the laws of nature* in my favour— John had again broken a blood-vessel—in lifting tables to save the servants trouble! Madman that he is!—it was a hanging in the wind with him for two days—and the communication of his state had to be made to his father thro' us—for fear of doing mischief to his Mother who you know has a disease of the heart that requires the utmost quiet— When the old fool came down here, after receiving Carlyles note I was prepared to be very sorry for him—but at the very outset he set all my sympathies against him by his theatrical fuss—clapping his hand on his *stomach* and declaring "*no!* this *heart* must not break *yet!* I cannot afford to sink under my griefs!— I have five *orphans* depending on me"[10]— So little of humanity did I show him—that I answered merely "bless me!—you had better see the end of it—they are not *orphans yet*"*!* And when he sent his servant for news the next morning I wrote—"since the accounts are favourable you had better give up your distracted project of setting out for Falmo[u]t[h][11]—Do keep yourself *quiet if you can*—it were the greatest kindness you can show to those you are interested in"—for *this* he writes to me all these little extatic pages!

—Dear I will tell you a secret but see that you keep it to yourself—Carlyle is no more writing about *Oliver Cromwell* than you and I are!— I have known this for a good while[12]— You will wonder that I should not have known it all along—the fact is his papers were a good time more resembling hierogliphics than finished manuscript I could not be at the trouble of making them out—then when I came to find, on days when I chanced to look pages about "*The present fashion of mens coats*[13]—about the rage for novelties—puffing every thing or any thing *except* "*Cromwell Oliver*"— I had no misgivings— I know he has such a way of tacking on extraneous discussions to his subject—but when I found at last a long biography of *that Abbot Samson!*[14] then indeed—I asked what on earth *has* all this to do with Cromwell—and learned that Cromwell was not begun—that probably half a dozen

10. John Sterling had five children; a sixth was b. two mos. later.
11. Letters omitted.
12. TC had spent well over a year preparing to write a life of Cromwell or history of the period, but toward the end of Nov. 1842 he had put this aside and begun to write what was to become *Past and Present.* JWC had in fact already told Jeannie about this, ca. 21 Dec.; see 15:246.
13. Cf. *Past and Present, Works* 10:216.
14. Samson (1135–1211), b. at Trottingham, mitered abbot of Bury St. Edmunds, 1182–1211, which he built up materially and spiritually. Bk. 2 of *Past and Present* is devoted to him. For TC's reading about him in Jocelin de Brakelonda's chronicle, see 15:129.

other volumes will be published before that— Nevertheless for I know not what Reason he lets everybody go on questioning him of his Cromwell and answers so as to leave them in the persuasion he is busy with that and nothing else. Absolutely I will not begin another sheet yours J. C.

Monday [9 January 1843]

Dearest I have opened my letter to announce the arrival of yours—for mine was written last night while *they* were drinking their brandy-punch up stairs and *sealed* last night that Helen might not edify herself with the contents in the morning[15]—according to her usual fashion— I have no time however to write a new letter—this has been one of my rushing about days, *cleaning* the Lamp &c &c (for we are returned to the poor lamp at *his* particular desire[16]) and now—"Babbie I want you to do my hair!" These words will give you the liveliest image of my state!— But instead of that soothing operation I must off to Sloan Street[17] to buy new stuff for blinds—for *his* room is to undergo a thorough cleaning tomorrow— "The troubles that afflict the just in number many be"[18]— For the rest strange to say the cold weather seems to suit me *this* year better than the *damp*— I am always *strongest* in the frosty days—and Maggie has made my *arms* so comfortable![19]— The pain has been better for the last week—*partly* the effect of the blue pills I suppose—but partly also the effect of a *new idea* I have lately taken up which I will unfold to you when I have carried it on a while longer— Geraldine was right not to let her ms. be read at Maryland Street[20]—the religious ideas set forth in it would have seemed very shocking to those who had never heard any thing said about religion except in the orthodox tone this *entre nous* [between ourselves]—

My *love* to Gambardella[21]

15. Helen Mitchell, the Carlyles' maid since 1837; see 9:376–77.
16. TC had complained that the lamp was foul-smelling; see 15:209.
17. In Chelsea, NE of Cheyne Row.
18. Untraced but possibly a hymn based on or metrical paraphrase of Ps. 129.
19. Margaret (Maggie) Welsh, Jeannie's sister.
20. Geraldine Endsor Jewsbury (1812–80; *DNB*), novelist; see 12:103–4. The MS was of *Zoe* (see 15:246), which she had written jointly with Elizabeth Paulet (see 13:189).
21. Spiridione Gambardella (see 13:300) was in Liverpool painting portraits, including those of Jeannie and John Welsh.

TC TO CAROLINE FOX

Chelsea, 9 jan*y*, 1843–

Dear Caroline,

Thanks for your excellent news.[1] We will not scold the poor fellow much,—at least not till he get fully well again.

As to the Hero Verran, I wish you to understand that, at such a distance, and with such friends' eyes close on the very scene, I cannot presume to form any farther judgement of his interests, but will leave them altogether to the eyes and hearts of said friends. Do, therefore, what seems to *you* wisest.— Perhaps if there be, as it seems there is, in Verran's personal neighbourhood, a good discerning man, who will take charge of this £20,[2] to do his best therewith for the poor Miner's behoof,—it will be wise, in several ways, to give it up to that man at once and for altogether; saying merely: "*Do* thy best with it for him." Verran may thus gain another friend, and occasional guide and patron; which may be worth more to him than several guineas. "Twenty," I think, is no bad result. To find twenty persons, in any locality, who reverence worth the extent of paying one pound sterling to it, is verily something in these days. Days (as I some times feel, when I reflect sorrowfully on them) altogether unexampled since the Creation of the World, in the respect! [Even the fickle Athenians did at least put Socrates to death, had a least the grace to hate him, did not merely seek to amuse themselves with him!][3] It is unutterable;—and will lead to conclusions by and by.

Meanwhile what the good Caroline has to do is happily utterable enough,—not abstruse or fearful at all! What I have to do is also, alas, too plain: namely to go about my business; and, with many wishes and salutations, *vanish,* as one in haste and double haste; subscribing myself cordially once more

Caroline's Friend,
T. Carlyle

TC-CF, 9 Jan. MS: Duke. Pbd: Fox 175–76; I. Foot, *Michael Verran . . . and Thomas Carlyle* 43–44.

1. About John Sterling's health.
2. For details of subscription to the Verran fund, see Foot 38–40.
3. Someone (presumably Caroline Fox) has overwritten this sentence with a comment beginning "O Thomas Carlyle why dost thou," the rest being illegible. Someone else, presumably at a later date, has written above the line those of TC's words that the superscription made illegible.

TC TO AN UNIDENTIFIED CORRESPONDENT

Chelsea, 11 jan*y*, 1843–

What a peremptory man: "–Receive the honour of Knighthood with this sword, or I will give you a cut with it!"–

You should give me more warning. Three days ago I was bespoken, unlucky that I am, to dine with fat Scotch Theologians, in Gower Street,[1] on Thursday! "Nobody can be in two places at once, unless he be a *bird*":[2] can he?

With sorrow, yet with blessings,
T. Carlyle

JWC TO JEANNIE WELSH

[ca. 12 January 1843]

Dearest Babbie

Both yesterday and today I am so sick–Elizabeth Pepoli might say *so "truly" sick!* that I absolutely cannot set myself to write a handsome letter such as your merits entitle you to expect– But I send you meanwhile something to keep your heart up–a scrap of my execrable handwriting–and a sight of Miss Fox's horror which she calls Carlyle![1] I say *a sight*–for it is my positive will and pleasure that when you have laughed your fill over it and all the rest have enjoyed the same "questionable" pleasure you are to lay it on the coals and there consume it until it be dead–the only fate which beseems such a chimera!– If you do not contrive to lay yourself up with a bad cold by means of all these temptings of providence with white muslim–I shall consider you quite an exceptional little girl–

Carlyle's *first* book[2] will be ready for printing in the spring–he is getting on like a house in fire–there is even a prospect of their giving

TC-UC, 11 Jan. MS: NLS 2883.148. Hitherto unpbd.

1. Unidentified; possibly in London in connection with the threatened disruption of the Church of Scotland. The Wedgwoods lived at 16 Gower St., and may have been involved through Mary Rich and her religious connections.

2. See 15:57.

JWC-JW, [ca. 12 Jan.]. Addr: 20 Maryland Street / Liverpool. MS: NLS 1892.319. Pbd: Huxley, *JWCLF* 236–37, where dated Feb.? 1845. Dated between the arrival of books from Moxon, 6 Jan. (see TC to EM, 7 Jan.), and Jeannie's comparison of Anna Fox's copy of TC's portrait to a murderer (see JWC to JW, [19? Jan.]).

1. Anna Fox had sent her copy of Samuel Laurence's drawing of TC of July 1838 to JWC, Oct. 1842; see 15:163.

2. *Past and Present.* JWC had told Jeannie that "half a dozen other volumes" might be pbd. before *Cromwell;* see JWC to JW, [8 Jan.].

him a little money for this one— Twice during the last week "we have had the visit" (as Mazzini[3] phrases it) of *Mr Chapman & Hall* (Helen announced him so) *to propose*— I may mention at the same time that Moxon another booksel[ler] took the opportunity of coming with Alfred Tennyson[4] and has since sent a magnificent *present of books,* his new editions of Shakspear—Ben Johnson—Massenger and Ford—Beaumont & Fletcher—Wicherly Congreve &c—Curiosities of Literature—Miscellanies of Literature—Charles Lamb's works—Cicero!!![5]— Does it not look as if the Millenium were at hand—attentions from Booksellers are a more infallible proof of *rise in the world,* for people in our time than a whole string of coroneted carriages at the door— Oh what a disgusting world it is after all! especially with ones insides all in a worry from continual blue pills—bless you my darling your JC

JWC TO FRANCES WEDGWOOD

[16? January 1843]

Drama in one Scene.

(A parlour in no 5 Cheyne Row. Enter M*r* Carlyle dressed for a dinner party at Philip van Artevelde's;[1] and looking as if *just setting out for "the thirty* years war"— M*rs* C—wife to the above—is seated at an oval table—strewn with litter—of coloured papers—leather—old books—&c—looking excessively bothered; as well she may—being in the thick of *binding* a copy of Pope's works in *seven* volumes!)

M*r* C: Oh dear *dear* me!

M*rs* C. Dont you think you are going to make yourself too late?

M*r* C: I shall be time enough for any good I shall get! *Certainly* I am

3. Giuseppppe Mazzini (1805–72), Italian revolutionary living in London, close friend of the Carlyles; see 11:225.

4. Moxon was the friend and publisher of Alfred Tennyson (1809–92; *DNB*).

5. *The Dramatic Works of William Shakespeare,* intro. Thomas Campbell (1838); *The Works of Ben Jonson. With a Memoir of his Life and Writings, by Barry Cornwall* (1838); *The Dramatic Works of Massinger and Ford,* intro. Hartley Coleridge (1840); *The Works of Beaumont and Fletcher,* intro. George Darley (1840); *The Dramatic Works of Wycherley, Congreve, Vanbrugh and Farquhar. With Biographical and Critical Notices. By Leigh Hunt* (1840); Isaac D'Israeli, *Curiosities of Literature* (1841) and *Miscellanies of Literature* (1840); *Works of Charles Lamb* (1840); Conyers Middleton, *The History of the Life of Marcus Tullius Cicero* (1839).

JWC-FW, [16? Jan.]. MS: Wedgwood Papers, Univ. of Keele. Pbd: Fielding, *FR2* 308–9. Dated by Wilson's recitals and the arrangements mentioned in JWC to FW, [ca. 25 Jan.].

1. Henry Taylor (1800–86; *DNB*), author of the dramatic poem *Philip van Artevelde* (1834); the Carlyles' friend since 1831; see 6:40.

a most unfortunate man! My dear, are you not sorry for me?

Mrs C: No—

Mr C. Well! I can assure you however, I am heartily sorry for *myself!*

Mrs C: I am sure you are going to be too late—

Mr C: (looking at his watch) hang it! So I am!—but there is something I should like you to do for me—in fact you *must* do it— Write to Mrs Wedgwood *how I am situated*—out today—shall be all shattered to pieces in consequence—and absolutely unequal to any thing more this week: but that *we* will come and dine some Monday (not the first—any other) and go all to Wilson's scotch songs afterwards!![2]

Mrs C. And who do you mean by *we?*

Mr C—*You* and myself. You will write *that* will you?

Mrs C *Me!* me with "my *interior*" (as you call it) in an everlasting worry of blue pills—much good Scotch songs in a cold winter night would do me!

Mr C You will write what I bid you?

Mrs C No—I will engage for you—but not for myself— Dear me you will be an hour too late!

Mr C I am afraid I shall (exit running)

Chelsea
Some Monday

JWC TO JEANNIE WELSH

[18 or 19 January 1843]

My best Babbie

I would have written to you yesterday forenoon; if it had not rained last Monday— The connection of cause and effect here will not be very apparent to you—what the rain of Monday had to do with the writing of yesterday—but so it was—as certainly, as that my husbands having received a *seductive* letter from the *Lady Harriet* a few days since will be cause of Mazzinis hearing a corn law lecture in the Strand tonight![1] "Ah" things are very curiously linked together in this

2. The Scottish singer John Wilson (1800–49; *DNB*) gave a series of recitals, "Wilson's Scottish Entertainments," at the Music Hall, Store St., every Mon. evening, 9 Jan. to 14 Aug., except for the last two Mons. of July.

JWC-JW, [18 or 19 Jan.]. Addr: 20 Mary Land Street / Liverpool. PM: 19 Jan. 1843. MS: NLS 1891.167. Pbd: Huxley, *JWCLF* 80–84 inc. Dated by the Corn Law lecture, 19 Jan., as happening "tonight" or "tomorrow night."

1. Lady Harriet Baring (1805–57; *DNB*), m. to William Bingham Baring (1799–1864; *DNB*), of the Baring banking firm; see 11:40. The lecture was to be in the Lowther Rooms, on the Strand.

little world—the Chinchinopoli[2] chains of invisible workmanship are not half so intricate as some of the connecting chains between the simplest causes and the simplest effects—and I cannot fancy a readier way of losing one's wits, than just sitting down to consider how *this* comes out of *that!* or a readier way of settling one's pride on the great question of man's *free-agency!*

If you would know how the rain of Monday produced the silence of yesterday—I should be sorry to balk your scientific curiosity—so attend and you shall hear— On Monday at one oclock there being every appearance of a clear, dry day I set out in an Omnibus—to buy tea & coffee at *Fortnum & Mason's,*[3] meaning thereafter to pay a *charitable* visit to poor Darwin who was (& is) confined to the house with cold.[4] but no sooner had I issued from the Omnibus according to programme, than contrary to all human expectation, it began to rain on me—so I made for the nearest refuge that offered itself viz: the London Library! being in the Library what could I do but choose myself some books?— every thing I asked for was as usual *"out"* so *as usual* it ended in bringing away french novels—a book of Sand's which I had not before seen and two of——Paul de Kock![5] Having still however some sense of *decency* remaining—I cooly entered my name in the ledger for these books *Erasmus Darwin!* to the wonderment of the bookkeeper doubtless, who must have thought me an odd sort of Erasmus! (this—by the way) Well having the books in the house, it was natural that I should read them—yesterday after breakfast I took up *Frere Jacques*—meaning to read in it only till the table was cleared for writing—but it proved so amusing that hang me if I could lay it down till dinner-time when I had quite finished it— So you see if it had not rained on Monday I should have gone to Darwins—if I had gone to Darwin's I should have had no time to go to the Library. if I had not gone to the Library I should not have fetched away *Frere Jacques* and but for the fascinations of *Frere Jacques* I should have written to you!— So now you see how the two things hang together the same as Lady Harriet Baring's love-making to my husband and Mazzini's hearing M*r* Fox on the corn-law![6] "but how is that again?"— Oh you cannot guess— Well. I

2. Literally, of the city of ceremonious greetings.
3. Purveyors of comestibles, in Piccadilly.
4. Erasmus Darwin lived at 43 Gt. Marlborough St., Oxford St.
5. George Sand, pseud. of Amandine Aurore Lucie, Baroness Dudevant, b. Dupin (1803–76), French novelist; see 13:154. Charles-Paul de Kock (1791–1871), popular and prolific French novelist and playwright of rollicking, often coarse tales of French life. JWC borrowed *Rose et Blanche* (Paris, 1831), written by Sand in collaboration with Jules Sandeau, and de Kock's *Frère Jacques* (Paris, 1825) and *Georgette* (Paris, 1821).
6. William Johnson Fox (1786–1864; *DNB*), unitarian minister, journalist,

will tell you that also—for it is good for your morality that you should be made to reflect on this subject of cause and effect— One can never be too much alive to the consideration that one's every slightest action does not end when it has acted itself, but propagates itself on and on, in one shape or other, thro' all time and away into eternity. Lady Harriet writes to my husband that she is ill—that she dines at four o'clock and is allowed to go nowhere in the evenings—to do nothing but speak—that "there is nobody—(she may really say almost nobody in the world) she likes so well to speak with as him"— Pray mark the fine truth-giving effect of the modifying parenthesis!— "So he sees what a work of *charity* and *piety* is cut out for him"! When a handsome, clever, and reputedly *most haughty* woman appeals to the *charity* and *piety* of a simple man like Carlyle you may be sure she will not appeal in vain— So he writes to her engaging to visit her on Thursday evening—and *forgets* to tell *me* he has done so— Then comes a ticket of admission for one gentleman and one Lady—to Mr Fox's lecture for the same Thursday evening—and he asks me would I like to go? The Devil puts it in my head to answer unexpectedly "yes"— In fact I have been long wanting to hear this Fox lecture—for I understand him to be a first rate speaker—and observing that his place was this time on the straight line of the Omnibus I thought I could never have so good a chance— "Very well says he rather perplexedly—but *I* cannot go with you— I promised to go to Lady Harriet tomorrow evening— Can you get any other man?— Mazzini is the never failing man in every case of need but I would not propose him—for young Italy[7] has been horribly out of favour this long while—seeing that I remained silent he himself however proposed him— As *he* was going *his* road he felt the fairness of allowing *me* to go *mine*— So now you see that chain of consequences also—so far as it yet extends—

But I myself have written a letter the consequences of which I feel more interested in than in any conceivable consequences that can follow out of the Lady Harriet's. After reading the Seaforth manuscript I wrote to Geraldine some of my notions about it, and she answered me in a whole *pamphlet* of witty, devil-may-care objections to my objections— "*C'est assez* [It is enough]" I said to myself "if she *will* run about the streets naked it is not I who am her keeper"— However

---

and politician; see 6:240. Fox was unable to speak "from sudden indisposition" and his place was taken by James Silk Buckingham (1786–1855; *DNB*), a popular lecturer and author of travel books (*Examiner*, 21 Jan.).

7. Mazzini's *Giovine Italia*, founded 1831, in support of republican principles and national unity and independence.

"she had sent on my protest to Betsy" and accordingly in a few days came a letter from "Betsy" also[8]—extremely clever—and what was more to the purpose perfectly *rational*—assuring me that I had merely "said in other words what *she* had been telling Geraldine all along"— Since my letters were sent from one to another I saw no need of writing to both—and Mrs Paulet being clearly the most reasonable of the two I addressed my next to her, and certainly did not conceal the displeasure which Geraldines levity had occasioned me— Now things said *at* one are more annoying than what is said *to* one—and so poor Geraldine "moped," and has had "sore eyes"—and seems to have been sincerely vexed—and finally writes me the best natured, most penitent little letter in the world As nobody knows better than I do the difficulty of confessing oneself *gravely* in the wrong, there is nobody more touched by such confession from another,—so I could not help reading a part of her last letter to Carlyle and declaring that she was after all a good little soul— Carlyle seemed never to have doubted it and winded up his praise of her with "you should ask her to come up here for a little while; it might be of great use to her"!—a proposition of such a *novel* character on *his* part quite took me by surprise, and I sat staring at him without making any answer— "Why says he you seem *doubtful* about it—she is very easy to do with is she not? and you like her company"? "Oh said I at last as to the *doing with*—have no misgivings about *that* but"— "but what"? "Why I am afraid that having her beside me from morning till night would be dreadfully *wearing"!* "You had Jeannie beside you from morning to night—what would be the difference"?!!— "Jeannie! Jeannie was not always in a state of emotion! dropping hot tears on my hands, and watching me and fussing me as Geraldine does!— "Oh as you like! only I think it would be a kindness to *the poor lonely girl*—and that her company might be useful to yourself when you have so little of mine"— I lay awake half the night endeavoring to resolve whether I should ask her or no—but there was so much to be said for and against!—a little of her would be very enlivening—but a continuance of her does really fatigue one—and then to say the truth—tho I am not jealous of my husband (pray read all this into yourself and burn the letter) tho I have not only his *habit* of preference for me over all other women (and *habits* are much stronger in him than *passions*) but also his indifference to *all* women *as women* to secure me against jealousy—still young women who have in them, as Geraldine has, with all her good and great qualities, a born *spirit of intrigue* are perilous sort of inmates for a married pair to

8. Elizabeth Paulet.

invite—they may make mischief in other ways than by *seducing the husband's affections.* Then again; it might as he said really be of use to her in several ways—and should I let my purely selfish misgivings hinder her of the possible good—professing as I do both to herself and other people to have a friendship for her? another argument *for,* the invitation arose out of my consciousness that I am letting myself grow too indolent—perhaps I should be the better of being roused out of my habitual still life and forced to exercise my faculties again in human speech—especially of the intellectual sort which Geraldine takes delight in— Still the thought of those ecstatics she goes on with introduced an immense questionability into the project— So that it was with a hesitating mind I wrote to her finally inviting her *in a sort of a way* to come *"for two or three weeks"*—and it is with an unsettled mind that I await her answer—not knowing whether I wish it be a *yes* or a *no*—and foreseeing that if she come, there will be consequences from her coming either good or evil— I took precious good care not to tell her that the invitation originated with Carlyle—that fact would have *been sufficiently* flattering for her to have founded a whole prospective Romance on it!—and really the sober sadness of this life weigh too heavily on me that I should have much patience with the romances of other people!— I wish I might talk with you for a couple of hours about this and other matters—ones mind does sometimes make such a foolish uncertain figure on paper!

But enough for the present— The watch stand was for *Helen*— I sent it to her instead of the small one which I could not part with— The *other Helen* has plainly not the slightest idea of going away[9]—and as she has behaved quite satisfactorily *since last time,* I had best I think let her be doing for the present—till some really desirable looking servant comes in my way— I should be very much put about in exchanging her for an entire stranger, while I am capable of making so little exertion in the house myself— I can never feel affection or confidence for her after her last misconduct—and should no longer keep her *for her own sake* As I have so often done before—but my own interest will be best served by taking the matter leisurely and keeping her such as she is and has shown herself till I have a distinct prospect of bettering not worsening my position— I was charmed at your discovering that gallows-expression in Carlyle's picture— I have all along been calling it *Greenacre-Carlyle*[10]—

9. Helen Welsh and the "other" Helen Mitchell; for JWC's irritation with the latter, see 15:233.

10. James Greenacre was a notorious murderer, executed 1837; the picture was Anna Fox's copy of Laurence's drawing of TC.

Your letter came in the midst of this— Bless you— Kisses to all— Write me instantly that you have news of Walter[11]

Your affectionate / Jane Carlyle

TC TO [HENRY DRUMMOND]

5. Cheyne Row, Chelsea /
20 jan*y*, 1843—

Dear Sir,

Many thanks for your kind message to me.[1] I had not seen the new Publication; as indeed I see almost no new Books except such as voluntarily come to me: but I find there already are in this several things which it might do me good to see. The Northampton slain at Stafford, for example;[2] he and his seven Comptons,—one of whom, I have read somewhere, was so orthodox even in infancy that he would not *suck* on the Church fast-days![3] One is fond of long genealogies, as of long rivers and Rhine-streams, when they *can* be traced clearly, when they pass by many a noble Drachenfels,[4]—should they even *end* in Dutch quagmires, which are very melancholy to see!— My friend "Hubert" must be of the Northumbrian region, I suppose;[5] Heaven knows what one's affinity to him is. My kindred, it would seem, is of the "Penersaughs Carlyles" (as poor old Nicholas calls them): my great grandfather lies in the churchyard of that place;[6] and beyond him there is no clear light at all. It struck me much, two years ago, standing amid the graves there, to find that beyond *two hundred years* or so there

11. Welsh.

TC-[HD], 20 Jan. MS: EUL. Hitherto unpbd. Addressee identified by the reference to Albury, Drummond's home in Surrey, 3 mi. E of Guildford. Henry Drummond (1786–1860; *DNB*), banker, politician, and prophet in the Catholic Apostolic Church, 36 Belgrave Sq.; see 5:341–42.

1. Inviting TC to visit Albury.

2. In 1842 Drummond pbd. pts. 1 and 2 of *Histories of Noble British Families,* a lavishly illustrated folio of five family trees, including the Compton family; they were later bound with pt. 3 to make vol. 1 of 2 vols. (1846). Spencer Compton (1601–43), 2d earl of Northampton, killed in a fight for the royalist cause at Hopton Heath, nr. Stafford.

3. See 15:191.

4. Mountain on E bank of the Rhine; 1,053 ft. high; scene of Siegfried's slaying of the dragon.

5. Unidentified.

6. Nicholas Carlisle, *Collections for a History of the Ancient Family of Carlisle* (1822); see 14:174. In his Journal TC wrote: "In Penner's Haughs Churchy*d,* I copied (hastily, *dimly*): John Carlyle, in Burrens, died 11 March 1727; age 40 (my grt-grandf*r;* left 2 sons, Thomas, my grandf*r* and Francis ('Capt*n* of Middlebie')." Pennersaughs is ½ mi. from Ecclefechan.

was no legible vestige extant of anything whatever. Two hundred years: and *dust* a thousand years old lay there;—and rocks perhaps a million years; and other invisible *realities* a whole Eternity of years old. We are of yesterday, and know nothing.——

Several months ago I had another favour from you; which I would not trouble you with writing about; but which I did not fail to appropriate and examine with due thankfulness. I find, what interests me not a little, that you and I, tho' starting as it were precisely from opposite poles arrive pretty nearly at the same centre; at this namely, That there must be an Aristocracy to govern, and even a *Land* Aristocracy,—tho' whether our present Land Aristocracy are adequate to do that, or only adequate to fail miserably of doing it, and have themselves and much else thrown into the ditch, we should probably dispute.[7]

A sight of Albury, according to your very kind invitation, could not fail to gratify, to interest me in more than one way. Why should I say that it is not possible yet some day? I heard of Albury long ago, from those that do not now speak to me any more![8]— At present, however, I sit in ninefold imprisonment; struggling with infinite Stupidities (that is to say, writing a Book or volume), and in a state of nerves that renders the duty of staying at home entirely imperative on me. Were the Book done, were the Spring Days come, with their silver radiance, and prophecy of Hope, who knows? The country, then, any kind of country becomes like a sort of unattainable Eden to me; the sunbeams struggling thro' Town-smoke are like a *rance-des-vaches* [smell of cows], and sometimes make me *desert* straightway without counting of costs.

If you ever pass this way, it would give me pleasure to see you. My garret citadel is open at two o'clock and for a while after.

I remain always,

Dear Sir, / Yours with thanks / T. Carlyle

7. Drummond had sent TC his pamphlet *Rights of Laymen* (1841) in April 1841; see 13:113. He had also pbd. *On the Condition of the Agricultural Classes of Great Britain and Ireland. With Extracts from the Parliamentary Reports and Evidence from 1833 to 1840 . . . Preface by H. Drummond,* 2 vols. (1842). Cf. *Past and Present, Works* 10:174, 245.

8. Mainly Edward Irving. See *Reminiscences* 287.

TC TO MARGARET A. CARLYLE

Chelsea, 20 jan*y* (Friday) 1843—

My dear good Mother,

I am sitting here with a nasty *rheumatism in the back*, what they call *lumbago*, which I caught the day before yesterday in the damp; and, what is far worse, with the obligation to go out into the country to dinner and stay all night:[1] so that I am good for nothing at all as the hours go; and after an attempt at a days work, have flung it by, and taken to answer Letters!— To whom ought I to write, in that case, if not to dear Mother withal? I will scribble you also a line before I go:—then I will go, and dine, and stay all night (as really I was partly bound to do, having already *refused* three times, in quick succession),—and they shall look with clear eyes that see me in any adventure of the sort again for a while!

This rheumatism is nothing but the fruit of my own negligence in the damp &c, and perhaps the very dinner will drive it away; for I feel still whole at heart; and am indeed getting on with my work in a reasonable measure— I have learned too not to tear myself in pieces, but to [take][2] a reasonable rest now and then: so, at bottom, there is nothing to be complained of; and I shall get my bit [little] Book done by and by,—and I hope it will be a useful kind of Book; which is the best of all! It goes rather in a fiery strain, about the present condition of men in general, and the strange pass they are coming to; and, I calculate, it may awaken here and there a slumbering blockhead to rub his eyes and consider what he is about in God's Creation: a thing highly desirable at present. I found I could not go on with *Cromwell*, or with anything else till I had disburthened my heart somewhat in regard to all that: the look of the world is really quite oppressive to me,—eleven thousand souls in Paisley alone living on three halfpence a-day, and the Governors of the Land all busy shooting partridges and passing Corn-Laws the while: it is a thing no man with a speaking tongue in his head is entitled to be silent about![3] My only difficulty is that I have far too *much* to say, and require great address in deciding how to say it.—

Jane continues on foot; really better than she has been in past win-

TC-MAC, 20 Jan. MS: NLS 521.10, 512.43. Quot: Froude, *Carlyle* 3:285.

1. At Lewisham, S of the Thames and SE of London, home of Stephen Spring Rice (1814–65), commissioner of customs and son of TC's friend Lord Monteagle; see 14:241.

2. Word omitted.

3. See 14:183 and cf. *Past and Present, Works* 10:3, 171. Paisley, then a textile town in SW Scotland, is 7 mi. WSW of Glasgow.

ters. Our winter here, indeed, is more like a nasty, slobbery sunless Summer; *glar*[mud] and damp are the only things we complain of, no *cold* to hurt even a sickly Jane. There have been only two days that I have noticed with decisive ice; no snow but one shower that lay only a few hours, and then was all *glar* again. I believe you have it harsher in the North: but I hope you, dear Mother, take *good* care of yourself; and as Jenny is there to light the fire, never rise till things are all aired about you. *Do* you follow this course? I have sent you no flannel jackets this year,—tho' I have good warm stockings of *your* spinning on me! I wish I knew what to send, or *any*thing I could do for you: it were surely *much* my part, a duty and a great happiness alike, to do it and send it. You look down from the picture-canvas here upon me, so patient and good;[4] and will not tell me what you want! I have more money now than I used to have; surely if money can get you anything, you *ought* to tell me! Jack says, in answer to my catechising, that you seemed snugly enough provided, and had money of your own,—but he's apt to be a hurried observer. My dear good Mother, what can I do for you?

This Note which I enclose is from an old friend of Edward Irving's,[5] whom I have not heard of for long before: he is very rich and vain, a good[6] devout-hearted man, but full of continual half-mad sallies of one sort or the other: he did Irving a great deal of harm; but shall not me,[7]—I am too old now for that kind of thing. One of my Notes today has been to decline the proferred visit till at least "bright summer weather come,"—if then!

Last night Jane went, under due escort, to hear an Anti-Corn-Law Lecture, which seemed to have amused her somewhat;[8] and I went, the while, to sit for an hour with a certain family called Baring (the American *Lord Ashburton's*[9] son is head of it), the Lady of which, a

4. Maxwell's portrait of Margaret Carlyle had been painted the previous summer and hung in Cheyne Row in Oct.; see 15:129–30 and frontispiece.

5. Henry Drummond.

6. NLS 521.10 ends after the first syllable of the next word.

7. In his *Reminiscences* TC uses almost the identical words: "He, without unkindness of intention, did my poor Irving a great deal of ill; me never any" (294).

8. The *Examiner,* 21 Jan., reported that Buckingham, the speaker, "concluded amidst tremendous applause . . . followed by three times three cheers for free trade and the repeal of the Corn Laws."

9. Alexander Baring (1777–1848; *DNB*), 1st Baron Ashburton, was trained in his father's financial house and later sent to the U.S. to extend its business operations. While there, he m., 1798, Anne Louisa (d. 1848), eldest da. of Sen. William Bingham of Philadelphia. He had concluded the Ashburton-Webster treaty with the U.S., 1842, which settled certain boundary differences between the U.S. and Canada (see 14:42).

considerable admirer of mine, and now very unwell, wished to see me in that way. It was melancholy enough, in my *rheumatic* humour, to look round on all that. A proud, clever woman, of great birth and wealth, in the middle of splendour there; and very probably dying of consumption; certainly very miserable in heart, independent of her illness. I said to myself, "What is the *use* of your greatness, poor Lady Harriet? Why *do* men fret themselves to death for what is worth, it would seem,—nothing!"— They are extremely polite people; and a little talk with *such* is really almost the chief good I get of talking at all at present. Very few men have any fund of truth in them. I prefer holding my peace, and following my work,—which gets on best always in *silence*.

Thank Jamie for his Letter till he get better payment. The Scotch Kirk it would seem is in a really alarming predicament;[10] a Mr Hamilton came here for me the other day to sign a requisition to Dr Chalmers to come and *lecture* here about it.[11] All, I suppose, will be in

10. For earlier crises in the Church of Scotland, see 12:43 and 14:205. The General Assembly, 24 May 1842, had passed the Claim of Right, which stated that civil actions taken in favor of patronage were a threat to the position of the Church guaranteed by the 1707 Treaty of Union and by the statutes of the realm. Its object was to seek protection from what was seen as the encroachments of the civil courts on the spiritual jurisdiction of the Church. The govt. took so long to reply that a convocation of ministers was called in Edinburgh, 17–24 Nov. 1842, at which 354 ministers signed a statement undertaking to resign from the Church unless the govt. accepted the Claim of Right and at which Thomas Chalmers (see below) put forward his plan for financing a Free Church. After this convocation preparations were made at local level for the threatened disruption. Sir James Graham (1792–1861; *DNB*), home sec., issued the govt.'s reply, 4 Jan., saying that they assumed that "nothing less than the total abrogation of the rights of the Crown and of other patrons will satisfy the Church" and completely rejecting the Claim of Right. A special meeting of the Commission of the General Assembly, 12 Jan., declared that the legislature could either force a disruption of the established Church, "with all its attendant evils," or restore the Church to the position of 1834–38, when the Veto Act of the General Assembly (which allowed rejection of a minister introduced by a patron) was still legal. The opposition of the civil courts to these claims was confirmed by the Stewarton decision in the Court of Session, 20 Jan., which declared illegal the setting up of *quoad sacra* (concerned with sacred matters) parishes by the Church and that the ministers of these parishes had no right to a place in Church courts. This threw into doubt every decision of the Assembly since 1834, when such ministers had been admitted. A petition containing the Church's grievances, agreed 31 Jan., was put before the House of Commons, 10 Feb., by Fox Maule (1801–74; *DNB*), M.P. for Perth, and debated 7–8 March, when by 211 to 76 (the majority made up of mainly English M.P.s belonging to the Church of England, a source of bitterness in Scotland) the Commons refused to consider the petition. The Disruption of the Church of Scotland duly took place, 18 May, when 474 ministers out of 1,200 seceded to form the Free Church of Scotland. It was a combination of theological principle and a substitute for a demand for greater national independence.

11. William Hamilton, a merchant of Scottish origin, of Laurie, Hamilton &

vain; and really it is a pity that *that* had been the end of it.– My brotherly salutations to Isabella, to Jenny; my blessings on one and all of you. Adieu, dear Mother.

Your ever affectionate
T. Carlyle

TC TO DAVID THOM

5. Cheyne Row, Chelsea
London, 20 jan*y*, 1843–

Dear Sir,

Your Letter, and still earlier the Book it was to announce,[1] arrived here several days ago. Many thanks for both. The friendly inscription you have prefixed to the Book is all the more gratifying to me, or rather is alone gratifying, as I can discern by clear indications, what I already knew by credible report, that you are a man of sincerity,—a very rare kind of man at present. I am accustomed to say, and do not mean any paradox, that Intelligence and Integrity are twin faces of the same thing, and cannot be divorced at all; a fact which is very important and very cheering to me in looking at these sad days. If praise be of any value, as certainly it sometimes is withal, then praise from such a man is precisely the kind for another man.

I have not yet got your *Divine Inversion* sufficiently examined; nor am I sure that I shall ever fully succeed in penetrating into the peculiar centre where you stand and look: but I already seem to myself to discern indubitable analogies with much that is deepest and most central in what I otherwise have come to believe; and I may venture already to express my persuasion that the Doctrine you state and enforce there, is, in the real essence of it, *true*.

Wishing you good success, wishing you faithful continual endeav-

---

Co., 127 Cheapside; see 5:302. Thomas Chalmers (1780–1847; *DNB*), Scottish theologian, one of the leaders of the evangelicals and first moderator of the Free Church. As convenor of the financial section of the provisional committee, Chalmers was working for the establishment of the Free Church. He did not come.

TC-DT, 20 Jan. Addr: Bold-Street Chapel / Liverpool. MS: Strouse. Hitherto unpbd. David Thom (1795?–1862), ordained, 1823, as minister of the Scotch Church, Rodney St., Liverpool; deposed for heresy by the presbytery of Glasgow, 1825; became minister of Bold St. Chapel, which had been formed in 1823; frequently engaged in theological controversy; author of many books on theology. See J. A. Picton, *Memorials of Liverpool* (1875) 2:245–46.

1. *Divine Inversion* (1842).

our, which is the best success, in all your strugglings, and strenuous life-battles (for such, I see, yours are), I remain, / Dear Sir,

Yours with thanks and regard,
T. Carlyle

TC TO JOHN A. CARLYLE

Chelsea, Tuesday Afternoon
[24 January 1843]

My dear Brother,

My rheumatic back was almost well; and now this morning, while I stooped washing myself, it grew all at once horribly ill again (as if some huge tiger had struck its claws into me,—there is a simile for you!)—and I have been very lame ever since. My persuasion is that I can cure it, by blue-pill and castor; for I feel as if the mischief, and even the very pain, were *within* as much as without; and I do not feel nearly so heart-sick as I did on Sunday. This night I mean to experiment.

I go on with my work; which is an infinite comfort, indeed the only comfort I have any need of. To be *weak* is miserable,[1] and there is no other misery.——

They have called me down to dinner; I have dined, and here in the ultimate dusk finish off my response to you.

There has a curious Book, *Bamford's Passages in the Life of a Radical,* come to me.[2] You may recommend it to Cochrane in my name:[3] it is to be had "at Middleton near Manchester from the Author."

Can you ask Cochrane too if he has got Robertson's account of Dr Francia (or whatever the title is)?[4]

TC-JAC, [24 Jan.]. Addr. 3. Chester Terrace / Regent's Park. PM: Chelsea, 25 Jan 18[43]. MS: NLS 524.42. Hitherto unpbd. Dated by TC's rheumatic back (see TC to MAC, 20 Jan.) and by the postmark.

1. Cf. *Paradise Lost* 1:157.

2. Samuel Bamford (1788–1872; *DNB*), poet and weaver; champion of the working class; unjustly imprisoned at time of Peterloo Massacre, 1819; worked as a journalist in Lancashire, beginning ca. 1826 and apparently giving up journalism, 1839; special constable in Middleton during Chartist troubles, 1839; moved to Blackley, nr. Manchester, ca. 1840, where JWC visited him, 1846; worked in London in inland revenue office, 1851–58, then returned to Lancashire and to his trade as weaver; author of poems and other writings, including *Passages in the Life of a Radical,* pbd. in pts., 1839–42, bound in 2 vols., 1843, and an extended edn., 1844. See W. H. Chaloner, intro., *The Autobiography of Samuel Bamford,* 2 vols. (1967).

3. John George Cochrane (1781–1852; *DNB*), first librarian of the London Library; see 5:123 and 12:346.

4. J. P. and W. P. Robertson, *Francia's Reign of Terror* (1839), pbd. as vol. 3 of their *Letters on Paraguay* (1839), of which TC used the 2d edn. (1839).

I hope you will get down some day soon after 2 o'clock.
Good bye meanwhile, and all blessings be with you!

Your affectionate / T.C.

JWC TO FRANCES WEDGWOOD

[ca. 25 January 1843]

Dearest Mrs Wedgwood

Here is Mrs Jameson's address,[1] which I have procured from her sister in Belgrave Place— If you can make out the word before *Cottage* I shall consider you qualified to read——your own beautiful little handwriting!

I am afraid we must postpone *the transaction* till a future Monday[2]— Carlyle went to *Lewisham* last week and staid all night—the consequences have been dreadful! "Rheumatism in his back," "indescribable qualms in his interior" and the Devil to pay ever since! We are still only getting the damage repaired thro' blue pill and castor oil. The Lewisham day was a fatal one for *me* also tho' I did not *stir* from home— *Robertson* came in the evening[3]—and Carlyle, who *does* all the talk *naturally*, not being there I was obliged to talk a little—this simple talking—and to Robertson—for whom anything is good enough—threw me into such a flurry that I went to bed as much excited as a young Lady after her first ball—and did not fall asleep till four in the morning!!

Did you ever hear of such a pair? fitter to be transfered to *Hunter's Museum*[4] than to live anywhere else on the earth—

TC lists them separately in "Dr. Francia," *Foreign Quarterly Review* 31 (July 1843):544–89. He borrowed both from the London Lib. in Jan. José Gaspar Rodriguez Francia (1761?–1840), Paraguayan lawyer and dictator.

JWC-FW, [ca. 25 Jan.]. MS: Wedgwood Papers, Univ. of Keele. Hitherto unpbd. Approximately dated after TC's back pain and his visit to Lewisham, 20 Jan. (see TC to MAC, 20 Jan.), and in reply to Frances Wedgwood's letter of "Tuesday," [24 Jan.].

1. Anna Brownell Jameson (1794–1860; *DNB*), author; see 7:144 and 10:196. She was staying at her mother's cottage in Ealing, ca. 8 mi. W of London; see 15:120.

2. In her letter Mrs. Wedgwood had said: "Most gladly will we accept the plan alluded to in the Dramatic Scene [16 Jan.?] transmitted to me through the medium of Rowland Hill [i.e., the penny post]—long ago now—for many days I have been hoping to come to you but that hope no longer exists . . .—so do you in the plural come next Monday & do the Scottish Minstrel [John Wilson] in Store Street— It is so mild that I do hope that you in the singular dearest Mrs Carlyle will come also. . . . I will expect you at ½ 4."

3. John Robertson (d. 1875), journalist; see 9:337 and 10:137.

4. In Lincoln's Inn Fields, founded by John Hunter (1728–93), surgeon and

I am wearying very much to see you—and what is more to the purpose I *will* see you before I am much older

Affectionately yours / Jane Carlyle

TC TO [HENRY DRUMMOND]

Chelsea, 26 jan*y*, 1843–

My dear Sir,

In one corner of your Note there is a gentle but very sad indication, which seems to say to me that *perhaps I ought* to come, and straightway![1] If I am right, pray consider that I have already consented; that after some two weeks, when your sorrow-stricken house is again set in order, I will come whenever you ask me.

These are horrible days and doings; and it is not the guiltiest who suffer, but the most innocent:[2]—as indeed which of us *is* "innocent"? Heavy afflictions fall upon you: as my good Mother would say in her dialect, so say I in mine, "May they be sanctified!"

With much sympathy and regard, / I remain always / Yours most truly

T. Carlyle

TC TO THE HON. SECRETARIES OF THE MANCHESTER ATHENAEUM

Chelsea, 26 jan*y*, 1843–

Sir,

I had the honour, several days ago, to receive your invitation to the Annual Meeting of the Athenaeum; for which I can now only return

---

anatomist, which later became part of the Royal College of Surgeons. It included medical curiosities.

TC-[HD], 26 Jan. MS: NLS 7197.2. Hitherto unpbd. Correspondent identified by TC to MAC, [28 Jan.], where TC mentions that he has had a second letter from Drummond and that he has undertaken to visit him in two weeks' time.

1. The letter stated that Drummond's son was dying and wished to see TC; see TC to MAC, [28 Jan.].

2. Probably an allusion to the death of Drummond's cousin Edward Drummond, 25 Jan., from an assassin's bullet; see TC to MAC, [28 Jan.].

TC-[HSMA], 26 Jan. MSS: EUL and NLS Acc. 5127, both written by TC on paper with the same watermark. The EUL MS has the subscription torn off, and the NLS MS has the subscription "J Parker Esq*r* &c &c" crossed through in pencil. Text: EUL. The NLS MS has two blots on the first pg., and probably therefore TC wrote it out again. A facsimile of the EUL MS was pbd. in Edward W. Watkin, *Alderman Cobden of Manchester* (1891), opp. 138, Watkin having presumably torn off the inaccurate subscription for the lithograph to be made my thanks and regrets. The state of my arrangements here rendered it impossible for me to come; and, in some accidental confusion, your Note itself has been lost, so that I have too long neglected even to reply. Pray accept my excuses; attribute my delay to something better than neglect.

Your Institution, if I rightly understand it, is one to which all rational men will wish success. To provide the working people with a Place of Reunion, where they might enjoy books, perhaps music, recreation, instruction; and at all events, what is dearest to all men, the society and sight of one another: this is a thing of palpable utility, a thing at once possible and greatly needed;—it is a thousand pities *this* were not brought to pass, straightway, in all working Towns! I have regretted much, in looking at your great Manchester, and its thousandfold industries and conquests, that I could not find, in some quarter of it, a hundred acres of green ground with trees on it, for the summer holidays and evenings of your all-conquering industrious men; and for winter-season and bad weather quite another sort of social meeting-places than the Gin-shops offered!— May all this, and much else, be amended. May good and best speed attend you and your benevolent associates in your attempts to amend some part of it.

I remain, with thanks and good wishes,

Yours very truly / T. Carlyle

JWC TO JEANNIE WELSH

Thursday [26 January 1843]

My Darling

I believe I should do wisely to make a sacred *week* of it—to wholly abstain, for eight days, from writing to man, woman, or child! Seeing that in the week past I have nearly written myself into *delirium tremens!* at least (to stick by *the fact*), I have written myself clean off my *sleep!* and *that* is a grave consequence in my particular case—the exception being so apt to become the general rule— This is one of the

without it. The Sotheby catalog for the auction, 3 Dec. 1974, at which the EUL MS (item 106) was sold, states that it was addressed to "Messrs. Watkin and Berlyn, Honorary Secretaries of the Manchester Athenaeum." Edward William Watkin (1819–1901; *DNB*) became director of the Manchester Athenaeum, 1843; later a successful railway promoter and an M.P.; knighted, 1868. He and Peter Berlyn served as hon. secs. of the great bazaar, 1843. The Manchester Athenaeum was founded, 1835, for the purposes TC describes.

JWC-JW, [26 Jan.]. Addr: Thomas Cooke's Esq*r* / 42 George Street / Manchester. PM: Chelsea, 26 Jan. 1843. MS: NLS 1891.176. Pbd: Huxley, *JWCLF* 84–87 inc.

*dis*advantages of that *"constant stillness,"* which you protest against; the less one is excited the less can one bear excitation— I have observed this in myself, in Carlyle, in all people that I have had opportunity of seeing into— Long continued stillness in *purifying the blood,* seems to have the effect of *thinning the skin,* so that the merest flea-bite pierces into one, and inflames, and irritates, as thick-skinned people cannot have the smallest idea of! A curious instance of this occured to both C. and myself a few days ago— *He* went to dine and *stay all night*—not with *Mrs Laing*—but with young Spring Rice, at Lewisham[1]—it was no party—quite a domestic transaction, and attended with no bodily fatigue. He returned with rheumatism in his back, nameless qualms "in his *interior*"—there has been the devil to pay ever since—and nothing less than a blue pill and doze of castor-oil have been needed—to counteract that quiet visit! Then, for *my* part in the illustration; it happened that Robertson[2] came the evening that C. was at Lewisham—and sat two or three hours— So that I was under the necessity of talking a little— C. not being there to take the trouble off me— Well! this mere talking—and to Robertson—for whom *anything* is good enough—threw me into such a flurry; that I went to bed as excited as a young lady after her first Ball—and never closed my eyes till four in the morning!— Did you ever hear of such a thin-skinned pair? Nor was this all the consequence to me of Robertson's visit that evening. He had come to request that I would put down in writing for him "my little history of the vinegrette"—to be published along with other documentary evidence he is collecting against the present order of pawnshops[3]— I promised quite readily, without considering the *quantity* of writing it would take—but it *made* me consider it when I found myself filling sheet after sheet—yet if I told the story at all I must do it in *my own* way—not in the dry way of a police-report— So *there* was *one* good spell of writing for me!—then just at the same moment Harriet Martineau took it into her head to involve me in writing *her two long* letters "in quick sucession" of the *reasoning* sort;[4] the sort of all others which are most apt to *murder sleep.*[5] Poor Harriet seems to me to be got into a dreadful state of *"self-consciousness"* of late—to be fancying always that the world has noth-

1. Presumably Mary Laing, b. Cowan, wife of the politician and author Samuel Laing (1812–97; *DNB*); see 15:155–56. Stephen Spring Rice.

2. John Robertson.

3. The story of the vinaigrette not traced. Presumably it had to do with its theft from JWC and discovery in a pawnshop.

4. Harriet Martineau (1802–76; *DNB*), author, living as an invalid in Tynemouth; see 6:305 and 13:42.

5. Cf. *Macbeth* 2.1.

ing more important to do than to occupy itself with *her*, and *her* "principles of action"!—that affair of *the pension* having subsided[6]—and full time that it should!—she has got up a new *excitement* for herself—fully as absurd it strikes me, as Gambardella's "letting his hairs grow" She is demanding thro'out the whole circle of her corresponence which is almost as wide as the world—that there should be a general thorough conflagration of her letters—for fear of their publication at her death—and this she calls—not what it really is, a diseased anxiety about her future *biography* but *"her protest against the laxity of society in the matter of letters"*[7] "She feels it her *duty* (varnish!) to set this example" &c &c— I felt it *my* duty (without varnish) to tell her that I considered the whole uproar *"unworthy* of her"—to tell her a great many very sensible things. which have been entirely thrown away— "She perceives that I think her a little *mad*—morally"—but the only inference she has drawn from that is that *I* must be a little mad—morally—and so she goes on exciting this letter-conflagration as if it were "the burning-up of all the sins of the world"[8]— I have *done* the *practical* in the matter—keeping only an autograph for Helen[9]—but for the rest, have told her that I must be allowed to retain my own *opinion.*

Besides the 'history' and these *controversial letters,* my acquaintance here have all *conspired* one would say, to write me notes at one time, requir immediate answers—more or less long! Even Anna Maria[10] of Falmouth writes "wilt *thou* have the goodness to inform me &c &c"— They are all settled with, now however,—having cost me a good deal in *valerian*—and I write to my Babbie not from duty but affection—

All this about Walter is heartily vexatious—the only comfort one has, is in hoping that a *moral* good may result to him from the *material* annoyance—a young man is all the better for having a little *struggle* for his future ease—that he may know what stuff this world is made of—but when the young man is ones *cousin;* one is apt to lose sight of

6. She had refused the offer of a pension; see 15:175.

7. For her views on the matter, see intro. to her *Autobiography,* 3 vols. (1877), and letters of Jan. and Feb. in *Harriet Martineau's Letters to Fanny Wedgwood,* ed. E. S. Arbuckle (Stanford, 1983) 41–55. She wanted Mrs. Wedgwood to read a part of a letter dealing with the subject "to all of our coterie who may chance to have any letters or notes of mine," including the Carlyles. "I have mentioned it to dear Jenny, but not at sufficient length" (43–44).

8. Like Ram Das; see 2:464.

9. Welsh, who collected them; probably the fragment of a letter signed H. Martineau, apparently written when she was still living with her mother in London at a time when JWC had been suffering from flu: "I do believe you have had more of it than any body in England" (NLS Acc. 8140). JWC also enclosed with this letter notes from Letitia Macready and Fanny Wedgwood.

10. Fox.

that *judicious* reflection!—to dwell rather on the hope of his struggle being speedily ended—by the approaching tumblement of all the non-intrusionists out of the Scotch Church[11]—

I pity my Uncle most of any body concerned— Your other piece of intelligence makes me really glad— I do not exactly understand how Alick should have fallen in love with Sophy[12] but if he have done so (entirely his own affair) I am sure she will make him a much better wife than many a showier person—in a more elevated position might have done— She will feel so *grateful* to him! and she has been so domestically brought up!—and then poor good M*rs* Martin will be so happy! I will not engage to *dance* at that wedding—my dancing-days being past—but I will bestow my warmest sanction on it—

Yes—of course—Geraldine comes! A perfectly exstatic acceptance by return of post made me almost angry with myself that I could not share her *transports!*[13] could only look into the thing with a *dubious* satisfaction— I hope it will turn out well for *her* at all events—such *faith* deserves fulfilment—the *when* is not settled—there were *shifts* to be provided!!— She seems herself to have some idea of my misgivings—for she assures me that I "will find her much *quieter* to *live* with than to see just for a day"—and that as she has two other invitations she will not be altogether "*on my arms*" as I once said to her! God grant! for "my arms" are of the weakest! God bless you my own good child my love to Helen—and please remember me to your beautiful-eyed cousin[14]— Ever thine / Jane Carlyle

TC TO ALEXANDER J. SCOTT

Chelsea, 27 jan*y*, 1843—

Dear Scott,

Many thanks for *Dunlop;* thanks also for your hint of this morning, which I understand!

I investigated forthwith, with much satisfaction, the "attempt to cut Oliver down"; a valiant and very honest attempt on the part of our

11. The delay between Walter Welsh's presentation (Nov. 1842) and ordination (13 Sept.) would be solved when his opponents (the "non-intrusionists," those opposed to the imposition of ministers by patrons) left the Church on the Disruption.

12. Alexander, Jeannie's brother, was to m. Sophy Martin, da. of Mrs. Martin (d. 1847), the Welshes' cousin and neighbor.

13. For JWC's invitation to Geraldine Jewsbury, see JWC to JW, [18 Jan.].

14. Walter Macgregor of Liverpool, Jeannie's cousin, toward whom she seems to have been romantically inclined.

TC-AJS, 27 Jan. MS: Berg. Hitherto unpbd. Alexander John Scott (1805–66; *DNB*), minister at Woolwich; see 5:351.

good John,—tho' the *rope* proves a little toughish for him, good man![1]

I did not write straightway in answer; because I had to be in Lewisham in a few days, and hoped to get across to Woolwich with the thing in my pocket as I returned. Alas, at Lewisham I found myself "seven miles of intimate country" from Plumstead;[2] with a sleepless night close in the rear of me, and a thing they call *lumbago,* as if the *Tigre National*[3] had struck his claws into my back: I was totally inadequate for Woolwich that day! I wrapt up the printed leaves, and laid them in the shelf with your address; hoping you might call soon; and now, failing that, here under the escort of your two blue stamps they return to you.

Do not fail to come and see me whenever you get to Town. I will see Woolwich too before very long.

I am writing a kind of "Tract for the Times," of some extent, *not* in the Pusey vein.[4] Wish me well thro' it.

The Maker of this Universe was wise,
He plann'd all Souls, all Systems, worlds and Particles;
The great Groundplan he used from end to end
Was the Rev*d* Newman's Nine-and-thirty Articles![5]

Adieu, dear Scott,

Yours ever truly / T. Carlyle

1. Scott had apparently sent TC a copy of *Oliver Cromwell: A Poem, in Three Books* (Edinburgh, 1829), by John Dunlop (1789–1868), Scottish-born author and temperance reformer (see 13:22). TC presumably refers to Dunlop's defense of Cromwell's reputation in his pref. as well as the poem: "No character in British history has been so mercilessly dealt with as that of Oliver Cromwell" (vi).

2. A parish in the borough of Woolwich, S of the Thames, where Scott lived.

3. Literally, "National Tiger"; unexplained.

4. *Past and Present.* The *Tracts for the Times* were a series of ninety pamphlets, pbd. 1833–41, written by John Henry Newman (1801–90; *DNB*), John Keble, Edward Bouverie Pusey (1800–82; *DNB*), et al., advancing the "Tractarian" or "Oxford Movement" claim for the catholic nature of the Church of England, i.e., for its authority and divine power similar to that traditionally claimed for the Roman Catholic Church. The last and most famous was "Tract XC," in which Newman argued that the Thirty-Nine Articles of Religion of the Anglican Church are not inconsistent with a "catholic" faith.

5. Scott replied, 22 Feb.: "I should count a Tract for the Times from you a public good. You have my Glückauf [wishes for success] most warmly. I am glad to see you condescend to take notice of M*r* Newman and his articles, for assuredly they show how the wind sits, at least one of the currents, the lower of the shorter-lived one."

TC TO MARGARET A. CARLYLE

Chelsea, Saturday [28 January 1843]—

My dear Mother,

I should send you half a word to say that my *lumbago* is all gone, by the aid of some medicines I took; that I am *terribly*, and every moment of my time, BUSY; and that my poor Book is going on apace. I expect to be at press with it before a couple of months and to have you a copy of it before the Summer come! It is a fiery thing; and tells lumps of the truth, in a franker manner than I have ever done hitherto. The time is come for it, I think! When men are dying round you of want of bread, and two millions of them sitting in workhouses or living otherwise on Parish Alms, and the Governors busy only with their partridge-shooting, I think one ought to speak.—

Here is the last Note I had from Jack: on the back of it are scribblings and preparatory scrawlings which have now gone safe into the Book. I scrawl on any bit of loose paper that is near me.

The day before yesterday I had a Note from Jean at Dumfries: she is better now, she says; your flannel gown and the shamoy leather waistcoat assisted her. Poor thing, she has a struggling time of it among those unhealthy *bairns*. A new *charge*, it seems, is awaiting her before long.[1]— Poor Isabella, I grieve to hear from her, is at present worse rather than better. Jenny, I calculate, still stays with you: I like better to fancy her there.

Curious enough, I happened, last time, to send you a Note of Henry Drummond's.[2] I had just answered him before I went off to my engagement (it was with young Spring Rice) at Lewisham: my omnibus, up in the town, was to start from this Henry's Bank at Charing Cross; on arriving there I found the street all in emotion,—the assassin Macnaughten had just fired his pistol into this Henry's brother! Nobody could give me the smallest account of it; the only thing too sure was that Henry Drummond's Brother was shot; and the criminal instantly taken up. Next morning, we read in the Papers, that there was no danger. Alas, in two days more, the poor man had died! Macnaughten, it appears, now confesses that he took his victim for Sir R. Peel. That is a fact for the Corn-Law men! M'Naughten is from Glasgow, not a poor man at all; I suppose, a fanatic for Corn-Law Repeal.[3] The world is getting to a strange pass!—

TC-MAC, [28 Jan.]. MS: NLS 512.61. Hitherto unpbd. Dated by TC to [HD], 26 Jan., where TC talks of visiting Henry Drummond within two weeks.

1. A son, John, b. April.
2. See TC to MAC, 20 Jan.
3. Edward Drummond (1792–1843; *DNB*), Henry's 2d cousin, not his

Poor Henry Drummond has written me a second time. He had but two sons; one of them is dead of consumption, the other dying,—and it was he, this last one, that wanted to see me.[4] Poor creature! I have undertaken to go, in two weeks.—

Blessings on you dear Mother; blessings on all my true Brotherhood;—and a hasty adieu just now.

Ever your affect*e* / T. Carlyle

TC TO JAMES G. MARSHALL

Chelsea, 1 feb*y*, 1843—

Dear Marshall,

Many thanks for your good hearty Letter; the sunniest I have read for a good many days. I hope that Forster will call upon you soon;[1] that you will find one another mutually supportable Phenomena in this world, where it is not pleasant to be alone!—

What you report of your recession from Public Radicalism is altogether agreeable to me.[2] You have chosen the better part, I do honestly think. It needs that you go on in the same, to higher and higher heights; that hundreds and thousands gradually fall into the same, and escort and encourage you thereon! This is actually my opinion. A *real* Aristocracy, in place of a false imaginary Aristocracy, is becoming and already become indispensable for English Society,—and the Captains of Industry, not the Captains of Idleness whatever array and honours they may for the present hold, are the men for that.[3] Not "arms and

---

brother; private sec. to the prime minister, Sir Robert Peel (1788–1850; *DNB*), was shot in the back, 20 Jan., as he was walking toward Downing St., by Daniel McNaughtan, age 27, a wood-turner of Glasgow, in mistake for Peel. Drummond was able to walk to his brother's bank, 49 Charing Cross, where the bullet was extracted, but d. 25 Jan. At his trial, 3 March, McNaughtan, who was under the delusion the tories were persecuting him, was acquitted on grounds of insanity, the case providing the so-called McNaughtan Rule for defining insanity as a defense in court. Though no link with McNaughtan was found, there was much speculation about the possibility of the Anti-Corn Law League's responsibility for incitement to violence. McNaughtan was the spelling he used in his signature; there are many variants.

4. Drummond had three sons—Henry (1811–27), Malcolm (1821–42), and Arthur Henry (1822–43), who d. 6 Aug.

TC-JGM, 1 Feb. MS: Yale. Hitherto unpbd. James Garth Marshall (1802–73), Leeds flax manufacturer; see 10:95.

1. William Edward Forster (1818–86; *DNB*), Bradford businessman; see 15:229. Forster, whom TC had met only a few mos. previously, was in the woolen trade and, like Marshall, lived in Yorkshire. TC considered them both enlightened businessmen.

2. See 13:288.

3. Cf. *Past and Present, Works* 10:271–72.

the man" now our epic; no, it is "Tools and the man."[4] Not "arms and the man"; how much less "White waistcoats and the man!" I counsel you to go on, and *be* a real King, and guide, and just *Law-ward* (antique for "Lord"[5]) or Preserver of God's Law, among your people. The first man that effectually accomplishes such an example will be a blessed man in England. Go on, and fear not! Indeed, "it is not pleasant to be alone," as I say; but every man must hold himself ready, on occasion, to be it. All good fellows I have ever heard of were oftentimes in that same "minority of *one*": they stood there, worked there, and it gradually became a minority of *two*, of many; gradually a *majority*, and at length a *universality!*—

The Book I am writing will be at Press, if I prosper, in some six weeks, and out before the summer. It is properly a development of the very things I am now writing here to you. I think of calling it "Past and Present," or some such title: it is partly historical, partly oratorical,—dreadfully difficult to bring under any of the "*icals*" or "*oricals*," and keep from looking too bedlami*cal!* A "Tract for the Times" full of the most portentous Speculative-Radicalism ever uttered in Governess-English, or even in *Carlylese* as they call it!— All this is a dead secret hitherto, and you need not speak of it to anybody.

Mrs Marshall sends me a beautiful Postscript; for which pray return her in my name most kind thanks;—I will thank her in speech again, some day, by and by.[6]

Good Speed to you always! Yours very truly

T. Carlyle

TC TO JOHN STUART MILL

Chelsea, 1 feb*y*, 1843—

Dear Mill,

I am about sending off those Berlin Autographs on Sunday first.[1] If you can find a Bentham, Brougham, or whatever you can find, will

4. Cf. *Past and Present, Works* 10:209. "Arms and the man": *Aeneid* 1.1.
5. TC's etymology is mistaken: "Lord" comes from "hlafweard," bread-keeper.
6. Mary Alicia Pery Marshall, b. Spring Rice (1812–75), m., Feb. 1841.

TC-JSM, 1 Feb. MS: NLS 618.105. Pbd: A. Carlyle, *CMSB* 81. John Stuart Mill (1806–73; *DNB*), philosopher; see 5:379.
1. To Karl August Varnhagen von Ense (1785–1858), Prussian soldier, diplomat, and biographer, who collected them; see 9:382.

you send it to me before that date.[2] Your Father's autograph, at any rate;[3]—your own I shall not need!—

Yesternight I heard from this Varnhagen a description of the Austins, whom he had met.[4] The "mistriss Sarah Austin" appears to have won laurels from him: the John Austin to have seemed perhaps—*etwas bedenklich* [somewhat serious], in a point or two!

Come soon again some evening or Sunday. Favonius and all the West Winds and Spirits invite you,—as do some other Spirits withal.[5]

The news from Sterling is again not so favourable: "weak," "recovery slow"—nothing worse as yet.

Yours ever truly / T. Carlyle

JWC TO JEANNIE WELSH

Thursday evening [2 February 1843]

Darling

Do you know, between ourselves, I am not at all sure that I have not got a little of—the spirit of prophecy! and why not? My Great Great Ancestor John Welsh the Covenanter had the gift of prophecy beyond all doubt—he displayed it on many remarkable occasions—once; I remember he foretold to a certain City in France which had used him scurvily that the Plague would devour it in a few days—as it actually did[1]— Now why not fancy a little of a turn for prophecy to be still in the blood as well as a tendency to consumption &c &c?—

2. Jeremy Bentham (1748–1832), leader of the utilitarian school. Henry Peter Brougham (1778–1858; *DNB*), Baron Brougham and Vaux, whig politician.

3. James Mill (1773–1836), utilitarian philosopher.

4. John Austin (1790–1859; *DNB*), jurist, and his wife Sarah, b. Taylor (1793–1867; *DNB*), trans. and enthusiastic advocate of German culture; see 5:386–87. They had been living in Germany for Austin's health and for economy.

5. In Roman mythology Favonius was the favorable west wind.

JWC-JW, [2 Feb.]. MS: NLS 1893.187. Pbd: Huxley, *JWCLF* 330–34, where dated 17 May 1849 because the letter is bound with an envelope postmarked 18 May 1849. Dated here by Geraldine Jewsbury's visit apparently beginning Mon., 6 Feb., by Thackeray's recent return from Paris, and by FitzGerald's visit to London (see below).

1. John Welch or Welsh (1568?–1622), presbyterian minister, m. Elizabeth (d. 1625), youngest da. of John Knox. JWC's ancestor was not John Welsh but his elder brother, David of Colliston; see 3:420. She may have confused several stories about John Welsh's prophetic gifts: two concerned the plague breaking out in Ayr and the turning away of two travelers who then took the plague to Cumnock; the other was about the second siege of St. Jean d'Angely by Louis XIII when Welsh prophesied that the city would fall. No story has been traced about the plague and a French city.

Even Carlyle tells me sometimes that I have "the intelligence of *Schuping sing*" (you remember that Chinese young Lady?)—"who *resembled* a disembodied spirit" in the accuracy of her insight;[2] being able to tell always what her enemies were plotting on the other side of stone walls— The occasion on which my spirit of prophecy—or Shuping-sing-intelligence—call it what you like—has just evinced itself, relates to you and your dose of physic—both Tuesday and Wednesday when I returned disappointed from the letter box I said to myself—there is something strange in this—if it be not that she has worn herself out in Manchester, and has had to take physic since her return!— When today I came to the *physic* in your letter I felt a sort of fear—of *myself*—really shuddered at the superhuman in me! Along with your letter today came one from Geraldine which I allowed to repose on the mantlepiece till I had read yours all thro, and behold when I opened it; the first words were that she would be here on Monday! good heavens and *this Thursday* I feel as if I should have little enough time to get up the steam—I do not mean the *house-steam* for *that* you know will not be put out of its natural course but my own internal steam— Carlyle now says "My dear I wish that girl may not fatigue you dreadfully?—" ! "it is needless to be getting up such apprehensions, after the matter has reached its actual stage— "Oh I hope not says I Jeannie like the judicious little soul she always is, has told her that it will be best she should let me alone, and not fuss me when I am ailing"— He reflected a moment and then asked—"would it not be better if *I* wrote to her myself and impressed the same thing on her before she arrived at all—"? Poor Geraldine! I declined this considerate offer—for really I thought if *he* should write to that same effect, she might be driven to carry the letting-alone system to an extreme—and I should be as much worried with her unnatural stillness as with her natural superabundance of emotion. Indeed I am so prepared for *the worst* that I do not think she will drive me out of my composure. At all events it is very absurd to ask her to come and then to take fright at the thought of it—the beautiful confidence of sixteen with [which][3] she is *rushing to my arms* on the first word—deserves a kinder return—

Now Babbie never pique yourself any more on the *crimping* of *that collar*—I grant you it was a *devoted* proof of affection but I flatter myself I have done as much, and more, for you in the copying of my whole correspondence with Robertson for your delectation!— I who have an absolute horror of copying—especially my own letters!—there

2. Shuping Sing, a fictional character who could see through stones; see 5:319.

3. Omitted in MS.

it is nevertheless! manuscript enough to curl your hair with for a month—besides the "intellectual feast" it will be to you!—a feast, by the way, not unlike that which was once set before me at a fine country-town-evening-party where I happened to find myself in appetite (I was young then, and not above feeling *hungry* at times) well supper came in due course, and each person received—a *wineglass* heaped with white froth (of milk) with a teaspoonful of redcurrant jelly at the bottom! devil a thing else!

I can sympathize with you in your Manchester—"miseries of human life"— Oh yes, I know the irritation of feeling oneself entirely superseded in the heart and life of an old companion by a little troublesome monkey of a child. I remember my first visit to Agnes Vetch after she became a *haus-frau* [house wife][4]—my *friend par excellence*—as I considered her—before I knew what the word *friend* meant—for ones first *friendships* are apt to be as great *spooneyisms* as one's first *Loves! That* does not however hinder one from thinking them life-and-death matters at the time, and so I had my heart quite crushed within me by being made to feel at every turn, that the vilest squall of her little slobbery red-coloured child was more precious music to her ears than the most eloquent language of my long-tried affection—but I learned, as you will do—just to take back my friendship from those who knew not the worth of it and to bestow it on such as did—"*That minds me*"[5] as Helen says—*I* am going to be found in a child!—without personal inconvenience however and—without possibility of detriment to my other affections—I am requested to be God mother to the new Macready! *Jane* Welsh Macready!![6]—what a strange combination—Tristram Shandy's Father might shake his head portentously over the poor infant that is to be launched in the world with such a name![7]

You have asked *more* than once about Darwin and *Craik* and never been answered— Darwin is better—not yet well—he has only been once here these last three weeks—a bad account of him—but I have been oftener than once to him— As for Craik your tender sympathies need not trouble your sleep on *his* account— A man *must* be *sorry* more or less for the death of his own child—but Craik is as uninteresting *in* sorrow as out of it— He has been here several times and ex-

4. Possibly Ann Dunlop, b. Vetch, wife of Alexander Dunlop; see 13:69. Agnes was her mother's name and possibly that of an otherwise unidentified sister.

5. Coterie speech.

6. Lydia Jane Macready (1842–58), da., b. 26 Dec., of Catherine, b. Atkins (1806–52; see 11:69–70), and William Charles Macready (1793–1873; *DNB*), actor-manager.

7. Walter Shandy, in Sterne's novel, believed that a child's Christian names affected his whole future.

cept that he has on black clothes, and minces his words a little more affectedly than usual I can trace no difference in him[8]— If you look narrowly at his countenance indeed—you find on it always a smile which seems to *challenge* your *warmest admiration* and *gets* your *heartiest disgust*—a smile which says as plainly as words—"look with what *manly cheerfulness* and *sublime resignation* I bear my trial—look and take example by me!" Bah!—Cavaignac stamping on the floor, and repeating his awful *"ce n'est pas just—Mon dieu* [it is not fair—my God]! was not a *perfect sufferer* But was one that I could sympathize with better than with this *"diffusion-of-useful-*RESIGNATION"—*Mr Craik!*[9]—

Thackery is returned from Paris he was here with Fitzgerald the other evening[10]—I was upstairs when they came in—and on coming into the room went to Thackery first, to shake hands *in enthusiasm*—as one does after a journey to Paris—but I gave a loud scream on finding a small cold, hard, hand—as of a dead fairy—laid in mine—it was *your* hand which he had fastened at the end of his sleeve! I declared the joke to be a *heartless* one—which seemed to vex him greatly—he repeated a dozen times during the evening that he wished he had not done it!

Fitzgerald had lost a good deal of his hig[h] colour[11] and was very *good* and, *rational.* I get to like him— Garnier also was here last week[12]—*saner* than I ever saw him in my life—he asked many questions about you and about *the German*— By the way my dear you will never do any thing *effectual* in german or in things in general until you muster courage and determination enough to lock yourself up—in *a cupboard*—if so be that you cannot be allowed *a room,* all to yourself— I see for ever before my eyes—in Mazzini—how little—all the talents and *good intentions* in the world can avail—so long as one submits to be *eaten up* as it were, by *little things*—one, two, twenty of them could not tell on ones general results—but let them become infinite—of daily recurrence and like the packthreads of the Lilliputians

8. George Lillie Craik (1798–1866; *DNB*); see 8:207. For his da.'s death, see 15:221.

9. Eléonore Louis Godefroy Cavaignac (1801–45), journalist and revolutionary republican; see 7:53. JWC refers to Craik's work for the Society for the Diffusion of Useful Knowledge (see 5:84).

10. The novelist William Makepeace Thackeray (1811–63; *DNB*) had returned from Paris in late Jan. Edward FitzGerald (1809–83; *DNB;* see 15:89), poet and trans., stayed with Thackeray at 13 Gt. Coram St., Brunswick Sq., until mid-May. They had been friends since undergraduate days at Cambridge.

11. Letter omitted in MS.

12. Joseph Henry Garnier (d. 1848), German refugee and journalist living in London; see 8:125 and 12:143.

they make a mesh that the strong man cannot tear himself loose from—Poor Mazzini! I declare I could weep over him sometimes—there in his enchanted Tancioni-Castle[13] holding no free communication with the world he lives in—*just* as you figured him in your dream!—and then I get angry—and scold—but it is of no use—he is born to make a Martyr of himself, and *the great* not having accepted his sacrifice he offers himself, bound hand and foot, to *the little*—which always *accepts!*—Love and kisses to them all—I am out of humour with Spiridione[14] entirely— Your own / J Carlyle

JWC TO HELEN WELSH

[ca. 4 February 1843]

Dearest Helen

One hears much fine talk in this hypocritical age about seeking and even *finding* [one]'s own happiness in "the happiness [of] others"—but I frankly confess to you, that I, as one solitary individual,[1] have never been able to confound the two things, even in imagination, so as not to be capable of clearly distinguishing the difference and if every body would endeavour [as] I do, to speak without *cant* I believe there would be a pretty general admission on the part of sinful humanity, that to eat a comfortable beaf steak when one is hungry yields a satisfaction of a much more positive character than seeing ones neighbour eat it!—for the fact is; *happiness* is but a *low* thing, and there is a confusion of ideas in running after it *on stilts!* When Sir Philip Sidney took the water from his own parched lips to give it to the dying soldier,[2] I

13. Pio and Susanna Tancioni. In the late 1830s Mazzini found a young woman who had collapsed in the street from cold and hunger and took her to his lodgings, where she remained as a servant. Da. of an Oxfordshire laborer, she m., 1839–40, an immigrant Italian, Pio Tancioni. Mazzini took board and lodging with them first at 26 Clarendon Sq., March 1840, then at 4 York Bldgs., King's Rd., Chelsea, July 1840 (see 12:194). In March 1841 Mazzini appointed Tancioni sec. of the Union of Italian Workingmen in London, a section of Young Italy. In time Tancioni deserted Susanna and their two sons. Mazzini found a house for her in which he lodged, and made himself responsible for the boys' education and apprenticeships. In 1849 they moved to Genoa, then Geneva, still with Mazzini's help.

14. Gambardella.

JWC-HW, [ca. 4 Feb.]. MS: NLS 603.257. Pbd: Froude, *LM* 1:386–89, where dated 20 Jan. 1847. The letter has been mistakenly bound with an envelope with PM Liverpool, 21 Jan. 1847. Dated before Jewsbury's 1843 visit when she apparently arrived on Mon., 6 Feb. The MS is ink-smudged in several places.

1. Coterie speech; see 9:278.

2. Sir Philip Sidney (1554–86), soldier, statesman, and poet, who, wounded, gave his water bottle to a dying soldier on the battlefield of Zutphen, 1586, saying, "Thy necessity is yet greater than mine."

could take my bible-oath that it was not *happiness* he felt—and that he would never have done that much admired action; if his only compensation had been *the pleasure* resulting to him from seeing the dying soldier drink the water—he did it *because he could not help himself*—because the sense of *duty*—of *self-denial*—was stronger in him at the moment than low, human appetite—because the *soul* in him said *do it* not because Utilitarian Philosophy suggested that he would find *his advantage* in doing it—nor because socinian dilettanteism required of him *a beautiful action!*[3]— Well! but if these moral reflections are not a preamble to something more relevant; I find such a commencement of a letter—"what shall I say—*strange*—upon *my* honour"![4]— Do you so? my sweet little Cousin—be thankful then! we live in a world of commonplace—a *strange* letter—a *strange* cousin, so far from being taken sharply to task, should be accepted graciously as a sort of refreshing novelty.

But if I cannot show you that my moral reflections lead to something, I *can* show you that *some*thing lead to *them.* I had been looking over the last budget of autographs that I had got together for you—Such distinguished names! To be sure, I said to myself, these will make her fortune—ni[ce] autographs. And then I felt a certain self-complacency—a certain presentiment of your satisfaction in seeing your collection swelling into something really worthwhile—and having the pen in my hand to write to you, I was on the point of putting on the paper some such *fadaise* [nonsense] as *this.*

"It was a capital thought in me dearest Helen, the making of this collection for you— My own pleasure in sending you the autographs being greater I am sure than any you can feel in receiving them" But the sentence having reached a full stop—in my head—my better judgement said—Bah! Beware of the socinian jargon MA CHERE [my dear] there is always "a *do* at the bottom of it"![5]—and so my pen dashed off, of itself, as it were, into a reactionary tirade against "the wellfare-of-others"-principle—

I have been long plaguing Carlyle to give me for you one of the letters of Varnhagen von Ense—for besides being the autograph of a distinguished Author and Diplomatist and *husband of Rahel*[6]—you

3. Utilitarianism, especially as formulated by Jeremy Bentham, maintains that the greatest happiness of the greatest number should be the basis of morality and legislation and that self-interest encourages benevolence. Socinianism denies the essential depravity of man and holds that salvation is to be achieved by virtuous action.

4. Coterie speech; expressions of Mazzini.

5. Coterie speech; see 8:330. A "do" is a trick.

6. Rahel Antonie Friederike Varnhagen von Ense, b. Levin (1771–1833), famed literary hostess in Berlin; see 9:382.

will find it curious for its perfect beauty— I never saw such writing—and in whatever haste in sickness or in health it is always the same—C was very grumpy about parting with one of his letters—but having taken a great deal of trouble for him the other day in seeking out some notes he wanted from his trunk of old papers—he presented me with this one as a *reward*—and also I suppose as an encouragemen to future exertions of like utility. Besides *Varnhagen von Ense* you have here—*Goethe—Sir Walter Scott—Rogers—Sir R Peel*—a *whole* note from *H Martineau* (*before* our friendship) *Charles Buller—Count D'Orsay—Milman*—A very *characteristic* note from *Mazzini*—Lord *Stanley*—Mrs *Austin—Lockhart—Thackey* (alias *Titmarch*) *Allan Cunningham*[7]

Tell Jeanie that when I informed Mazzini yesterday that Geraldine was to be here on Monday—he first stared—then said "well! after then I come for *ten minutes* only"! and then looking into the fire gave a *long clear whistle!*— Jeanie can figure the sort of mood in which alone Mazzini would dream of whistling!

But alas I must go and clean the Lamp! a much less agreeable occupation than writing to you my Dear— But such consequences of the fall of Adam *will* always exist— Nothing will Go on any time without human labour

Ever your affectionate
Cousin J. Carlyle

TC TO KARL AUGUST VARNHAGEN VON ENSE

Chelsea, London, 5 Feb*y*, 1843—

My dear Sir,

Many thanks again for your kind present of Books; for your two kind Letters, the latter of which arrived with Asher's Book-parcel duly, a few nights ago.[1] The only unfriendly news you send is that of your own health; which I wish you had been able to make a little pleasanter to me! Summer weather at the Baths, and no permission to enjoy it ex-

7. Sir Walter Scott (1771–1832), writer. Samuel Rogers (1763–1855; *DNB*), poet and banker; see 8:322. Charles Buller (1806–48; *DNB*), TC's former pupil and politician; see 2:4–5. Count Alfred D'Orsay (1801–52; *DNB*), artist and society figure; see 11:54. Henry Hart Milman (1791–1868; *DNB*), clergyman, poet, and historian; see 12:69. John Thomas Stanley (1766–1850), 1st Baron Stanley. Sarah Austin. Thackeray used the pseud. Michael Angelo Titmarsh in several of his works of the 1840s. Allan Cunningham (1784–1842), misc. writer; see 3:94.

TC-KAVE, 5 Feb. MS: Jagellonian Univ., Cracow; longhand copy: Jagellonian Univ. Pbd: Preuss 418–20; *Last Words* 213–18.

1. Adolf Asher (1801–53), German bookseller, founder of Asher & Co., Berlin, book importers and exporters.

cept thro' carriage windows, is very sad work. And you are still a prisoner in Berlin, or nearly so;—yet, thank Heaven, not an idle one, not a discontented one: this too is something to be thankful for. We have to take the Light and the Dark as they alternate for us here below; and try to make the right use of both. I say often of myself that if I had suffered no ill health, I should have known nothing. The stars shine out, as Friedland's did, when it is grown rightly *dark* round us![2]—Yet I hope to hear, as the summer advances, that you emerge again, and see good under the Sun. Nay, so long as you can continue writing, with whatever pain it be, how many sons of Adam are there who ought to *pity* you; who are not rather called to envy you?—

I know not if I ever reported with what pleasure I read that little Delineation of the Prussian Field-Marshal Schwerin.[3] One has pleasure in it because it *is* a 'Delineation,' which so many Books only pretend to be: one *sees* a certain section of Human Life actually painted, rendered credible and conceivable to one. That last Battle is clear to me as if I had fought in it:[4] there is a kind of gloomy dumb tragic strength in the Phenomenon, as in some old Norse-Mythus, for me,—as if I looked into the old Death-Kingdoms, whereon Living Prussia, with what it can say and do, reposes and grows! Those long ranks of speechless Men standing ranked there, with their three-cornered hats and stiff hair-queues and fighting apparatus; dumb, standing like stone statues to be blasted in pieces with cannon-shot:—there are 'inarticulate meanings' without end in such a thing for me!—— Surely I much approve your farther Biographic projects; and bid you, '*Frisch zu* [Go ahead]!' How true also is that of Goethe in his advice to you:[5] I have felt it a hundred times;—indeed it is properly the grand difficulty with my own poor *Cromwell* at present; that he lies buried so deep; that his dialect, thought, aim, whole costume and environment are grown so obsolete for men. What an English Puritan properly *meant* and struggled for in the Seventeenth Century: I say to myself, "Is all that dead?

2. From Schiller's *Wallenstein;* see *Works* 25:133.

3. In Varnhagen's *Leben des Feldmarschall Grafen von Schwerin* (Berlin, 1841). Count Kurt Christolf von Schwerin (1684–1757), created field marshal by Frederick the Great.

4. See *History of Frederick the Great, Works* 17:133–35.

5. Johann Wolfgang von Goethe (1749–1832), "Varnhagen von Enses Biographien," vol. 6 of *Über Kunst und Alterthum* (1827): "We wish that he [Varnhagen] may proceed, with his biographical representations, more and more to the eighteenth century, and promote, by delineating the individualities and the spirit of the time with which they stood in action and reaction, clearness of the whole state of things. Clearness necessitates insight, insight creates tolerance, tolerance alone is able to procure a peace active in all parts and talents" (trans. *Last Words* 215).

Or is it only *asleep* (not entirely with good consequences for us); a thing that can never *die* at all?" If it be *dead,* we ought to leave it alone! "Let the dead bury their dead"[6] is as true in Literature as elsewhere. Hence indeed so few *Histories,* and so many *Pedantries* and mere Sham Histories,—which, if men were resolute enough, they would verily fling into the fire at once, and make an end of!—

Stuhr, as you predict, is heavy; but I find him solid and earnest, I believe I shall find it well worth while to travel thro' him.[7] One's *desire* to know about the old days is so unquenchable; the average of *fulfilment* to it grows at length so very low! Stuhr is very far indeed above what I have to call "par" in late times.

Some fortnight ago I sent off the *Life of Richter* by the channel you pointed out.[8] There was not another copy readily procurable; so I sent you the one we had ourselves been reading here. There was a Mitchell's *Life of Wallenstein* added, which perhaps you may find partly interesting even in its very short-comings.[9] Mitchell is an honest man; but his indignation against much inanity that he has to witness here throws him into somewhat of a cramp antagonism now and then. He is distinguished here by his deadly enmity to the bayonet, which he declares to be a total chimera in war,—false, damnable, heretical, almost in the old ecclesiastic sense!—

My stock of Autographs which I have had much pleasure in gathering for you is of much more bulk than value! Hardly a half dozen of men very interesting to you will you find here; the rest are transitory notabilities,—on many of whom, as they are like to be entirely unknown out of their own Parish, I have had to mark some brief commentary in pencil. Pray use your *Indian-rubber* there, where you find needful; for it is of the nature of free speech to a trusted friend, not of *litera scripta* [the written letter]. Perhaps, even thro' the Trivial, you with your clear eyes will get here and there a glimpse into our English Existence: the great advantage is, that you can and ought to *burn* some nine-tenths of the bundle so soon as you have looked it over. As occasion offers I will not forget to gather you a few more

6. Matt. 8:22.

7. Peter Feddersen Stuhr (1787–1851), Prussian historian. TC probably alludes to Stuhr's most recent work, *Forschungen und Erläuterungen Über Hauptpunkte der Geschichte des Siebenjähringen Krieges,* 2 vols. (Hamburg, 1842), or possibly to *Die Brandenburgisch-Preussische Kriegs-Verfassung zur Zeit Friedrich Wilhelms des grossen Kurfürsten* (Berlin, 1819).

8. Eliza Buckminster Lee (1794–1864), *Life of Jean Paul Frederic Richter* (Boston, 1842); see 15:161.

9. John Mitchell (1785–1858; *DNB*), Scottish army officer, *The Life of Wallenstein* (1837); see 15:240.

autographs: Byron, Fox, Pitt I do not yet give up;[10] indeed the first of these, with some others, are already promised me.

Your reading of the Austins is altogether correct.[11] Mrs Austin came first into vogue among us by translating Puckler Muskau (if that is the right spelling),[12] and has risen ever since by her sunny hopeful vivacious character, and a good share of female tact and the like. Her husband, as you say, is truly painful,—a kind of *Prometheus Vinctus* [Bound],[13] bound *not* by any Jupiter! The man is faithful, veracious, energetically almost spasmodically laborious; but of an egoism which has, alas, proved *too* strong,—which has made him unhealthy unhappy; which, as I say, "has eaten *holes* in the case of it." Poor Austin,—a brave man too: but able to bring it no farther than hard isolated *Pedant*hood! Nay, as Sir Toby in Shakspeare has it, "because *thou* art *virtuous*, shall there be no more cakes and ale?"[14]

I am very busy; and hope to tell you about what (it is a poor volume,[15] perhaps *preparatory* to something farther) in a month or two. Adieu, my good Friend: better health to both of us; unabated heart to both of us!

Yours ever truly / T. Carlyle.

TC TO THOMAS BALLANTYNE

15 Feb. 1843

Can you without much difficulty ascertain for me *how many persons were killed* at the old Manchester Peterloo?[1]

10. George Gordon (1788–1824), Lord Byron. Charles James Fox (1749–1806), statesman. William Pitt the Younger (1759–1806), statesman.
11. See TC to JSM, 1 Feb.
12. Prince Hermann von Pückler-Muskau (1785–1871), *Tour in England, Ireland, and France,* trans. Sarah Austin (1832); see 8:43.
13. Tragedy by Aeschylus.
14. *Twelfth Night* 1.3.
15. *Past and Present.*

TC-TB, 15 Feb. Pbd: A. Carlyle, *NL* 1:282 inc. Thomas Ballantyne (1806–71; *DNB*), newspaper ed.; propagandist against the Corn Laws; see 11:32 and 13:216.

1. See 15:22 and TC to TB, 28 Feb.

JWC TO JEANNIE WELSH

[18 February 1843]

My dearest Jeanie

I hardly know what I am going to write—only I feel a need to write something by return of post— Your news of this morning[1] has quite confused me— I feel only one thing quite distinct[l]y[2] that you are the best wisest little soul that ever was made— Oh yes let none of us ever more have concealments!— You were right to tell me the whole truth—but how few in your circumstances would have told it in such a wise considerate way!—told anyhow, it could not fail to make me very anxious, and, somehow, just in this particular month—when my heart is quite full of last february it could not fail to make me very sad[3]—but I am better pleased—to be ever so anxious and sad than to be kept in the dark— Oh if all people had had your sense—what bitter regrets would have been spared me for my life long!

—My child you are an example to me—for all so much older and more experienced I am— Your quiet affectionate good sense rays itself into my mind even at this distance, thro all the tumultuous nonsense that is fussing round about me and thro all the natural temptations I have to get nervously excited myself— I say with you in calmness and faith "let us hope the best"— Yet it is hard for me to have to wait till Monday for further intelligence[4]— Oh that I were beside you—to see how things go on with my own eyes— If my uncle does not get better *soon*—and if you feel that my company would be of the slightest use or comfort to you say so without hesitation— I am quite aware that every one of you makes a better *nurse* than I do—that in fact I am a very helpless being—but I feel myself so much your elder sister that it seems unnatural for me not to be beside you all, to take my turn in reading to him and all that, and to share your anxieties on the spot— You understand? I would not officiously set off in the Geraldine fashion—to "*do*" what will be perfectly well done without me, or may be perfectly well left *undone*—or to parade *my* anxieties among anxieties which must be naturally still greater than mine—but if my going to you could in any conceivable way make you more comfortable—you have only to bid me—I will not say any more for indeed I am very confused—

JWC-JW, [18 Feb.]. Addr: Maryland Street / Liverpool. PM: 18 Feb. 1843; 19 Feb. MS: NLS 1891.185. Pbd: Huxley, *JWCLF* 87–88.

1. Saying that her father, John Welsh, was seriously ill.
2. Letter omitted.
3. JWC's mother died 25 Feb. 1842.
4. JWC is writing on Sat.

Only that I pray God to make this danger pass swiftly away—and to have you all in his keeping— Your own
Jane Carlyle

TC TO LADY HARRIET BARING

Chelsea, Saturday [18? February 1843]

Dear Lady Harriet,

Luckily I can, and right gladly I will! I have been out nowhere these three months; but my term expires before Friday.— I will also treat myself to a sight of you in the interim, perhaps on Monday evening. I am just finishing a dreadful *Book* on these Times and Aristocracies; which (tho' we by no means will have *you* killed in this general Twilight of the Gods) will most likely deprive me of your friendship for evermore:—wherefore I must make the best of my few opportunities that remain!

You get Bamford's Book by applying, or directing any Bookseller (I suppose) to apply, to the Author himself, "Samuel Bamford, Silk-Weaver, Middleton, near Manchester." If you have the smallest difficulty, let me know, and I will find a man in Manchester to do it.[1] You deserve to be saved for reading such Books, were it for nothing more.

I remain ever / Yours with true regard / T. Carlyle

TC TO [WILLIAM HALL]

Chelsea, February 20, 1843.

I want you to take a copy of my Chartism with 'from the Author' in it and dispatch it addressed to 'Mr. Samuel Bamford, silk weaver, Middleton, Manchester' . . .

A copy of the *French Revolution* is wanted, elsewhere; but this must first be bound, not in a sumptuous but in a reasonably handsome manner; and I must first write the name in it myself . . .

The new book we were speaking of is coming near a conclusion. I

TC-Lady HB, [18? Feb.]. MS: Marquess of Northampton. Hitherto unpbd. Tentatively dated by the near completion of *Past and Present* and the similarity of Bamford's address to that given in the next letter; see TC to [WH], 20 Feb.

1. See TC to SB, 13 April.

TC-[WH], 20 Feb. MS: Sold at auction, Charles Hamilton, Inc., New York City, 13 Dec. 1966, catalogue 16, item 237, from which the text incl. ellipses is given. 4 pp. William Hall (ca. 1801–47), partner of the publishers Chapman & Hall.

think it were as well if the Printer very soon had a piece of it, to go through his preliminaries upon; for I desire much that there should be no delay in it. I have yet mentioned the matter to no bookseller whatever but yourself;—nor probably shall I. You must consider what is the utmost you can do for me; and let us try if we can settle it soon!

The book will be as large, I calculate, as a volume, perhaps as any volume of *The French Revolution;* I propose to call it *'Past and Present';* and it might be announced in the Papers with this addition, *'A Chartism,* Part Second,' which would probably explain the purport of it there. I consider that probably it will be found readable: but that is *your* field of prophecy rather than mine . . . compliments to Mr. Chapman, which of course he will not fail to get notice of, reading this along with you.[1]

JWC TO JEANNIE WELSH

[22 February 1843]

My dearest Babbie

Your *long* letters ev[ery][1] day are dearly welcome—but you are not to plague yourself with writing long ones—I know when one's mind has been shaken all topsy turvy, as yours must have been at present, that writing even to those one loves is often irksome— I cannot be generous enough to dispense you from *writing* constantly, till my dear Uncle is going about again I do beg that I may be written to by one or another every day—but understand that *three lines* will suffice when you are not disposed for more.

What makes me more delicate in my exactions, is my incapability of making you an adequate return—one while it is Helen's illness,[2] then my own—with the continual running accompaniment of worry—that makes me feel really as if the faculty of letter-writing were a thing I *had* possessed in some previous state of existence!

My cold is gone—but yesterday and today—I am quite stupid with headach—attributable however to *natural causes*— In fact *the* presentiment seeming in fair way to work itself out—without leaving me *one* exceptional day—

I will not enter on details today— I am not in a humour to turn

1. Edward Chapman (1804–80), Hall's partner. Chapman tended to take care of literary matters and Hall to look after the business side.

JWC-JW, [ca. 22 Feb.]. PM: 22 Feb. 184[3]. MS: NLS 1893.101. Pbd: Huxley, *JWCLF* 299 inc., where dated 22 Feb. 1847. John Welsh's illness and Geraldine Jewsbury's visit to Chelsea confirm the PM.

1. Letters omitted.
2. The maid's.

these or to turn anything into *amusement*—and in presence of the great anxiety hardly well over yet—petty annoyances sink into their due insignificance—one can no longer make a serious grievance of them— In a calmer time I shall have a great deal to tell you that,—passed into the sphere of *things well over,*—will make you laugh—"like a cuddy eating thistles" belike,—but still *laugh*— Meanwhile let us thank God my Uncle is so far recovered!—if this attack leave no worse consequences than it seems likely to do—it is to be taken as a merciful warning—a warning to him to take better heed of a life so precious to us all and a warning to us to make much of him—to love him with all our hearts and all our strength while it is yet time—that when the inevitable parting comes, the bitterness of *remorse* may not be added to the bitterness of death.

Yes Mazzini is a friend worth having—one that is always best in the hour of need— If he had heard of the illness of his Mother in Italy he could not have been more anxious than he has been in these days to learn the last news from Liverpool[3]— He has a power of *identifying* himself with those he loves—at least in *their sorrows,* which I never saw equalled— Thanks for the little packet which seemed to me like a *fragrant kiss* from my own babbie— God keep you my good child—love to them all—a dozen kisses to my uncle "to be taken at intervals" Geraldine sends her love—"and pray tell her how *very* anxious *I* have been for her"—

[no signature]

TC TO ALEXANDER CARLYLE

Chelsea, Wednesday [22 February? 1843]—

My dear Brother,

Here is an Order for Two pounds on Postie; which cash when you have got into your hands, I wish you to dispose of it for me as follows:

One pound to Mary Carlyle, our poor Cousin,[1] whose Weaver husband and household must be, I fear, in a state of *unusual* wreck at present. She comes into my head sometimes; and I say, Why dost thou

3. In an accompanying undated letter Mazzini asked JWC, "Will you be so kind as to let me know what news, if any, you had this morning from Liverpool? May God bless you with strength and affection like that of / your / Joseph Mazzini."

TC-AC, [22 Feb.?]. MS: MUL. Pbd: Marrs 546–47. Dated tentatively by the sending of "the first portion" of *Past and Present* to the printer "this morning," which JWC mentions as having already been sent in JWC to JW, [24 Feb.].

1. Mary Harkness, b. Carlyle (d. 1847), TC's paternal cousin; see 12:364.

not assist her according to thy poor means?— I would have you give her the money without mentioning much of me,—without mentioning me at all, if you could help it;—simply as a gift that comes to her from Providence by your hands. Poor creature: one *cannot* assist her or hers: nobody can.

The other pound I wish you to cut into two halves: give five shillings each to poor Rob Scott and the poor old Plate Morrison, if they are still alive;[2]—the remainder, in such proportions as you like, to such wretched objects as you think may be most benefited by it. My heart is sore for them. I send this to buy *myself* some ease from pain; I cannot call it charity at all. Be you my Almoner,—as I think you once before were. And may a blessing be in the poor mite, far beyond its own value!

This morning I sent the first portion of my Book off to the Printer.[3] There are still two good weeks or more of right hard labour before the *last* portion be got written: but the Printer will not overtake me; and I want to be *out* as soon as possible, that I may have quite done with it. Great things are announced in it, more or less clearly; I hope it may tend to the stirring up of here and there a human soul! My soul, at any rate, is very anxious to *have done with it.*[4]— I deal with my old Booksellers (present ones, I mean);[5] they are to give me £200 for an Edition of 2,000 Copies;—which is no great shakes of a bargain; but I cannot go hawking about for a better.

Yesterday there came a Note from Jenny; for which, and the news it brought, I am very thankful. Tell our good Mother to keep out of the cold! We have had rigid grim weather even here, tho' it is now gone again in mud and thaw. Jane keeps pretty well; the young lady from Manchester is still here.[6] Jack was well and brisk on Sunday. I am in good heart for my Book; and able for the rest of it yet.

Adieu dear Brother. God keep you all.

Your affectionate / T. Carlyle

2. Rob Scott the blacksmith and Jamie Morrison; see 11:211.

3. Levey, Robson & Franklyn, 23 Gt. New St., Fetter Lane.

4. A dated note on the Forster MS f.119v. shows that TC may have been eager to get back to working on Cromwell and certainly that he had not given this up entirely while writing *Past and Present:* on "20 feby" he made "almost a complete copy" of "*Harl Mss.* No 265."

5. Chapman & Hall.

6. Geraldine Jewsbury.

TC TO JOHN STERLING

Chelsea, 23 feb*y*, 1843–

Dear Sterling,

Blessings on your pen once more! You have given us a terrible fright, and must not make any fresh "experiments" of that nature! We are right glad to see your hand again; to understand that you are steadily tho' slowly getting built together again. Possess your soul in patience there: it is actually a better "progress" a thousand times than you are aware of! I cannot get you to understand this of SILENCE; but the Fates, I hope will,—for it is of the highest moment to you. *Festina lente* [Make haste slowly],—O Heavens there is a thousand times more in Silence than that: "Self-Annihilation, the beginning of all good and wisdom,"[1] this is in it among other things. The gods have somewhat in store for you,—if you will not spill it! Be quiet, I say, and thankful to the gods.

No man was lately busier, and few sicklier, than I now am. Work is not possible for me except in a redhot element, which roasts the life out of me. I have still three weeks of the ugliest labour; and shall be fit for the hospital then.

This thing I am upon is a volume to be called "Past and Present": it is moral, political, historical &c;—a most questionable, redhot, indignant thing: for my heart is sick to look at the things now going on in this England; and two millions of men sitting in Poor-Law Bastilles[2] seem to ask of every English soul, "Hast thou no word to say for us?" On the whole, I am heartily sorry for myself,—sorry that, I could not help writing such words, and had none better to write.— Whether any *Cromwell* or what lies in the rear of this? The Fates know.

It was John Sterling, I think, that first told me my nature was Political; it is strange enough how, beyond expectation, that oracle is verifying itself.[3]

If you lay within distance of me, what better could I do than run into the Spring sunshine and your neighbourhood, were this horrid load of hodwork off my shoulders! But you are two hundred miles away; and my vehement speeches would do you no good at present.

I have seen nobody, except in glimpses, these several months. Today I am going over the river, to crawl about in the Lethe Flats of

TC-JS, 23 Feb. Addr: Falmouth. MS: NLS 531.60. Pbd: A. Carlyle, *NL* 1:281–82; quot: Froude, *Carlyle* 3:285–86.

1. Cf. Harrold, *Sartor* 186ff.

2. Workhouses established under the poor law act, 1834, where the poor were given relief and set to work; named after the Bastille.

3. Caroline Fox paraphrased the letter in her journal, 26 Feb. (Fox 178).

Battersea,[4] if nothing better. Your Brother called yesterday; complaining of slight cold; otherwise brisk, hardy, victorious as ever.[5]

Adieu, dear Sterling. Be quiet, I say; thankful to Heaven,—and mindful as often as you can of ME!

Yours ever / T. Carlyle

JWC TO [JOHN FORSTER]

[ca. 23 February 1843]

The Devil is in the man![1] palpably—never does he let any thing stand according to the original scheme! However excellent *the idea*, if time be allowed him, as sure as death, he will remodel it! Verily things go on under that cranium of his, as under a juggler's hat—eggs one moment are shaken into live chickens the next, and the next there are neither eggs nor chickens but only a little empty box!

The Macreadys are angels!—to think of coming all this way, to tea, in such cold weather, is one of those enthusiastic instances of friendship which the grateful heart stands amazed before as in presence of the infinite![2] On that side the new arrangement is good, beautiful! But my Husband says "as to Forster *himself* it is a bad arrangement—when a man comes to dinner one gets into a sort of stream of conversation with him" (that is when one does not dine up stairs on beef tea) "but no talk can be carried on at tea except of the most fractionary unprofitable sort. This is *his* notion who I suppose "is always in the right"— Well! you will come another day and get into "the stream" will you not?— And on Wednesday[3] be it your own way

Truly yours / J Carlyle

4. On the S bank of the Thames, opp. Chelsea. Lethe is the river of oblivion in Hades; cf. *Hamlet* 1.5.

5. Anthony Coningham Sterling (1805–71; *DNB*), capt. in 73d Foot, on half pay from Dec.; see 9:103.

JWC-[JF], [ca. 23 Feb.]. MS: NLS 602.95. Hitherto unpbd. Approximately dated by the Macreadys' visit, 26 Feb. (see JWC to HW, [27 Feb.]). John Forster (1812–76; *DNB*), historian, biographer, and ed.; see 6:118 and later vols.

1. Referring to TC.
2. Coterie speech.
3. Presumably 1 March.

JWC TO JEANNIE WELSH

[24 February 1843]

My dearest Babbie

If by the alchymy of affection, or other alchymy, you can manage to extract any comfort at all, out of such rags of letters as it is possible for me to send you under the actual circumstances—have them, my child, and welcome, Only I wish you could teach me your secret for transmuting stupidity into comfort—it is a secret as well worth discovering as the philosophers-stone.

I opened your letter today with less agitation than usual— I felt myself quits with destiny in the way of fright before I broke the seal of yours—for I found in the box along with it, one of those horrid black bordered notes which make ones heart jump into ones mouth—addressed to *him* and bearing the *Ecclefechan* postmark—nervous as I am in these days you may fancy the dreadful things that crossed my mind—but when I opened it—myself—I found it nothing worse than the announcement of the death of a Brother of William Graham's[1]—bad enough for poor Graham—but for us who never saw him! accordingly your news was more disappointing that I was not prepared for any falling back—it seems indeed to have been the result of imprudence—but that is small comfort— Oh dear me how I wish for all our sakes that he[2] were going about again— The little touch of *impatience* about the Doctors was the most comfortable part of your intelligence—I hate to see a man who is not naturally a *Job*—behaving like one—it is always a good sign when a patient begins to get cross

Hang that cook—to be plaguing you with enquiring after servants just now— Be sure to tell me if Helen[3] have got one—with *two* good ones left you have not such reason to dread changing as I have—still on any principle changing is bad— Helen[4] has not plagued me with her temper much of late—but the reason of that is only I am afraid, that she is conscious of having been a sufficient plague to me in another way—for a great many weeks back she has not been at all up to her work—part of the time up to nothing— I am rather disposed to think that she will never be again the servant she was some years ago

JWC-JW, [24 Feb.]. Addr: 20 Maryland Street / Liverpool. PM: 24 Feb. 1843. MS: NLS 1891.188. Pbd: Huxley, *JWCLF* 88–89 inc.; Bliss, *JWC* 114–15 inc.

1. William Graham of Burnswark (1770–ca. 1857). His brother John, who d. 19 Jan., aged seventy-one, had been a merchant in New York; see 1:274.
2. John Welsh.
3. Welsh, who as the eldest da., was chiefly responsible for running the household.
4. Mitchell, the maid.

in point of work—these drinking bouts have undermined her constitution—and *nerves coughs* &c &c are likely to be henceforth her portion— I am not brute enough to *be angry* with the poor wretch for having her house all in a mess—and doing no one earthly thing as it ought to be done—while she is liable to be choked with coughing at every turn!—but—as she has got to the end of my affection for her which could have made me overlook such inconveniencies for the sake of having her beside me, I see very clearly that an easier place would suit her better—and a healthier woman would better suit *me*— However—*laissez fair* [let be] is my motto for the present—till the summer plans have assumed some positive shape—

Carlyle has sent the first part of his Book to press in a month or so I hope it will be off his mind—and then he will take to revolving fifty different projects—out of which I shall find some one I hope compatible with my private wishes and make that one predominant— What think you of a cottage on the other side of *your* water?[5]—why not there as well as elsewhere?—it were near Annandale for *him*—near Maryland Street for me—Maryland Street being all that remains for me— But at present the chief thing is to get my uncle well again—it were also a good thing if Geraldine would lay it to heart that I asked her just for two or three weeks—it will be three weeks on monday since she came[6]—three most uncomfortable weeks—and when she received a note yesterday from a M*rs* Green in St Johns Wood[7] reminding her of her promise to spend some time there and saying that she had actually accepted an invitation for her to a ball on the 3*d* of March she asked *me* what she was to do?— "of course you should go" I said "a ball is not to be lighted on every day"—"and stay *all night*? said she— "but then the long visit?—when is that to be executed?"— I wonder said I that you should go at all on a *long* visit to a person you dislike so excessively"—for she had been *abusing* this woman the whole morning— "Oh my dear said she I shall only be too happy to stay on here—till you *desire* me to go"—a pleasant footing to have her stay set upon! My astonishment is that he[8] she is not as thoroughly enraged at me as I am weary of her—for I have a hundred times been quite unable to conceal my provocation— Of Carlyle she sees very little for ever since she came he has sat up stairs in the evenings as well as in the forenoons—and of other people she has seen very few—and all of these decline *taking* to *her*— One would say she had the poorest

5. I.e., across the river Mersey in Cheshire.
6. She apparently came on 6 Feb.
7. Unidentified. St. John's Wood, suburb in NW London.
8. Thus in MS.

life of it here that can be figured—all the mornings she scribbles letters on her knees—and all the evenings she lies on the sofa and—sleeps! I speak little with her—for her speech is so extremely insincere that I feel in our dialogues always as if we were acting a play— —and as we are not to get either money or praise for it and not being myself an amateur of play-acting I prefer considerably good honest *silence*—intellect! Carlyle made a grand mistake when he held this Geraldine up to me as something superlative—she is sharp as a meataxe—but as narrow—there is no *breadth* of character in her and no basis of truth—in fact she is what Dunlop described the dumfries-womans hen—"nothing but just a fluff of feathers"[9]— She is off today to wheedle M*rs* Sterling[10]— She is also wheedling John Carlyle at a great rate pretending all the while to have the greatest dislike to him—every sunday and on no other day—she makes a *grande toilette* [dresses elaborately]—comes down *in the forenoon* with *a bare neck*—and a black satin gown—or coloured silk!—all wasted I assure you— I wish tomorrow were come that I might have another letter Your own

J C

TC TO MARGARET A. CARLYLE

Chelsea, Friday [24? February 1843]

My dear Mother,

Take another brief word from me, rather than none at all! I am driving along my poor Book, and in a terrible pucker and puzzle, every minute of my time occupied:—but I ought to be busier than I ever yet was, if I could not send my dear good Mother a syllable of salutation now and then! In few weeks I shall be more at leisure, and be able to write as before.

We have got very nasty weather since February came in; plashy sleets, cold east-winds, reek and mud: I do not care much for all that; but it is somewhat hard on Jane;—who however still keeps her feet, and even goes out when the Sun by chance shews himself. Ellen our servant has got a cold in these days; and cannot even be kept lying in her bed: she is a very distracted kind of creature, under any pain or pressure of the nerves, and runs about almost as a poor burnt whelp might do,—entirely astonished at the state it finds itself in! To add

9. See 8:85.
10. Hester Sterling.

TC-MAC, [24? Feb.]. MS: NLS 511.82. Hitherto unpbd. Tentatively dated by TC's final work on *Past and Present* in Feb., Geraldine's visit "these weeks," and the recent receipt of "Jenny's Letter."

somewhat to the perplexity we have a vister in these weeks; a Miss Jewsbury from Manchester, a great friend of Jane's and mine, whom Jane had invited lately to come and pass a three weeks with her. But she is a good lively young woman, and perhaps rather *likes* messing about in the kitchen on such an occasion: we do not in the least put ourselves about for her. Jane has, today, got in a good handy little girl of the neighbourhood, who is used to the house: all will get on pretty well now. I proposed to her: "Cannot you put Ellen into bed, and turn the key upon her?"——

I am myself in fully the average state of health; often in rather good spirits about getting forward with my Book! I walk considerably, and do not overwork myself. Jack Ritchie's maxim is decidedly good: "The slower thou ridest, the sooner thoul't get to thy journey's end!"[1]—— This Book will probably be of some use: it "gives up" a good many classes of men and things, "their *fit*,"[2] as you say in Annandale; tells them what *measure* they are of,—which they are terribly ignorant of, at times. At any rate, it will as usual be a great relief to me *to get rid of it;* to say, "There, that is what *I* had to do with the business: and now—what you have to do, let us see that!"—— Peel will not change the Corn-Laws this year: but next year both he, it is likely, and they, and much along with them, will go! He has certainly no very blessed place of it at present.[3]

If Alick can get me another quarter of a stone of that Tobacco without much trouble, tell him he may do so. The present stock is done; and I am thrown on London again. I have found a rather better kind than usual, and *can* do, however.

Jack is well; I had Jenny's Letter, and Jack sent me the one he got about the same time. I will write to her by and by. I will write to Jamie,—to everybody, so soon as I am "my own man" again! To Jean I am indebted a Letter too: be patient with me!

Dear Mother, keep out of the bitter weather. Take care of yourself for my sake. Blessings on you, on one and all of you. My sympathies and regards to poor Isabella. And so adieu dear Mother!—— Your affectionate T. Carlyle

1. Coterie speech (see 8:271), attrib. to John Richie, evidently an Annandale neighbor. "Vister" in the preceding paragraph is thus in MS.

2. "Gives up their *fit*," meaning "rebukes."

3. Because of the widespread hunger and continued agitation for repeal of the Corn Laws.

TC TO WILLIAM GRAHAM

Chelsea, 27th Feb'y, 1843.

My dear Friend,

You wrote me a very kind but Melancholy letter about the New Year time, which I was almost of Mind to write and admonish you about;[1] and now another brief, but too emphatic missive announces that a new great sorrow has fallen upon you,—your good Brother lives no more under this sun. Alas, Alas, what are all human sympathies? the friendliest pity of one man for another? It is a great loss that has fallen on you, a bitterness which no sympathy can sweeten. He was your Eldest Brother, I think, the Pioneer of you all in this adventurous life-pilgrimage, and a dark cloud has suddenly hid him from your sight. He is away with God who made us all!

The reflection that can tend to compose a man and Brother in such extremities is this, of the ancient Psalmist we shall go to him, he shall not return to us![2] No, not to *us,* but we are travelling swiftly towards *Him,* out of a long Eternity he has but gained a little hour upon us, we have to bow our heads and keep silence, or say only God's great and just will be done.— Your reflections and speculations in the former letter were full of undue gloom. You were wont to be of a cheerful hoping heart, and have often admonished me for my despondences, and what was far nobler, encouraged me under them. I would fain here, if it were in my power, do the like for you. A rational man is bound by all considerations and necessities to look fixedly and with the unspeakable awe into that great Eternity, towards which at all moments he is travelling, and of which his whole earthly work is as it were a symbol, but reverence, not fear or despondence beseems us nevertheless.

My despondences have been many and long continued, and will not quit me while I live, but looking into Eternity, I could never see it to be other than a still home, unknown, but still and safe where the weary were at rest. I consider that we do know nothing more of it,

TC-WG, 27 Feb. Typescript: David L. Graham. Hitherto unpbd.

1. Graham had written from Burnswark, 7 and 9 Jan., about the death of his sister, Jane Howatson (in 1841; see 13:221), his own deep conviction of sin, and his faith in TC: "you are the only living man to whom . . . I could unbosom my deep grief & Sorrow, to this extent; if I had loved you less, my confidence would have been in proportion, perhaps altogether withheld." The second part of his letter, 9 Jan. was about the churches, the distress in the country, Allan Cunningham's death, and David Hope and Margaret Carlyle at church, "looking really *well.*" He ended by asking TC not to show the "enclosed sheet," that written 7 Jan., to "any mortal." TC wrote on the cover: "Await the issue. In all battles if you await the issue, each fighter has prevailed according."

2. Cf. 2 Sam. 12:23, a favorite quotation of TC's; see, e.g., 3:68, 5:219.

that no man ever did or will know more of it while in this life; and that in all ways our attitude towards it is that of Hope, the very essence of us seems to be HOPE,[3] God is love and *Hope,* I had almost said; we have ever more to trust in God.

My dear friend, you must not let gloomy remembrances, gloomy anticipations overcloud you. On the whole I wish the sun would shine out, that you could get abroad in the fields, to the Hillsides again, look if that be a world made by one unkind to us! I find the green grass and the blue sky worth a thousand homilies to me when in distress.

My hurry in these weeks & months is enormous. I am writing a book again—near done now, let that account for all things.

My true sympathies and regards to Miss Graham,[4] God bless you both.

Your affectionate,
T. Carlyle.

JWC TO HELEN WELSH

[27 February 1843]

My dearest Helen

After (in Dumfries & Galloway-courier[1] phraseology) "taking *a birds-eye view*" of all modern literature, I am arrived at the conclusion; that to find a book *exactly* suited to my Uncle's taste I must—*write it myself!* and alas, that cannot be done before tomorrow morning!

"La Motte Fouque's *Magic Ring*"?[2] suggests Geraldine—"too mystical! My Uncle detests confusion of ideas"— *"Paul de Kock?* HE is very witty"— "Yes but also very indecent!—and my Uncle would not relish indecencies read aloud to him by his daughters."— "Oh!— Ah!— Well! *Miss Austin*"?[3]— "Too washy—watergruel for mind and body at the same time were too bad"— Timidly and after a pause— "Do you think he could stand Victor Hugo's *Notre Dame*?[4]— The idea of

3. Cf. Harrold, *Sartor* 158–59.
4. His surviving sister, Elizabeth Graham, who lived with him.

JWC-HW, [27 Feb.]. Addr: 20 Maryland Street / Liverpool. PM: 27 [Feb.] 1843. MS: NLS 602.96. Pbd: Froude, *LM* 1:186–91, where dated March; Bliss, *JWC* 116 inc., where dated March. Dated here by the visit of the Macreadys, 26 Feb.; the continuing visit of Geraldine Jewsbury, who left Chelsea, 11 March; and the postmark.

1. A Dumfries newspaper.
2. Baron Friedrich Heinrich Karl de La Motte Fouqué (1777–1843), German writer and romanticist, *Der Zauberring* (Nürnberg, 1812).
3. The novelist Jane Austen (1775–1817).
4. Victor Marie Hugo (1802–85), *Notre Dame de Paris* (Paris, 1831).

my uncle listening to the sentimental monstrosities of Victor Hugo!—a smile of scorn was this time all my reply.

But in my own suggestions I have been hardly more fortunate— All the books that *pretend* to *amuse* in our day come in fact either under that category which you except against—"the extravagant clown-jesting" sort or still worse under that of what I should call the galvanized death's-head-grinning sort— There seems to be no longer any genuine, heartfelt mirth in writers of books—they sing and dance still "*vigoureusement* [vigorously]"—but one sees always too plainly, that it is not voluntarily but only for halfpence.— and for halfpence they will crack their windpipes and cut capers on the crown of their heads—poor men that they are!

I bethink me of one book however, which we have lately read here, bearing a rather questionable name as a book for my uncle—but nevertheless I think he would like it— It is called "*Passages from the life of a Radical*"—by Samuel Bamford—a silk-weaver of Middleton— He was one of those who got into trouble during the Peterloo time, and the details of what he then saw and suffered are given with a simplicity, an intelligence and absence of every thing like party-violence, which it does one good to fall in with—especially in these inflated times— There is another book that might be *tried*—tho' I am not sure that it has not a little too much affinity with water gruel—*The Neighbours*— A domestic novel translated from the Swedish by Mary Howit[5]— There is a "*little wife*" in it, with a husband whom she calls "*Bear*" that one never wearies of altho' they never say or do anything in the least degree extraordinary. Geraldine strongly recommends Stephens's *Incidents of Travel in Egypt Arabia and Petrea* as "very interesting and very short"— Also *Waterton's Wanderings in South America.*[6] There are *two* novels of *Paul de Kock* translated into English, which might be *tried* at least, without harm done—for they are *unexceptionable* in the usual sense of that term—*the Barber of Paris* and *Sister Anne*[7]— I have read the *last* not the first—and I dare say it would be very amusing for any one who likes Gil Blas[8] and that sort of books—for *my* taste it does not *get on* fast enough—

5. Frederika Bremer, *The Neighbours: A Story of Every-Day Life,* trans. Mary Howitt (1799–1888; *DNB*), 2 vols. (1842).

6. John Lloyd Stephens, *Incidents of Travel in Egypt, Arabia Petraea, and the Holy Land,* 2 vols. (1837). Charles Waterton, *Wanderings in South America, the North-west of the United States, and the Antilles in the years 1812, 1816, 1820, and 1824* (1825).

7. *The Barber of Paris; or, Moral Retribution,* trans. unidentified, 3 vols. (1839); *Sister Anne: A Novel,* trans. G. W. M. Reynolds (1840).

8. Alain René Le Sage, *L'Histoire de Gil Blas de Santillane,* 4 vols. (Paris, 1715–35).

There! enough of books for one day— Thank you for your letter Dear— If I had not wee angels to write me consolatory missives at present I should really be terribly ill off. My Maid continues highly inefficient—myself *ditto*—the weather complicates every thing—for days together not a soul comes—and then if the sun glimmers forth a whole rush of people breaks in, to the very taking away of ones' breath!—yesterday between the hours of three and five we had old Sterling—M*r* & M*rs* Von Glĕhen—M*r* and M*rs* Macready—John Carlyle & William Cunningham.[9]— Geraldine professed to be mightly taken with M*rs* Macready—not so much so with "*William*"— Poor dear *William!* I never thought him more interesting however—to see a man who is exhibiting himself every night on a stage, blushing like a young girl in a private room is a beautiful phenomenon for me!— His wife whispered into my ear as we sat on the sofa together—"do you know poor William is in a perfect agony today at having been brought here in that great coat!—it is a *stage-greatcoat*—but was only worn by him twice— —*the piece it was made for did not succeed*—but it was such an *expensive* coat I would not let him give it away—and does'nt he look so well in it?— — I wish Jeanie had seen him in the coat!—magnificant fur neck and sleeves—and such frogs on the front!— He did look *well*—but so heartily ashamed of himself!

Oh I must tell you for my uncles benefit a domestic catastrophe that occurred last week—one day after dinner I heard Helen lighting the fire which had gone out in the room above—with a perfectly unexampled vengeance!—every stroke of the poker seemed an individual effort of concentrated rage. What ails the creature now? I said to myself—who has incurred her sudden displeasure? or is it *the red-herring* she had to dinner which has disagreed with her stomach? (for in the morning you must know when I was ordering the dinner she had asked might *she* have a red herring? "her heart had been set upon it this good while back"!—and of course so modest a petition received an unhesitating affirmative—) on her return to the subterranean the same hubbub wild[10] arose from below which had just been trying my nerves from above—and when she brought up the tea tray she clanked it on the lobby-table as if she were minded to demolish the whole concern at one fell stroke— I looked into her face inquiringly as she

9. Edward Sterling. Probably Mr. and Mrs. Robert von Glehn, 34 Upper Harley St.; he was a merchant, his business located at 2 Hercules Ct., Threadneedle St. William Coningham (1815–84), John Sterling's cousin; see 11:207. Macready wrote in his diary, 26 Feb.: "Called at the Carlyles, where we saw Mrs. C——, a Miss Jewsbury, Mr. Commyn [probably Coningham], Carlyle and his brother. I was amused" (*Diaries,* ed. W. Toynbee [1912] 2:197).

10. Cf. *Paradise Lost* 2:951.

entered the room, and seeing it black as midnight (*morally* that is) I said very cooly—"a little less noise if you please—you are getting rather loud upon us!"— She cast up her eyes with the look of a martyr at the stake, as much as to say "well if I must be quiet, I must! but you little know my wrongs"! By and by Geraldine went to the kitchen for some reason.— She is oftener in the kitchen in one day than I am in a month—but that is irrelevant— "Where is the cat"? said she to Helen— "I have not seen her all night"—she takes a wonderful most superfluous charge of the cat as of everything else in this establishment—"the cat"? said Helen grimly I have all but killed her!"—"how?" said Geraldine— "With the besom" replied the other— "Why? for goodness sake?—" Why? repeated Helen bursting out into new rage "Why indeed? *because* She eat my red herring! I set it all ready on the end of the dresser, and she ran away with it, and eat it every morsel to the tail—such an unheard of thing for the brute to do! Oh if I could have got hold of her she should not have got off with her life"! "And have you had *no* dinner asked Geraldine—"oh yes! I had mutton enough—but I had just set my heart on a redherring"!— Which was the most deserving of having *a besom* taken to her the cat or the woman— My love to Babbie her letter to day is *most* com[f]ortable[11]— blessings on you all— Your affectionate Cousin

J Welsh

TC TO JOHN FORSTER

Chelsea Monday [27 February 1843]—

Dear Forster,

On Saturday, with a view of conquering the biliary Demon by sheer force, I walked the whole day,—as far as Croydon[1] or farther: and have in consequence made myself much worse. Add to which, I had yesterday *eleven hours and half of* continual talk with individuals of various complexion, to not one of whom did I, or do I for a long time to come, wish to speak one syllable! The result is, that even our early hope for Thursday[2] has become impossible at present,—ay de

11. Letter omitted.

TC-JF, [27 Feb.]. MS: FC. Hitherto unpbd. Tentatively dated by the meeting "yesterday" of "individuals of various complexion," presumably 26 Feb. (see JWC to HW, [27 Feb.].

1. Ca. 10 mi. S of the Thames, in Surrey.

2. Presumably when Forster was to come to dinner or they to dine with him; cf. JWC to [JF], [ca. 23 Feb.].

mi!— Eleven hours and a half by the Shrewsbury Clock![3] Yours most afflicted

T. Carlyle

TC TO THOMAS BALLANTYNE

Chelsea, 28 Feby., 1843

My dear Sir—Many thanks for your Notes; which were sufficient for my purpose. I had already written down "some 13" as the cipher of the Manchester business;[1] and so it may now stand.

The Book is to be called *Past and Present:* one stiff volume, treating of the grand "Condition of England Question,"[2]—I suppose, in a somewhat unexpected way. But you will see in not many weeks. The Printer is already at work,—though the poor *Writer* has still a rather heavy fortnight in store before ending; and was seldom busier.

The Booksellers Chapman and Hall have forwarded, from me, a copy of *Chartism;* addressed "Mr. Samuel Bamford, Silk-weaver, Middleton near Manchester." The Book, they tell me, now lies or will straightway lie, at the shop of Syms and Dinham (if I remember the name right) in Manchester, "to be called for." Will you be so kind as call for it, or apprise Bamford that he must call.

I could rejoice to hear that Bamford had decided on sticking to *authentic* Prose; writing down many a thing that he with his own heart and eyes has *known:* that seems to me his true vocation as an Author; for Poetry I could trace no decided call in him. You need not mortify the brave man by telling him this straight out;—but if he could get in some oblique way convinced of it, I feel certain there were good and not harm done to him. He is certainly a remarkable man; calculated, one would say, to be the spokesman of much that lies dumb at present,—with no way of speaking itself but Chartist Insurrections, Trades Unions and such like; which are a very imperfect way indeed! It will be well worth your while to go and see him, to

3. See *1 Henry IV* 5.4.

TC-TB, 28 Feb. Pbd: A. Carlyle, *NL* 1:282–83.

1. The number killed at Peterloo, the meeting held at St. Peter's Field, Manchester, 16 Aug. 1819, in favor of parliamentary reform. TC said in *Past and Present:* "Some thirteen unarmed men and women cut down,—the number of the slain and maimed is very countable: but the treasury of rage, burning hidden or visible in all hearts ever since . . . is of unknown extent" (*Works* 10:16).

2. The title of ch. 1 of *Chartism.*

keep your eye upon him, if at any time there be possibility of helping him on his way.

I am spending my allotted minutes *here*,—and must end!

Yours always truly, / T. CARLYLE.

TC TO FRANCES WEDGWOOD

Chelsea, Monday [March 1843?]—

My dear Mrs Wedgwood,

Thanks for your Ticket; which I shall strive to make use of. Thanks too for your kind invitation:—but consider whether it would consist with Scotch prudence to walk up to Gower-Street in order to be conducted to Albemarle-Street?[1] Alas!——

I think of putting myself under the protection of Erasmus, if perhaps he will, on sollicitation,[2] hold out a hand to me. Marlborough Street and a quiet pipe were no irrational preliminary. Perhaps I may meet you all there, on your road?

Yours ever truly / T. Carlyle

JWC TO JEANNIE WELSH

[2 March 1843]

Dearest

The cover of my yesterdays letter was in my uncle's handwriting was it not? I laid it by in that idea—for having never received a letter from him in all my life, even a cover with my name to it in his handwriting—especially when he is sick—seemed a thing to be kept—if not with all the *Werterean* tenderness which Creek[1] exhaled over my old newspaper covers, and note of invitation to dinner,—with at least a sincerity of natural affection not liable to violent *reactions* making it out of the question that some fine day I should *send it back!* Indeed darling your description of the bed-gallows is quite enough for me—I

TC-FW, [March?]. MS: Yale. Hitherto unpbd. Dated tentatively at a time when the Carlyles record frequent visits or outings with the Wedgwoods.

1. Regular Fri. evening lectures were given by a variety of lecturers at the Royal Inst., 21 Albemarle St., from 1825. The scientist Michael Faraday (1791–1867; *DNB*), for example, began the lectures in 1843 on 20 Jan., and they went on till 3 June. The distance from the Wedgwoods' home was approx. 1 mi.

2. Thus in MS.

JWC-JW, [2 March]. Addr: Maryland Street / Liverpool. PM: 2 March 1843. MS: NLS 1891.194. Pbd: Huxley, *JWCLF* 90–91 inc.

1. Werther is the hero of Goethe's novel *The Sorrows of Young Werther* (1774). Creek was the Carlyles' nickname for G. L. Craik.

should *not* like to see it "the least in the world"[2]—and I hope it will very soon have fulfilled its mission—and return "into the womb of uncreated night."[3] I could not sleep a wink under it—*moi* [I]! Give him a kiss and tell him from me; he is a dear angel to—wish for bacon! it is an honest, healthy, rational wish!—as Carlyle would say, it is *"indicative of many things"!* How I should like to share my present ham with him!— John Carlyle; suddenly taken with I know not what movement of superhuman generosity—sent lately to Carlyle a *Tweed!*—if you know what sort of a garment that is—and to *me some* oranges—figs—french plums and a Yorkshire Ham from Fortnum & Masons—which ham is the "very best I ever eat— —" I believe it was a sort of *amende honorable* [reparation], for certain purblind, impertinent criticisms which he had been making to C. on his book—the which, by the way, he has *never read* and so was in no very competent state to pronounce an opinion of it—but he was sure that Carlyle "formed a wrong judgement of the Aristocracy—he had not had the same opportunities which he (John) had had of observing their dispositions and proceedings!!![4] To which Carlyle who had been fretted too long with his *blether* [nonsense] answered "No! perhaps not Sir I was never attached to any nobleman or noble woman—in capacity of flunky or in any menial capacity whatever."!!— The result of this quarrel was the above mentioned *Tweed* and eatables— Geraldine I dare say secretly persuades herself—that *her* Sunday's bare neck—and *grande toilette* was the moving spring of his generous proceeding—but that is incredible truly! Oh no—Geraldine does no execution on either man woman or child here— No living soul takes to her—Severals Mazzini, Elizabeth,[5] Darwin testify a sort of *sacred horror* of her—and the curious part of it is that every newcomer after surveying her with questioning eyes, begins immediately to ask me a hundred questions about *you!* Even Carlyle has come to the conclusion that, "that girl is an incurable fool—and that it is *a mercy for her she is so ill looking!! There* was a remark *"indicative of several things"!*— I really wish she would go away now for she places me entirely in "a false position"— Besides so long as she remains I am not likely ever to have C's company except at meals— From all which several practical inferences may be drawn—1*st* Beware of "swearing everlasting friendship" on "a sudden thought"—(a thing I might have known at this time of day without any new expe-

2. Coterie speech.

3. *Paradise Lost* 2:150.

4. John Carlyle was personal physician to the countess of Clare, 1831–38, accompanying her abroad (see vols. 5–9), and to the duke of Buccleuch, 1838–39 (see vols. 10–11).

5. Pepoli.

riences)—*2d* Put no faith in the intellect which is *purely theoretical;* when you ask it for bread it will give you a stone—*3d* Choose your friends by their qualities to *excite* love and esteem—not by the love and esteem which they profess to *feel*—or may even in reality feel for *you*—*4th* follow your first impulses—not the impulses which you have cockered up in yourself by dint of special pleadings— —That is to say—if you be a reasonable woman—if you be not a reasonable woman all will be folly the first impulses as well as the last—your best course in that case were to tie your hands together, and deliver yourself over to some wise person, begging him or her, to take the responsibility of living off your shoulders—to *order* you in the way you should go[6]—

Has Helen got a cook?

Poor Darwin is still very suffering—he came one day a week ago bringing with him three beautiful hyacinths in pots—a white, a blue, and a pink— The smell of them makes me sad somehow— Forster has also been ill, and is ill—all that prodigious "Brummigam enthusiasm" and foaming vitality bottled up in a sick arm chair,—very deplorable to see! for I actually went to see him.— One is so sorry for a man *ill* with only a tiger to look after him—tho *his* is the pink of Tigers![7]— Poor M*rs* Sterling is confined to bed at present.— Indeed every body seems ill or miserable— Bless thee my sweet wee Babbie—I would give a crown-piece for a kiss of you at this instant—J C

When is that monster of a Gambardella to come home with my picture?[8]

It is too bad to make you write every day still—but so pleasant!

TC TO JOHN STERLING

Chelsea 9 March / 1843—

Dear Sterling,

Here is your Verran's Epistle to the Cornubians[1] again: I fear the poor man will go mad; but he has at least a better chance, keeping

6. Cf. Prov. 22:6.

7. John Forster, still a bachelor, who lived at 58 Lincoln's Inn Fields, was ill for much of 1843. "Brummagem [Birmingham] enthusiasm" was the phrase used by Rosina, Lady Bulwer (1802–82; *DNB*) to describe Forster in *Cheveley* (1839) 3:291; see 13:291. A tiger is a liveried boy acting as a footman or groom.

8. Of her uncle John Welsh.

TC-JS, 9 March. Addr: Falmouth. MS: NLS 531.61. Pbd: A. Carlyle, *CMSB* 266–67; quot: I. Foot, *Michael Verran . . . and Thomas Carlyle* 49.

1. Natives or residents of Cornwall. TC refers to a letter, dated 9 Feb. at Callington, from Michael Verran to Caroline Fox in which he says: "The twenty-fifth day of this month it will be three years since the lord spok peace to my soul I was three months before I received the second blessing and the week fowolling

cows, in sight of green fields, skies and other actualities, than imprisoned in the bowels of the Earth, and his own Magic-lantern Phantasms merely. If the Subscription can contribute to save him, it will do well; which may the gods grant.

I finished my poor Book yesterday, in a very sick condition (it and I); and today have corrected the first sheet of it: we find there are to be some 19 in all; and it will be towards May, I conjecture, before the sluggish people let me quite free of it.

Tonight I go to the House of Lords to hear old Wellington speak: I want to hear the voice of that old blade, what kind of sound it has; once, while we are still both in this world.[2]

My poor little sweetheart, whom I remember, as if still seeing her: it is bad news this you send me of her![3] I long for the Southwest winds for all your sakes. The weather here is infinitely too vehement to admit of *you* yet for a while, were all the rest propitious.

I have quantities of Letters to despatch today; and have already pored my eyes out, rectifying "Copy."

Adieu, dear Sterling. Get strong again, and come to see us.

Yours ever / T. Carlyle

I am attending a Lyell's Course of Lectures on Geology, too;—in our old shop up in Edwardstreet Portman Square.[4] The audience a square-jawed harsh male company of near 200; the Lecturer clear—but of kin to Neptune, I fear![5]

I received the third blessing and my path is like that of the just shining briter and briter but I must confess I am a brand pluck*d* from the eternal burning but thanks be for the Lord I am more than concueror through him that so love me and the language of my heart is O that my head was water and mine eyes a fountain of tears I might weep day and night for the slain of the daughter of my people I am determing at this time to spend and to be spent to the Glory of God may he ever keep me humble and all his fellow-travelors for his name and mercy sake may the Lord Bless you and yourse my feelings is more than I can express" (MS: Strouse).

2. Lord Monteagle had written to TC, Friday [3 March?]: "I should have had peculiar pleasure in sending you an order for the House of Lords, but that your note did not reach me till after the proper hour. / I shall look out for the first good night when the 'old Hero' is likely to speak again & I shall take care that you are provided with the proper certificate for admission." Thomas Spring Rice, 1st Baron Monteagle (1790–1866; *DNB*), Whig politician; see 10:28. Arthur Wellesley, 1st duke of Wellington (1769–1852; *DNB*), spoke against the motion condemning Edward Law, 2d Baron Ellenborough (1790–1871; *DNB*), gov.-gen. of India, 1841–44. Monteagle voted for the motion, which was defeated.

3. John Sterling's da., probably Charlotte, who was ill; see 9:120.

4. A course of eight lectures on geology, 7–31 March, given by the geologist Charles Lyell (1797–1875; *DNB;* see 12:335), at the Marylebone Inst., where TC had lectured, 1838–40.

5. I. e., watery.

TC TO [THOMAS BALLANTYNE]

Chelsea, 9 March, 1843–

Private

Dear Sir,

At present I am much too busy for any extraneous kind of writing: nor indeed, tho' my convictions about Free Trade as they well can be, should I, most probably, prove worth much as a writer on it.[1] I am as it were *too* well convinced for speaking on the subject at all, with the due patience. *It* lies before me as an axiom;—and innumerable things lie behind it!

None wishes your Cause speedier success than I; but I think as before that perhaps *my* best on behalf of it is to be done *here*.

For the rest I shall rejoice to see a set of competent Papers, together or apart, on this matter, set in circulation. The heavy public ear must be flagitated and agitated: there seems to be no other way of getting even Bread for England, but that somewhat melancholy one.

Believe me, / Dear Sir, / Yours very truly

T. Carlyle

JWC TO JEANNIE WELSH

[9 March 1843]

Dearest

I was very disappointed yesterday forenoon, when no letter arrived from you—and over and above, a little out of humour—but my humour was quickly restored to its natural calm, by what was meant to aggravate it. The fussy officiousness and superfluous enthusiasm with which Geraldine struck into the concern, wondering how it ever should happen that "any one whose letters I was at the pains to wish for should not feel it worth the pains to write" &c &c produced a speedy reaction in your favour, just as the wife who getting herself beaten by her husband—fell foul of the stranger who interfered in her behalf—demanding what it was to *him* if her husband chose to beat his own wife"?— After dinner came the parcel—truly a beautiful and most luxurious wrapage! but in spite of my admiration of it, I did not will-

TC-[TB], 9 March. MS: NLS Acc. 9086.25. Hitherto unpbd. "Thos Ballantyne" written on the last page, possibly by TC, but almost invisible because now obscured by the mounting.

1. Evidently TC had refused to write anything on free trade for Ballantyne because he was busy.

JWC-JW, [9 March]. Addr: 20 Maryland Street / Liverpool. PM: 9 March 1843. MS: NLS 1891.206. Pbd: Huxley, *JWCLF* 92–95.

ingly leave off shaking it, and shaking the books, in hopes that a letter would fall out— "Perhaps, I said the letter will be coming by tonights post"—and at this same moment Helen who had come in without my noticing her, my attention being absorbed in the shawl, put the letter into my hand—*then* finally my contentment was complete! When I had finished reading it I put on the shawl drew the delicious little hood over my head—and stretched myself on the sofa to be supremely comfortable— I had been in the forenoon to the Chinese exhibition[1]—which like all *exhibitions* had tired me dreadfully— I was soon asleep— Carlyle was stretched on the green chair and two others—he had yesterday finished his book! he also slept profoundly—as he had good right to do— Geraldine makes herself a bed with the *priedieu* [prayer desk]-chair and a sofa cushion and the hearth rug—*every day* after dinner—and sleeps like a person under the influence of liquor—or drugs—a singular phasis of a young lady—yesterday evening she was stretched out and sound as usual!— Into this enchanted looking room walked Garnier—considerably distracted—singling out me to chatecise he asked "why do you *tender* yourself in this way? or are you really not well?"— Geraldine who had got on her end, and always bursts out of sleep into volubility—poured forth a torrent of words a[bout] "the poor creature having been to that *confounded* Chinese exhibition &c &c"—but she was cut short by Garnier's uplifting his two hands, and saying to me with an affectation of dismay—"Oh my goodness! how fast that Lady does talk! it is quite impossible for me to follow her! Mrs Carlyle is she a relation of yours"?— She pretended to be vastly amused—and vastly amused with the quizzing which he carried on the whole evening—but I believe she had her own private misgivings about it! After tea Carlyle and Garnier went down to smoke—and in the interim a gentleman sent in his card—Helen whispered it was the gentleman of next door[2]—and that you may understand all the awfulness of this announcement for me—I must tell you that Carlyle had yesterday put into effect his long matured purpose of trying the fair musician with a letter! I was out at the time and did not see it—but he gave me to understand that it was of the most chivalrous discription, professing his conviction that "a young beautiful female soul working in the most beautiful element that of *music* would not willingly give annoyance to any fellow worker"!! &c &c

1. The Chinese Collection, Hyde Park Corner, advertised in the *Athenaeum*, 4 and 11 March, as a collection "of objects *exclusively Chinese*, [which] surpasses in extent and grandeur any similar display in the known world."

2. The Lamberts lived next door, 6 Cheyne Row, and had two das. who sang and played the piano to the Carlyles' great annoyance; see 15:191.

&c— What he required of her practically to do—or rather to not do was to refrain from playing all days of the year till after two oclock!!!—a modest request to a young lady whose whole existence seems to be in practicing!— I feared "the gentleman next door must be come to make *a shine* [scene]. But the first glance at him as he entered, hat in hand, reassured me— He lookd at me most benignly from head to foot—sat down on the chair I motioned him to and then observed "We have had a delightful day Mam"!— I myself led the conversation to the piano—saying that I understood my husband had been invading his house today with a most unheard of remonstrance—but the amiable gentleman would not let me finish—he bewailed the annoyance his daughters must have given us—bewailed our patience in having suffered so long without protest—would do unheard of things to spare us in future—the piano should be drawn into the middle of the floor—the *top* should never be opened—there should be no playing in forenoons unless when the mistress came on Wednesdays—and if *she* could possible change the hour it should be done—in short there never was such a complaisant gentleman as "the gentleman of next door" since this world began!— When Carlyle came he seemed ready to fall on his knees before him to implore his forgiveness for having daughters who played on the piano— I assure you we were quite melted by his superhuman politeness and he seemed to find himself quite melted by our grateful sense of it—and he staid talking—till suppertime!—and then there was such a shaking of hands—and repetition of civil speeches on both sides—nobody knows what he can do till he tries! the putting down of a piano under such circumstances would have seemed desperate even to me!— Today the *faintest* sound of it was heard as if for trial for about a minute—it was hardly audible— Heaven knows how they have deadened the sound— So pray my dear have a fly at your chimney cans [pots]!—that is an insupportable thing and ought not to be tolerated for twentyfour hours—

Geraldine goes on Saturday thank heaven[3]— — I did not absolutely give her notice—but I took precious good care to avoid uttering a word that could be a second time misconstrued into an invitation to stay longer.— On monday she said "I *must* write to that *horrid* Mrs Green[4]—to say when I am to pay her the long visit— She wanted me before tomorrow evening for a music party"—the "*horrid* Mrs Green you should know is a pretty, gentle—rather silly—but very innocent and goodnatured looking young woman who has shown her first and last a deal of kindness—and who when she came here the other day

3. JWC is writing on Thurs.
4. Jewsbury's friend in St. John's Wood.

was caressed and flattered all over by Geraldine—just as she caresses and flatters *me!* before my face too—but *that* I *think* was an oversight she afterwards bethought herself of—certainly it was a sad oversight, for the credit of her *sincerity* considering the atrocious things she had said to me of the poor young woman— I was reading when she began to speak of her visit to her— I turned over a leaf and made no answer— She scribbled a few lines—then looked up to me pen in hand—and asked—"well! *when?*—will you tell me *when* you would have me go"?— I answered dryly—"surely it is for *you* to decide on the *when* not for me"—and continued my reading—she wrote a note naming Saturday then handed it to me to read— I glanced it over, and giving it back said merely—"it seems all quite right"!— This I think was the next thing to "giving notice"!—but indeed I am sick to death of her—and I have not her gift of showing kindness where I feel only annoyance and disgust— Your own JC

A passionate kiss to my uncle for the shawl and dozen for abstract affection Love to all the rest— Mary's note was too short to entitle her to any special thanks[5] The devil fly away or rather fly home with Gambardella—home first and then away after—beyond the realm of chaos and of night[6] if he like

TC TO G. L. CRAIK

[ca. 9 March 1843]

Dear Craik— I break up this Note to say that all is right in regard to the "hand," that "Miss A. Winward's natural hand" (on this paper) will do perfectly well and that she can have a large mass of the *Ms.* whenever she sends for it. The other point of *time* will decide whether *all* the *Ms.* or not.— Ever yours

T. C.

5. Mary, youngest da. of John Welsh.
6. Cf. *Paradise Lost* 1:543.

TC-GLC, [ca. 9 March]. MS: Univ. of Calif., Los Angeles. Hitherto unpbd. Dated by TC's employment through Craik of a "young lady" to copy part of *Past and Present;* see TC to GLC, [14 March], and TC to MAC, 24 March. The note is written on the cover of a sample of her hand, which has a note, presumably by Craik: "Miss A. Winward / (Natural Hand)."

TC TO RALPH WALDO EMERSON

Chelsea, London, 11 March, 1843–

Dear Emerson,

I know not whose turn it is to write; tho' a suspicion has long attended me that it was yours,[1] and above all an indisputable wish that you would do it: but this present is a cursory line, all on business,—and as usual all on business of my own.

I have finished a Book, and just set the Printer to it; one solid volume (rather bigger than one of the French-Revolution Volumes, as I compute): it is a somewhat fiery and questionable "Tract for the Times," *not* by a Puseyite, which the horrible aspect of things here has forced from me,—I know not whether as preliminary to *Oliver* or not; but it had gradually grown to be the preliminary of anything possible for me: so there it is written; and I am a very sick, but withal a comparatively very free man. The Title of the thing is to be *Past and Present:* it is divided into Four Books, "Book I. Proem," "Book II. The Ancient Monk." "Book III. The Modern Worker"; and "Book IV. Horoscope" (or some such thing):—the size of it I guessed at above.

The practical business, accordingly, is: How to cut out that New-York scoundrel, who fancies that because there is no gallows it is permitted to steal?[2] I have a distinct desire to do that;—altogether apart from the money to be gained thereby. A friend's goodness ought not to [be][3] frustrated by a scoundrel destitute of gallows.— You told me long since how to do the operation;[4] and here, according to the best way I had of fitting your scheme into my materials, is my way of attempting it.

The Book will not be out here for six good weeks from this date; it could be kept back for a week or two longer, if that were indispensable: but I hope it may not. In three weeks, half of it will be printed; I, in the meanwhile, get a correct Ms. Copy of the latter half made ready: joining the printed sheets and this *Ms.*, your Bookseller[5] will have a three-weeks start of any rival, if I instantly despatch the Parcel

TC-RWE, 11 March. Addr: Concord / Massachusetts / Steam. MS: RWEMA. Pbd: Norton, *CE* 2:21–24; Slater, *CEC* 336–38. Ralph Waldo Emerson (1803–82), American philosopher and man of letters; see earlier vols.

1. Emerson had written a note of introduction for the Rev. Orville Dewey, 26 Feb., which was not used till June. Emerson had last written on 15 Oct., TC on 17 Nov. 1842.

2. The New York publishers, D. Appleton & Co.; see 13:103, 140.

3. Word omitted.

4. Emerson had told TC, 30 April 1841, to have his MS copied and sent to the U.S. in time for simultaneous publication in England and America.

5. Little & Brown, of Boston, Mass.

to him. Will this do? This with the announcement of the Title as given above. Pray write to me straightway, and say. Your answer will be here before we can publish; and the Packet of Proofsheets and Manuscript may go off whether there be word from you or none.—And so enough of *Past and Present.* And indeed enough of all things for my haste is excessive in these hours.

The last *Dial* came to me about three weeks ago as *Post-Letter*, charged something like a guinea of postage, if I remember; so it had to be rejected, and I have not yet seen that N*o*;[6] but will when my leeway is once brought up a little again. The two preceeding N*os* were, to a marked extent, more like life than anything I had seen before of the *Dial.* There was not indeed anything, except the Emersonian Papers alone which I know by the first ring of them on the tympanum of the mind, that I properly speaking *liked;* but there was much that I did not dislike, and did half like;[7] and I say, "*I fausto pede* [Go auspiciously];[8] that will decidedly do better!"— By the bye, it were as well if you kept rather a strict outlook on Alcott and his English *Tail,*[9]—I mean so far as we here have any business with it. Bottomless imbecils ought not be seen in Company with R Waldo Emerson, who has already *men* listening to him on this side of the water. The "Tail" has an individual or two of that genus,—and the rest is mainly yet undecided. For example, I knew old Greaves myself; and can testify, if you will believe me, that few greater blockheads (if "blockhead" may mean "exasperated imbecil" and the ninth-part of a thinker) broke the world's bread in his day.[10] Have a care of such! I say always to myself,—and to you, which you forgive me.

Adieu my dear Emerson. May a *good* Genius guide you; for you are *alone, alone;* and have a steep pilgrimage to make,—leading *high,* if you do not slip or stumble!

Ever your affectionate / T. Carlyle

6. *The Dial* was a quarterly magazine, founded 1840, as the organ of American transcendentalism, ed. by Emerson, 1841–44; see 12:267–68. TC evidently refused vol. 3, no. 3 (Jan.).

7. For a list of Emerson's many contributions to vol. 3, see G. W. Cooke, *An Historical and Biographical Introduction to Accompany THE DIAL* (Cleveland, 1902) 2:203–07. Cf. 15:57.

8. Horace, *Epistles* 2.2.37.

9. Followers of Amos Bronson Alcott (1799–1888), American transcendentalist, who had visited England the previous year; see 14:230.

10. James Pierrepont Greaves (1777–1842), mystic and vegetarian (see 5:91), lived his last days at Alcott House, Ham, Surrey. His disciples Charles Lane (1800?–70) and Henry G. Wright (1814?–46) came to the U. S. when Alcott returned, autumn 1842, bringing with them about 1,000 vols. of Greaves's library. A partial list of these books by mystics was pbd. in *The Dial,* 3 (April 1843):545–48.

JWC TO JEANNIE WELSH

Sunday [12 March 1843]

My Babbie!

"Thanks God,"[1] the house is quiet again! Oh so quiet! so quiet!—How worthy of being remarked is that apparent platitude of a remark that "all happiness is comparative"—the mere *negation of worry* is indeed as much happiness for some of us, as for others would be a rich succession or the realization of "loves young dream."[2] She went yesterday, according to programme—on *her* side, *of course* the parting was a dreadful business!—floods of tears—even a sort of *mild hysterics*—on our side it was transacted with dry eyes, with a composure of soul impassive even for the claims of sympathy— In fact, it must have been from seeing *such* women as Geraldine in tears that old Burton came to his conclusion that "the spectacle of a woman weeping was no more moving than that of a goose going barefoot."[3] Some few times in her life I will believe she has *wept*—really wept from heart-fullness—unconsciously—not "according to programme"— But all the tears that I have seen her shed have been of the programme-sort—with no more *real* sorrow in them than there is in drops of rain or in the *drops of steam* that gather on the lid of a tea-kettle!—they are the same sort of half-constitutional half voluntary thing, these tears of hers, as the little nervous cough on the strength of which some women set up for being interestingly consumptive!—and which they carry about them all their lives without being either better or worse for it!

"Dear me! how hard-hearted Cousin is this morning"!— No my angel-babbie—I am not harder-hearted this morning than any other morning—*thy* soft true tears—the tears of no true woman—would suggest to *me* on this or any other morning "a goose going barefoot"—But I am, very naturally, in a state of reaction against the *cant* of sensibility, which has lead me such a devil of a life for five weeks back.—It is come to an end now however— She is gone and my good wishes go with her and abide with her—so long as she keeps far away! But never let us try to live under the same roof again! this time the trial has passed over without bloodshed, or any very flagrant outrage—but it might not be so always!— That we have not already quarreled outright, I will say in her praise is to be attributed to *her goodnature* or *self-possession* (I know not which) rather than to any virtue of mine—

JWC-JW, [12 March]. Addr: 20 Maryland Street / Liverpool. PM: 13 March 1843. MS: NLS 1891.213. Pbd: Huxley, *JWCLF* 96–99 inc.

1. Coterie speech, an expression of Mazzini's.
2. Title of Thomas Moore's lyric.
3. Proverbial; Robert Burton, *Anatomy of Melancholy* 3.2.3.4.

My behaviour to her as my guest—and on my own invitation—has been very far from perfect—from the first day I have been for her cold, cross, ironical, disobliging—and this evil disposition on my part, instead of getting itself disarmed by her unfaltering flatteries and caresses has rather been aggravated thereby—flatteries and caresses so out of reason and so ill responded to appearing to me in truth a what shall I say?—*bassesse* [lowness]—*toadyism*—or else a hypocrisy in either case a thing alike incompatible with an *honest friendship,* which would have found itself *enraged,* and with good right, by such repulsive behaviour— Carlyle seems not a whit less relieved than myself—altho he had so little of her— He said to me last night with a beautiful *naivete* "Oh my dear what a blessing it is to be able to sit here in peace without having that dreadful young woman *gazing* at me"! To be sure she did *gaze* at him—and try all sorts of *seductions* on him, with a hope that seemed to "spring eternal in her human breast"![4]—but the poor man proved absolutely *unseducable*— Even when she took the strong measure of stretching herself on the hearth rug at his feet and sleeping there—in the manner of Ruth[5]—all that came of it was a remark to me afterwards "that he looked at her face when she was lying sleeping on the rug and could not help thinking how like she was to an old snap-wife"![6] But more than enough of her and her *Pattenisms*[7]— I only wish that I had seen into her in the beginning as I see into her now—that I might not have committed the memorable folly of taking her for my confidential friend!—

And would not one say to read all this much ado about *her* that I had not an uncle in the world to think about and write about? and nevertheless he is not out of my head for an hour together— He and all the babbies are really as much before my eyes as the portraits hanging on the wall are The weather has not been weather for mending *rapidly* and besides rapid recoveries are not always the surest—so I suppose we should content ourselves with the progress he makes—still I should so like to hear of his being out again—if it were only for a drive in a carriage.— *Men* shut up in a drawing-room put one so in mind of the wild animals in the zoological gardens! Have you ever tried for Bamfords book?—or the *Neighbours?*[8] You will soon have a new one of our own—in four or five weeks—the printing is going on rapidly—I consider it a *great* book—calculated to waken up the Soul

4. Cf. Pope, *Essay on Man* 1:95.
5. See Ruth 3:7–11.
6. A woman who sells gingerbread snaps.
7. Manners like those of the Pattens, Jewsbury's friends in London, presumably relatives of her friend Patten in Manchester; see JWC to JW, [17 Aug.].
8. See JWC to JW, [27 Feb.].

of England if it have any longer a living soul in it—and *"thanks God"* he has got thro it with less bodily harm than was to have been anticipated— He intends sending a copy to the Young lady of No 6—as an acknowledgement of the extraordinary courtesy of that house-ho[l]d[9] I do not think they have played an hour in the day since the remonstrance was sent in—sometimes I could find in my heart to send round a request that they would play—the silence becomes so oppressive to me in fancying what it must be costing them—

Monday

The foregoing was written yesterday by way of taking Time by the forelock[10]— I was interrupted by The Editor of the *Tablet* and an *Artist* whom he called Herbert[11]— Robertson came just as we finished dinner, and an hour or two later Mr Spedding[12]— After Robertson came in I rose to go up stairs—John followed me, saying he wished to talk with me a few minutes— We went into the Library where there was a good fire—I wondering what he was about to say—judge of my amazement when he fell to asking me more questions about my side and all my et ceteras than he had done from first to last putting all together since I first complained to him!— The more I told him my side was much better than it used to be, the more he showed himself *inquisitive*—almost anxious about it!! and the result of the consultation was his inviting me—I should rather say prescribing for me that I should take part of— —his cigar!!—"there were certain states of the stomach in which a little *mild* tobacco-smoke was extremely good for one!—I had better take a little more!—I had not had enough yet to do me any good"— —I protested that more of it would make me sick— "Oh no!—I would find it *highly* useful for me—*provided I did not send it through my nose,* which was very dangerous—very dangerous indeed"— Can he be going out of his wits? such attentions to me would almost make one think so—

He spoke of Geraldine as "a very *unfortunate* young woman"— "Did I know how she had been brought up? it would be curious to know how she had arrived at her present absurd figure!— Perhaps the best she could now do were to go into the Catholic Church, it might be the means of keeping her out of worse mischief—"

9. Letter omitted.

10. Proverbial.

11. Frederick Lucas (1812–55; *DNB*), ed. of the Roman Catholic weekly the *Tablet;* see 12:145. John Rogers Herbert (1810–90; *DNB*), portrait and historical painter, a recent Roman Catholic convert like Lucas.

12. John Robertson. James Spedding (1808–81; *DNB*), close friend of TC who had retired from the colonial office, 1841, to devote himself to the study of Bacon; see 8:196, 14:42, and K. J. Fielding, "Carlyle and the Speddings: New Letters," *Carlyle Newsletter* 7 (1986):7–20 and 8 (1987):51–66.

I am going today to dine *in the family way* with the Wedgwoods and attend a lecture on Music in the Evening[13]—O Dio!—it looks a vast vast enterprise!

Carlyle is tomorrow—*again* going to sit for his picture—to Linnell!!![14] at the request of William Cunningham "who is a good sort of fellow that one does not like to disoblige—but it is really an unspeakable hardship"!!!

—Here is your letter—no darling I was not provoked with you on Saturday—I had one the day before and did not feel myself entitled to another— From what you tell me I flatter myself that my uncle will soon have a drive in this beautiful spring weather— Pray tell me if you find *my* picture as like as *yours*—I am always fearful of something evaporating in a *copy*[15]— I am happy that Walter has been to the Fergus[16]—for in the country intelligent people are so scarce and the Ferguses *are intelligent* whatever else— Bless you my child— Your own J. Carlyle

What I paid for the parcel was simply eight pence! You are getting as ridiculously punctilious as myself—so much for keeping bad company

TC TO AN UNIDENTIFIED CORRESPONDENT

[13 March 1843]

Dear Sir— Some time ago your letter was delivered me; I take literally the first free half hour I have had since to write you a word of answer.

13. Hensleigh and Frances Wedgwood lived in Gower St.; for the musical lecture see TC to GLC, [14 March].

14. John Linnell (1792–1882; *DNB*), portrait and landscape painter. See frontispiece for the portrait which TC confirmed was "done for a Mr. Cunningham [William Coningham]," who "would not have anything to do with it when finished" (*William Allingham's Diary*, intro. G. Grigson [1967] 267). It was exhibited at the Royal Acad., 1844.

15. Apparently JWC's copy of a picture of Walter Welsh, based on Hick's sketch; see 15:170, 200.

16. Walter Welsh had visited the Carlyles' old friends John Fergus (d. 1865) and his sisters Jessie and possibly Jane (see 10:162), in Kirkcaldy, Fife; see 9:246.

TC-UC, 13 March. Pbd: *Chambers's Edinburgh Journal* n.s. 1 (1844):239, rptd. from *Cupar and St. Andrews Monthly Advertiser*. Text: *Chambers's*. TC wrote to R. Richmond, 18 Sept. 1845, about *Chambers's* that "the young student [to whom the letter was addressed] had used the somewhat questionable freedom of printing this Letter: of which step whatever I might think, there was no doubt but the Letter (written I knew not and know not how, when, or to whom) was mine."

It would give me true satisfaction could any advice of mine contribute to forward you in your honourable course of self-improvement, but a long experience has taught me that advice can profit but little; that there is a good reason why advice is so seldom followed; this reason namely, that it so seldom, and can almost never be, rightly given. No man knows the state of another; it is always to some more or less imaginary man that the wisest and most honest adviser is speaking.

As to the books which you—whom I know so little of—should read, there is hardly anything definite that can be said. For one thing, you may be strenuously advised to keep reading. Any good book, any book that is wiser than yourself, will teach you something—a great many things, indirectly and directly, if your mind be open to learn. This old counsel of Johnson's is also good, and universally applicable:—'Read the book you do honestly feel a wish and curiosity to read.'[1] The very wish and curiosity indicates that you, then and there, are the person likely to get good of it. 'Our wishes are presentiments of our capabilities;'[2] that is a noble saying, of deep encouragement to all true men; applicable to our wishes and efforts in regard to reading as to other things. Among all the objects that look wonderful or beautiful to you, follow with fresh hope the one which looks wonderfullest, beautifullest. You will gradually find, by various trials (which trials see that you make honest, manful ones, not silly, short, fitful ones), what *is* for you the wonderfullest, beautifullest—what is *your* true element and province, and be able to profit by that. True desire, the monition of nature, is much to be attended to. But here, also, you are to discriminate carefully between *true* desire and false. The medical men tell us we should eat what we *truly* have an appetite for; but what we only *falsely* have an appetite for we should resolutely avoid. It is very true; and flimsy, desultory readers, who fly from foolish book to foolish book, and get good of none, and mischief of all—are not these as foolish, unhealthy eaters, who mistake their superficial false desire after spiceries and confectionaries for their real appetite, of which even they are not destitute, though it lies far deeper, far quieter, after solid nutritive food? With these illustrations, I will recommend Johnson's advice to you.

Another thing, and only one other, I will say. All books are properly the record of the history of past men—what thoughts past men had in them—what actions past men did: the summary of all books whatsoever lies there. It is on this ground that the class of books specifically named History can be safely recommended as the basis of all study of books—the preliminary to all right and full understanding

1. Cf. Boswell, *Life of Johnson* 393–404, 1080.
2. Untraced.

of anything we can expect to find in books. Past history, and especially the past history of one's own native country, everybody may be advised to begin with that. Let him study that faithfully; innumerable inquiries will branch out from it; he has a broad-beaten highway, from which all the country is more or less visible; there travelling, let him choose where he will dwell.

Neither let mistakes and wrong directions—of which every man, in his studies and elsewhere, falls into many—discourage you. There is precious instruction to be got by finding that we are wrong. Let a man try faithfully, manfully, to be right, he will grow daily more and more right. It is, at bottom, the condition on which all men have to cultivate themselves. Our very walking is an incessant falling[3]—a falling and a catching of ourselves before we come actually to the pavement!—it is emblematic of all things a man does.

In conclusion, I will remind you that it is not by books alone, or by books chiefly, that a man becomes in all points a man. Study to do faithfully whatsoever thing in your actual situation, there and now, you find either expressly or tacitly laid to your charge; that is your post; stand in it like a true soldier. Silently devour the many chagrins of it, as all human situations have many; and see you aim not to quit it without doing all that *it,* at least, required of you. A man perfects himself by work much more than by reading. They are a growing kind of men that can wisely combine the two things—wisely, valiantly, can do what is laid to their hand in their present sphere, and prepare themselves withal for doing other wider things, if such lie before them.

With many good wishes and encouragements, I remain, yours sincerely,

THOMAS CARLYLE

CHELSEA, 13*th March,* 1843

TC TO G. L. CRAIK

Chelsea, Tuesday [14 March 1843]—

Dear Craik,

We had gone out last night to hear the Scotch songs;[1] which was unlucky.

3. Cf. "Sir Walter Scott," *Works* 29:30.

TC-GLC, [14 March]. Addr: Old Brompton. MS: Strouse. Hitherto unpbd. Dated by John Wilson's recital "last night," 13 March; see below and JWC to JW, [12 March].

1. Wilson's Scottish Entertainments, "Highland Melody and Song," Music Hall, Store St., 13 March.

On Saturday, after I saw you, there came a young man, apparently with satisfactory copying talents;[2] whom, however, I apprised of the state we were in, and put off without any final response till Wednesday. He too was ignorant of the rate 'per 1000 words'; nor have I yet learned that anywhere.

But the question at present is, How much *Ms.* can the young lady copy *before the evening of the* 29th *of March?* The American Packet sails on the 1st of April; and I hope to get the Printer, with his share of the job, driven up to the mark at that time. The 'words' are probably about 50,000; not fewer! If the young lady cannot do them all, the young man might have a share of them. But indeed I have not yet got the Printer's response;—his devil having absented himself yesterday. At all events I wish you would ask your young lady, and let me know as soon as possible.

Wilson is a capital singer; but last night we had only his Highland Songs, an inferior sample of the article. It was on an old engagement with the Wedgwoods that we went.[3] You and I must go some night, and hear the Jacobites.[4]

Yours ever truly / T. Carlyle

TC TO MARY RICH

Chelsea, Tuesday [14 March 1843]

Alas, my dear Mrs Rich, I find that I *have* already two engagements for Saturday, "The British Authors' Society" at 2 o'clock, "The London Library Committee" at 4;—so that we must stand by Thursday for Woolwich after all![1]

2. For copying the MS of *Past and Present;* see TC to GLC [ca. 9 March].
3. See JWC to FW, [16? Jan.].
4. The 6 Feb. and 6 March concert had been billed as "Adventures of Princes Charles," i.e., Jacobite songs.

TC-MR, [14 March]. MS: Penn. State Univ. Lib. Hitherto unpbd. Dated by the Carlyles' attendance at Wilson's concert of "Highland melody" (see TC to GLC, [14 March]), and TC's visit to Woolwich, 16 March (see JWC to JW, [16 March]).

1. The London Lib. committee met on 18 March but TC did not attend. The Society of Authors was proposed in early 1843 to help protect such writers against American piracies (see 14:92–94). The original group included the antiquarian John Britton (1771–1857; *DNB*), G. L. Craik, the poet and journalist Charles Mackay (1814–89; *DNB*), and John Robertson. This meeting on Sat. must be the informal one of 18 March between Robertson and TC, noted in Robertson's letter to Mackay, 19 March (Charles Mackay, *Forty Years' Recollections* [1877] 1:170), not the first formal meeting of 25 March held at the British Hotel, Cockspur St., as there was no London Lib. committee meeting on 25 March. The poet

I shall probably see Scott today at the lecture:[2] but at any rate this will find you in time.

The wild Highland Songs are sounding thro' my head strangely this morning.[3]

In great haste / Yours ever truly / T. Carlyle

TC TO RALPH WALDO EMERSON

Chelsea, 15 March 1843—

My dear Emerson,

About four days ago I wrote to you about a new Book to be called *Past and Present.* I learn now that this letter, which I will make "N*o.* 2," can still go along with the former: and so, having made a variety of calculations and arrangements, I will now with all brevity (my haste being boundless) communicate to you the practical result of them.

Our next Steamer for Boston will sail on the 1st of April. I have secured a copyist for the second portion of *Past and Present,* who is to be ready with his work all done, in time for that conveyance; the Printer, a punctual man, undertakes on the other hand to be ready with his share of the operation: wherefore, in brief, you can instruct your Boston Bookseller to expect a Complete Copy of the work by that said Steamer, so that his Printers may fall upon it, tooth and nail,—and overtake ours if they can; at all events, completely distance the New-Yorker, it is to be hoped.

This is the essential of "N*o* 2." I will do what is in me to be punctual; and as my subordinates are steady people, I think we shall manage it.— Our Book, as I compute, may be still some four weeks, after the April Steamer goes, in a hidden nascent state. If a Letter of yours in answer to this arrived before Publication, as is possible, and in-

---

Thomas Campbell (1777–1844; *DNB*) presided on 25 March and TC was one of the speakers; John Robertson read a draft prospectus, and a subcommittee (with TC) was appointed to revise it. The proposed prospectus announced four objects for the society: (1) to register the names and works of all British authors; (2) to see that all the laws for the protection of authors and their works were kept; (3) to encourage the enactment of needed new laws; and (4) to establish an international correspondence among authors about the society's aims. See Mackay, *Forty Years' Recollections* 1:168ff, and Walter Besant, *Essays and Historiettes* (1903) 271–307.

2. Alexander Scott at Lyell's lecture; see TC to JS, 9 March.

3. Wilson's concert.

TC-RWE, 15 March. Addr: Concord / Massachusetts / N*o* 2. MS: RWEMA. Pbd: Slater, *CEC* 338–39.

formed us that another week or two of delay will be essential, that too can easily be granted.

I send no "Apologies": for they would but occupy my time and yours. I am very busy. Among my other operations I have undertaken to hear Lyell lecture on Geology,—a somewhat superfluous enterprise, at once wearisome and ineffectual; our Geologist being dreadfully *Neptunean* in his qualities, I fear!—

John Sterling arrived yesterday, to see his Mother who is very poorly. I have not got eye on him yet, but shall attempt it today.[1] Blessings and desert of blessings on you!

Yours ever / T. Carlyle

JWC TO JEANNIE WELSH

[16 March 1843]

My dear good Babbie to write me such a big letter! But *ecco la combinazione* [here is the combination]! In reading your paragraph about the servant I said to myself like you "that sounds well"—and I felt strongly minded to prosecute the scent—for even when Helen is not in a temper I have no longer any comfort with her— I do not know whether it be that she is fallen into that sort of chronic ill health which shows itself in listlessness and "*confusion of ideas*" more than in any other way—or whether it be that she has lost all care about pleasing me and so does not exert the faculties she has but certain it is the work of the house is always trailing behind her—herself always untidy—and nothing going on in the kitchen department as it ought to go on— Carlyle as well as myself is out of all patience with her, and for a long while back, I have only kept her because I *have* kept her, because I have a horror of changes— Plainly however this posture of affairs could not be allowed to last for ever—waited only *the fullness of time*[1] to have itself altered—and the result of my cogitations as to *when* it would be best to part with her has always been that something would be finally settled when we should be leaving

1. On his return to Falmouth, Sterling told Caroline Fox that TC was "very unhappy about the times, thinking everything as bad as ever, and conducted on the least happiness for the greatest number principle; the only thing good is, that people are made to feel unhappy, and so prove that enjoyment is not the object of life. His book is now being copied, and is to be printed simultaneously in England and America, so that he, being the Prophet to both lands, may receive the Profits from both" (24 March, Fox 179).

JWC-JW, [16 March]. Addr: 20 Maryland Street / Liverpool. PM: 16 March 1843. MS: NLS 1891.199. Hitherto unpbd.

1. Gal. 4:4.

town— I should try to find her a place then and get rid of her in a peaceable way—for to leave *her* in the house to invite all the thieves of Chelsea into it by publishing her terrors about them, was not to be thought of— —and to "clatch [move awkwardly] her about the country" with me as I did formerly, at great expense and trouble, required that she should be worth the expense and trouble— Always understood however, in mental reservation, that someday I might give her her leave "quite promiscuously"— If she broke out on me with any more insolence, my mind was made up to bring things to a termination at once—and let her seek herself a place where she could find one—

When I received your letter this morning then—tho pleased to hear there was such a promising-sounding woman in the world—I did not immediately jump at her— In all probability she would be hired, before I could conscientiously put Helen away—unless she committed some new *violence* and that was not to be calculated on— I meant to write then that all I could do in the matter for the present was to beg that you would keep an eye on her— But *ecco la combinazione* as I said before— The sun being shining very bright this morning—Helens *dirtiness* showed itself more flagrant than usual— Already Bingham Baring has been and others were likely to follow in so beautiful a day—so for the credit of the house I begged her to get herself cleaned a little as soon as possible—she was going to the door at the moment to speak to the Butcher—she finished a long confabulation with him and then flouncing open the parlour door she presented herself with an air of fiery determination and asked me "what was dirty about her? what I meant by desiring her to get herself cleaned—her cap (a great frouzy yellow night cap) was clean—her face was clean—what did I mean at all"? I told her; "I *meant* that she had been going about for months back in a state of untidyness that gave the house the air of a dirty Lodging-house—and that I wished her to reform herself in that particular "I do not at all know what you would have?" said she furiously—"I can keep myself no cleaner than I am—and if your not content I cant help it—you are always finding fault with something, and in short there is no pleasing of you"!— "I will tell you how to please me" said I—"by going and seeking yourself another place"— "Oh! thank you—thank you kindly," says she making a curtsey (!!) I want nothing better for *my* part"— "Very well then said I—let it be understood you leave this house"— She slammed the door and ran down stairs— In half an hour after she came flying up again—with her face crimson and her eyes sparkling like a wild cats— —"Do you wish me to go *to day* said she, or am I to do out the clothes?—if you do not want me I can be ready in half an hours time" "You will do out the clothes and you will do your work for *a month,* said I very cooly— I do not choose you to run out into the streets again like a wild animal as you have done on former occasions"— —"Oh" says she saucily I can get myself a lodging—you need not keep me a moment longer than you like"— "Compose yourself said I—it is not for *your* sake I am keeping you but for *my own*— I do not choose to be without a servant—go down stairs and remember that for another month you are *my servant* neither more nor less"!— So under these sudden and *decisive* circumstances—I fling aside a coat I was lining for Carlyle (who is gone to Woolich)[2] and write to you by return of post—to beg that you will throw yourself vigorously into the matter of investigating this woman—the account of her qualifications is perfectly satisfactory—but can it be ascertained if she be *honest—sober*—and not an absolute *fury*—a little heat of temper I do not mind—all good servants have it—and will you see her—and judge whether *I* should like her countenance—I never saw any good come of a disagreeable-*looking* servant with whatever recommendations. And find whether she be really *inclined* to take a single servants place—and *willing* to wash as well as *able*— The wages I give Helen *now* is twelve pounds—but I should prefer *beginning* with ten—that the rest might be *a reward* for good conduct if she pleased me— If you find on inquiry that she still *sounds* promising in all the particulars I have mentioned and above all if you like her looks—it might be best for me perhaps to engage her to come a month hence—but unless you think her *specially* desirable—there would be no sense in bringing her *before* we leave the house— I could get some body here to fill up the interval between Helen's going and our going— —send the valuables out of the house and lock it up as formerly—it would stand no worse chance locked up than with a person like Helen to take care of it—and then start with a new one on my return—

But tell me what you can learn and what you *advise*—and then I will answer positively—engage her or let her go—

I have plenty of other things to say—but must leave them in abeyance for the present—my *passion* has set my head a-aching—and my letter is already so long— who *are* the men you are to have for god's *sake?* and who is the young lady?

My congratulations and a shower of kisses to my Uncle for his descent to breakfast—

Bless you all and believe me even in the abyss of *prose* your poetically loving J C

2. For the promised visit to Mary Rich, see TC to MR, [14 March].

TC TO JEAN CARLYLE AITKEN

Chelsea, Friday, 17 March / 1843–

Dear Jean,

Here is another little Note, written in a small minute which I have been able to snatch from the general gulph; for I am still kept incessantly busy, and have no time at all to spare, of late days. Our Printers are hard at work; and I think have now about the fourth part of their job done: perhaps the worst with them is over, which generally is the getting of them fairly set under way,—in the *way* they are to travel. But I have also had a good deal of *fash* [trouble] with certain *Copyists;* persons, namely, that I had to get in great haste to copy a portion of the Manuscript for the use of the Americans; to prevent a certain 'free and enlightened citizen' there from stealing the Publication of the thing from me. In short, I am and shall be kept in a perpetual *fike* [fidget] till this business be off my hand: I send you a printed leaf to shew what kind of look it is like to have;—and will say no more about it at present.

The other day I had a letter from John Carlyle, our half-brother in Canada:[1] poor fellow, he does not explain much of his situation; but writes in an affectionate manner; and does seem to be busy and in health, and making the way about as long as the day, in a tolerable manner. His first Farm-lease is out; but he has taken another Farm, and planted himself there, about 5 miles from the old place,—his former *address* still serving. He says he has not money enough to buy a cleared Farm; and his sons rather incline "to be mechanics" than farmers.[2] I sent the Letter over to Jack, and he was to forward it to Alick.— Alick seems to have made up his mind to quit his present business at Ecclefechan; but nothing other that is satisfactory hitherto suggests itself to him. Poor Alick, I wish greatly he could fall into something: but I cannot give him any advice; indeed nothing but his own choice could give him a fair chance in whatever enterprise he took to. A small Farm might suit him: but I doubt there is none attainable in your part of the world at present.

Jane keeps tolerably well; and now we have got sunshine again too, beautiful spring weather. Our servant Helen is about to bundle; she has long been discontented, very useless, inclined to insolence withal;

TC-JCA, 17 March. MS: NLS 512.1. Hitherto unpbd.

1. John Carlyle (1791–1872), TC's half-brother, had emigrated to Canada via the U.S. and settled nr. Brantford, Ontario, 1837; see 1:139 and 12:228.

2. His eldest son, John, became a farmer; James and William became, respectively, a school principal and a school inspector. John and Peggy Carlyle also had two das., Janet and Mary.

so yesterday she was finally apprised to make ready. Jane thinks a good successor may be procured from Liverpool, by aid of her cousins. We can do either way, for a while, as it is not our expectation or purpose to continue thro' the summer here, but to flit somewhither towards the sea-coast.

Jenny I suppose is come up to you by this time: give her my kind regards, and encourage her to write again. Sucess to James at Thornhill.[3] Sucess to you too! I hope to hear good news by and by.—— Jack was here, as usual, on Sunday: all well and cheery. Adieu dear Sister. Ever your affectionate

T. Carlyle

JWC TO JOHN FORSTER

[18 March 1843]

My dear Mr Forster

Geraldine told me the day of the Lecture[1] that she was to go into Essex on Tuesday. She returns to London but not for some six weeks or a month. She engaged to come here on Sunday morning (soon after breakfast) and stay till three She had to dine at the Pattens at four on that day—so there remains only Monday evening, in case you cannot come on Sunday morning—and I don't know if she be disengaged; I *rather* remember that she was to dine with Mrs Gore (!) on that day[2]—and then *could you* come on Monday? I will ascertain if she is attainable at all rates and send you a line by post on Monday morning—unless you can come as I hope tomorrow morning I have a note from Mrs Macready this morning—all well— for myself I am nearly dead of gaities, two Balls since I saw you *a Fancy one* (!) and a plain one—and my Cousin to be *done* every day![3]

Ever yours affectionately
Jane Carlyle

3. Apparently James Aitken had taken a lease of a business at Thornhill (13 mi. NE of Dumfries), using a tenant; he abandoned it a year later; see TC to AC, 3 May 1844. TC spells "success" twice as "sucess."

JWC-JF, [18 March]. MS: NLS 605.431. Hitherto unpbd. Apparently written on Sat. as the invitation for "Sunday morning" and "tomorrow morning" is clearly the same; dated between Jewsbury's departure from Chelsea, 11 March, and her visit to Chelsea, 20 March (JWC to JW, [20 March]), before going to Essex, 21 March. At the top of the MS someone has written "May 1840" in pencil and then TC wrote "(No!—*inquire of* Geraldine &c)" above it in blue pencil.

1. Wilson's Scottish Entertainments, 13 March, referred to by JWC as a lecture in JWC to JW, [12 March].

2. Catherine Gore (1799–1861; *DNB*), novelist; see 12:350.

3. Presumably daily letters to Jeannie.

TC TO EDWARD STRACHEY

CHELSEA, Monday morning,
March 20, 1843.

MY DEAR SIR,—I wrote on Saturday to my Russian; he called yesterday with his answer. I, unfortunately, had gone out, and he had to leave it with my wife. Still more unfortunately, the answer itself proved to be entirely negative, and very little better than zero.

He does not think that there is on sale in any shop in London a single Russian book. Nobody learns the language here; a few English merchants about Petersburg are the only English persons that do. He knew of a teacher of Russian here at one time, but he could get hardly any shadow of encouragement, and after long struggling had to withdraw to Brighton, where probably he now is.

My Russian (probably a *German* merchant, and a most obliging man)[1] is persuaded that there must be extant some kind of Russian-English grammar, Russian-English dictionary, for the use of the St. Petersburg English clerks, if no otherwise, but he himself is entirely ignorant of any. The like as to Russian-French, though probably the hope is greater on that side. This is all that he knows. For the rest, he will "send to St. Petersburg" for me, "send to Paris," do all that a zealous man can do. If you think, in these circumstances, it is worth while prosecuting such an outlook, pray entrust me, and I will most cheerfully employ this gentleman, who, I think, will like to be employed by me. If your brother be *determined* to learn Russian,[2] it might be possible for him, but such books as we are like to get will almost infallibly be *bad*, and the difficulties will be greatly increased thereby. They can be got, it seems, by sending to St. Petersburg, and St. Petersburg can be sent to.

I am afraid I shall not get so far eastward to-day as to see you again this time.[3] Let us hope you will return before long. Pray take care of yourself; keep up and encourage the improvement you are already making; exercise and regimen, not medicine or doctors.[4] And so Good speed you.

Will you offer my affectionate remembrances to your mother,[5]

TC-ES, 20 March. Pbd: E. Strachey, *LC* 829. Edward Strachey (1812–1901; *DNB*), author and nephew of Isabella Buller; see 10:91.

1. Possibly Robert von Glehn, merchant; see JWC to HW, [27 Feb.].
2. Probably William (1819–1904), who joined the colonial office, rather than George (b. 1828), still at school but later minister at the Court of Saxony; there were three other brothers, all of whom served in India.
3. Strachey at Mount St., Grosvenor Sq.
4. Strachey was partly crippled by inflammation of the knee.
5. Julia Strachey, b. Kirkpatrick (1791–1846); see 2:4–5.

whom I will always reckon among my chosen ones? May Good be with you and yours.

I remain, my dear sir,

Yours with true good wishes, / T. CARLYLE.

JWC TO JEANNIE WELSH

[20 March 1843]

"Forgive your last"!—upon my honour you *are* modest! Any one but yourself with such an *awful* day's work before her; to say nothing of *an earthquake* over night! would have thought it much to write at all![1] Henceforth, Babbie of my soul, you shall be *placed* under the same category with Cavaignac[2] who once answered an invitation which I had sent him for a particular night; "tho an earthquake should intervene I will come not the less"—for you an earthquake *has* intervened and you have written not the less!—and your merit is greater than his—in the proportion that *have done* is better than *would do.*

Let us not seek to lessen it your merit by asking invidiously—whether you *slept* thro the earthquake?— I will believe no such thing tho you *did* sleep sometimes thro the electrifying shock of Carlyles rusty bell-string!

I meant to have written you a long long letter yesterday by way of going to church—but Geraldine jumped in about twelve oclock and staid till—she had a glimpse of the D*r!*[3]— She was as foolish and every way unsatisfactory as usual—saying all sorts of improper things about the people she is staying with who appear to be excessively kind to her— Bah!—one of Cavaignac's growls is the only fit criticism to make on her—

JWC-JW, [20 March]. Addr: 20 Maryland / Street. PM: Chelsea, 20, 23, and 25 March 1843. MS: NLS 1891.220. Hitherto unpbd. JWC forgot to write "Liverpool" on the envelope so that it is covered with conjectures in various hands as to where it should be sent; see JWC to JW, [29 March].

1. The *Times,* Mon., 20 March, reported that after a small earthquake in Lancashire on 10 March more violent "shocks . . . were felt" just before 1 A.M. on "Friday last . . . in Liverpool . . . and . . . almost the whole of Lancashire and Cheshire . . . ; they followed each other in such rapid succession that to many they appeared to be simultaneous. In Liverpool and the neighbourhood they were very distinct, an interval of from 10 to 15 seconds having elapsed between each. . . . [T]he effects in all cases appear to have been similar in many respects—namely, an agitation of the floors, windows, and furniture of home, and a lifting up of the beds."

2. E. L. G. Cavaignac.

3. John Carlyle.

God bless me! What a stramash [uproar] in your kitchen!— I *am* heartily sorry for it!— I had hoped that G. and H.[4] would be fixtures for a long while especially the little one. I wish that this world would return to the simple habits of its forefathers—so that we might have *cerfs*[5] again instead of servants—or serve ourselves, which were perhaps the best way of all.— They seem to be all alike ungrateful & unreasonable— If here and there be one who has better dispositions than the rest—bad example soon corrupts her down to the general standard— — Helen is working like a Turk and getting the house cleaned famously—as she always does when in a rage—it is the only principle on which I have been able to get any thing effectually cleaned for months back— She has taken no step yet that I know of to seek herself a place— But I only await your letter to take *my* steps decisively— On the whole I think it will be best if this woman[6] do *not* turn out excessively desirable or the best of all were if she turned out desirable and would consent to engage with me at six months hence or so— —It might happen that she would *like* coming to *London* and might stretch a point to get there— I really think the house would be safest locked up as formerly—and it is besides a very severe trial for a servant to leave her for months with nothing to do and bad neighbours about her— If we leave town in the end of May as Carlyle speaks of doing at present—there would be such a little while to fill up, and not long enough for a servant to have got *hefted* [adjusted] (ask my uncle) in the place— *My* plan—and I hope to make it paramount is that we should go direct to Liverpool—and then that *he* should go on to Annandale for a week or two leaving me with you to seek a cottage by the seaside at Formby or Conway[7] of some of those places where we might rusticate two or three months—within possibility of Liverpool— Perhaps one might get a cottage all to oneself in which case one would need a servant at once—at all events I should need one to bring back with us. —I know nothing of these localities or their resources—*Lancashire* hitherto has meant for me simply 20 Maryland Street—but with a strong determination and such light as you could give me or get for me I feel sure we might find the sort of upputting we want there—as well or better than anywhere else— — But it is time enough to take up this branch of the subject—and my

4. Recently employed servants at Maryland St.

5. Thus in MS.

6. One mentioned by Jeannie as a possible replacement for Helen Mitchell; see JWC to JW, [16 March].

7. Both on the coast, Formby 10 mi. N and Conway (N Wales) ca. 30 mi. W of Liverpool.

head is not clear enough for it today anyhow— I must out into the *Freie* [open air]! where I hope my uncle is also at this moment Bless you dears

Your own J C

TC TO EDWARD STRACHEY

CHELSEA, *March* 21, 1843

MY DEAR MR. STRACHEY,—I have received your beautiful little book, and am far indeed from "thinking less of you" for writing it.[1] The little book is the product of a generous, pure, loving heart, and will speak good only, and not evil, into other hearts. Thanks to you for writing it; thanks to you for sending me a copy of it.

I have been exceedingly busy with printers, with copyists, and other confused persons and things ever since I saw you, or I should have been in Mount Street again. In a week or so I hope to be freer, and then—

With many thanks, with constant good wishes,

Yours most sincerely, / T. CARLYLE.

JWC TO JEANNIE WELSH

Thursday [23 March 1843]

Dearest Babbie

I cannot make out from your Tuesday's letter whether you had received mine of Monday—or no. Appearances are against your having received it—for you make no allusion to any part of its contents nor yet to the letter of our immortal Cousin James which was enclosed in it[1]— Yet I cannot fancy how it could have miscarried—or failed to arrive at the right time (Tuesday morning) being that I as good as put [it][2] in the post office with my own hand—on Monday at midday—that is to say I saw with my own eyes Robertson put it into the post office with his hand— But perhaps I had forgotten to address it! I sometimes do such things. —yet no—for I remember Robertson asking

TC-ES, 21 March. Pbd: E. Strachey, *LC* 829.

1. *Holy Matrimony: Its Duties and Dignity as set forth by the English Church* (1843), the first of Strachey's many books, written under F. D. Maurice's influence.

JWC-JW, [23 March]. Addr: 20 Maryland Street / Liverpool. PM: Chelsea, 23 March 1843. MS: NLS 1891.224. Quot: Sanders, *CF* 239.

1. James Baillie, JWC's maternal cousin; see 12:196. JWC had forgotten to put Liverpool on her letter of 20 March.

2. Word omitted.

me in looking at the letter "Where is Maryland Street"?— Am I sure however that I put *Liverpool?* if not—the letter of course *would* have a rather discursive progress—

In the case of your not having had that otherwise of-no-consequence-letter you will be thinking me no better than I should be—and to put an end to such misappreciation I write to day merely to say that I had written—for today my head is specially bad and I am not up to a decent letter—in compensation I send you a document from Thackeray—which has wit enough in it to make up for any sort of scrap— To understand it aright I must tell you that he and Fitzgerald came here that evening we were at the musical lecture[3]—the *only* evening in which they *could* have failed to find at least one of us at home— Ever since I had been thinking occasionally that I should write him a note of regrets and fix an evening—but my intention like too many others during the last week had gone to the paving of *the bad place!*— To sharpen my sense of hospitality there arrived this letter from Fitzboodle[4] two days ago which would have made even old Pistrucci "in the Character of Heraclytus" laugh.[5] Pray return it to be present among my genuine treasures—

I have a great many things I am sure to tell you—but my headach today puts a veto on everything— Bless you dearest—and in the meanwhile write to me on credit. Love to all—

Your own J C

TC TO MARGARET A. CARLYLE

Chelsea, 24 March, 1843.

My dear Mother,

Having a few minutes to myself today, I will again scribble you a line. The Doctor sent me down Alick's Letter; the best news in which was that you were in your usual tolerable state of health; that you had walked out with him "to the top of the Potter Knowe."[1] I am very glad to hear so much authentically particularized.— Since yesterday, in order to be farther from the fire in these warmer days, and have my *side* to the light, which I like better, I have shifted my writing-table;

3. 13 March; see TC to GLC, [14 March].
4. One of Thackeray's many pseudonyms.
5. Filippo Pistrucci (ca. 1777–ca. 1857), actor and improvisatore (see 8:360) in Mazzini's circle, nicknamed Heraclitus, after "the weeping philosopher" of Ephesus (fl. 500 B.C.).

TC-MAC, 24 March. MS: NLS 512.2. Pbd: A. Carlyle *NL* 1:287–88 inc.; quot: Wilson, *Carlyle* 3:18.

1. The hill behind Middlebie, a few mi. NE of Ecclefechan.

and now every time I look up, *your* affectionate sorrowing face looks down on me from the Picture-frame above the mantel-piece:—my dear good Mother! It has a sorrow in it, that face, which goes into my very heart. But it is not to be called a mere "sorrow" either; it is a noble *weariness* rather, as of much work *done*. I will wish all men and all women such a "sorrow."

Our Printing here goes on with tolerable success; and is now about half finished. He is a good clever man my Printer, whom I discovered several years ago, and whom I have insisted on sticking to ever since.[2] They say, "He is a little dearer."— "Well," I answer, "ought he not; being considerably *better?*" A *better* man ought to be had in respect, and by all methods encouraged, whereever we fall in with him.— My Copyists (for the American Market) give me somewhat more trouble: but they also, as I trust, will be all over in about a week. The Packet of Paper will then go off from Liverpool, and I shall have no more to do with it: if they can thereby save themselves from the American thief, it shall be well: if not, why then he must steal; *I* could not hinder him!— One of my chief Copyists is a poor young woman who has been bedrid for almost a year, totally unable to stir from the spot, with a disease in the back-bone. There are two sisters of them; daughters of a Widow: the Widow married again, and they could not live with the new Father; accordingly they removed into a lodging of their own to support themselves by being governesses in Schools: they were doing extremely well, till this one was lamed in the way I speak of,—and now, poor thing, she is striving to write, or to sew, or to do anything she possibly can for herself, lying fixed on her back! The writing she makes is not good; but it is very pains-taking: how can I complain of it? By and by I mean to go and see the poor girls myself, and ascertain whether any other aid be possible for them.

The distress of many thousands of people is extreme at present. The silent distress, as usual, is often the worst. Jane, walking out the other day, was struck with the look of a poor middle-aged woman, crawling along the streets with a staff, who seemed to be "more dead than alive"; one of the saddest wasted spectres, Jane said, she ever saw in this world. Jane went to her house; found the woman lying on some tatters of clouts on the floor, patiently "dying of a deep decline": the Doctor had ordered her mutton-broth, but she could not get any, so the Doctor ceased to come near her. Her husband was a farm-servant, 18 miles off,—her eldest daughter, fifteen years old, was at a kind of charity school, out all day; they had to pay 2/ a-week for rent

2. Robson, of the printers Levey, Robson, & Franklyn, had printed vol. 3 of *The French Revolution* and done most of TC's printing since 1839.

of their garret-room: the rent-payment had gone with their last penny, that day Jane had seen her out on the street,—ever since which exertion she had been obliged to lie still, "being rather worse for the exertion." Jane managed to get her an old bed-tick and fill it with clean sound straw, an old blanket,—also to get the daughter a besom, and charge her to clean up the house: finally, what was best of all, to get the poor woman a little broth;—and now *both* of them are in hopes the poor creature may not die; for her "decline" seems first of all to have been cold and hunger, with some slight ailment in the winter time! The woman has a good character; and, Jane thinks, a hard proud temper, which perhaps has driven her husband, who was a dissipated fellow, away from her, tho' he still sends 10 shillings a-week, an astonishing sum of money for him,—but inadequate here for a mother and four children.— I must not omit one other feature of the business: the wretched people, neighbours of the woman, seemed struck with spite that *she* had got anybody to look after her; and one of them, probably some boy or the like, out of some window had *spat* upon Jane's shawl as she came out! Nothing more miserable was in all the concern than that.— I suppose such cases exist by the thousand in all quarters of this ill-fated country at present.

Alick's Letter, both his Letters are very gloomy, as indeed is not surprising: he seems decided for leaving Ecclefechan, and does not know yet whitherward he shall go. Jack wrote to me that he did not think Haregills Farm would do,[3] the land being all scourged out, and the requisite outfit of capital very large. He seemed to think, however, that perhaps some small farm of a feasible sort, like the Gill[4] or so, might be worth looking after. As for me I do not know how to give a word of advice to Alick, this way or that: I can only give him my deep sympathy, and be ready any moment to assist him in what *he* advises himself to do. Certainly he has need of forming a manful decided resolution; but it is *he* that must form it, if there is to be a fair chance of his succeeding in it: we cannot much assist him, poor fellow, in that! There is a gloomy energy in his late Letters, which is very painful, but is not without hope to me. I prophesy sometimes, with inexpressible satisfaction, that he will get *sight* of the thing that has been *wrong* with him; and rise, in the name of God, and rectify it! If he can, it will be a victory more glorious than all he ever yet contemplated even in his boyish dreams. God assist him, my poor much-erring, much-enduring, brave, kind and truehearted Brother! I believe

3. Ca. 4 mi. N of Ecclefechan.

4. The farm 4½ mi. NW of Annan where TC's sister Mary (1808–88) and her husband, James Austin (see 5:68), had lived since Oct. 1839.

it really will be useful for him to quit Ecclefechan, at any rate: he ought never to have gone thither; among such a set of "infamies," as he himself correctly names them.— You will give him my heart's love, dear Mother: and as for yourself, you will behave in this matter henceforth as you have done hitherto, in the brave silent manner he describes to us.—

Poor Isabella gives us all much uneasiness;[5] but we will hope whatever is good nevertheless. My blessings and prayers with one and all of you! Adieu, dear Mother, for this day.—

Ever your affectionate, T. Carlyle

TC TO AN UNIDENTIFIED CORRESPONDENT

My dear Sir,

On the foregoing leaf is a piece of German writing,[1] which, if you please, you may slit off, and forward to Col. Mitchell by the first Packet you chance to be sending.[2] One real Soldier and Writer may, with satisfaction, hear any word that another of the like character will say of him or of his work.

Yours always truly / T. Carlyle

Chelsea, 27 March, 1843—

5. Generally unwell, Isabella was expecting a baby within four or five weeks. She had evidently asked John Carlyle for his advice, for he wrote to her, 3 March: "there can be little room for expecting any decided improvement till after your confinement but I hope you will then recover your health & strength again as you did under almost similar circumstances before" (NLS Acc. 9086.199).

TC-UC, 27 March. MS: Yale. Hitherto unpbd.

1. An extract of a letter to TC from Varnhagen, dated Berlin, 12 March 1843, and copied in TC's hand. In trans. the extract reads: "The life of Jean Paul is a [word illegible] very painstaking piece of work, which I greatly prefer to the German sources from which it is drawn; thus also the Hon. Mitchell's life of Wallenstein, which provides the nucleus from the uncritical desert of Forster's biography and, as it were, presents it purified. The documents regarding this historical figure are not yet available for a complete winding-up; for that, further publications from the Austrian archives, or, failing these, freer points of view, must be awaited, than those which our historians now have. Schiller the poet has without doubt correctly seized the character of Wallenstein as such, and through empathetic creative power penetrated to the historical situation. Exactly seen, the most vigorous historian is on the whole the most certain. The mind is always a master of circumstances and objects are formed through perception" (MS: Yale). The life of Jean Paul was by Eliza B. Lee, and the life of Wallenstein by John Mitchell; see TC to KAVE, 5 Feb. Friedrich Christoph Förster, *Wallenstein . . . Eine Biographie* (Potsdam, 1834).

2. Mitchell, on half pay since 1827, was an unattached lt. col. He spent part of each year on the Continent and part in Edinburgh.

JWC TO JEANNIE WELSH

[27 March 1843]

My Hearts-Babbie

Never apologize to *me* for being "*cross*"—I should not like you half so well if you were always the same sweet placid Babbie 'without shadow of change'—I should not feel *sympathetic* with you, if you had either an *imperturbable temper* or what is called "*a* SUBDUED *temper*"— As Darwin says "defend me from *a subdued temper*"!—and the *imperturbable* is nearly as bad! your last note I assure you was very much after my own heart—and I would have sent you a little word of encouragement by return of post—only that I had something else to do for you, which I considered would be of more permanent use— What?—"Ah that is the mystery

Of this wonderful hystory
And you wish that you could tell"![1]

But it were cruel to keep you puzzling your bits of brains!— Well then—know that on Saturday I sat from twelve till four to—Gambardella—for my picture!—to be given to *you!*—and again yesterday from eleven till four!—and you all the while expecting him in Maryland Street on his way to London!!

On Friday morning he scampered up to this door on a grey horse—and took the house as it were by storm— I found him fatter—more hairy—and more in love with himself than ever—but the same good hearted fellow as ever— He spoke of you all in grateful and approving terms!—but it is my Uncle who is his *passion* in the family— *He* was "a *grand* man"—"a *noble* man—*especially when excited*"—"Oh there was nothing in Liverpool he liked so well as to see *Welsh* excited"— He talked a vast quantity of nonsense, not without flashes of good sense—and ended by telling me that I *must* come to him *immediately* to sit—"without any words about it"—he had "promised the picture to *Jeanie*, and if he did not do it before he began to other *wo-k* he would never probably find leisure to do it at all"— Of course I was quite ready to sacrifice my *humility* or as you consider it my *vanity*—when

JWC-JW, [27 March]. Addr: 20 Maryland Street / Liverpool. PM: 27 March 1843. MS: letter NLS 1891.247, envelope NLS 1891.232. Pbd: Huxley, *JWCLF* 101–04 inc., where dated end of March. Date confirmed by Gambardella's beginning his painting of JWC "on Saturday" and continuing "yesterday," apparently Sun., following the Thurs. of his arrival in London, almost certainly 23 March (see JWC to JW, [29 March]), and his calling on JWC the next day.

1. Untraced rhyme; see 13:121.

"Jeanie" was to be the gainer—so I appointed to go to him the following day—I was very unwell however the morning he came—but as he complimented me on my looks, I thought it needless to call myself ill—and besides I hoped to be better by the time I should need to go to him— Thack[era]y and Fitzgerald were to dine with us that day (Friday)[2]— I baked a mutton pie and a raspberry tart in a state of great suffering got thro the dinner—hoped to get thro the tea—and then promised myself to go to bed—but just before the men came up stairs, my affairs reached a consummation—I fainted—and had to be carried to bed—and lay for three hours alternating between fainting and retching—Helen blubbering over me, and the men, increased by the arrival of Spedding and Robertson,[3] raging and laughing in the adjoining room— Oh I assure you I have not passed such an evening for a good while. The following morning I felt too *broken* to get up to breakfast and was still in bed at ten oclock, when down came G. again— Helen told him I had been ill and was not up— "*Well* then"—says he—"you tell her not to be later than *twelve* and to be sure to bring the black veil I have seen on her head"!—"Lord preserve me" says Helen "you can never be expecting the mistress to sit for her picture to day!—*the thing's an impossibility!*"— "Did *She* bid you say that?" says he—"No", says Helen, but anybody may see by her that she is not fit for any thing of the kind"!—"Oh never *you* mind" says G. "you tell her what I say"—and off he went like a passing whirlwind— —Nobody knows what he can do till he tries thought I—and so I rose—and dressed myself and actually went and sat four hours! and yesterday again five hours!—and I am not dead—only near it.

—I hope the result will be satisfactory for you— One is not a good judge of ones own likeness and no one else has yet seen this of mine—I incline to suppose it is e[x]tremely[4] ressembling—but not very well conceived—the features are every one of them exactly what I see in my looking glass—but the expression he has given them I never saw there—it *may* be that my "habitual look" is as he says it is, this which he has painted me with—the look of a rather *improper female* DOING a sort of St Anthony's ecstacy![5] and *doing* it not well—but you will see it in good time and perhaps it will strike you differently— However it strike you you will be pleased with the great pains which he has

2. MS reads "Thacky." In a letter dated from London, "Friday," probably 24 March, FitzGerald said in a postscript to a friend: "Just off to dine with Carlyle—on sheep's head" (Terhune, *LEF* 1:387).

3. James Spedding and John Robertson.

4. Letter omitted.

5. St. Anthony (ca. 250–350), first Christian monk, is usually portrayed in art as transfixed and ecstatic.

bestowed on it— If it had been to have yielded him fifty guineas he could not have taken more—

But all this while I have said nothing of my uncle's picture—my own more immediate concern.

—In the first moment—I was disposed to quarrel with the eyes—he held it too near me—and I was not used to the want of the spectacles—still I thought it a good likeness on the whole, and was fully as content with it as I had expected to be—but after a while, rising to warm my feet at the fire, my eyes fell on it unexpectedly where he had placed it behind a screen, which let in the light on it only from above—and absolutely I gave a little scream—and ran forward to kiss my own identical little uncle— Oh it is perfect in that light—the dearest little life-like kissable thing!— If Gambardella had not been by; I must have cried over it when I recognized how good a picture it was—you can understand why— Oh I am so much obliged to him—give him a whole smotherment of kisses for me (my uncle I mean)— I have not got it home yet—it was framed—beautifully framed—but he must send the frame he said for a few days as a pattern to make the others by—for he meant to frame my picture for Jeanie himself—"as a present"[6]—This is equal to "Authors giving *bound* copies of their works"!

Speaking of Authors—tell my uncle for god sake that the name of our book is to be

Past and Present

The subject as you have rightly heard is the condition of England—only there is a long biography of your old friend Abbot Sampson of St Edmund's Bury introduced into the heart of it— I will tell him more of it next time and perhaps send a specimen but here has been Mazzini keeping me up till near post-time and I have still an enquiry to make in Carlyles name of Alick[7]— Will He (Alick) be so good as discover to a nicety the last day on which it would be quite safe—without the smallest chance of being belated for a packet[8] to be in Liverpool to go to America. Carlyle thinks it is the fourth of April on which a vessel will sail but is not quite sure—also will he mention the name of the steamer—and give a guess if he can at what would be the probable charge for carriage from Liverpool to Boston of a packet weighing some three or four pounds—the last query is the least im-

6. Gambardella's portrait of JWC, given to Jeannie Welsh, who m. Andrew Chrystal, is owned (along with his portraits of Jeannie and John Welsh) by Jeannie's descendants.

7. Welsh, Jeannie's brother.

8. Above "packet" JWC wrote "parcel" and enclosed the two words in a single square bracket.

portant to have answered with precision— Moreover could you tell me all this if possible by return of post—as I shall have no peace till he knows about it—

I have a great deal more to say—and do not end—only interrupt my writing— Bless you loveliest Your own / J C

JWC TO JEANNIE WELSH

Wednesday [29 March 1843]

My darling

I do not wonder that my uncle is suffering from this weather—it is very cruel on all ailing people— To the east wind I impute my own increase of discomfort of late days—the pain in my side as bad as ever—continual nausea from morning till night—and a "confusion of ideas" that "heats the womb"[1]— —all yesterday I lay on the sofa fairly given up to despair—for the time being—and today it is only by a strong effort of *will* that I can hinder myself from doing the same feat—

Here is *the* letter—come back to me—having like the Dove of the ark[2] found no rest for the sole of its foot!—to think of the botheration I have caused to so many poor post-men thro this *betise* [stupidity] of an address! Our own postman had been tried with it, he told me, from its bearing the Chelsea post mark[3]— But for James Baillie's letter inside they would not even have known where to *return* it—for it has no signature—nor date!— What I feared was they might perhaps have sent it to James whose letter *has* a date!! —I have read it over with some curiosity—and should rather like to know if *"The Officers appointed by Her Majesty's Postmaster General for opening letters" read* this one as well as *opened* it! and if he be a man that one is likely ever to meet in society!

And now Babbie I have something on my mind to tell thee—a sort of confession—at the thought of which I feel a certain delicate carnation steal over what Geraldine calls my "horribly pale face"!—in what words to put it?—best out with it at once!— I have again been got the better of by Helen!!!— Plainly it is now a hopeless thing that I shall

JWC-JW, [29 March]. MS: NLS 1891.266. Pbd: Huxley, *JWCLF* 115–17 inc., where dated April. Dated here by TC's packet to Alick to be sent "on Saturday," 1 April, put on a ship from Liverpool to America, 4 April (see JWC to JW, [27 March]).

1. Untraced.
2. Gen. 8:8–9.
3. The letter to Jeannie Welsh of [20 March], on which JWC had forgotten to write "Liverpool." At least six postmen signed with various comments, such as "No such Street in Chelsea," and "Not known in Marylebone St. Golden Sq."

ever have the force to emancipate myself! I seem to have got into the relation with her of the gentleman and his old Butler of seventy who on being told by his Master that his temper was become absolutely insupportable and that they two *must* part—asked his Master in ironical astonishment—"Where the deevil wud ye gang to"? *Helen* asks *me;* "if I cant let alone *greeting* [weeping] to see you ill when I am here to take care of you, I should like to know what would become of me—away from you, fancying you ill, and not knowing whether you were taken right care of or not?—" by this puzzling question, and a declaration that she had made up her mind *not* to seek a place—but if "a new woman" came to go into a lodging! and "let anything come of her that liked"—and by the usual promises of perfect infallability for the future, and lyrical recognitions of herself being "just the stupidest *unluckiest* cretur that ever lived"—by all this, and plentiful tears—and *kisses* even—for I was lying on the floor entirely at her mercy—she moved me at last to say "well well—be quiet and stay there"— So now we are going on beautifully again—as always after a Stramash [uproar]—her faculties have been awakened up into new activity—she does her work as well as any one could desire—and is ready to lay the hair of her head under my feet—if it could but last!

Anyhow—it would really seem that I do the poor blockhead injustice in ever suspecting that she is not very heartily attached to me—she *exploites* her attachment somewhat—but to make much ado about everything is her way— I believe the fact that touched me most on this last occasion—was her having gone out one evening *all dressed*—as if to offer for a place—(to save her poor little dignity) and as I afterwards came to know having passed all the while of her absence with one of the *numbers*—No 4[4]—in the city!—there was something really affecting in that poor little struggle between angry pride and unsubduable affection! dont you think so?— Geraldine would laugh at all this spoonyism on my part—but you dear Babbie will not laugh—will you?

On the very morning before my fainting fit,[5] in course of which our reconciliation took place, Geraldine had written me of a paragon which her Miss Darby had found for me in Essex[6]— The woman seemed really most suitable—and was most anxious to come—and would have gone to her friends during our absence and returned when

4. The maid at 4 Cheyne Row.
5. Fri., 24 March; see JWC to JW, [27 March].
6. Margaretta Darby, who since 1840 had been living at High Laver Rectory, nr. Ongar, Essex, keeping house for her brother-in-law. Geraldine Jewsbury had earlier attended the Miss Darbys' boarding school nr. Tamworth. See S. Howe, *Geraldine Jewsbury: Her Life and Errors* (1935) 12, 115–16, 143.

I wanted her again— But *"I could not do otherwise"* like Luther *"und so Gott helf mir* [and so God help me]"[7]

I think I will send you Geraldine's last letter just to show you her *admirable toleration*—I only regret that I have not the letter to which it is an answer—to send also to show you—how her fire can burn as bright as ever not only without new fuel but under plentiful application of cold water—the last page gives you *her* interpretation of my reserve—it is my *nature* to be *silent*— — Does she really in her heart so interpret it?— *chi sa* [who knows]?

—Your gladness over the picture is very pleasing to me—an ample remuneration for any *"trouble"* I had with it—I must go and see it again finished, for there was still a good deal to do to it— — But I must tell you it has cost me more than *trouble*—it has cost me—the adoration of—old Sterling! —Yes Babbie—that picture has made a breach between us which can never surely be healed in this world!— "Devil may care"!— Sterling called here during my last sitting, and was stupidly enough told by Carlyle where I was gone and how occupied—OF COURSE he came puffing off to Michael Place and demanded admission[8]— G. had given orders to his maid that "nobody whatsoever" was to be let in to him that day—that he was "not at home"—and that point settled he had turned the key of his door on me— —Well Sterling insisted—persuaded the woman to take up his name— G. indignant at having his *fiat* protested against—roared out *"No!*— I repeat to you stupid woman as you are—I am not at home"— Sterling thereupon ought certainly to have gone away—but the thing which he *ought* to do is seldom that which he does—very curious to see the picture doubtless—for *he* has long been wanting a picture of me the old fool—he again sent up the poor maid to say it was Mrs Carlyle whom he wished to see for a few minutes— "Are you mad"? cried Gambardella now perfectly furious—"go back you vile woman, and repeat that I am not at home"—this order was given with an authoritative wave of his hand to *me*—on my compliance with which, I felt that the fate of *your* picture depended—so I kept my seat and left the thing to take its course— —Tho' every word he said must have been heard at the street door and far beyond it— Sterling nevertheless, as willful as himself, persevered—actually proceeded to ascend the stairs—*without a search-warrant*—to look for a woman whose pleasure it was, clearly enough, not to be found!— This was too bad—for it was a liberty he would not have dared to take in the house of a pri-

7. Martin Luther's reply at the Diet of Worms, 18 April 1521, to the demand that he recant.

8. Gambardella's studio at 8 Michael Pl., Brompton Sq.

vate Gentleman—it was showing Gambardella that he regarded his study merely as a *shop*— I cannot then be angry with G. for what followed—his behaviour was savage—*brutal* if you will—but he was in a state of justifiable *excitement*— He stood with the door in his hand looking like a concentration of a hundred lions—facing Sterling, whom I *heard* but did not *see* on the stair— "I wish to see M*rs* Carlyle" said S. in a tone of forced politeness— "*I* am engaged Sir said G. fiercely— I am painting— I desired my servant to tell you I was not at home"—

—"Sir"—repeated Sterling warming into wrath—"it is M*rs* Carlyle that I wish to see"!

—"Sir" repeated Gambardella in a voice of thunder: "I tell you I am painting—I am engaged—*I have a sitter*"—and with that he—slamed the door in the man's face!!—the pause that followed was awful!— G. snatched up his brushes and began to paint—but his hand shook like the leaf of the lime—he rung his bell—told his maid she was "a vile creature"—then tried it again—but his hand still shook, so he laid aside his brushes, took a pinch of snuff and burst into a perfect earthquake of laughter—Sterling has not been heard of since—in fact I do not see how he *can* come here again—for tho it was not personally *I* who so insulted him, he must know that I was witnessing the insult and letting it take its course— But his own conduct was far from perfect— Gambardella bade me tell you that he could not have called for you in his way thro Liverpool without putting off his journey a day and he had *two wagers* depending on being in London on the Thursday[9] On the one day he staid he began and finished a picture—which left him not a moment to go anywhere—

I send you a sheet of C's book but my Uncle will not be able to make either head or tail of it I fear in that disjoined state— And now dear I had better stop before I become entirely illegible

—Never mind the marmlade at present—it will keep as well with you, as with me and I am not at the end of Helen's—but do not be *cold* in returning my thanks to Mrs Martin— She is a kind good soul—but the fact is, all of you are a hundred times kinder to me than I deserve— —Distribute kisses, as usual and little Benjamin's share to yourself[10]—my Babbie

J C.

Carlyle will send off his packet to Alick's care on Saturday

9. 23 March; see JWC to JW, [27 March].
10. Benjamin's was the largest share; see Gen. 43:34.

TC TO CHAPMAN & HALL

Cheyne Row, Chelsea
[late] March 1843.

Gentlemen:

I request and hereby authorize you, to give on my behalf to the Honourable the Commissioners of Her Majestys Customs, such notice as you may deem necessary to prevent the importation of Foreign editions of the following publications, that is to say—

The French Revolution, a History
Sartor Resartus; the Life and opinions of Herr Teufelsdrockh
Wilhelm Meister's Apprenticeship and Travels
On Heroes, Hero Worship and the Heroic in History
Chartism
Critical and Miscellaneous Essays
Life of Frederick Schiller, comprehending an examination of his Works

I am / Gentlemen / Your obd Servant
Thomas Carlyle

To
Mssrs Chapman & Hall
186 Strand—

TC TO RALPH WALDO EMERSON

Chelsea, 1 April, 1843—

My dear Emerson,

Along with this Letter there will go from Liverpool, on the *4th, inst*, the promised Parcel, complete Copy of the Book called *Past and Present*, of which you already had two simultaneous announcements. The name of the Steam Packet, I understand, is *the Britannia*. I have addressed the Parcel to the care of "Messrs Little and Brown, Booksellers, Boston," with your name atop: I calculate, it will arrive safe enough.

About 100 pages of the *Ms.* Copy have proved superfluous, the text

TC-C&H, [late] March. MS: Huntington Lib.; only the signature is in TC's hand. Hitherto unpbd. The copyright act, 1 July 1842, section 17, decreed that only the proprietor of the copyright or someone authorized by him could import for sale or hire into the U.K. or any part of the British dominions any book first composed in the U.K., as a protection against the import of pirated copies of British works. This letter was presumably TC's authorization to Chapman & Hall as his new publishers.

TC-RWE, 1 April. Addr: Concord / Massachusetts. MS: RWEMA. Pbd: Norton, *CE* 2:25–27; Slater, *CEC* 339–40.

being there also in a printed shape; I had misestimated the Printer's velocity; I was anxious too that there should be no failure as to time. The *Ms.* is very indifferent in that section of it; the damage therefore is smaller: your press-correcter can acquaint himself with the *hand* &c, by means of it. A poor young governess, confined to a horizontal posture, and many sad thoughts, by a disease of the spine, was our artist in that part of the business: her writing is none of the distinctest; but it was a work of charity to give it her. I hope the thing is all as correct as I could make it. I do not bethink me of anything farther I have to add in the way of explanation.

In fact my prophecy rather is at present that Appleton the gibbetless thief at New York will beat us after all![1] Never mind if he do. To say truth, I myself shall almost be glad: there has been a botheration in this anxious arrangement of parts, correcting of scrawly manuscript copies of what you never wished to read more, and insane terror withal of having your own *Ms.* burnt or lost,—that has exceeded my computation. Not to speak of this trouble in which I involve you, my Friend; which, I truly declare, makes me ashamed! True, one *is* bound to resist the Devil in all shapes; if a man come to steal from you, you will put on what locks and padlocks are at hand, and not on the whole say, "Steal, then!" But if the locks prove insufficient, and the thief do break thro',—that side of the alternative also will suit you very well; and, with perhaps a faint prayer for gibbets where they are necessary, you will say to Appleton, next time, "*Macte virtute,*[2] my man!"

All is in a whirl with me here today; no other topic but this very poor one can be entered upon.— I hope for a Letter from your own hand soon, and some news about still more interesting matters.

A young man, named Philips,[3] I think, wrote to me from Nottinghamshire about two years ago, with a most absurd *Manuscript,* in flagrant imitation of my *Chartism;* a thing to be or not to be 'published,' &c: I answered swiftly, "Not to be"; and the young man became silent. The other day there comes a new enthusiastic Letter from the same party, and a *printed* Paper this time, of very greatly improved quality,—and in flagrant imitation, this time, of Waldo Emer-

1. D. Appleton & Co.

2. "Go on and increase in valor"; *Aeneid* 9:641.

3. George Searle Phillips (1815–89; *DNB*), b. at Peterborough and educ. at Trinity College, Cambridge; went to U.S., where he became a journalist in New York City; returned to England and became ed. of *Leeds Times,* 1845; apptd. sec. of People's College, Huddersfield, 1846; arranged for Emerson's lectures at Huddersfield, 1848; lecturer at Yorkshire Union of Mechanics' Institutes, 1854; returned to U.S., ca. 1857, and worked as a journalist; became insane, 1873, and confined till death to asylums; most of his works, including *Emerson, His Life and Writing* (1855), pbd. under pseud. "January Searle."

son! I wrote to the young man; "*Benissime* [very well], Do as thou hast *said!*" for it is all about the greatness of the soul &c &c. Men are very strange. Thi[s] Philips seems to be of the schoolmaster profession; has really a sincere sound in him now;—and may perhaps be heard of again by and by.

Adieu my Friend; I feel still as if, in several senses, you stood alone with me under the sky at present!

[signature cut away]

TC TO [JAMES BOOTH]

Chelsea, 4 April 1843

[Requesting a House of Commons order allowing John Carlyle and Robert Arbuckle to attend Charles Buller's speech and debate,[1] giving their addresses, and asking about correct procedure.[2]]

JWC TO JEANNIE WELSH

[4 April 1843]

Great news for thee, "insinuating" Babbie![1]—my family has received an addition of *four* new members! Carlyle made the grave discovery some three weeks ago that the cat—our "*he* cat" was "*all full of kittens*"—and accordingly yesterday *he*—or as we must now I suppose call him—*she* brought forth—modestly—in the coal-hole four little angels of kittens—black and white—the tender images of their parental[2] parent, whom I observed this morning, sauntering with a melancholy, reflec-

TC-[JB], 4 April. MS: Offered for sale by C. A. Kyrle Fletcher, London, catalogue 233 (1971), item 45. TC wrote other such requests to James Booth (1796–1880; *DNB*), counsel to the speaker of the House of Commons, for admission to the public gallery.

1. Robert Arbuckle, physician, John Carlyle's longtime friend (see 5:341), who had been in Brazil (see 8:218). Charles Buller, M.P. for Liskeard, opened the debate, 6 April, on systematic colonization, proposing it "as a remedy for the distress of the country," though he withdrew his motion at the end of the debate, 12:45 A.M.

2. Replying, 5 April, Booth said that he had put their names down "on the Speakers list for tomorrow. . . . Buller's debate will not commence before 5 [but] I would advise them to be there not long after the opening as there is great eagerness to be present . . . . The Members list has been full for the last week & more & the Speaker has many more applications than he can comply with."

JWC-JW, [4 April]. Addr: 20 Maryland Street / Liverpool. PM: 4 April 1843. MS: NLS 1891.240. Pbd: Huxley, *JWCLF* 107–11 inc.

1. Helen Mitchell's phrase for Jeannie Welsh; see 15:167.

2. Thus in MS, probably intending "paternal."

tive, air thro the back-premises—as if foreboding the untimely end of his innocent offspring!— To be sure they must be drowned in the course of the day; and that is piteous to think of!—

For the rest; your picture is finished—I sat again on Friday[3] from ten till two! and *he* worked at it by himself all the rest of that day! so in point of *finishing* you may fancy it has had all manner of justice done to it—indeed I think M*rs* Millner Gibson looks coarse beside me![4] As for the *likeness;* you are to know, for your comfort that he has now worked the *estasi* [ecstasy] pretty well out of it—and it looks *simple* enough—Carlyle thinks too simple *"for anything"!* (as you say in Lancashire)— The eyes he says "want expression" the mouth "wants character"—but for one person that finds it less *inspired-looking* than the original there will be twenty finding it excessively flattered. Gambardella's own criticism on it when finished was, (with a look of ineffable self-complacency) "It looks too young! I must put in some wrinkles!"— The frames are not yet ready—and besides he seems to wish that I should keep it here for a few days that the visitors may see it—a harmless vanity in which it were but fair to indulge him. So be patient—it is not even dry yet—

My last days sitting was enlivened by the most extraordinary of all *excitements* he has yet found out for himself— I do not speak of the *"wittels"*[5] he produced for me—About a hundredweight of rusks in a great paper-bag—A whole hoop of figs—Guiness's Porter, Scotch Ale—Indian Ale—Cyder and something else with an incomprehensible Italian name!— This gigantic lunch was laughable enough but not to be recorded as in the sphere of the absolutely extraordinary—however that you may have a clear understanding of what I am about to tell you, we must begin further back—!

At my second sitting,[6] he was telling me of sundry new household arrangements which he contemplated— He had engaged the two upper rooms in addition to those he had—partly that he might [have][7] a place to show visitors into besides his studio, and partly because the gentleman and his wife who at present occupied them are so—dreadfully *ugly* that he cannot endure to meet them in the stairs! Then he was going "to have a gu-l all to himself; the lodging-house gu-ls being vile creatures who left finger-marks on every thing"—and this gu-l should wash his brushes, mend his linen, make fancy-dresses for his

3. 31 March.
4. For TC's opinion of Gambardella's portrait of Susanna Milner-Gibson (1814–85; see 15:67), see 15:174.
5. I.e., victuals.
6. Sun., 26 March.
7. Word omitted.

pictures, according to his own directions, out of "very rich *stoffs*" which he intended to buy—and most important of all should "have beautiful fo-ms" and sit to him for model whenever he needed one— In fact he had already sent an advertisement for such a person to the *Times* newspaper!

Poor M*rs* Sterling's two hundred and eighty nursery-governesses[8] rushed thro my mind—and I thought; God help you! you know not what you are bringing on yourself— But as the thing was *done* I saw no use in frightening him about the consequences beforehand—they would disclose themselves only too soon— I asked merely how his advertisement was worded—

"Wanted a very genteel girl to do *very genteel work*—not under fifteen nor exceeding eighteen years of age—wages from twenty to thirty pounds per annum"!!![9] Could there be two ideas as to what sort of functionary this advertisement had in view?— I groaned in spirit for the poor blockhead who, without having the smallest ill meaning (I am very sure) was thus exposing himself to the most atrocious imputations!

I called on Thursday forenoon to ask when I was to be needed again—the door was opened by himself—as mad looking as a march-hare—his eyes were gleaming like live coals—his "hairs" in a state of wildness—his whole figure expressing the most comical excitement blended with perspiring perplexity.

Tho heretofore so respectful of my *years;* he on this day flung his arm round my person—as if I had been the reed of a drowning man, and almost *carried* me up stairs! I sat down and asked "Well? what on earth is it?"—but he *turned* his head to a side as if listening, then darted down stairs again to the door—then back—then down again— and so on for half a dozen times before he could find two spare minutes to tell me his story— At length I got it out of him, but with innumerable parenthesis of opening the street door That morning at eight gu-ls began to troop into the streets from all points of the compass—congregated in groups of threes and fives—till the clock struck nine—and then there was a general rush of *fifty* to demand admission!— and fresh ones were continuing to pour in,—as I saw— "The people of the house were furious"—no wonder!— "M*r* Blore[10] had sent him up

8. Who, presumably, answered an advert. placed by Susannah Sterling, b. Barton (d. 1843), John's wife (see 8:140).

9. The advert. in the *Times*, 30 March, read: "WANTED, a respectable genteel GIRL, from 15 to 18 years of age, to do genteel house work and sewing. Wages from £20 to £30 a year. Inquire at 8, Michael's place, Brompton-square."

10. Presumably the landlord.

a most impertinent note"—"neither mistress nor maids would go to the door any more and so he had to open himself"—and then if I could only have seen "the detestable ugliness" of all that had come!—"vile wretches calling themselves *eighteen* who were *thirty,* if they were a day"!— To make a long tale short he had from three to four hundred applicants that day and not *one* of "beautiful forms"—or even passable forms among them!—he had also six and thirty letters from the Country! not containing a single inquiry as to the nature of the "*very* genteel work"—but all passionately eager to have the place, whatever it was, for some daughter, or sister, or friend!— Does not this give one a horrible glance into life—as it is at present—even worse it seems to me than the *boiling of the dead dog!*[11] *that* at least involved no immorality!— On the following day which was that of my last sitting, they were still coming—but not in such numbers—and the people of the house having been heaven knows how restored to good humore M*rs* Blore was opening the door to them herself—and by his desire showing them all in succession up to the painting room—"that I might just see what ugly wretches they were"!— But Fortune favoured me—for among the *twenty* who were thus shown up, I found *three* very pretty—they[12] rest certainly were hideous!— One of the three himself even was pleased with—but tho she looked to *me* as improper as improper could be; she expressed some hesitation about *sitting as a model*—she would consider it and let him know in a couple of days—the fact was she prefered transacting with him without witnesses, I believe—for she came back the same afternoon and declared herself ready to come— But when he (much to her astonishment doubtless) proposed to *see her parents* on the subject before coming to a final engagement she answered that they were *both ill in bed* and could not be spoken with—which he thought "sounded ill for her *respectability*" and so he would have no more to do with her! The last of the three pretty ones was a very sad spectacle indeed she was a gentle innocent looking girl—not more than sixteen—brought in like a sheep to the slaughter by a wicked-faced devil—as to whose business in life there could not be two opinions— Gambardella hardly looked at the girl—but told the woman in a grave imperative manner that he was already suited—and the pair went off to seek a less scrupulous customer—leaving me very much shocked upon *my* honour!— I was at his house again yesterday—went with Carlyle to see the picture in its finished state—and stayed awhile behind him, helping the *Unfortunate* to concoct a new advertisement! more *precise,* and not so liable to misin-

11. Probably referring to a newspaper story about the eating of a dead dog.
12. Thus in MS.

terpr[et]ation[13] as the first— In addition to the female help he is minded now to have a—tiger! Lady Morgan[14] having laughed at him for having the door opened by a maid with a *baby* in her arms!! It is impossible to make him conduct himself like a reasonable being—and so he must just flounder along like a very unreasonable one— The only comfort is that sort of headlong—unbalanced character has a wonderful knack of lighting always like a cat on its feet—— There I must stop abruptly—Mazzini has been here and as it pours down rain I had best send the letters with him—

You *might* have written today if you had liked—for your last was short / Your own / Jane Welsh

TC TO MARGARET A. CARLYLE

5. Cheyne Row, Chelsea, 5 April, 1843

My dear Mother,

I will send you a little Bulletin today, tho' there has nothing new fallen out, that you do not know of; I ought to tell you expressly so, when there is nothing else to tell.

Our bad easterly weather has given place to rain, and that again is about issuing in sunshine: Jane, always when the easterly wind is blowing, gets back the old 'pain in the right side' (it is something in the liver, we understand); and always when the westerly wind and warm weather takes up its tale, she recovers again. In general she is much better than in some or most former years. She is very quiet; and tho' her Mother's death dwells constantly with her, I think, yet it is now in a quieter form, and does not tear her in pieces as it did. I hope the sorrow indeed has done her good: we ought all to know, and be taught even by severe suffering and stripes, that our possession is not in this world; that very truly it is all a poor shadow that we did or do or can possess in this world.— John Welsh at Liverpool had a kind of palsy-stroke, not unlike what poor Mrs Welsh's was, and in the month of February just as hers was: it frightened them all very much; but he is now for the present getting well again.

As to me I do not feel that this Book has hurt me so much as Books are wont to do: I fancy I shall be able for another in shorter interval than the last was. I was terribly cut up with the *French Revolution;* I should not like to get such a shaking again, if I could help it!— There has been a great deal of ugly trouble getting the American Copy made

13. Letters omitted.
14. Sydney, Lady Morgan (1783?–1859; *DNB*), novelist; see 15:247.

TC-MAC, 5 April. MS: NLS 521.11. Hitherto unpbd.

fairly out; I had it all to examine minutely, to correct &c, and was heartily sick of it: but happily, last saturday, I got it all fairly tied up, and despatched once for all to Alick Welsh at Liverpool; and now it is tumbling about, on the waste Ocean waves, in the Boston Steamer;—and the people may make of it what they can, when it arrives. If the New-York man manage again to steal it from us,—he shall have the *next* on still readier terms: he will save me a world of *fash* [trouble] at any rate!— In some two weeks now, I think, the Book will be about ready; and your Copies, we may hope, will get along to you by the beginning of May. It is a fiery enough Book; and speaks home into the heart of many a big-wigged looking thing,—the big-wigged thing can take it as it likes! I wish now, we were upon something *else*, and had that fairly all lying behind us.

Jack wrote to you, I understand, that his present engagement[1] was going to terminate; suddenly the end of *it* has come in sight. We cannot profess here that we are sorry for it: plenty of money did come in, but the rest was all an unmitigated stupidity; the ugliest work I have seen any man of abilities set to spend his days in doing. Jack has already plenty of money to live upon where and how he likes; he need not be anybody's slave, at any price whatever. I rather think too he has improved himself somewhat in this long dealing with these foolish things and persons, where his own wisdom, courage and decision such as it might be, had to form the basis of whatever good result would realise itself: I think I notice him more silent, more *angry*,—more like *working*, and conquering difficulties, than he used to be! He will fall on some useful thing by and by. A great deal of talent lies wasted in poor Doil,[2]—all trampled out of sight, in the scattery way of life he has had. My notion, too, is that, at bottom, he feels glad enough to be off from this Ogilby concern; but that as a *volunteering* to cast away such a salary, he durst hardly have ventured upon freeing *himself* from it: and now behold, by indifferent Destiny, without fault or without merit of his, he is freed! By a Note from yesterday, I find they have paid him up all his salary, and a quarter over and above, which is a very handsome way of winding up the business. Jack talks as if he would have a "run," or bit of travelling, in some direction or other, by way of shaking the thing out of his head.—

Jane's "poor woman," of whom I wrote to you last time, turns out to be a poor creature that brought on her woes by drink! At least so the Clergyman's Wife, who is a most charitable lady, but somewhat *swift* of judgement, assured Jane. Jane determines to continue her

1. As William Ogilby's physician.
2. John Carlyle's nickname.

gifts,—in the shape of *soup* &c; the poor woman, drunken or not, is dying, as John says on examining her; a great part of her lungs already wasted away. The miseries of poor mortals are many, in this world!

Jenny sent me a small Letter from Gill; which I neglected to answer at the time; being terribly busy. She was expecting to be instantly summoned to Dumfries; but perhaps is not gone yet. Will you thank her for her little missive till I get time for more.

Alick may, for aught I know, bring over this Letter too himself; and help you to read it. In any case, you can remind him again, of my brotherly heart-sympathy with him; my prayer that he may be led to decide for *what is wisest*, and my readiness to farther him in whatever *he* may deliberately judge to be such. Jack is not making money as he was; but there is money among us yet; and surely in such a case it ought to be ready!—— Jamie gets a Newspaper today: a Letter *by and by*. We send our kind wishes and regards to Isabella. It is long, dear Mother, since I read your hand, is it not? All good be with you, dear good Mother; take care of yourself, and we will all love you! Your affectionate

T. Carlyle

TC TO [JOHN ROBERTSON]

CHELSEA, *April* 7, 1843.

I ought have explained more distinctly what I did state in the way of conversation on Sunday week,[1] that in my present great bustle of business and total dimness as to this matter in hand, I cannot attend your committee[2]—that, in fact, I do not see what any committee or person can do in the present stage of the business except inquire, in a distinct manner, of the literary notabilities of the country whether they consider such a project to have any feasibility in it; whether they will take the trouble to meet or consult at all on the subject, or will not take any such trouble. If they all answer no, then clearly the project is unexecutable. If yes, if many, or even several of them answer yes, then

TC-[JR], 7 April. Pbd: Walter Besant, *Essays and Historiettes* (1903) 282–83.

1. 26 March. Robertson had been calling frequently at Cheyne Row; see JWC to JW, [3 May].

2. The second meeting of the Society of Authors, 8 April, when Charles Dickens (1812–70; *DNB*) was chairman, and Robertson was named hon. sec. A proposed prospectus was approved to be sent to the chief writers of the country for their suggestions, neither TC nor Dickens enlisted as members; see Besant 281–88 and *DL* 3:470. For TC's impression of the first meeting, 25 March, see TC to JJ, 4 June.

is the time come for a meeting. As it at present stands, I really and truly cannot help you at all, and therefore beg to be off and excused.

The prospectus[3] which arrived this morning is unexceptionable in character, but seems to me to offer little practical basis for any operation beyond what I have above indicated. I have written a sentence at the bottom of the page which embraces my own opinion of the matter and nearly all the opinion I yet have of it.

Yours ever truly, / T. CARLYLE

JWC TO JEANNIE WELSH

[8 April 1843]

My goodness Child! why *do* you make bits of apologies to me for writing about the servants—as if *'the servants'* were not a most important—a most fearful item in our female existence! Do you forget how I was always, while you were here,[1] finding fault with Helen[2] and the rest, that they would not tell us about the servants?—whether they were doing well or ill? I think, talk, and write about my own servant as much as Geraldine does about her lovers—and make myself sure that everybody that cares for me will sympathize with me in the matter—that way everybody who asks me with a real interest "how are you"?—would ask also if it were passed into a fashion of speech "are you comfortably *suited*"? With respect to these damsels of yours; I have to remark for the thousandth time what a mercy it is for us, that we never discover all the misconduct of the "vile creatures" till they are gone or going!— I shall be really anxious to learn your hopes from the new-comers—or your fears. But I confess my faith in Mr Miles[3] is somewhat shaken by this *stramash*—and I feel *surer* of the wisdom of my conduct in forgiving Helen for the thousandth time— She (Helen is going on of course beautifuly for the present—doing

3. See TC to MR, [14 March]. A proof of the prospectus in the Free Lib. of Philadelphia includes an open letter from John Robertson, 3 May, asking for comments, and a list of the provisional committee chosen, 29 April, as well as a list of members.

JWC-JW, [8 April]. Addr: 20 Maryland Street / Liverpool. PM: 8 April 1843. MS: NLS letter 1891.227, envelope 1891.252. Pbd: Huxley, *JWCLF* 104–7 inc., where dated 27 March. April date confirmed by Gambardella's portrait of JWC, not finished till 31 March or later; by Gambardella's "mistresses" who called in answer to his advert. (see JWC to JW, [4 April]); and by Hester Sterling's "dying very fast," her death occurring 16 April.

1. From mid-March to mid-Oct. 1842.
2. Welsh.
3. From whom JWC had hoped to get a servant to replace Helen Mitchell; see 15:234.

her work in a quite satisfactory manner, and conjoining to the daily, recognised services, a world of little delicate attentions more easily conceived than described— Especially she keeps a watch over my "*happetyte*"— When toast is left at breakfast, which has happened pretty constantly of late, she is sure to bring in a small tray between twelve and one—and if I can eat her improvised pancake—cupful of soup or whatever else it may be, verily she has her reward!! But alas one knows so certainly that these halcyon days cannot last for ever!—three months is the natural term—perhaps this time they may run to four months, for her fright was stronger than usual last occasion: as she says herself "I never absolutely told her before to go and seek herself *a place*—and fixed the very day for her going—"!

Darwin came the day before yesterday apparently to ask me "if I had found Gambardella a mistress yet"—for it was his first question—He carried me with him to Michael Place[4] to see the picture which he pronounced a master-piece—"the only picture of G's he had seen that gave him any idea that he could ever become a good artist"!—"from which" says Carlyle "it is plain that Darwin knows nothing at all about you"!!— G told Robertson who asked, that his charge for such a picture would be forty guineas! and Darwin thought it not at all dear!— "He must be very much in love with Miss Welsh says Darwin to bestow so much work on her gratis"— He must be very much in love with *the subject*" says Carlyle that is all"!— I suppose Miss Welsh and *the subject* have *the love* between them.

—I went to *a party* at the Chadwicks on Wednesday evening[5]—and the misery of it I cannot express to you— Carlyle has been for a long while shewing himself excessively discontented at having to go every where alone— I really think he was getting afraid that people would suspect him like Mr Liston of having made his wife into an anatomical preparation[6]— Some months ago I undertook at his particular desire to go to a party at the Proctors' (Barry Cornwalls) but when the night came I sent him as usual with my apology[7]—and as I was really plainly, to outward eyes even, extremely unwell, he did not force me— On wednesday then—I determined to go—to sacrifice myself for

4. Gambardella's address.

5. Edwin Chadwick (1800-90; *DNB*), sanitary reformer (see 6:450), and his wife Rachel (see 14:82).

6. Robert Liston (1794–1847; *DNB*), surgeon (see 4:347), prof. of clinical surgery, Univ. of London, since 1835. Neither his wife nor the accusation has been traced.

7. Bryan Waller Procter ("Barry Cornwall") (1787–1874; *DNB*), poet and barrister (see 3:84–85 and 6:219), and his wife Anne Benson, b. Skepper (b. 1799; see 2:451).

one time and then be done with it for months to come—as I can now say to him under the next score of invitations "I went to the Chadwicks—I have publicly testified that I am *alive*—what more would you have?" If you had seen me getting under way you would not have known whether to laugh or cry over me—I rather fancy you would have prefered the *latter* thing— I went off at half after eight to dress myself, as pale and trembling as if I had been preparing for the scaffold—my hands could not put in the pins—and then I had forgotten how to *dress for a party!*— My head? first of all—to go with it in its usual state of bare simplicity—would pass for *affectation*—the black scarf came most naturally to hand—but no—the spiteful people would say "M*rs* Carlyle being desperate of enacting the *girlish* any longer with advantage, is now for *doing* the *nun-like*— I bethought me of the wreath of *your* old black bonnet (the bonnet by the way Helen had sorted up for herself with coloured ribbons and it has been her Sunday's bonnet ever since)—*that,* I twisted round my small knob of hair—with what effect those who found themselves *behind* me only know— Then my silk dress, which has not been on since I was in Suffolk![8] your chimesette[9]—in its pristine *unwashed* purity!—and Helen's beautiful little pocket-handkerchief finished my decoration— When I heard my name bawled from Servant to Servant I was really within a trifle of fainting—and instead of getting slipped quietly into a chair, to recover myself; I was presently surrounded with acquaintances all expressing the most importunate *surprise* over me— "*You* actually come" says one "I declare it almost frightens one like seeing a gohst"!— "How *is* this" says another— "Are you *well* now"? "But good heavens" says M*rs* Booth[10] "will you explain it to me? *how is it* that I see you out?"—&c &c—till I was tempted to start up like a wild deer, and rush down stairs, and out of the house again, and home to my safe bed! Oh dear dear when I *did* get home to bed I cried like a child that had been *lost* for so many hours! And this was what people call *pleasure!* a pleasure to be purchased with *eight and sixpence for a fly!*— And next day I was so ill—no wonder—for I really *suffered* that night—horrible things— —To make not only the impression but to have the sensations of a gohst—while one is yet alive is a state of contradiction which those only who have felt it can appreciate the horror of!— I shall not do such violence to myself in a hurry again—indeed with such continued ill health as I have I do not see that I need any got up ex-

8. At Troston, Aug.–Sept. 1842.
9. I.e., chemisette, a kind of bodice, or piece of lace or muslin covering the open front of a dress.
10. Jane Booth (d. 1872), wife of James; see 12:49–50.

cuses for avoiding *general society*— If nobody else can see that I am *too ill* for going about to soirees and late dinners and all that *I* at least see it, and feel it and know it—and *that* should suffice to justify me in staying at home, and saving my small stock of strength for more essential purposes than visiting—

Meanwhile I have got back my Sunday mornings *congregation*— Plattnauer[11] presented himself unexpectedly the last sunday and had the door opened to him by Carlyle (Helen being gone to church) He looked much better—and *strangely* glad to see me again— — He asked most cordially after "*her*" nodding towards your picture,[12] and expressed unmitigated disgust over Geraldine's letter to him,—"one *half line*" from myself would have been better than all that *strange stuff—which of course required no answer*" He never saw Cavaignac!!![13] C. *twice left a card for him* But he dined sometimes with George Sand and found her "really very charming—for a French woman"—

Poor M*rs* Sterling is dying very fast— I never see her now—have not seen her these three weeks— She still comes into the drawing room but is too weak for receiving any one— Alicia Campbell[14] is with her— William Cunningham comes here very often—he came in yesterday and found Lord Jeffrey (who also just arrived) kissing me *à plusieurs reprises* [over and over again] and calling me "my darling"—mercifully however with the grave presence of M*r* Empson to justify or at least palliate the procedure[15]— William nevertheless looked perplexed— Love to them all

Your own J C.

What is the meaning of a blister on the back of my uncle's neck?— if he be so well why blist[e]r[16] him!

11. Richard Plattnauer, a German émigré, tutor to the Marquess of Ailesbury's son; see 13:234.
12. Either the one by Gambardella or the oil painting of Jeannie Welsh as a child that apparently was hung in the drawing room at this time (see JWC to JW, [25 April]).
13. In Paris, where Plattnauer appears to have been since Nov. 1842; see 15:167. For Jewsbury's letter see JWC to JW, [13 April].
14. Hester Sterling's nurse or housekeeper.
15. Francis, Lord Jeffrey (1773–1850; *DNB*), Scottish judge and critic (see earlier vols.), on his annual visit to Haileybury and his da. Charlotte, m. to William Empson (1791–1852; *DNB*), ed. and prof. of law (see 5:378–79 and 10:127). Jeffrey had unsuccessfully called on the Carlyles on Fri., 24 March, during a "two days' *lark*" in London (Henry Cockburn, *Life of Lord Jeffrey* [Edinburgh, 1852] 2:378–79).
16. Letter omitted.

TC TO JANET CARLYLE HANNING

Chelsea, 11 April, 1843—

Dear Jenny,

I am right glad of your little Note of yesterday; and return you many thanks for it. We have long been waiting for the like of it! I hope all goes well still; and that Jean will soon be on her feet again, and have the whole business safely by.[1] I will write to her in her own person, you may say, before long.

Another little Note came from you a while ago from Gill: I meant to send you some answer; but was too busy at the moment; and then afterwards I did not know for certain whether you were still there or gone to Dumfries. I had no news to send at any rate; nothing except that we were all well, which I think signified by a Newspaper.— Jamie and Mary send us no word whatever from Gill. We suppose it must be a very bad time for Farmers this, while all things are at so poor a price and so difficult to sell.

The Doctor, as I think you have learned, is now out of his situation: he often talked of leaving *it,* and probably if it had not been that there needed some kind of quarrel and discussion for that, and he never could be at the *fash* to make a quarrel, he might have done so long ago; but now, without any quarrel, altogether in a quiet manner, the situation leaves *him,* and he is free of it. A great deal of money annually he foregoes;[2] but also a very great deal of entirely ugly obstruction and confusion,—not *work* so much as *forced idleness,* which is far worse. On the whole I am not sorry; nor, I believe, is he.— What he is to do next? Yes, that will be a question; and need a screed of talk by and by!

For the present he is gone off with the Prussian Ambassador (an old Roman acquaintance of his) for a short visit into Sussex;[3] about 70 miles south of us: to breathe the fresh air a little, and shake the *Stour* [dust] out of him, after his Ogilby concern. We do not know but he may come here tonight: or perhaps he "may go on into the Isle of Wight, and not be home for several days."— He talks of having a "run into France or somewhere" next; he is also about advising me to go with him and recreate myself by a look at Germany this Summer: but I hardly think it will take effect in my case; I am very poor traveller

TC-JCH, 11 April. MS: Univ. of Toronto Lib. Hitherto unpbd.

1. Jean Aitken had given birth to a son, John.

2. £1,000.

3. Christian Karl Josias Bunsen (1791–1860), Prussian ambassador to Britain since 1841; see 11:29. John Carlyle had met him in Rome, 1835 (see 8:47) and was a close friend of him and his wife, whose country home was at Herstmonceux.

for my own share. Sunshine and free air anywhere, with some composure to follow my affairs, is all I bargain for at any time.

The Printer promises that I shall see the last of my Book *tonight.* I know not whether he will keep his word; he has not quite two sheets of it to do now. There will copies of it be probable for you, therefore, before long,—by the beginning of May *at latest;* sooner, I rather guess. My disgust with the whole job has grown considerable; I shall be very glad indeed to shake it all to the winds.[4]

You will stay, I suppose, a while with Jean, then back to Scotsbrig? Some money is due to you (or perhaps far *over* due?):[5] I must ask Jean about it;—but if there be any need, you can consider it procurable at a moment's notice.

I send my kindest regards to Jean, my welcome and true wishes to the small New Man; my blessing to one and all of you; and am ever

dear Jenny / Your affectionate
Brother
T. Carlyle[6]

TC TO ROBERT BROWNING

13 April 1843

[Arranging for an hour's stroll with Browning.]

TC TO SAMUEL BAMFORD

5, Cheyne Row, Chelsea, London,
13 April, 1843.

Dear Sir,—Will you be so good as send by the earliest convenience you have two copies of your book, "Bamford's Life of a Radical," ad-

4. TC noted in his Journal, 11 April: "My book called *Past and Present* is to be out of the Printer's hands today. The writing of it, accomplished with unusual ease for *me,* was done about six weeks ago. The Book is full of fire and zeal; but amounts to very little."

5. Probably for sewing she had done for TC.

6. TC wrote in his Journal, 11 April: "Was out dining at L*d* Monteagle's last night; ended in a soirée, dull as ditchwater. Does not seem to have done me much hurt, accordingly. Saw Horner, a good frank man; saw Lyell,—had been hearing Lyell on *Geology* thro' eight Lectures." Leonard Horner (1785–1864; *DNB*), geologist, educational reformer, and chief inspect. under the factories act.

TC-RB, 13 April. MS: Offered for sale by Sotheran, London, catalogue 737, item 373. Robert Browning (1812–89; *DNB*), poet, whom TC had known since 1836; see 8:332–33.

TC-SB, 13 April. Pbd: *Manchester Guardian,* 16 April 1881, p. 9; *The* dressed to "The Hon. W. B. Baring, 12, Great Stanhope-street, London." Two copies have been wanted there for some time.[1] Probably you have some appointed conveyance by which your books arrive here without additional cost; if so, pray use the earliest of these. Nay, perhaps your books are themselves procurable somewhere in London? That would be the shortest way of all. At any rate the coach or railway remains, and will be of no enormous amount. Be so good as apprise me by post what way you have adopted, and on what day the books may be looked for in Stanhope-street, not forgotting to enclose an *account* withal. I read your book with much interest, with a true desire to hear more and more of the authentic news of Middleton and of the honest toiling men there. Many persons have a similar desire. I would recommend you to try whether there is not yet more to be said, perhaps, on some side of that subject, for it belongs to an important class in these days. A man is at all times entitled, or even called upon by occasion, to speak, and write, and in all fit ways *utter* what he has himself gone thro', and *known,* and got the mastery of; and, in truth, at bottom there is nothing else that any man has a right to write of. For the rest, one principle, I think, in whatever farther you write, may be enough to guide you; that of standing rigorously by the fact, however naked it look. Fact is eternal; all fiction is very transitory in comparison. All men are interested in any man if he will speak the facts of his life for them; *his* authentic experience, which corresponds, as face with face, to that of all other sons of Adam.

Another humbler thing I will suggest—that it seems to me a pity you had not your book in the hands of some bookseller; such a one could sell it for you much faster than you yourself will. A friend of mine, for example, could not find your book in Liverpool at all; and, unless he have written to Middleton, as I suggested, may still be in fruitless search of it. The commission charges of booksellers are in truth entirely exorbitant, unexampled among any other class of *sellers* or salesmen in the world; but, as I said once, "If you have a wagon to drive to York, you had better pay the tolls, however unconscionable, than try to steeple-hunt it thither!" This, too, is not to be neglected, tho' a very secondary side of the business.

Wishing you a right good speed in all manful industry with hand or with head or with heart, I remain, yours very truly,

T. Carlyle

Autobiography of Samuel Bamford, ed. W. H. Chaloner, (1967) 1:26–28. Text: Chaloner.

1. See TC to LadyHB, [18? Feb.].

P.S. What is curious enough: this note was just folded, but not yet sealed, when your letter was handed in to me! Many thanks for your gift. Your remarks on *Chartism* are also very welcome to me. I have now only to add that you had better send Mr. Baring's two copies to Mr. Ballantyne[2] along with the other, and request him to forward them all to me without delay. Do not forget to enclose your account, which will be paid thro' the post-office.

T. C.

TC TO CHAPMAN & HALL

Chelsea, 13 April, 1843–

Dear Sir,

I bethink me that the American mail-packet sails in these very days (on Tuesday, I think): it will be well to let that be fairly under way before we publish, in order to give my Boston friends a better chance.[1] With this postscript I stand by what was written yesterday.

Yours very truly / T. Carlyle

JWC TO JEANNIE WELSH

[13? April 1843]

My beloved Babbie

There is a tone of *weariness* in your last letter—weariness with "Things in general"—which has something more than *cold* at the bottom of it. But *whatever* be at the bottom of it; I long to have you in my arms, to cover the babbie's face of you with kisses!— I feel so sympathetic with you *thus!*—not that you were not loveable for me in your *placidity*—that "*beautiful equability of temper*"—that "*disposition to be pleased with every thing*" which gained you such approbation from Carlyle and the rest was not thrown away upon *me*, only— For

2. Thomas Ballantyne.

TC-C&H, 13 April. MS: Yale. Hitherto unpbd.

1. TC wanted delay in pbn. of *Past and Present* (the printing being complete) to give Emerson and Little & Brown more time for printing the Boston edn. before its piracy from the British edn.

JWC-JW, [13? April]. MS: NLS 1891.233. Pbd: Huxley, *JWCLF* 111–15, where dated Mon., early April. JWC seems to be writing on Thurs., the day after Geraldine Jewsbury's visit on Wed. Dated here after JWC to JW, [8 April], where JWC first speaks of Jewsbury's letter to Plattnauer, and before Walter Macgregor's arrival at Cheyne Row, Mon., 17 April.

your *normal state* (as Mazzini would call it), such equability, such disposition to be pleased is good—the very best, and in an utilitarian point of view even, it was almost indispensable for living along side of *me,* whose *normal state* is unfortunately very different—but if you had never exceptional moments, hours, days, of longing after an unrealizable *ideal,* of protesting against the mean, worrying *actual*—I could never have felt thoroughly sympathetic with you—there must always have remained a Bluebeards Chamber[1] in my heart of which I durst not have given you the key—you would have remained my *Babbie*—literally— You could not have become what you are, my *friend* my *sister*—the one being alive that I can turn to in *every* mood with assurance that neither her kindness nor her sympathy will fail me—

I have been thinking this morning that I have written very little from *me* to *you,* this long while back—and that with all my writing you are not kept up as you ought to be with the current of my *personal concerns*— The fact is, ever since my Uncle has been confined to the house—my letters have been more for *him* than for *you*—I have written more with a view to making him laugh than to relieving my own mind of what I had a *besoin* [need] to say— Hence long stories of Gambardella &c—while much more important things have remained untold— Just to think for instance, that I should not yet have told you of the breaking up of Johns engagement with Mr Ogilvie altho it took place a fortnight ago and will excercise a rather malign influence on my individual comfort for a pretty while to come, I am thinking!— Mr Oglevie went off to Cheltenham some weeks ago, with his *maternal* uncles—(There are two sorts of them *maternal* and *paternal*—the former considering their nephew an exceedingly wise man—the latter those who appointed John to *keep* him—) Well the maternal uncles wrote from Cheltnam that they considered Mr Oglivie needed nothing now, "except to learn to *think* and *act* for himself" (a pretty considerable of a need one would say) and that the companionship of a man of his own years—not a physician—would perhaps help him better to that end— —Of course John at once acceded to the suggestion—considering that "on the whole perhaps they were in the right"— Mr Oglive sent him thereupon, his half year's salary with a quarter's over and above as "an expression of his sincere gratitude and affection"—and so the thing smoothly terminated— John left their house in Chester Terrace some days ago—and went into the country for *a week* with Bunsen the

1. As in "Blue Beard," first pbd. in Charles Perrault, *Histoires, ou Contes du Temps Passé* (Paris, 1697), trans. Robert Samber (1729).

Prussian Ambassador—but finding Bunsen's house *"too full"* he arrived here last evening—with bag and baggage—when Helen was in the midst of *a washing* and myself in the midst of a headach—and now the question presses itself on me with some emphasis "what will he do or attempt to do next? above all how long will he stay *here*"?—running up and down stairs—fretting me with distracted queries and remarks—making the house—what he has on so many former occasions made it—a scene of *worry* world without end!— When one has renounced all the gaities of life one does hold rather grimly by one's *quiet*—and where John is, you know whether there *can* be any quiet.

That he will ever muster energy to take up house for himself—altho he is now as able in point of money to keep a house as we are—I have not the smallest hope— He finds it always much easier and less expensive to live as *our* visitor—and what suits himself he is in the habit of thinking must perfectly suit other people—so that this time, as on former occasions, I see no deliverance from him, except in Providence—sending unsought the offer of some new tempting *situation*—Unless indeed Carlyle gets provoked into telling him flatly that he cannot keep him here—now that he is well enough off to keep himself elsewhere—and it would be long before Carlyle's brotherly nature could get itself provoked to *that* point—while for *me* in the meanwhile—the *Sister-in-law*—nothing of course remains but to submit, and even with a good grace—

All our summer schemes however are tumbled topsy turvy by this untoward chance—there is talk now of a voyage to Iceland even!—instead of the cottage at Fornby (I never spoke of *Seaforth*)[2]—indeed it is all up with a *cottage* any where if *he* is to go with us!—it is bad enough to be pent up with such restlessness in a town house—in a country cottage it would blow the roof off— Indeed Babbie I am at my wits end!— I know not what to advise even—if *they* would but *decide* on anything for themselves—and leave me to decide for *myself*!—one thing grows only the clearer for all the general uncertainty: that *I* must see you this summer if I would preserve my soul alive—

Geraldine was here yesterday She wrote from Essex the beginning of last week; that she was "dreadfully anxious about me" I would not tell her about myself—but "thank God" she would now be able to see with her own eyes how I was—as she was coming to town on the morrow, and would be with me the first leisure moment after her arrival— Well! she *did* arrive on the Wednesday and her leisure moment turned up for her only yesterday a week after!! and even then,

2. Fornby in MS, meaning Formby. Seaforth House was the Paulets' home, 4 mi. NNW of Liverpool; see 13:189.

she went round by M*rs* Hall,[3] so as to arrive here after two oclock when she knew that if well enough I should be *out!*—unfortunately I was *not* well enough and so she found me in! And then the *excuses!*—she had been "mad to get to me—absolutely mad" but without making "the most horrible grievance" she could not absent herself for an hour till that day; there were such endless schemes for her amusement!—(she is with the *Pattens* at present)— What would she have said to *you* had you let difficulty or even impossibility keep you away so long— I was heartly obliged to her for having staid away—but such flagrant inconsistency between her words and her deeds disgusted me to a degree that I did not even try to conceal—as for Carlyle he went out to walk without coming in to the room!! Her staying with these Pattens after the way in which the *Man*[4] has shown his utter contempt for her, insulted her—even by her own showing,—is in itself a horror!—even now "he will not be a moment alone with her"! But to keep a footing in the house she is laying the hair of her head under the feet of his wife and daughter—his wife! whom she told me, when here two years ago "was absolutely *loathsome!* a creature that made your blood run cold to think of any man being bound to her for life"—an excellent woman all the while—as I told her even *then*— She goes back to Manchester on Monday—whence *I* will never thro' all eternity be the means of bringing her again—she is "a vile creature"—and that is the short and long of it—

I thought I had told you of the letter to Platnauer at the time— It was one day soon after she came that after having fussed me in all sorts of ways she said suddenly—"now what *can* I do for you? tell me some thing to do for you"!— I was thinking of Platnauer at the moment she spoke—how long it was that his letter from Paris had lain unanswered and I said in *perfect jest* of course—"really I can give you nothing to do unless you will write a letter to Mr Plattnauer"—"Well" said she jumping up "tell me where to get a sheet of paper"—"goodness Geraldine said I you are not going to do it"?

"Why not"?

"Because you do not know the man—and how is it possible you can write to him"?

—"My dear there is no such word as *impossible* where your convenience is concerned"— Seeing she was in earnest I determined on letting her proceed just to see how she would get thro it—and she

3. Anna Maria Hall, b. Fielding (1800–81; *DNB*), novelist and misc. writer; m., 1824, Samuel Carter Hall (1800–89; *DNB*), author and ed.; good friend of Geraldine Jewsbury. They lived at Old Brompton, N of Chelsea.

4. Mr. Patten.

wrote not only a letter but a very *long* letter—most *free and easy*—and I let it go—to amuse the poor youth—and had better have thrown it in the fire as it did *not* amuse him at all but made him vexed at *me*—

My darling I am not half done—but I must stop for my head is getting bad again—

I do wish the weather would grow milder for my uncles sake and yours and mine— If *I* cannot sympathize in your feelings of cold who can?

According to Geraldine it would seem that "fellow-feeling makes us wondrous *un*kind"[5]—which is quite a new reading of the proverb— I am glad that Walter[6] *even speaks* of coming—shall I try to keep him out of mischief by engaging him in a *platonic* affair with *me*?—a woman of a *certain age—married* and above all *three hundred miles off* is the *safest* of all possible *divinities* for an excitable youth like him— Bless you dearest—love to them all

Your own / J C

Give Alick the enclosed—from Carlyle[7]

JWC TO JEANNIE WELSH

Tuesday evening [18 April 1843]

My darling

There is a sort of hurry scurry in my moral as well as material atmosphere just now which makes it prudent for me to take advantage of any quiet hour that turns up—so I write to night, tho the letter cannot go off till tomorrow— I was meaning to write yesterday (Monday) but could not; so being that *Walter* was with me all the day!—at least all the available part of the day— On my return from the poor Sterlings where I went for a few minutes immediately after breakfast, I found a cab at the door, the driver whereof had betaken himself to the gin-shop while the horse was placidly devouring a bundle of hay that had been thrown down to it. "M*r* Macgregor up stairs with M*r* Carlyle"— I brought M*r* Macgregor down stairs to *Mrs* Carlyle—the cab was dismissed—and behold us DOMESTICATED after a sort!—as if it had been the most natural thing in the world!—

5. Cf. David Garrick's "An Occasional Prologue on Quitting the Theatre, 10 June 1776."

6. Macgregor.

7. Probably concerning the packet for Emerson; see JWC to JW, [27 March].

JWC-JW, [18 April]. MS: NLS 1891.257. Pbd: Huxley, *JWCLF* 117–20 inc. Dated by Hester Sterling's death, 16 April, "last Sunday."

Where the five Quakeresses[1] were all those *hours* he staid is a question which curious minds might urgently demand the solution of—and perhaps in vain! It might also be asked what he had done with his '*excitement*'—for a *calmer* young gentleman I never sat beside—as calm as Mazzini himself! whom by the way he saw and expressed decided approbation of— He had also a spell of Forster[2] whom he liked less because he was too *tumultuous*. In fact he seemed like myself "a lover of all quiet things"[3]—and I could have gone to sleep on the sofa, if *necessary*, knowing him to be in the room—which is my test of "*compatibility of temper*" in the choice of my friends!— All this will sound to you "most *mis-tai-rous*"!— Well! there is common-place matter enough in the world without *my* adding to it—better that I should be able to tell you something *new* to exercise your *speculative* faculty upon. I only wish he could have known how I had been spending the four or five previous days—between heart-wearying visits at Knightsbridge,[4] and lying on the flat of my back with headachs, at home—that he might have estimated at its full value my gladness to see him and the immensity of human speech which I bestowed on him! I shall tell you what I think of his palpitations and quakermania after I have seen him again— He will dine here on Sunday—but I expect him some morning before then—hitherto I have not tried my gift of "*divination*" on him—only my common-place faculty of *observation*—and by this, I judge him in no very alarming way either physically or morally.

You have seen in the newspaper what has happened at Knightsbridge?— Perhaps not— M*rs* Sterling died last Sunday morning—not unexpectedly—her end had been foreseen for many weeks— The poor old fool of a man is in such a state as you can figure. —Anthony[5] mercifully arrived on Thursday last— John is still detained at Falmouth by the confinement of his wife who is critically situated at these times— I had not been seeing her[6] for a good while back—no one was allowed to see her except her husband and Alicia Campbell who has been her most unwearying affectionate nurse—the last looks I got of her was from the open door of her room—where she was asleep in an easy chair—with her mouth wide open— I wish they had not made me look at her *so*—it was a sad almost horrible look to have itself fixed for ever in my mind as *the last*— I came home with a bad headach which

1. Unidentified; presumably friends of Walter Macgregor.
2. John Forster.
3. What Basil Montagu (1770–1851; *DNB;* see 2:451) wished written on his tombstone; see 3:399.
4. To visit the dying Hester Sterling.
5. Sterling.
6. Hester Sterling.

lasted all thro the night and next day I was too ill for rising out of bed, which is eternally to be regretted—for on that day—just that one day on which I *could not* go she expressed a wish "to shake hands with me"—adding "tomorrow I shall not be able"—but they did not tell me the latter words till after, or I would have gone at night when I *was* able to get up—but Anthony came down here at night and from the way he spoke I flattered myself that she would be able to see me and know me next morning— And when I went next morning—she was quite unconscious—alternating between stupor and delirium— I was in her room but came away again without looking at her— She was talking wildly—and *seeing* her in such a state had no consolation in it— To add to my regrets they told me that she had said that morning during a little interval of consciousness: "there now!— I said that I would *see* Mrs Carlyle yesterday and you see she has not come"!—so like her!—the pettish affectionateness of her nature still strong in death! Anthony who seems for his Mother's sake to have suddenly taken to behaving towards me as if I were their sister, promised that if she recovered her consciousness before death he would instantly come himself with a cab for me—but she never recovered her consciousness. —I went up on the evening of the day she died—and saw Anthony and Alicia—but not the old man— Anthony and William Cunningham[7] walked home with me, trying to talk on—indifferent subjects!—what unnecessary restraints people lay themselves under in this world for sake of something that they account manhood!—as if manhood could consist in talking about the favourchange in the weather and the effect of St Luke's[8] Steeple against the blue sky when their hearts were full of the dead— Truly we live all our days in a vain show[9]— I went next morning to see the old man for I was sure he would be better for getting a good cry with me—which he had; with his head on my shoulder poor old fellow—but at such a moment he was welcome to make any use of me that he pleased— Anthony speaks of leaving the army, and bringing his wife to live there—and really I do not see what else can be made of his Father[10]— *He* is as unfit to keep up a house about him as a child of five years old—

Today I had Jeffrey again and several others besides—and among them my purposed letter to you again fell to the ground—so you see between the solemn and the frivolous I have had my hands full—

7. Coningham, Mrs. Sterling's nephew.
8. St. Luke's, Chelsea, Sydney St.
9. Pss. 39:6.
10. Charlotte Sterling (d. 1863); see 11:138. Anthony Sterling retired on halfpay, 5 Dec. and bought the elder Sterlings' home at South Pl. His father was to move to a smaller house, but eventually returned to be looked after by his son.

Geraldine made her farewell visit on Sunday, along with her Miss Patten— She had written that *"grievance or no grievance;* she *would* and *must* come for two hours *alone* on Sunday immediately after breakfast." She came at *two* oclock— I said "I had ceased to expect you,"—"Oh yes" said she I meant—but *could* not get sooner"— With my heart at Knightsbridge I was in no humour to make even an attempt at patience with her— "Really" said I "it is a consolation to my self complacency to see you in *action*—when you tell me there is 'no such thing as *impossibility*—no such word as distance where *I am* concerned.' I look at MYSELF, not only recognising *impossibilities* at every turn, but even giving way before very slender *difficulties*—and think what a cold blooded, ineffectual character must *I* then be in comparison!—but when it comes to the test of *doing*—I find that the difference between us has been merely in *dialect of speech* not in *matter of fact!*"— For the first time in her life she had not a word to answer—but sat looking not unlike a fool— What think you Walter made the very same observation that Carlyle John and Mazzini made on her—each for himself—that "it was a *mercy* for her she was so ill-looking—"! Do not however in speaking of her ever *quote* me to her disadvantage—not to do her any mischief in her own circle, even at the cost of being supposed a bad judge of women, is the last duty that imposes itself on one who committed the imprudence of constituting myself her friend before knowing anything about her— Her friend I have ceased to be for ever and a day but from the consequences of having been it in the beginning I cannot wholly emancipate myself— Heaven grant that the *consequences* may be only *boring*—not *"fatal"*— But our *imprudencies* often enough cost us dearer than our *crimes*—

John is at the Isle of Wight for a couple of days—a precious deliverance!—only alas too *brief!*— His long sojourn with a madman[11] has worked no improvement in his own ways—he is if possible more restless, more indifferent, more selfish, more destructive of every thing like regularity and quiet in a household than ever he was! My hope lies in the very *magnitude* of the nuisance—his own Brother is so tormented by him that I am persuaded *he* will not be able to hold out many *months* without fairly turning him out of doors— Jeffrey delivered me from him originally by getting him sent off with Lady Clare.— yesterday the same kind friend suggested to me a new situation which *he* could get him if his magnificent Doctorship would accept it[12]—unfortu-

11. William Ogilby.

12. For the new situation, which John Carlyle did refuse, see next letter. After his unsuccessful call on the Carlyles, 10 May, Jeffrey wrote to TC, 12 May: "it was distressing to have so poor a report of my Dear Mrs C's health to take

nately there will be less *money* rather than *Honour* connected with it—and John likes *money* above all other things. We shall see!—

I hope my uncle does not see or hear much of all these visitors— I do wish he could get away into the country for a while—but *where now?*— Does he never think of getting summer quarters beside Walter[13]—cousin Walter I mean? *You* also should be in the country somewhere— Walter tells me you are *coughing* again—and not looking well—indeed he seems as *uneasy* about you in *every way* as you are about *him*.

The box came perfectly safe—*sweetness* for many days! and kindness for life long— Do not fail to tell M*rs* Martin that I feel her kindness very gratefuly— I see Maggie's[14] hand on the Damsons—will she tell me what on earth does *W S* denote—in Scotland it signifies *Writer to the Signet*[15]—but there cannot surely be a *writer to the Signet* enchanted into these pots—large as they are!

Your Picture[16] is here—and will go back I hope with Walter—but Gambardella has not yet got the frames— I am afraid that some day he will *shoot* the frame-maker or "send an arrow right thro' him"— Every body likes the picture except Carlyle and Elizabeth[17]— *She* says "it is a *young* lady that never knew a days sorrow or a days ill-health"— My kindest love to all— Your own

J C

TC TO JEAN CARLYLE AITKEN

Chelsea, 19 April, 1843—

Dear Jean,

You may fancy we were very glad to hear from Jenny what had taken place. I trust all is going on well; that you are getting out again, and the little fellow thriving. I shall expect a Letter now before very long,—some day when the cradle is steadily going.

It is above a week since I had entirely done with my Book; but the

---

away with me. . . . Do cheer your fair spouse and let me hear soon of her being better and gayer.— I have been haunted almost ever since, by the air of suffering and deep depression I discerned in her, the last day I saw you together. . . . with kindest love to your too fragile patient—and her Doctor brother."

13. Welsh, his son in Auchtertool.
14. Margaret Welsh's.
15. A member of a society of solicitors in Edinburgh, having special functions in regard to signet writs and drawing up crown writs.
16. Of JWC.
17. Pepoli.

TC-JCA, 19 April. MS: NLS 512.3 inc. Hitherto unpbd.

Press-men, the Binders, the &c, it appears, are all taking holiday and heavy-wet[1] in these Holy times (what they call the Easter week);[2] so that work is hard to be got from them: besides, I believe, our Booksellers were in no haste till the American Steam Mail should be fairly off *without* one of our copies in it: on the whole therefore we are not to appear till about Saturday first at soonest. You will get a bundle of copies straightway; with the beginning of May, I should think, they will be sure for you: and then much good may the thing do you! It is one of the most outspoken writings that ever came from me; and has a "dibble of a temper"[3] in it, whatever else. The times require plain speech.

Jack is off these two days on an excursion to the Isle of Wight, where he has some friends,—especially a Mrs Richardson, whose husband I think is a Dumfries man, a Doctor that sailed once towards the North Pole.[4] Jack is to return perhaps tonight, perhaps not tonight: we had orders to keep all Letters except those of the first day. He is very restless; goes about like a *thunder-spaik,*[5] making an agitated atmosphere wherever he is. He is ill off for a house to hold by, for a wife, for a profession, for any sort of fixation! I do not think he looks in the least like settling himself to anything, of *himself*. What is somewhat singular, yesterday there turned up the offer of a new place for him in the "family physician" way! Little Jeffrey was down here, and spoke of it by accident; is to come again tomorrow, and see if he can catch the Doctor himself. The salary is very miserably defective, only £250 a-year; but the honour is great and conspicuous, that of being Lady Holland's Doctor, forsooth,—an old cruel-looking insolent *touchan,* at whose house all the wits and wonders and dignitaries assemble, and where many blockheads are immensely ambitious to be![6] Probably Jack will decline at once; I know one man whom nothing would tempt

1. Strong ale.
2. Easter Sun. was 16 April.
3. Coterie speech; see 2:316.
4. Mary Richardson, b. Booth (d. 1845), niece of the Arctic explorer Sir John Franklin (1786–1847; *DNB*), and second wife (m. 1833) of John Richardson (1787–1865; *DNB*), Arctic explorer and naturalist; b. Dumfries; M.D., Edinburgh, 1816; surgeon and naturalist to Franklin's polar expedition, 1819; F.R.S., 1825; accompanied Franklin on his second expedition to NW Canada, 1825; apptd. physician to Royal Hospital at Haslar, 1838; inspector of hospitals, 1840; knighted, 1846; led a search for Franklin, 1847–49; pbd. his *Arctic Searching Expedition: A Journal,* 1851, and works on polar exploration and icthyology.
5. Pieces of wood tied to twine and whirled round by children to mimic thunder.
6. Elizabeth Vassall Fox (1770–1845; *DNB*), Lady Holland; see 12:77. Holland House, in Kensington, was a great political, literary, and artistic center; see 9:364.

to accept: but I do not mean to offer any hint of advice on the subject.

Our poor Mrs Sterling is gone from us; one of the first *friends* we have lost here by the all-destroyer. She died on Sunday morning last; her life, as it were, rapidly dissolving away in these latter weeks, into deeper and deeper languor, seemingly without much pain: her illness a disease of the heart. Jane looked on her once, about 8 days ago, *asleep* (for the poor Patient had no strength to see or speak with anybody), and that was their last interview. She was a right kindhearted, honest, loving soul; her loquacities, her whims and all her bits of weaknesses are now grown beautiful to us. The old fellow, who is a noisy, fiery whirlwind ('enormous *gunpowder* and considerable *shot*'), gets great pity from us; left solitary so in his old days, a forty-years partnership suddenly cut thro'. Alas!

My paper is ending; and I have not mentioned my chief errand at all. It is that you and Jenny would go and buy a right *good* black silk gown for our Mother, and get it made up for her all in due order. She has had several gowns from me; but never one that was *good:* pray take pains to ascertain what is really the right article, and take that at the price fit for it. I said black silk gown: but if you and Jenny, who

TC TO JOHN FORSTER

Chelsea, 19 April, 1843–

Dear Forster,

I have Docters' devilry in my interior today, and such a total despair of everything, that I conclude we must give up Horton for the present![1] It seems to lie within six miles of the Great Western Railway, some two miles from Colnbrook, perhaps not above five from Honslow; and might be attainable enough: but we should make a right Literary Party of the Expedition thither,—should we not? And choose the best of weather for it, and the best of humours. Perhaps Dickens would go, and other chosen men. And then ought not, as in the case of the Todgers people, "our rugged natures to be softened" (probably) "by the presence of lovely woman," on such an occasion?[2] If you and I go at any time ourselves, we must take in Chalfont too, and even Great

TC-JF, 19 April. MS: FC. Quot: *DL* 3:473n.

1. Horton, approx. 23 mi. W of London, where Milton lived for five years and where his mother is buried.

2. See Dickens's *Martin Chuzzlewit* ch. 9. The novel was pbd. in pts., Jan. 1843–July 1844.

Hampden, all of which lie in the same region.[3]— In short, for the present, all is shoved over the horizon again into the sunny continents of Hope; and nothing remains certain but the "early chop" for some day next week,—*which,* if it please the Pigs,[4] we will not neglect!

Adieu. In spite of blue-pill horrors,

Yours ever truly / T. Carlyle

TC TO CHAPMAN & HALL

[ca. 20 April 1843]

The Book looks very beautiful.—

The only *reviewer* I remember at present to whom I am under special promise is "Thomas Ballantyne Esq, Guardian Office, Manchester"; pray despatch him a copy with from the Publishers on it.

Forster, I conclude, has already got a copy: he seemed to be in haste for it.

There is one Editor at Dumfries,—to whom, if you are *professly* sending copies, one might be despatched: "Thomas Aird [Aird] Esq, Herald Office, Dumfries." Nay there are two Editors there, but the other is a blockhead:[1]—— I shall probably bethink me of several others by and by; and need a few Friends'-Copies more; but am in a great bustle at this moment.

You will of course lose no time in despatching these parcels according to their address.

With many thanks for your punctuality.

T. C.

3. Chalfont St. Giles, approx. 25 mi. WNW of London, site of the cottage in which Milton lived, 1665–66, to escape the plague in London. Great Hampden, seat of Cromwell's cousin, the parliamentary statesman John Hampden (1594–1643).

4. Coterie speech; see 9:376.

TC-C&H, [ca. 20 April]. MS: Huntington Lib. Hitherto unpbd. Dated by the completion of *Past and Present,* ca. 19 April (see TC to JCA, 19 April), copies of which TC had sent to his family, 21 April (see TC to JC, 28 April), and to reviewers, presumably at the same time.

1. Thomas Aird (1802–76; *DNB*), poet and journalist; see 6:361. The other ed. of the Dumfries *Courier* was John M'Diarmid (1790–1852; *DNB*); see 1:307. The brackets are TC's, the first "Aird" being blurred.

TC TO LADY HARRIET BARING

Chelsea, Friday, 21 April [1843]

Dear Lady Harriet,

Tomorrow I think of pilgriming on foot to a certain Shrine; the name of it is Addiscombe,[1] and it is not the Military College there. I shall arrive all dusty, weary, woebegone; but if the light of your looks fall on me,—and if I had my hands washed,—I shall become quite cheerful again; and stay with you to dinner; and go home, according to the Yellow Ticket,[2] at half-past eight,—in an improved frame of mind. It is probably the last I shall see of you—?— For the Book is no longer to be hidden; I have just addressed a copy of it to Stanhope Street,[3] and there it will arrive this night!—

If you are to be from home Tomorrow, or in any way engaged, never mind me and my pilgrimages. I shall at least hear the larks sing, see the green face of my old Mother Earth undefaced by soot, once again; discover where you dwell; and return with profit sufficient. The gypsey existence has considerable charms for me; roving in the open air, even with no company but Silence, is not so bad. Indeed I have thoughts of pitching a marquee somewhere on the slope of the Addiscombe Hills, for a week or two, this summer; and there, in perfect savage liberty, "communing with Nature" and some other things! Verily it would be worth trying, even with a brown loaf and well of water for one's diet,—if one had the heart!

Buller[4] did not seem to be sure even of Wednesday; but I hope he has got out nevertheless.

The Sun is extremely polite to you, is he not?— If I do not come tomorrow, consider simply that the Demons have run thro' this beautiful project, and that somehow or other I am in the worst luck.— With blessings

Yours ever / T. Carlyle

TC TO CHAPMAN & HALL

[ca. 22 April 1843]

[Directing that a copy of *Past and Present* be sent to Charles Dickens.]

TC-LadyHB, 21 April. MS: Marquess of Northampton. Hitherto unpbd.
1. The Barings' country villa nr. Croydon, Surrey.
2. The railway ticket.
3. The Barings' London residence, 12 Gt. Stanhope St.
4. Charles Buller.

TC-C&H, [ca. 22 April]. MS: Sold at auction at American Art Galleries, New

TC TO CATHERINE DICKENS

5. Cheyne Row, Chelsea
24 April, 1843–

Dear Mrs Dickens

We are such a pair of poor sickly creatures here, we have to deny ourselves the pleasure of dining out anywhere at present; and, I may well say with very great reluctance, even that of dining at your house on Saturday,[1]–one of the agreeablest dinners that human ingenuity could propose for us!

With many kind reg[ard]s

Yours most truly / T. Carlyle

JWC TO JEANNIE WELSH

14 [24]*th* April [1843]

My Babbie– Tomorrow is your birthday– I have not miscounted?– Well do I remember your last birthday–here beside *me*–how you looked, and what you said, and every thing about it as if it had been but yesterday– above all I remember gratefully how your gladness over the pretty gifts they sent you was saddened into tears at seeing the sorrowful impression which these things made upon *me*.[1] God bless you my good child– You will shed no tears tomorrow I hope– not even over the benediction I send for your new year in shape of a *Venus's girdle!*[2] Would that I could send you along with this talisman for charming the heart of man–a heart of man deserving to be charmed by *you!*– But having married Elizabeth to Pepoli, I consider myself to have done considerably more than enough in the match-making line–so I should abstain *on principle*–were there no other reason–

York City, 21 April 1910. 1 p. Approximately dated by the completed printing of *Past and Present,* 19 April, and by similar requests made by TC to his publishers about this time.

TC-CD, 24 April. MS: Pierpont Morgan Lib. Quot: *DL* 3:473n. Catherine Dickens, b. Hogarth (1815–79), m., 1836, Charles Dickens and bore him ten children before their separation, 1858.

1. TC is writing on Mon.

JWC-JW, 14 [24] April. Addr: 20 Maryland Street / Liverpool. MS: 1892.143. Hitherto unpbd. Dated 14 April by JWC in error for 24 April, Jeannie Welsh's birthday being 25 April, "tomorrow."

1. Because of JWC's mother's death, Feb. 1842.
2. Evidently an article of woman's clothing, named after Venus's girdle or celebrated "cestus," which gave beauty, grace and elegance when worn by even the most deformed.

from charging myself with the matrimonial interests even of Babbie.— Unless indeed she had as in the above mentioned instance attained an age at which she was clearly no longer adequate to shift for herself— Good Elizabeth! it is a shame in me to jest about her—if she *did* commit one supreme absurdity in her existence—she has at least left nothing undone to redeem it—

I took Walter[3] there yesterday before dinner— She had repeatedly expressed her opinion that he was "a most interesting creature" and a wish to see more of him— Walter liked her better this time—as I knew before hand that he certainly would.— Be kind to Walter and do not provoke him by *Waltzing* with Mr Benson[4] more than you can help— I hardly think you do justice to his *grave interest* in you! at all events he is *ill* just now—and requires not only to take care of himself, but to be taken care of— Amidst the fevering maddening turmoil of his *economical* life he needs a quiet, safe, loving heart to repose himself upon—his Mothers?—his Sisters?— I am afraid there is no such heart for him in his own family!— But for want of it—he is going to his death— I can see that he has grown up under the most withering influences—that it would need now almost a miracle to be operated on him—to make him feel his *own worth,* independent of his *outward successes*— And yet there is *great* worth in him—a beautiful ardent spirit!—which one weeps to see getting itself strangled amidst a mesh of cobwebs! Dear Walter! I *love* him actually! and you know that by that word *I* mean something!

Here is old Sterling—ever ever the same thing over again! I will finish tomorrow

Your / J. C.

ask Helen to wear out with *humility* for me the gown I send by Walter I remember her once admiring it

JWC TO JEANNIE WELSH

Tuesday [25 April 1843]

My dearest

I was hurried off yesterday at the early hour of twelve oclock before I had got well begun— In fact I begin to be sick of the extraordinary occupation that has been appointed me for these last ten days, viz: dry-nursing my great, big, obstreperous infant of an old Sterling!

3. Macgregor.
4. Presumably a young man in Liverpool.

JWC-JW, [25 April]. MS: NLS 1891.253. Pbd: Huxley, *JWCLF* 120–22 inc.

Actually I have not had five minutes speech with Mazzini for the last week! At first I went to him from the impulse of my own compassion—then I ceased to go; really thinking that at least until the funeral was over they would be better without visitors— On Tuesday forenoon I was desirous of having a mouthful of quiet talk with Elizabeth[1] whom I had not got a sight of for many days— I had not been seated more than ten minutes when we were startled by the sound of Carlyle's voice in the lobby enquiring for me— I thought the house must have taken fire, such an occurrance as C's coming to seek me anywhere was so unprecedented—"My Dear" says he opening the drawing room door "here has old Sterling been to seek you *roaring and greeting* [weeping]! and I have had to bring him after you! You must go away in the carriage with him somewhere and keep him quiet"! I departed with a sigh on my difficult mission—and we drove—all thro *the streets!* crying the whole way (that is to say *he* crying.) and I bottled up beside him in his very small carriage—looking I am sure the very picture of what Harriet Martineau defined Queen Victory[2] to be "a young woman in prodigiously difficult circumstances"! On Wednesday Mazzini had just come in and we had just placed our two pairs of feet on the fender when the little carriage drove up again and in *rushed* the old man exclaiming "Oh my friend—my dear dear friend comfort me! Sooth me!" I was on the point of lifting up the poker to kill him—when he disarmed my wrath by adding—"I have a NEW disaster! John's wife has been carried off by inflamation"![3]— You know *I* never felt any affection for M*rs* John but the news of her death under such circumstances was truly shocking—and I became quite sick— "Oh come with me says he come and let us walk a few turns in the pure air of Battersea Bridge"!![4]— "I am *unable* to walk at this moment" says I—"Then I wont go—I must not separate myself from you! We will drive since you cannot walk—only for the love of God let me stay by your side"!!—Mazzini was *standing* all the while—*staring* as you can fancy—the sound of his voice was not heard any more! So off we set again—*thro the Streets!* Thursday ditto—friday ditto—Saturday ditto—on Sunday he came with M*rs* Anthony[5] who had arrived—but mercifully I was already gone with Walter to the Pepolis— And yesterday he came again while I was writing to *you*— But I begin to see he is merely prolong-

1. Pepoli.
2. Victoria.
3. Susannah Sterling died 18 April of complications following childbirth. The news of Hester Sterling's death arrived just a few hours before she died; see *Life of Sterling, Works* 11:246–47.
4. See 12:168.
5. Charlotte Sterling.

ing his wailing in the view of exploiting my compassion and getting better treatment from me than he has been used to— His real sorrow is already pretty well cured!! Already!— Yes it will be just as his son Anthony told me —"You will see that in a few weeks he will be back to his Carlton Club[6] and all his old haunts and the past will be for him as if it had never been"— I thought Anthony cruel to say so but he knew his Father better than even I did— In the depth of his despair he proposed to me to go away with him to the Isle of Wight or some secluded place for a few weeks—and I in my simplicity actually did not positively refuse and Carlyle in his simplicity—said "yes it would be well done"— But my last drive with him has given me other thoughts— And now I am going to say a horrible thing which I entreat of you not to read aloud—"Upon *my* honour" Babbie I do not think I should be— "what shall I say"—*safe* travelling alone with him old as he is—!! Plainly for all so old as *I* am, I have not yet arrived at a thorough understanding of human nature for it is always revealing itself to me under new and *a priori* incredible phases—

John is still here and to all appearance without the remotest idea of ever taking himself off into an establishment of his own— The situation (as physician to Lady Holland) which Jeffrey managed to get offered to him, he at once and peremptorily declined— —If the Queen should take a fancy to have him, and press him very much, and bribe him very high—perhaps he *might* condescend to engage with *her*—but otherwise I see nothing that is likely to be good enough for him—in this lower world— Meanwhile he treats both Carlyle and myself as pieces of furniture—*appendages to the house* which he cannot conveniently rid himself of or he would— To respect our privacy to study our habits in any one respect—in fact to let alone tormenting us continually forms no part of his programme. How long Carlyles patience will hold out under all this—or rather I should say how long his *im*patience will rest satisfied in venting itself in tirades against him addressed to *me*—and in general ill-humour heaven only knows. But the house is made almost uninhabitable for me—and I have not even the consolation of thinking that I am victimized in a good cause—

I hope my Uncle has by this time entered into possession of his book— I do not mean Bamford but *Past & Present* which letter[7] was to go in the Booksellers parcel to Liverpool— He will find it I should think a piece of tolerably tough reading—indeed I should not wonder tho' he could not make away with it at all—

You have seen Walter? And heard from him perhaps that all the

6. A tory club; see 9:299.
7. Thus in MS, for "latter."

Laings were in raptures over your Babby-picture[8] on Sunday—taking it for a youthful likeness of Carlyle! in his "indivisible suit of yellow serge"—made mention of in Teufelsdrock![9]— —By the way your old Lover[10] inquired after you in the very first breath—and the young Mamma (now)[11] had heard you were to be married to Gambardella —What do you think of Walters likeness?[12]— I hope Helen was not affronted by my sending her a half-worn gown—if it had not been made by that dear departed Madame Chardonnell[13]—I should not have thought it worthy of her graceful acceptance—give her my love and six kisses—and go thro the like ceremony with my uncle and the rest—

Your own / J Carlyle

TC TO JAMES CARLYLE

Chelsea, 28 April, 1843

Dear Jamie,

We are delighted to hear that poor Isabella has her work safely over;[1] we have been in no small anxiety about her here for a long while back. I am right glad to pay you the Letter I have owed for a great while, in answering such a piece of news. If she now take care of herself, and rally valiantly to her new occupation, she will grow greatly better, we trust.—

At present nothing of importance is stirring among us here. I got my Book fairly shoved out to take its fate with the Public on Monday last; three days before that (on friday, this day gone a week) I had already despatched Copies, one for every one of you, towards Dumfries by Edinburgh, to James Aitken's care: I conjecture that if you did not get them on Wednesday (which indeed is hardly possible), you may partly expect to have them on Wednesday next, or at all events Wednesday *second;*—and that you will read them with eagerness! If any undue delay occur, and you are sure it is not *at Dumfries,* you can let me know, and I will twitch up the Edinburgh man. People seem to get themselves considerably *struck* by the Book,—and "look two ways for

8. Samuel Laing (1780–1868; *DNB*), author and traveler, and his son and da.-in-law, Samuel and Mary Laing. The picture is presumably the one of Jeannie Welsh sent from Templand; see 14:68, 227.
9. See Harrold, *Sartor* 92.
10. Samuel the elder; see 15:155–56.
11. Mary Laing. Their first child, b. 23 Jan., was Samuel (1843–70).
12. JWC's copy of a sketch of Walter Welsh; see JWC to JW, [12 March].
13. Louisa Chardonnel, London dressmaker and stylist; see 13:226.

TC-JC, 28 April. MS: NLS 1763.227. Quot: Froude, *Carlyle* 3:297.
1. Isabella Carlyle had given birth to a da., Jessie or Jenny (1843–74).

sunday":[2] which is a very proper result for them! But indeed I for one care but little what becomes of them with it: that is *their* outlook now, not mine. I mean to make the Booksellers pay me down their cash, the first day I care to walk so far; and then the whole business can go whistle.

We have been much grieved here by the sad things that have happened among the Sterlings. Poor Mrs Sterling grew rapidly worse, and died about ten days ago. The eldest son had come over from Ireland, as [he][3] was there; but the other son, John, who is our more special associate, could not come up from Falmouth, 200 miles off, where he lives; his own health is always precarious, and his wife about that very time was waiting daily to be *confined:* alas, the poor man heard of his Mother's death, while his Wife lay almost at the point of departure; in four hours more he had lost his Wife too! It was her sixth child,—the child is living. We have not written to Sterling yet. They are of course all in great distress. Poor old Mrs Sterling was one of the kindest motherliest women we knew anywhere, and Jane's chief friend here. She had much trouble in the world, she loved and sorrowed much,—and seemed to have her eye always in a good direction in this pilgrimage; and, we hope, is at rest now.

Jack is with us, at least he breakfasts, writes letters and sleeps here; but we seldom see him at dinner here; he is roving about like a blazing torch all day, and only comes home at night. Lady Clare wants him to go with her to Italy again in autumn: he seems to have little mind for that. A certain Lady Holland (illustrious Whig dame and chief of dames in these parts) wanted him, on Jeffrey's recommendation, to take up his abode here in London, on a small salary, as *her* physician: but she is a wretched, unreasonable, tyrannous old creature, for whom, as I said on hearing her case, there seemed to be no remedy but getting to *drink brandy and water;*—so Jack, very wisely I think, *declined.* He speaks now of a short expedition to Annandale; in which I encourage him. He has only to steady *himself,* and then all will be steadied.

I got my dear Mother's Letter; and will answer it: tell her so,—and to keep out of the cold weather, and wrap herself effectually up, till the sun shine out again. We heard from Jean two days ago: all was well there, except that our Uncle John seemed to be ailing, and had gone out to Mary Tait's for country air.[4] Alick, she told us, was sowing

2. "He was born in the middle of the week, and looked both ways for Sunday"; Scots for someone who squints.

3. Word omitted.

4. John Aitken (d. 1843), maternal uncle; he died 9 May. Mary Tait was possibly his married da.

for you: is the ear better? Adieu dear Brother. My blessings on one and all of you. Yours ever, T. Carlyle

TC TO CHARLES REDWOOD

Chelsea, 29 April, 1843–

My dear Sir,

A Book of mine called *Past and Present* has just come out here; which I now warn you not to buy, inasmuch as a copy addressed to you is already under way, and indeed may probably arrive in Bristol before this Note. It bears your common address; it will lie, if there do any delay occur, at that Bristol Bookseller's who distributes our Chapman and Hall's *Chuzzlewits* and other *Pickickeries*[1] there,—whose name, unknown to me, you will easily discover if need be. Probably at Cowbridge they know it. But I hope no delay will occur, or at least none that you cannot easily abide. When the Book does arrive, will you be so good as despatch me a Newspaper (without writing any letter, which is not worth while), to signify that all is right.

Speech and speculation have again arisen about a visit to the Glamorganshire coasts this summer: I really do not think it is impossible; but you shall hear of it more expressly by and by. I speak of coming by myself, and having some small crib of a lodging with some neat peasant or farmer in a desart part of the coast,—if with a horse to ride, so much the better, and within riding distance of you!— We shall see, if the sun were once out in his strength.

With very kind regards to you and your good Mother,[2]

Most truly / T. Carlyle

JWC TO JOHN FORSTER

[May 1843?]

My dear M*r* Forster

I quite forgot to tell you about the M S which I could not take with me being to *go round* by the Lecture[1]—

TC-CR, 29 April. Addr: Llandough / Cowbridge / S. Wales. MS: NLS Acc. 9294. Pbd: Faulkner 152–53. Charles Redwood (1802–54), Welsh solicitor; see 12:13.

1. Thus in MS; Dickens's novels.
2. Elizabeth Redwood (d. 1846).

JWC-JF, [May?]. MS: NLS 605.432. Hitherto unpbd. Dated tentatively after Jewsbury's visit, Feb.-March, and before TC's departure on holiday in July and the publication of the sonnet in Colburn's magazine in Sept. (see below). At the

You may safely recommend the thing as an amusing sonet, with quite *moral intentions*—for the execution, between you and me I am afraid it is dashed with a spice of—what shall I say?—*rouéism* [rakishness]—which in poor Geraldine seems to be as incorrigible as it is *unconscious*—but there is nothing that a Publisher need be afraid of in it—only an innocent attempt to comply with Mr Colburns demand for "*a good deal more power and passion*"—which should satisfy him better or worse[2]—

What a pleasant day we had with you.[3]

Ever your affectionate / Jane Carlyle

TC TO [JOHN ROBERTSON]

1 May 1843

I wish it to be distinctly understood that I cannot be a member of the Committee of the Authors' Society nor of the Society itself, nor, indeed, embark any labour at all upon it, under its present aspect.

TC TO KARL AUGUST VARNHAGEN VON ENSE

Chelsea, London, 1 May, 1843—

My dear Sir,

Almost a month ago your three beautiful volumes of *Memoirs* were safely delivered to me here, and in all ways cordially welcomed.[1] I reckon it a healthy sign of your German Public, in spite of all its con-

---

top of the MS someone has assigned the date May 1840, above which TC wrote: "No!—inquire of Ge [Geraldine]."

1. Thus in MS. The lecture is unidentified.

2. Henry Colburn (d. 1855; *DNB*) owned the *New Monthly Magazine,* 1814–45, of which he himself was ed., Sept. 1843–June 1845. The previous ed., Thomas Hood, had complained that Colburn interfered with his editorship. The *New Monthly Magazine and Humorist* 69 (Sept. 1843):47 has an unsigned "Sonnet" ("My heart is sick with longing"), which might well be by Jewsbury, as it is much in the style of her letters to JWC. JWC might have thought it unseemly as addressed to a woman: "But when, dear lady, I am near thy heart / Thy smile is time, and then so swift it flies, / It seems we only meet to tear apart, / With aching hands, and lingering of eyes—." Jewsbury may have submitted an earlier version to Colburn on her visit.

3. The Carlyles saw Forster frequently.

TC-[JR], 1 May. Pbd: Walter Besant, *Essays and Historiettes* (1903) 283 inc.

TC-KAVE, 1 May. MS: Jagellonian Univ., Cracow. Pbd: *Last Words* 218–21.

1. The first 3 vols. of the second edn. of Varnhagen's *Denkwürdigkeiten* (Leipzig, 1843), first pbd. 4 vols. (Mannheim, 1837–38) and 2 vols. (Leipzig, 1840–42).

fusions, that it demands a new supply of such Writings: there is everywhere a great heart of Truth living silent and latent amid the noise and tumult of world-wide Inanities literary and other; this we shall always know, and quietly trust in this.

Last week there was consigned to your Berlin-London Bookseller here a new volume of mine with your address on it; probably in a fortnight it may be looked for. I now, by the direct conveyance, write to announce it;—enclosing a few more Autographs, which have come to me since your last packet.[2] None of them is like to be of almost any interest; but they are gathered here, without trouble, and I say always, You can at worst burn them. From time to time when such an object turns upon my path, I will not fail to lift it; to send it over sea, to the man of all living men who can extract most meaning out of it, for his own behoof and ours!—

Since the finishing of that Book, I have been reposing myself with various *imaginary* kinds of work;—among others a daily spell at reading Danish, with a view to get acquainted with the old Norse world. Müller's *Sagabibliothek*, I had hoped, was in German; but, alas, it proves to be in Danish;[3] and I have to learn that new dialect first,—which turns out to be an almost ridiculous mixture of *Scotch*, and broken *Teutsch* [German], artfully disguised; the whole broken down, seemingly *so as to give the speech-organs a minimum of trouble!* I get into it without difficulty; but find Müller unluckily to be no perfect oracle after all. *Nials Saga* in Icelandic is also here;[4] and the Abstract of it in Müller gives me great curiosity to penetrate into a sight of it, and of the strange old world it belongs to. We are without due helps in English for introducing ourselves to old Scandinavia; nor do I find hitherto in Germany any effectual notice of such. Do you know the magazine *Bragur;*[5] and what is the worth of it? Has anybody written, or translated, or in any way made accessible a solid word on that old province of things, in German speech? Geijer's Swedish History in its German dress[6] is already ordered from the Bookseller: I have also read with attention the German Version of one Strinnholm, a Swede, on the

2. Varnhagen collected autographs; many that TC sent him are now at the Jagellonian Univ.

3. Peter Erasmus Müller, *Sagabibliothek,* 3 vols. (Copenhagen, 1817–20). Karl Lachman had trans. vol. 1 into German from Müller's MS, *Sagaenbibliothek* (Berlin, 1816). TC had known of this trans. in 1840; see 12:28.

4. *Njáls Saga* (ca. 1280), a long, complex story into which are woven several tales, the chief of them being that of Njál, the hero who upholds the law.

5. *Bragur. Ein litterarisches magazin der teutschen und nordischen vorzeit,* 8 vols. (1791–1812).

6. Eric Gustaf Geijer, *Geschichte Schwedens,* trans. S. P. Leffler (Hamburg, 1832). For Geijer (1783–1847), see 13:326, 329.

Wikingszüge,[7]—it is something, not much. This; and some nine or ten Books of Travels in Iceland, from not one of which can I gain the smallest distinct insight even as to what specially the outward look of the Island is!— If in your circle, you happen to know any real Master in Scandinavian things, you could perhaps question him for me, on some convenient occasion: perhaps even a German Book-catalogue, if I knew which, might instruct me in several things.

There was one other matter, of the smallest possible weight, about which I have often forgotten to ask you a small question. In the Supplement to Creuzer's *Symbolik*, written I think by one Mone[8] (which I found to be but a stupid book), there is account given of an ancient German Body having been dug up from some morass, I think in the neighbourhood of Paderborn;[9] in which, or some such Museum, says Mone, the Body yet lies; due account of the business having been given in printed 'Transactions,' or the like, to which he refers. If I remember rightly the date is 1817. But I have not Mone's Book at hand; and, as you see, the matter has got somewhat dim for me. The purport of my request is, that if there was any Pamphlet published about it, any Paper in some Society's Transactions, or other attainable Article descriptive of this singular affair, you would indicate it to me. This poor old Cheruscan brother man,[10] apparently some horrible miscreant, plunged down to be *tanned* in peat-bogs, and then to be dug up into daylight again after 2,000 years; this is a thing I shall never forget; this is almost all that I now remember of Mone and his grey dreary Book.— In Dublin Museum, I believe, there is the analogous figure of an antique nearly naked Celt, dug out of bogs, in like manner; but this, from my account of it, seems much less notable than the Cheruscan.

I ought earnestly to caution you against taking much or any *trouble* about all this; but I am afraid, that will be almost of no avail! In verity, these matters are so unimportant to me, you can hardly take *too little* trouble with them; and if I find, as is still to be dreaded, that you have taken too much,—why then, in that case, I will not employ you again! Actually that shall be your punishment.——

7. Anders Magnus Strinnholm (1786–1862), historian; his work was trans. C. F. Friesch, *Wikingszüge, Staatsverfassung und Sitten der alten Skandinavien*, 2 vols. (Hamburg, 1839–41). TC mentions it in his Journal.

8. Georg Friedrich Creuzer (1771–1858), *Symbolik und Mythologie der alten Völker besonders der Griechen*, 6 vols. (Leipzig and Darmstadt, 1810–23), vols. 5–6 being the Supplement by Franz Joseph Mone (1796–1871). For Mone, see 13:194.

9. Prussian town, Westphalia prov.

10. The Cherusci were an ancient German tribe, whose country was bounded by the river Elbe on the E and the Weser on the W.

Today however, in my haste, I must bid you adieu,—in hope of meeting again, on paper at least, before long.— Poor Schelling![11] I really fear you are *right* regarding him! As for us, by God's help,

Dringen wir *vorwärts* [Let us push onward]
Yours ever / T. Carlyle

JWC TO MARY RUSSELL

5 Cheyne Row / Monday
[1? May 1843]

Dearest M*rs* Russel

I am wearying to have some news of you— Absolutely; willing or unwilling, busy or lazy, you *must* sit down and write me a letter! How are you? and what are you all doing there in Thornhill? Where is Margaret;[1] and what sort of industry is she following? And old Mary?[2] Is she still able to creep about? And have you any money for her remaining? My husband says you were to give her two shillings a week which you considered would suffice for her with what she had— Maybe so—but two shillings a-week would not keep a London poor woman in *"beer"!* A woman whom I found lately lying on a little mouldy straw with not a single blanket over her—only an old cloak—and sharing *that* and the straw with three children—owned to having *ten shillings* a-week allowed her,—besides some bread and cheese from the Parish,—while her eldest child received both food and clothing at a charity school—and—the youngest being only five years old could not consume very much— Tho' I never *tried* living and keeping *two* children on ten shillings a-week, I could not but think I would have made a better job of it than she seemed to be making, and took pains to ascertain how the money went—four and sixpence went to the grocer for tea and sugar! "And then" said she "As long as I live I must have my pint of *beer* (Brown stout) in the day— I cannot wa[nt] my pint of beer for anything." And so she lay all thro' the winter in the state I have mentioned—with a bad cold too—which turned to con-

11. Friedrich Wilhelm Joseph von Schelling (1775–1854), German philosopher; see 8:213.

JWC-MR, [1? May]. MS: NLS 602.98. Pbd. A. Carlyle, *NLM* 1:99–103 inc. Approximately dated by TC's having sent *Past and Present* "two weeks ago," when he had dispatched copies via Edinburgh, presumably one of which would have gone to the Russells (see TC to JC, 28 April). Mary Russell, b. Dobbie, m. to Dr. James Russell, of Holmhill, Thornhill; see 6:145.

1. Hiddlestone, servant at Templand when Grace Welsh died.
2. Mills, also Grace Welsh's servant.

sumption and the other day she died![3] And I am afraid this is no exceptional case of unthrift— A woman to whom I gave some money to get her children flannel petticoats out of pawn went home and within a quarter of an hour's time had fried herself a panful of mutton-chops off it!—mutton being at that time ninepence a pound—and ever so many instances of the same improvident spirit have come under my own observation— But tho' old Mary may get more good of two shillings than a London woman of ten—still even in Scotland, and under your good care, it is a very slender amount of capital to front the world with! And if she fall sick or become quite helpless I trust to your getting her whatever is necessary, and applying to me for money whenever she wants it—not that I doubt but you would be ready to help her yourself— My Mother often told me how good and charitable you and your husband were— But this old woman is *my* concern—not *yours*— I cannot supply to her the place of the friend she has lost[4]—but it is both my duty and my pleasure to do it as far as lies in my power—

Did you hear of the sad fright which we had with my uncle in Liverpool? He was taken ill one night, just as She was last year, and in the same week of the same month— Tho the daily accounts I received of him were always that he was a *little better* and a *little better*, for a long while I could not open their letter without terror— I remembered always how all *her betterness* had terminated, and made little doubt but *his* would prove alike fallacious—now however, months having passed without any new attack I begin to trust that he may be spared a few years longer to his poor children, who are too young to find themselves orphans in the world. His D*rs* tell him that he must live very sparingly—must guard himself from all sorts of excitement—leave off card-*playing* &c &c—and he does their bidding—*for the present*—while the danger he has run is still fresh in his mind— But God knows whether his patience and docility may not wear out! and then!—Poor children! They have quite got up their hearts again—are dancing away at balls, and all the rest of it, as if there were no drawn sword suspended by a hair over their heads!— For me who see both *the dancing* and *the sword* it is an anxious spectacle!

I shall probably go to Liverpool for a week or two in the course of the summer. There was a talk at one time of summer-quarters to be taken somewhere in Cheshire—but my Brother-in-law John—who has a particular knack—like the *pigs*—of *"running thro"*[5] things came to

3. For JWC's first meeting with the woman, see TC to MAC, 24 March.
4. JWC's mother.
5. I.e., creating havoc; coterie speech.

live in the house till some new employment turned up for him; proposing to my husband this and that excursion on the continent—till we are all at sea again with our plans — Wherever John *is*—there is *uncertainty* also!

Only think! I have still the same little maid! Indeed I need never speak of her *going* again till she be actually *gone*. Nothing could be more determined than I was to part with her that time when I wrote for Margaret.[6] But she absolutely *would not go! would not seek herself a place!* She seems really to have much the same notion of the indissolubility of our relation—that the old scotch Butler had of his and his masters—in whose service he had been forty years—when his Master told him, his temper was become absolutely insufferable, and they two must positively part—he answered with a look of disdainful astonishment; "and where the deevil wud ye gang to?" Helen did not exactly ask *me* where *I* wud gang to? but she asked me in a tone of the most authoritative remonstrance "What would become of me, I should just like to know—fancying *you* ill—and *me* not there to take proper care of you?— I think *that* WOULD be a *farce!!*"— To tell her what would become of her under such astonishing circumstances, quite exceeding my gift of prophecy; what could I do but just to bid her "stay where she was then; only trying whether she could not behave herself more like a reasonable creature." And to do her justice, she *has* been *a little* more reasonable latterly—

I have kept quite free of *Influenza* this Spring—for a wonder—and since I gave over swallowing my Brother in laws blue pills which had no effect but that of making me *uncomfortable all over*—I have been pretty much in my average state— The pain in my side still sticks there—better and worse—and I have not much strength to speak of— But I am able to keep on foot—and my mind is quieter—and on the whole I have reason to be thankful—

I hope you have got my husband's new book by this time—he sent it to you by a bookseller's parcel two weeks ago— To think that he should have finished a book and no copy sent to Templand!— When I saw him writing *your* name instead I could do nothing but cry. He asked "is that all the congratulation you have to give me on having got to the end of it"?— But *I* also had *got to the end* of so much! I enclose half a sovereign for a pound of tea to Mary and another to Margaret. God bless you all and believe me always gratefully and affectionately yours

Jane Carlyle

6. In Dec. 1842; see 15:231, 255.

Be sure when you write, to mention when more money will be needed for Mary— Do you ever hear of Mary Milligan?[7] Has she any child yet?

TC TO EDWARD FITZGERALD

Chelsea, 2 May, 1843—

Dear Fitzgerald,

You have not drawn Cromwell's House at all! It seems to be Stewart's House at Stuntney, Cromwell's Uncle's, but not Cromwell's own! This is a great mistake. The real House that Cromwell occupied (according to Noble, and to all likelihood) is in Ely City itself, about a gunshot west of the Cathedral; abuts on St Mary's Churchyard with its one gable, and on the big Cathedral Barns with its other: an old, much humbler House, which "Mr Page" used to live in;[1] which is now empty, and will soon be ruinous, abolished, and altogether expunged from human memory,—unless your friend Peacock[2] or you will take a real portrait of it while it yet stands. There is a huge old wreck of a horseblock still lying in front towards the western end; there Oliver doubtless now and then mounted his horse, 203 years ago; there I, last year,[3] took the liberty of smoking a cigar, under the starlight and gaslight, with several reflexions. A fraction of the old stone came home in my pocket, and is now here.

Bobus[4] is an exquisite painting; no better likeness need be desired.

7. Another of Grace Welsh's servants; see 8:254. Probably the Mary who married Nov. 1841; see 13:307 and 14:220.

TC-EF, 2 May. MS: Trinity. Hitherto unpbd.

1. In a letter of late April to a friend FitzGerald tells of visiting Ely and Cromwell's house, "two miles from Ely," and making "a drawing of it for Carlyle" (Terhune, *LEF* 1:387). In *Cromwell* TC writes: "As Sir Thomas Steward, Oliver's Uncle, farmed the tithes of Ely, it is reasonable to believe that he, and Oliver after him, occupied the house set apart for the Tithe-Farmer there; as Mark Noble, out of dim Tradition, confidently testifies. This is 'the house occupied by Mr. Page' [Noble 1:106]; under which name . . . the inhabitants . . . now know it. The House . . . is still standing; close to St. Mary's Churchyard; at the corner of the great Tithe-barn of Ely. . . . Of his House, for Oliver's sake, some Painter will yet perhaps take a correct likeness:—it is needless to go to Stuntney out on the Soham road, as Oliver's Painters usually do; Oliver never lived there, but only his Mother's cousins!" (*Works* 6:94–95). Mark Noble, *Memoirs of the Protectoral-House of Cromwell*, 2 vols. (3d edn.; London, 1787).

2. George Peacock (1791–1858; *DNB*), mathematician and dean of Ely, FitzGerald's host.

3. 6 Sept. 1842; see 15:68–69.

4. A caricature perhaps by Thackeray of TC's fictitious Bobus Higgins in *Past and Present* (see *Works* 10:31, 33). FitzGerald had been reading *Past and Present* in late April (Terhune, *LEF* 1:387).

Unadulterated ugliness adorned in the highest degree; ugliness, obesity, and an earnest energy withal, as of a reforming man and sausage-maker; and then the vision of the gig:—seldom, it seems to me, has either Raphael or Snoggins[5] hit anything better on the head. It is to be framed, and carefully preserved in some place of honour.

We were much grieved on Sunday to learn, from Bobus and Plugson, that Thacker[a]y[6] and you had been here,[7] and we had missed you! It was a great pity. Something might have been contrived about Naseby;[8] for really I am not indisposed to go for a couple of days, now the Sun is shewing face again. How long are you to be here? Perhaps we might manage it in the beginning of next week. I am engaged on Wednesday and then on Saturday;—and really most frightfully *dyspetical* and atrabiliar! I wish I had a swift horse, nay some Highland pony or even a Highgate ass,[9] to ride about upon, in green places, for six months to come, and not speak a word to anybody!—

Except on the nights above mentioned we are always at home here.

Yours most faithfully / T. Carlyle

TC TO FRANCES WEDGWOOD

Chelsea, 3 May, 1843—

My dear Mrs Wedgwood,

On Saturday,[1] it is already settled, we are to dine in the *Snuggery* way, with Forster, in Lincoln's Inn Fields, at *five* o'clock,—a much fitter hour for a poor broken-hearted Dyspeptic Radical-Reformer like myself! I wish you would bring Horner[2] down hither with you some Wednesday Evg; that would be far better than a 7 o'clock Dinner, or any such frightful phenomenon!—

Has Wedgwood any Icelandic Grammar? I am deep in Norse *Sagas.*

Yours ever truly / T. Carlyle

5. The High Renaissance Italian painter (1484–1520) or a fictitious English hack painter; the sublime and ridiculous.

6. Letter omitted.

7. FitzGerald was staying with Thackeray in London; see *Letters of Thackeray,* ed. G. N. Ray (1945–46) 2:109. Plugson of Undershot, the cotton manufacturer interested in nothing but money, is also in *Past and Present* (see *Works* 10:188–95).

8. The battlefield, which TC said he would visit "next summer"; see 15:116.

9. Highgate, suburb in N London.

TC-FW, 3 May. MS: Wedgwood Papers, Univ. of Keele. Pbd: Fielding, *FR2* 309 inc.

1. 6 May.

2. Leonard Horner.

JWC TO JEANNIE WELSH

[3 May 1843]

My darling

I was hindered from writing to you yesterday by headach, the day before by Robertson—who has been hanging about us of late like a physical malady—time after time he has come here—*always out of season* (which is his peculiar faculty) to bore Carlyle into taking active part in something which he calls—*Association of British Authors*[1]— If C be either out or "engaged" when he comes he doggedly sits down to wait for him—three or four hours it may be—an hour or two makes no difference to him!— And so on Monday he came in at twelve and sat till three—in spite of all that I could prudently suggest about the risk he ran of wearing out Carlyle's patience by urging him too pertinaciously— I knew in fact that C's patience had already reached its *Ultima Thule* and that at one word more on the hated subject he would certainly explode on the unfortunate Blockhead— Accordingly when C came down at three, and was passing out *determined* not to see him, Robertson intercepted him in the Lobby and thrust a paper on him like a bailiff serving a writ— Had you seen C's look!! *"Oh Heavens"!* and then how he fell to brushing his hat saying the while—"Sir! I have told you already I will have nothing more to do with that business"—"Why?" says the other; "because nobody but a madman can expect any good out of it under the present circumstances"!—how far a conversation commencing in such terms would go, you can imagine without being told—suffice it to say—Robertson went off in a *red* fury and left Carlyle in a *green* one— It is to be hoped however we have seen the last of him *now*—

Walter?[2]— Why! to be sure!— Another case of *wasted commiseration* it would seem! for *palpitations* arising from a prosperous passion are neither very distressing for the time being, nor likely to terminate fatally— Poor fellow! I trust in heaven that this "emanation from the Moon" (as the Chinese call a beautiful woman) is one who will do him good—not harm— If she be an *ambitious* woman (that is to say ambitious on the small scale) he will be not unlikely to follow in the path of George Rennie[3]— and end in a restless acrid egoism— She will have

JWC-JW, [3 May]. Addr: 20 Maryland Street / Liverpool. PM: Chelsea, 3 May. MS: NLS 1891.273. Pbd: Huxley, *JWCLF* 122–23 inc.

1. The Society of Authors.
2. Macgregor, who had fallen in love with "a Quaker lady" (*JWCLF* 122).
3. George Rennie (1802–60; *DNB*), JWC's old Haddington lover; see 13:68 and 15:37.

much in her power at the present turning point of his life to make him or to mar him— God grant she may use her power like a sensible woman and a true one!— His letter to me was excellent—I will answer it soon—

What you say of my Uncle is far from satisfactory—I wish I saw him—I wish I knew what we are to do— The idea of Carlyle's going abroad anywhere with John is now very unlikely— He may go abroad *to get away* from *him* but hardly with him!— John is no more companionable for him than for me His behaviour since he has been here is really too much for any patience to put up with— He treats us exactly as if we were persons keeping a lodging house for *his* accommodation! only that most people show more politeness to the persons they *lodge* with— Actually—since he came to live he has not asked me *one single question* respecting my side—or my health in any particular—has not even gone thro' the universal courtesy of saying 'how do you do' of a morning—meanness selfishness and illbreeding is what one sees in him, unredeemed by any saving grace from morning till night— Well it is some comfort to think that he is going to Annandale for two or three weeks— *You* will be favoured with a sight of him most probably the day after tomorrow— If I had my will I should go away somewhere and *lock up the house* before he come back—for nothing short of *that* will keep him out of it, so long as he has not another house equally *cheap* and more convenient open to him—*our* pleasure in the arrangement he does not feel the slightest necessity for consulting—

I do not at all wonder at what you say of Geraldines reticence with M*rs* Paulet— The part which Geraldine has taken is plainly to ignore all she finds unpaletable in my behaviour towards her— And being decided not to admit it too[4] *herself* no wonder that she does not admit it to M*rs* Paulet who moreover according to Geraldine's own account of her is "excessively indiscreet *tells every body whatever she hears said of them*—thinking it for their good"! This may be true or false of her—but you will be no the worse for acting upon it as possibility— I shall need to see more of M*rs* Paulet with my own eyes before I can give over liking her and even admiring her—but I confess that five weeks of Geraldine is enough to *shake ones faith* in those whom she retains for bosom friends—knowing her as M*rs* Paulet must do *thoroughly*— Since G's return to Manchester—she has written me either *four* or *five* long letters—to not one of which have I yet sent one line of answer!—nor is there a word of remonstrance in her letters—the pro-

4. Thus in MS.

testations of eternal tenderness are considerably modified but her letters do not look the less kind for the modification—on the contrary!—They have now an air of *credibility* which they never had before— I I shall send you the last for sample Burn it after you have read it—

I have still a dozen things to say—but I am headachy today and so worried— Helen continues on good behaviour—how are *yours*[5] performing?

God bless you my Babbie—and all that belong to you

Ever your own / J C.

TC TO JANET CARLYLE HANNING

Chelsea, 4 May, 1843—

Dear Jenny,

I had your Letter the other day, and was glad to hear you had got back to Gill, where Mary as we understand has need of you at present. These are terribly hard times for Farmers; but they must not be downhearted: it is not likely the times will continue so bad; and if they do, some new arrangement will have to be fallen upon,—not by them alone but by the whole farming world. Tell Mary to take care and not overwork herself in her present state. Do you for her whatsoever you can in the way of help and support; I know you will without my telling you.— I like well to hear of your teaching the two little Bairns[1] to read; that is a right good work, in which there will lie a blessing if in any work whatsoever.—

But the grand object of this fraction of a Note was to let you know that you are likely to see the Doctor again very soon. He is off this morning to Liverpool; and may perhaps be over in Annandale on Monday or Tuesday if there be Steam[2] on either of those days. He will of course look in upon the Gill not long after that. He it is who will tell you all our news much better than I can write them He talks of staying "for a week or two"; that is to say, as long as he finds it pleasant and useful for him and for all of you: he is in very good health and spirits; but full of uncertainty as to fixing himself,—which I wish much, but hardly hope, he could now do.

We had a Box from Scotsbrig last night; all safe, and the contents excellent. I add no other word today; but a hearty salutation to one

5. Her servants.

TC-JCH, 4 May. MS: Yale. Pbd. Facsimile: Copeland between 152–53.

1. Either Mary Austin's son William (b. 1837 or –38) and her fourth da. (b. 1838 or –39), or Janet's das. Margaret (b. 1838) and Mary (b. 1840).

2. Steamship to Annan.

and all at Gill, Jamie, Mary, Jenny, and all the Bairns down to the youngest.[3] Your aff*e* Brother T. Carlyle

TC TO ALEXANDER CARLYLE

Chelsea, 4 May, 1843–

My dear Brother,

Yesternight the Parcel which your Letter had announced came safe to hand: all right, and the charge only 5/6. We found the fowls still uninjured; we were at the ham this morning, and you are to tell our dear kind Mother, till she be better thanked, that it is of first-rate quality, as good a ham as we ever ate,—and sent, we are sure, with a blessing too. The second, of course, will be like it. Jane has been among the Peppers too and *sweeties;* and the Tobacco is excellent. All is right therefore. Many kind thanks to you all.

We rejoice to hear of Jenny's happy proceedings, and hope she and the little Newcomer will both continue to do well.[1] The poor little Stranger comes into the world in a time of distress and disaster to many, when the Father and Mother themselves are at a loss to what hand to betake them;[2] may it be a blessing nevertheless, and a token that better days are coming!

There is not a moment's time for writing today; but I must mention, as our chief piece of news, that Jack did actually set off this morning (Thursday) with a bright sun, and we hope will be safe in

3. The other children were Margaret (b. 1831), Grace (b. 1833), and Jessie (b. 1834) Austin.

TC-AC, 4 May. MS: MUL. Pbd: Marrs 551–52.

1. Janet (Jenny) Carlyle, b. Clow (1809–91), m. to Alexander (see 1:166), had borne Alexander (1843–1941) on 29 April. He was educ. at the Univ. of Toronto, took first class hons. in natural science, and became a teacher. He visited Britain in 1871, met TC, stayed at Cheyne Row while his uncle was away, and became engaged to his cousin Mary Aitken. On a second visit, 1878, he stayed with TC and Mary at Dumfries: "she was willing to go to Canada" with him, but "my uncle could not spare her," so in 1879 TC invited him to live "in Cheyne Row with dear Mary as my Wife." TC went with them on their honeymoon, and they lived with him till he died. Later Alexander helped C. E. Norton ed. the *Reminiscences* and *Early Letters,* and he himself ed. many other such vols., constantly pursuing a campaign (with his wife), for which there was much justification, against Froude's work on the Carlyles. Mary d. 1895. He went to Canada, 1901, and m. Lilias MacVicar (d. 1929). His only son d. 1928, leaving two das. He gave most of his large collection of Carlyle papers to the NLS ("Jottings on Alexander Carlyle's Life and Work. By Himself").

2. Alexander's shop in Ecclefechan, started in Oct. 1837 as an alternative to emigration (see 9:284–85), had failed, and he needed some other means of support.

Liverpool before this leaves London. He will write to you when to look for him; it will probably be about Tuesday or Monday, according as the Steamer suits. He is full of desire to advise and further you in your procedure at present.[3] We have often talked together about what was possible for you: the fruit of all is, that the resolution, whatever it is, must be your own, and that it beseems good brothers to forward you with all heartiness therein. May Wisdom guide your counsels, my dear Brother, and may Good come of it and not Evil, if God will!—Not a word more today.—— Ever your affectionate

T. Carlyle

TC TO EDWARD FITZGERALD

Chelsea, 4 May, 1843—

Dear Fitzgerald,

I will go next week, if you like, and if Spedding will go with me,[1]—so soon as the coast is clear. Thursday or Wednesday would do well enough for me:[2] but we ought to wait till the Rent affairs and etceteras are all settled; and you alone are left upon the ground:—to wait, were it even into the following week. Get Spedding to undertake it, and to come down to me and consult. I will vote for being lodged where the Tobacco is; that is to say, in the Farm establishment.[3] I know of no other likely man but Spedding; a man that will sit silent, and let his fellow creatures sit dull and silent, "as stupid and ugly as they like to be";[4] an invaluable kind of man!

3. John Carlyle had written to Alexander, 22 March: "From the first I never had strong hopes of your succeeding at Ecclefechan and for years past I have felt convinced that you would never be able to do any good there. . . . I am therefore glad that you persist in the resolution of quitting at Whitsunday next and seeking some other better way of gaining a livelihood. What you are to do is a question you must, of course, mainly decide for yourself. Canada has many drawbacks, especially at present, and perhaps it might be better to seek some farm work at home. . . . In your former trials at Craigenputtock and Catlinns the times were against you and partly hindered your success, but I think there also was considerable mismanagement in various respects on your part that had a share in your failure, and that you yourself would be ready to acknowledge, and anxious to avoid in future" (Marrs 551).

TC-EF, 4 May. MS: Trinity. Hitherto unpbd.

1. TC had tentatively proposed a visit to Naseby in TC to EF, 2 May. James Spedding had been FitzGerald's friend since schooldays.

2. 11 or 10 May.

3. Presumably the farm of Charles Watcham, whom FitzGerald described to TC, 2 Oct. 1842, as "an old (not very old) servant of ours" whose family were "willing and accustomed to wait on us. I keep a store of tea, candles, brandy etc., here: which use—come when you will" (Terhune, *LEF* 1:369).

4. Coterie speech; see 13:196.

You mentioned some Pamphlets about Okey etc.[5] which you had seen. If you will give me the titles or description of them, I will spend another headache in the Museum in examining what they say. I have all your Letters; if you have mine,[6] we can read them together, and make the whole matter alive again, which has grown somewhat dimmer with me than it was last year.

Settle with Spedding; and let him take the affair on his shoulders!

Yours always / T. Carlyle

TC TO JOHN A. CARLYLE

Chelsea, Friday, 5 May 1843–

My dear Brother,

Examining the *Courier* and its Steamers,[1] I do not think you will go till Monday: wherefore I send off these two Letters, tho' neither of them came in time for yesternight's mail. The small one arrived this morning at breakfast time.

All yesterday I was very sad about your way-going. "We cannot go, we cannot stay!" I was weak and in bad spirits at any rate. As I saw you roll off in that confused manner, it was an emblem to me of all the partings, bodily and other, men have in this world;—summed up at last by the grand Parting, which awaits us all;—*which*, if it be God's will, may perhaps prove but a *Meeting* under happier omens! Amen.

I wrote to all the three Scotch Post-offices of our kindred; *shortest* notices that you were fairly underway towards them. I also read many pages in Holberg's Danish History,[2] *without* the Dictionary, for that is a briefer and very nearly as illuminative a way now: I can understand the *Dansk Sprog* [Danish language] about as fast as Tim Bobbin's Lancashire,[3] rather faster, and take the meaning very respectably along with me.— Jane and I then went both into the City; she to buy clothing, I to get my cash; these things done we came home by the Steamer, and except a little walk of mine amid showers passed one of

5. John Okey (d. 1662), regicide; see 15:115. The British Lib. catalogue lists, for example, *The Full and Exact Relation of the Apprehension . . . Tryal . . . and Execution of I. Barkstead . . . I. Okey, and M. Corbet* (1662) and *The Speeches, Discourses, and Prayers of . . . J. Okey* (1662).

6. Of Sept.–Oct. 1842.

TC-JAC, 5 May. MS: NLS 524.43. Quot: Froude, *Carlyle* 3:297.

1. The list of steamships between Liverpool and Annan.

2. Ludvig Holberg, *Dannemarks Riges Historie,* 3 vols. (Copenhagen, 1732–35).

3. Pseud. of John Collier (1708–1806), who wrote in Lancashire dialect.

the stillest evenings. Fitzgerald will have me go to Naseby next Thursday: perhaps I shall. Redwood also wants me over at the very same time in Glamorganshire; but that must be a later adventure. Do you see any eligible lodgings about the coasts where you now are? We have rain this morning; a damp strong wind, which the Sun is even now getting dried. Adieu dear Brother. All my love to our dear good Mother!

Your affectionate / T.C.

What Letters may now come (as today's *mail* delivery is past) I will forward to Scotsbrig

TC TO JOHN STERLING

Chelsea, 5 May, 1843—

My dear Sterling,

It is but some four weeks since I one day bade your Father say that, having now a little leisure, I meant to write to you straightway;—and alas, since then, there has fallen out so much about which there was no writing. We have had to think of you in silence. "Man goeth to his long home, and the mourners go about the streets."[1] It is the old story; as old as the first existence of mankind in this Earth; and yet to every one of us it arrives with a strange originality, sharp and astonishing as if it had never happened before. Ah me!— You must take care of your health more than ever: all kinds of grief weigh on one with double pressure when the body is weak. Grieve not, all grief is useless;—we are but a little way behind. As the old Psalmist said, "We shall go to them, they will not return to us";[2] there is in this an everlasting source of composure: death would be intolerable otherwise.

Probably you will be better within reach of London; and if so, Southampton surely is an eligible region. You are but four hours from us there, and yet almost a hundred miles. I have often thought of a cottage for myself on the beach of some cove in the Isle of Wight: but I believe I shall never get it, or anything resembling it; my notion begins to be that I am doomed to this spot, unlovely as it is to me: alas, few places are very lovely in late times; the Earth all growing into a kind of Golgotha for me;[3]—a golgotha which is a flaming Sinai[4]

TC-JS, 5 May. MS: NLS 531.62. Pbd: A. Carlyle, *CMSB* 267–69.

1. Eccles. 12:5.
2. Cf. 2 Sam. 12:23.
3. Cf. Harrold, *Sartor* 164. For Golgotha, see Matt. 27:33.
4. The mountain where Moses received the Ten Commandments; see Exod. 19:20–24.

too, however: let us complain of nothing! We must not complain, we must march on like men:

> —stille
> Ruhn oben die Sterne
> Und unten die Gräber.[5]

All Gospels and religions, as it were, lie included for me in those words. Courage!—

My health is not so much bad, as painful, depressing; to which, I suppose, the solitary life I have been long leading, and still insist on leading, must somewhat contribute. The speech of men does nothing for me in general; it grieves and distresses me, on the contrary, for most part. I am positively almost frightened now and then at quack speech! The remedy of course is: Avoid it. Yes; and yet there is much to be said on the other side withal. I think of doing two things: first, slinking off into the country so soon as the Sun comes fairly out; and then secondly endeavouring to get forward with some fresh work or other. There is always work enough for a man,—thank God! And plenty of comfort for a man accordingly. I do not feel unable for new work, were I once rested a while.

For the present I get along mainly by help of *Danish,* in which I have got a master (or rather got one lesson, for that was all that proved necessary) of Müllers *Sagabibliothek* in that language, and all manner of perplexed shadows out of Scandinavia. It is as good as "worsted work"[6] for a weak man! I really delight greatly in the essence of that old Norse World, where I can get a glimpse of its essence. Agamemnon and Achilles seem to me lucky in their Homer; I have fallen in with as good fellows, if not better, that remain entirely *unsung!* Besides, compared with Exeter Hall, are not *Gimle* and *Valhalla* really respectable places?[7]——

We saw your Brother often, and liked him better than ever. I do not think he knows completely what regard is entertained for him here. Adieu, my Friend: be careful of your health; the rest you will do without advising.[8] Yours ever T.C.

5. "Stars silent rest o'er us, / Graves under us silent." Goethe's "Symbolum"; see 15:252–53.

6. Knitting.

7. Exeter Hall, 372 the Strand, used for large religious meetings; see 14:144. In Scandinavian mythology Gimle was the home of the blessed after the final destruction of the world by the war between the gods and the giants; Valhalla was the home of Odin where he received dead heroes.

8. Sterling visited London in mid-May, presumably on his way to and from the Isle of Wight, where he was to settle at Ventnor (see *Life of Sterling, Works* 11:249). He returned to Falmouth, 23 May. Caroline Fox recorded in her diary,

TC TO JAMES JOHN GARTH WILKINSON

Chelsea, Wednesday Evg
[early May 1843?]

Dear Wilkinson,

I am still a long way off Denmark; tho' continuing to talk about it, and even to read a little Danish, in the midst of other new business.

Friday night we are here; and shall be very happy to see you, and any Danish or other friend of yours. Tea occurs, as usual, about 7 o'clock.

Yours ever truly / T. Carlyle

TC TO MARGARET A. CARLYLE

Chelsea, Saturday, 6 May, 1843

My dear Mother,

It was only the day before yesterday that I wrote a Letter or rather fraction of a Letter to Alick, in which there was an account of all that we could call new here: but it seems so long since you and I had a special word together, I will now before going out send a small bit of writing to yourself, particularly for *your* behoof. I got your good little Letter; and found it still in my breast-pocket this morning: my dear Mother, it would take *you* much more trouble to write me that than it will me to write you this!—

John, as you have heard, left us on Wednesday: I think by the Newspaper account of the Steamers, he will not get across to you till Monday, so that probably it will be Tuesday when you meet. Or indeed perhaps he may go over into Galloway, with a certain Dr Arbuckle, a comrade of his; so arrive by way of Dumfries on some other day: but this I do not consider likely. He will himself write you warning of his arrival. He is in capital case every way; but very much in want of some steady place to live at, some fixed thing to do. Both these wants, I hope, will be supplied to him by and by, poor fellow. He will have a glad meeting with his good Mother at any rate.

---

25 May, that his "London time was an extremely bustling one. Carlyle does not seem quite happy; though he has blown so loud a blast, and though it has awakened so many deep echoes in the hearts of thoughtful men, there are other trumpets yet to sound before Truth can get itself fully recognized, even by those who have gone far" (Fox 181).

TC-JJGW, [early May?]. MS: EUL. Hitherto unpbd. Conjecturally dated by TC's learning to read Danish (see TC to JAC, 5 May). James John Garth Wilkinson (1812–99; *DNB*), English Swedenborgian; see 10:141.

TC-MAC, 6 May. MS: NLS 521.12. Hitherto unpbd.

He and I were often speaking about the want you must have of somebody to do the work of the house for you, to take care of you every way. We think it a great pity that Jenny and you could not get *fettled* together in some house of your own: her children will be growing bigger, and no longer troublesome: she has at present nothing special to do, and surely could not be better employed than in taking care of her mother! If you had a nice house fit for you, not too far off the rest, I think you might be a comfort to one another. You might be near Jean at Dumfries, if you liked that. You might be wherever you liked. The *expense* &c I would most cheerfully pay myself; and indeed, dear good Mother, I wish very much you would give me some opportunity of serving you: if ever a son deserved to be grateful to his Father and Mother, it is I. In whatever use I am of in this world I trace *their* honest handiwork, and often thank them in silence. My brave Father is no longer here to be helped or cherished; but by the great mercy of the Supreme Power, my Mother still is.— Jack will speak to you about all that; and I hope some kind of result will come of it. Jenny is not well where she is, I believe; and one may fear, she will never more get good of her absurd fool of a husband:[1] it were far better I think, that she attached herself to her mother again, and gradually forgot him. I pray you think of this; and when you take a house anywhere, see that it be a *right* house: five pounds a year will be terribly *ill* saved off the comforts of the House where my Mother has to live!—

You have got your Book now, I suppose, and are reading it. The people are considerably astonished with it here, I imagine, and were not altogether expecting such a thing! They will need to get another thing or two, perhaps, by and by.

In your Letter you ask me whether I am not thinking of a look at Scotland this year again. I do think of getting out into the country somewhere, and considering in solitude about *the next Book.* I have yet settled about nothing; but I shall certainly be rather *disappointed* if I do not get a glimpse of my good Mother this year again. So we will leave it in hope.

Alick would tell you what excellent ham it was: it will do me good, I think,—many good thanks to my Brother for that! I am getting stronger in these days, tho' the weather has become very wet: indeed there never was much the matter with me; this Book has done me almost no mischief at all.— They tell me you have had a fit of cold, dear

1. Robert Hanning. In fact, Janet and their two das. joined him in Canada in 1851. They stayed together after this, and Hanning was employed by the Great Western Railway of Canada from 1853 until his death in 1878.

Mother; I wish I could be as sure that it has left you fairly! I hope the good weather will come for your sake among others. It is still rather ungentle here. How is Isabella? How are all? Adieu, my dear Mother; blessings be ever with you! T. Carlyle

TC TO EDWARD FITZGERALD

Chelsea, 8 May, 1843—

Dear Fitzgerald,

Alas, the weather, instead of raining itself out, seems only to be raining itself in! Here is such a day as would do honor to Kendal or the Isle of Skye;[1] and tho' tomorrow there is no likelihood of "Snow," yet I conclude all fields that rest on clay subsoil must be in a state of puddle, and the country in a pleasant state for no class of creatures but ducks and fishes. Accordingly, is it not best that we give up this enterprise altogether "for Tuesday,"[2] and postpone it again into the Indefinite? After much deliberation, not without sufficient regret, I have decided so—for you, who are not here, as well as for myself who am. Is it not right? As we have no particular cause of haste, there ought to be moderate assurance of good weather to see the place in. I am at your bidding whenever that may arrive and you like it otherwise.

I only hope this letter may arrive in time tomorrow morning; at lowest that the carriage may not wait for me inconveniently either at Crick or Rugby.[3]

If you are coming back to Town, come straightway and let me see you. If you are still rusticating at Naseby for a week or so, and the weather should *dry* in the interim, we will make a new appointment,—and keep it in spite of all but Fate!

Yours very damp and sorrowful
T. Carlyle

Have you any Tory Squire of your neighbours, who has *not* lowered his rents, to whom, by way of solacement in wet weather, you could lend this somewhat interesting Pamphlet?[4] It were well done. Forster gave me the thing on Saturday; and now I give it to you. "The Chartists," I suppose, have done it—poor fellows! We are like to get

TC-EF, 8 May. MS: Trinity. Hitherto unpbd.

1. A town in the Lake District and an island off the NW coast of Scotland, both renowned for wet weather.

2. Evidently the date for visiting Naseby had been changed from Wed. or Thurs., 10 or 11 May (TC to EF, 4 May), to Tues., 9 May.

3. Both nr. Naseby.

4. *Hunger and Revolution. By the author of "Daily Bread"* [*John Lhotsky*] (1843). For Lhotsky (1795–1865?), émigré and explorer-naturalist, see 14:242.

serious enough by and by, I think. God give us sense to look even a little way ahead!

JWC TO JEANNIE WELSH

[9 May 1843]

My sweetest

Here is a letter for Walter[1] which I consign to your keeping. not knowing his proper address— To yourself, I have hardly any time remaining to write—Plattnauer having been cheated out of his Sunday visit by a sudden whim of the Marchionesses that he should go *with her* to church—made himself ammends by putting his baby-Lord in a street cab this wet morning and bringing him here *for exercise!*[2] The dearest, prettiest *kissablest* little Lord it is that ever I set my eyes on! no wonder he always calls him "*my* boy"—he is worth the appropriating— Now he is gone I must go out on diverse business—the most noteworthy an investigation about houses— Since it became wholly indifferent to me, whether we remained in this house or not, Carlyle seems to have been growing in attachment towards it—even the accursed piano which "must be got rid of" does not always d[ri?]ve his imagination forth into new streets or a new country, but only ON TO THE ROOF—or *up to the top of the garden!* One day he is for building a sort of well deafened observatory aloft—and the next he will build a good-sized room at the end of the garden!— But preparatory to so strong a measure, there would be need of our having the house on some other principle than from six months to sixmonths.— It would be best he says to *buy* the house!!!—*this* house which he has a thousand times over sworn to be "out of before he was a month older" as if his life depended on being out of it!— Now however he wants to buy it—and then he will build the room in the garden—and "throw the Library and *my* bedroom into "one reasonable drawing room"— He would like he says "to have a soirée now and then"!! "once a fortnight or so"!— Is he going mad? or is it I who have been mad all this while in fancying that he disliked company—and cared nothing about "appearances"? If I cannot get any satisfaction about this house I am to enquire after one *in the same street*—it seems we are attached even to the street!— I am at my wits end! my bedroom turned into a drawing room—soirees once

JWC-JW, [9 May]. Addr: 20 Maryland Street / Liverpool. PM: Chelsea, 9 May 1843. MS: NLS 1891.278. Pbd: Huxley, *JWCLF* 124–25.

1. Macgregor.

2. Maria, b. Tollemache (d. 1893), marchioness of Ailesbury, second wife (m. 1833) of Charles Bruce Brudenell-Bruce (1773–1856), 1st marquess of Ailesbury. Plattnauer was tutor to her son, Charles William (1834–97).

a fortnight with *one maid* servant? The realization of these wild dreams is still a great way off—but I confess they appal me! And this particular day I am not ill to appal—for I went to Charles Bullers to dine yesterday—the father and mother are returned[3]—and instead of dining at six as I had laid my account with we were kept starving till eight—and eating *then* made me sick—and Mrs Buller insisted on my telling *three* long stories which I had told to *her* at Troston—and when I went to bed I could not sleep and today I am "heavy and displeased"— Thank heaven John is not here to "*aggravate*" me!

So goodby to you love till a more auspicious moment— — A kiss to my uncle for the envelope—which was anything but a comforting sight to me! only do not tell *him* that!— — I had a furious quarrel with old Sterling on Sunday gone a week— I went to dine there with Mrs Anthony[4]—at her earnest entreaty—her husband having left her with the old goose alone— Well the way he took of testifying his gratitude was to fall foul of my husbands book which *I knew that he had not read*—and utter the most monstrous impertinencies about it— I gave him of course as good—or a pretty deal *better* than he brought and came away—abruptly—telling him that he must learn good manners before I visited his house or received him into mine again— He had been in fact *brutally insolent*—as his nature is when he loses command of himself—two days after he stopped his carriage a few doors off—came to the door on foot—rung the *bell*—handed in a letter and walked away miserable in spite of Helen's officious entreaties that he would "come in and rest himself"— I enclose the letter—to show you what sort of arrant fools are the Rulers of our Israel![5] Ever your own Jane C

3. Charles (1774–1848) and Isabella Buller, b. Kirkpatrick (d. 1849); see 2:4–5.

4. Sterling.

5. JWC had turned inside out and reused Edward Sterling's black-bordered envelope addressed to her at 5 Cheyne Row for her letter to Jeannie. His letter has not survived, but JWC later sent Jeannie his letter of 25 May, which is also gloomy: "My wretchedness, dear friend, becomes insupportable— It darkens upon me every hour. . . . She flits before me in all shapes—& at each turn of Eye or person—Oh God have mercy. . . . I have confined myself to bed all this afternoon—with cold & fever, aggravated by the cruel condition of my spirits—you who are full of resources & of humanity—what can you do for me?— . . . I dare not ask you hither." But it also included news of John's safe return to Falmouth and his own intention to go to the Isle of Wight, 29 May, "to meet John and his family by the middle of the week."

TC TO EDWARD FITZGERALD

Chelsea, Wednesday [10 May 1843]—

Dear Fitzgerald,

On a calm prognosis of the weather-symptoms, and survey of all the circumstances, I say, No for this time. Come you off straightway, and leave Rutput and the other Hills[1] to drip a little. So soon as the Sun does decisively shew himself, we shall be ready to give him meeting.

I am off to the Museum today, to investigate Col. Okey and certain other persons.— Is not *Hunger and Revolution*[2] a comfortable piece? Be sure you leave it with some Tory of the kind specified.

In immense haste,

Yours always / T. Carlyle

TC TO JOHN FORSTER

Chelsea, 12 May, 1843—

Dear Forster,

The Book upon Dr Francia which is indispensable for me, that of *Rengger and Longchamp*, was translated into English, and published as I find by "Hurst and Chance, St Paul's Churchyard, 1827."[1] It is a small Book, that may have cost originally 5 shillings. I make no doubt your people will be able to rake up a Copy;—and the sooner the better! This is entirely indispensable, this *Renger;* the Robertsons[2] are asses of the first water, and their braying cannot be changed into *speech* well otherwise.— I get notice also of another Book, "Grandine's *Briefe aus Paraguay**[3] (1823–4) with an Introduction by Humboldt,"[4] which would be very desirable; but this, I fear, is *un*attainable?

TC-EF, [10 May]. Addr: Naseby. MS: Trinity. Hitherto unpbd. Dated by TC's plans to visit Naseby; see TC to EF, 4 May, and 8 May.

1. Hills on the battlefield of Naseby; see 15:91.
2. Lhotsky's pamphlet.

TC-JF, 12 May. MS: FC. Hitherto unpbd.

1. Johann Rudolph Rengger and Marcelin Longchamp, *Essai historique sur la révolution du Paraguay, et le gouvernement dictatorial du docteur Francia* (Paris, 1827); *The Reign of Doctor Joseph Gaspard Roderick de Francia, in Paraguay; being an Account of Six Years' Residence in that Republic, from July, 1819—to May, 1825,* trans. unidentified (T. Hurst, E. Chance, 1827). Forster's copy of the trans. has marginal pencil notes said to be possibly by TC (*Forster Collection . . . Printed Books* [1888] 418).
2. J. P. and W. P. Robertson; see TC to JAC, [24 Jan.].
3. In the margin TC has written: "*'Letters from Paraguay' (German,—or perhaps this too is only a French book translated?"
4. Untraced. F. H. Alexander von Humboldt (1769–1859) travelled with the French botanist Aimé Bonpland (1773–1858) in C and S America, 1799–1804.

The *Funes* (or *Fynes*) that I named to you seems also to be published in English: "Gregorio Funes's *History of Buenos Ayres, Paraguay and Tucuman,*" with an Appendix about the S. American Revolution (year of Publisher not given):[5] can this be laid hold of?

Mazzini speaks of a French Book he has seen expressly a *Life* of Francia:[6] but he can tell me nothing more about it whatever. It is not in the British Museum that I could see. I should of course like greatly to read it, or even to have the correct title and description of it: is either the greater or the less of these two things possible?

I will plunder Cochrane to a considerable extent;[7] I will also go thro' Ass Robertsons again, and look at their new Braying you have sent me;[8] if I had *Rengger,* still more if I had the others withal, I think I could manage. The sooner the better! For I have a notion to take the Books all with me, and fly into the country, out of this dusty uproar, and there write in the name of Heaven!

Yours ever truly / T. Carlyle

TC TO CHARLES REDWOOD

Chelsea, 15 May, 1843—

My dear Sir,

I duly received your Letter, and then your Newspaper with the announcement of the Cardiff Steamboats; and thank you heartily for your kind promptitude in regard to that matter. I have still several things to do in London; and indeed the Sun is hitherto so drowned in vapours and rains, there is but little invitation towards the country. I was to have gone last week to explore the region of Naseby Battle in

5. Gregorio Funes (1749–1830), Argentine priest and historian, *Ensayo de la historia civil del Paraguay, Buenos-Ayres y Tucuman,* 3 vols. (Buenos Aires, 1816–17). TC refers to "Historical Sketch of the Revolution of the United Provinces of South America, from the 25th of May 1810, until . . . the 25th of March, 1816, written by Dr. Gregorio Funes, and appended to his History of Buenos Ayres, Paraguay and Tucuman, with a Continuation made . . . by Dean Funes . . . to the Battle of Maipo," which was Appendix A to *Reports on the Present State of the United Provinces of South America; drawn up by* [*C. A.*] *Rodney and* [*John*] *Graham . . . and laid before . . . Congress of the United States* (1819) 137–215. The history itself was apparently not trans.

6. Untraced.

7. J. G. Cochrane. TC borrowed from the London Library, 12 May, John Miers, *Travels in Chile and La Plata,* 2 vols. (1826), listed among works reviewed in "Dr. Francia" (*Works* 29:261).

8. *Letters on South America* (1843).

TC-CR, 15 May. Addr: Llandough / Cowbridge / S. Wales. MS: NLS Acc. 9294. Pbd: Faulkner 153.

Northamptonshire; and all was adjusted, and my hospitable conductor on the spot, would the weather but have grown dry. The weather did not grow dry, and still does not.

I by no means give up Glamorganshire yet;—altogether the contrary. But there will be several adjustments to make here first. For the rest, I have a Friend in Clifton, whom I must try to see as I pass;[1] it is likeliest I may stay a day there, and so have ample time to choose my Steamer, and give you warning about it.

Does Glamorganshire produce good horses? If you should hear of any modest stout eligible riding-horse on sale in that quarter, I could half wish you would give me notice about it. I have a feeling again as if I ought to have a horse; and to purchase one in Tattershall's[2] is very far beyond my commission at present! Nay the whole matter is still so much in the state of a mere imagination, that I will expressly forbid your taking any *trouble* about it, or treating it as other than an altogether loose affair. My price for a horse has hitherto been somewhere between £20 and £30; and their qualities are quite dark to me till I have tried them!

Still hoping to see you in Wales before long,

Yours always truly / T. Carlyle

TC TO JOHN A. CARLYLE

Chelsea, 15 May, 1843—

My dear Brother,

Your Letter which came on Saturday was very welcome. Your ideas and proceedings as to our Mother and Jenny have my most hearty concurrence; and I cannot but desire very much that Jean may

1. Julia Strachey, who had written to TC, 7 May: "I shall hope to be favored with a visit whenever you do come, & you may depend upon *a cordial* reception, although I regret to say the *enthusiasm,* of which up to present I have always been conscious of possessing a large share, seems just now either extinct, or in a quite dormant state— Whether it is that there are in fact *no Heroes left* upon this poor Earth, whom one can by any possibility think worthy of enthusiastic reverence, or whether it was that my former all but adoration of such supposed personages, was an illusion, which now shares the fate of all other illusions, I know not, but so it is. . . . I left London somewhat prematurely . . . but I found the noise & confusion of Mount S*t* all but intollerable . . . & so I took my flight in a sort of melancholy despairing state. . . . You said nothing about M*rs* Carlyle accompanying you here but should she propose doing so, my pleasure will be greatly enhanced. . . . Pray remember me most kindly to your brother . . . always a great favorite of mine."

2. Horse auctioneer's, Hyde Park Corner, founded 1776, by Richard Tattersall.

TC-JAC, 15 May. MS: NLS 524.44. Hitherto unpbd.

succeed in finding some suitable sort of house at Dumfries: the rest I think might all be managed; in fact, might go on better and better if it were once fairly *set* agoing.[1] It would be a very easy thing to settle all the rest. To me, and no doubt to you also, it would be a real solacement to pay 10 or 15 pounds apiece at stated times in the year, if by so doing we could make our good Mother even a little comfortabler! Twenty or thirty pounds a year added to what she already has, would keep her and Jenny very well. The money I think ought be paid to my Mother, and to be hers, that *she* might continue in form as in fact mistress of the establishment: Jenny I believe might feel that to be the comfortablest way for her; she would then consider herself as *working* and doing good service for her keep. But I am far too remote from the scene to take any right hold of the minute circumstances, or give any advice that is worth much. Only it does seem, and has always seemed, very desirable to me that Jenny and our Mother should be with one another; and I cannot believe but it *is* possible to get some rational arrangement contrived for their being so. You will be right well employed in arranging that if you can manage it.

I also very much participate your notion about Alick:[2] I am truly glad moreover to hear what you say about his improved mood of mind. Pray Heaven there may be something good arranged on that side also! Our poor Alick; a brave man too,—but drifted far awry by the currents of Life. I never can do other than pray with my whole heart that better days be yet coming for him. It is evident at least that he is right in leaving Ecclefechan.— I have to write a word to him one of these days, for indeed I have some money to pay him.

I did not design writing to you today; but that Letter came by the Post, and I would not send it without a word.— There is a brief Note

1. John Carlyle wrote from Scotsbrig, 11 May, to say that their mother needed someone in the house with her at all times, for which "we must try to make arrangement . . . as soon as possible. . . . I have written to Jean & asked her to look for some cottages about Dumfries that would be large enough for our mother & Jenny & have a spare room. Of course there will be reluctance to move, but Isabella's continued illness & the restraint it imposes renders moving more & more desirable. Our mother says that she is like a 'cloker [broody hen] *in her old nest*' & unable to make up mind to leave it."

2. He had written that Alexander Carlyle had let his house and would soon sell the contents of his shop at auction. "He speaks of going to Canada but with no strong heart or healthy purpose & our mother, though she will not interfere & prevent him hears of it with dismay. . . . The only rational plan for him is to go & look at Canada alone. . . . Though there has been much to blame in his management of all the farms he has hitherto had one must confess that he never had a fair chance of succeeding on any he has tried, the times having turned so much against him. . . . He seems to me at present in a better mood of mind too than I have seen for years & all things considered, if he were to give up Canada, I should not regard another trial in a farm as at all desperate."

from Dickens, in very good humour:[3] is not that right? Item one from Jeffrey in a "*mixture* of good and evil, Mother";[4]—and finally one from Bunsen, just come, which I have not yet got read.[5] These if they seem worthy I will send you directly: I have only got them half read yet.—— Darwin is here waiting to take me up to Town; and the day is altogether muddy.

My blessings and love to my dear Mother, and one and all of them.

Your affect*e* / T. Carlyle

TC TO [J. S. BUCKINGHAM]

5. Cheyne Row, Chelsea
16 May 1843—

Dear Sir,

Accept many thanks for the kind gift of your Book on Canada, which I received last night with much pleasure. I have already perused with due attention the Chapter and the Supplements on Colonization;[1] and am happy to express not my assent only but my zealous

3. Dickens had invited Bulwer, 14 May, to attend a meeting of authors and publishers, 17 May (*DL* 3:489), and may have invited TC to the same meeting; see TC to [CD], 18 May.

4. Coterie speech; see 3:412. Jeffrey wrote to TC, 12 May, of *Past and Present:* "I agree more with it, I think, than with any of your other lucubrations—and have better hope of its making an impression in favour of your genius—and your doctrines—altho', with regard to the greater part of the last, I must not let you suppose that I am as yet anything of a convert—or indeed other than a decided and, I rather fear an inconvertible heretic—and even as to the matter of genius—tho' there can be no doubt that it has that stamp, both broad and deep, almost on every page, I am yet so far from being satisfied with the taste and style of your writing, that I am absolutely provoked with you for wilfully putting obstacles in the way both of your fame and the efficacy of the many great truths you deliver. . . . If I had had to deal with your M.S. I should have struck out at least a third—and yet have left you all your poetry and pathos, and originality—and most even of your *oddness*—which is often very piquant—and awakening—."

5. Bunsen wrote, in German, from Carlton Terrace, London, 15 May, to thank TC for his copy of *Past and Present.*

TC-[JSB], 16 May. MS: NLS 1808.116. Hitherto unpbd. Addressee identified by references to his *Canada, Nova Scotia, New Brunswick, and the Other British Provinces in North America, with a Plan of National Colonization* (1843), pbd. early May.

1. Ch. 29 was on "Capacity to relieve the mother-country of her surplus population. . . . Decline of great empires from neglect of Colonization, Commerce, and Education," and other ideas which TC sympathized with. A supplementary ch. was added on national colonization, written after Charles Buller's speech to the House of Commons on the subject (see TC to [JB], 4 April), critizing the govt.'s inadequate response to his proposals, and a postscript quoting the *Sydney Morning Herald*'s criticism of the ignorance of colonial matters of Lord Stanley, sec. of state for the colonies.

consent to all that I find there; it seems to me as if I would have spoken every sentiment of it myself,—as if all rational men ought on all fit occasions to be speaking and inculcating them! My notion is that there is an immense *silent* assent to all that, lying latent in the country, only waiting to be spoken to, that it may answer. In my own case the business is fifteen years old or older; and on all hands I have had the like reflected on me from persons of insight and sincerity, when the matter came in course.

If we had a Government that could and would give the word in such an enterprise, it were very happy for us at present. But in the absence of that, are there not others that can *give the word*, tho' in a less direct way? I think I know one man whose excellent popular talent might do real service in this matter![2] There ought to be a Course of Lectures on Emigration and Colonization delivered in these years in all quarters of Britain and Ireland. It seems to me of the last importance that the Corn-Law be *swiftly* abrogated, and that this of Emigration follow swiftly in the rear of it. This, and much else—alas!

With many thanks and good wishes, I subscribe myself,

Dear Sir, / very truly Yours
T. Carlyle

TC TO C. K. J. BUNSEN

5. Cheyne Row, Chelsea
17 May, 1843—

Dear Mr Bunsen,

Accept many thanks for your kind and wise word about my poor questionable *Berserk* of a Book![1] You answer with calm light and recognition where there is, along with the insight and veracity, so much wrath and smoke. It is a clear reflex of my meaning, from a most friendly intelligence;—a far worthier response than I could look for in such a case. Many thanks to you;—and may the Supreme Power turn many a thing, both in England and in Deutschland, to better use than we have cause to dread at present! "The Devil invented *Must*":[2] that is a fact I shall try not to forget.

My Brother is in Scotland, safe beside our good old Mother there;

2. Buckingham. JWC had heard him lecture on the Corn Laws; see JWC to JW, [19? Jan.].

TC-CKJB, 17 May. MS: Yale. Hitherto unpbd.
1. TC is replying to Bunsen's letter, 15 May.
2. Bunsen had written: "'*Muss hat der Teufel erdacht*' ist ein tiefes deutsches Sprüchwort [*The Devil invented necessity* is a profound German saying]."

and seems to be nearly stationary; imprisoned, I suppose, by the ever-active rains and mud. He meant to go to Edinburgh, and see the venerable old Kirk *suicide* herself in these days,—like a noble old Kirk, accepting death rather than dishonour; a highly tragic operation:[3] but the time is unpropitious, and John, it seems, is not to be here[4] to witness. He told me of the Icelandic Grammar: whenever it does arrive, will you be so kind as forward it direct by the *Parcels Company:* I can read Danish now; I have got a *Nial's Saga* in Icelandic, and know where to borrow a Rask's Dictionary; I want only the Grammar to begin reading.[5] What a poor fellow was Agamemnon, was good Achill[es], to many of these unsung forgotten Scandinavians: *vate caruerunt sacro!*[6] I find sermons on "Silence" wherever I go or stand in this world.

You are very kind to offer me such a "Coffeehouse"! I am seldom in your quarter[7] early, or indeed at all, of late months; but I will try to call some morning and find you. Will Madam Bunsen accept my sincere respects, and acknowledgements for her remembrance of me, the official Proof of which arrived here shortly before your Note.[8] We have unluckily a sort of general engagement here ourselves to be at home on Wednesday Evenings: nevertheless I do speculate on some attempt at escaping towards you on occasion.

With many true wishes and regards,
Yours always / T. Carlyle

3. The expected Disruption of the Church of Scotland took place during its General Assembly at Edinburgh, 18 May; see TC to MAC, 20 Jan.

4. Meaning "there."

5. R. K. Rask (1737–1832), Danish scholar and philologist, ed. *Lexicon Islandico-Latino-Danicum* (Copenhagen, 1814), and had also written an intro. to an Icelandic and Old Norse grammar, *Vejledning til det islandske eller gamle nordiske sprog* (Copenhagen, 1811); a trans. had been pbd. by P. Marsh (Burlington, 1838), and George W. Dasent pbd. another in 1843.

6. "*Vixere fortes ante Agamemnona / Multi; sed omnes illacrimabiles / Urgentur ignotique longa / Nocte, carent quia vate sacro* [Many brave men lived before Agamemnon, not a few; but on all alike, unwept and unknown, eternal night lies heavy because they lack a sacred poet]" (Horace, *Odes* 4.9.25).

7. Nr. the Prussian embassy, Carlton Terrace, Pall Mall.

8. Evidently an invitation for Wed., 24 May; see TC to JAC, 29 May. Frances Bunsen, b. Waddington (d. 1876); see 11:29.

TC TO SAMUEL LAURENCE

5. Cheyne Row, Chelsea / 17 May, 1843—

Dear Lawrence,

I know not if I have a right to say that anybody in America specially "wants my Picture." Gambardella meant to give his work to Emerson, I believe, had he succeeded: "R. Waldo Emerson, Concord, near Boston."[1] But Emerson is not a rich man; not a picture-buying man, I should think. On the other hand, there was once an American,[2] whose name I have forgotten, that did send, by a Scotch friend *whose* name also has now escaped me, some request that I should sit for a Likeness: but the whole matter, as you see, has gone into the vague; and I can recall nothing more than the impression that my American was a Bostonean. On the whole, your friend's best way will be to inquire of the Boston Booksellers (Little & Brown is the title of one House, Munroe and Co of another), who will probably be able to set him on the track of discovering who is the suitable man, if suitable man there be. I cannot in the least estimate the probabilities: but perhaps the adventure of inquiring into them by this opportunity will not be very heavy. Your Portrait of me, sublimely ugly as it may be, is the only decent attempt at a likeness I have yet fallen in with; and indeed seems to me to contain in it, very visibly, the elements of an excellent Picture.[3] Sterling, I think I have told you, prizes the chalk Sketch at an enormous rate.[4]

[signature cut away]

TC-SL, 17 May. MS: Pierpont Morgan Lib. Hitherto unpbd. Samuel Laurence (1812–84; *DNB*), portrait painter; see 10:115, 118.

1. For Gambardella's praise of Laurence's 1841 portrait and his intention to paint TC, see 13:300–1; for the attempt, see 15:166, 188–89.

2. Unidentified.

3. Probably the oil portrait shown at the Royal Acad., 1841, which is also probably the portrait of 10:frontispiece (though there dated 1838) since it is the only known portrait in oils, and for which TC sat, March 1841 (see 13:60–61, 208). Laurence also made several crayon portraits in 1838. There is still some uncertainty about identifying which are which and when they were painted.

4. Made July 1838, now in Carlyle's House, Chelsea; see 8:frontispiece. For John Sterling's acquisition of it, see 15:163.

TC TO JOHN FORSTER

5. Cheyne Row, Chelsea
17 May, 1843–

Dear Forster,

There is not a *gleam* of new light in Rengger, the unfortunate Rengger; and Funes is all about the Abipones[1] and old Jesuit and Ante-Jesuit days! Francia will continue dim till after far wider inquiries. What is to be done?

Will you look among your Indexes, and see whether, since the year 1839, there was any article on Oehlenschläger's *Autobiography* (not his Plays, but his Autobiography first published then).[2] I have just been reading that; and might make a shortish readable story out of it;—and will do it, if your perverse Indexes hold their peace, or even almost if they do not![3] Yours ever

T. C.

TC TO [CHARLES DICKENS]

Chelsea, 18 May, 1843–

Dear Sir,

I think your Project looks, especially in your hands, much more feasible than the other did;[1] one may hope too that, if realized, it may

TC-JF, 17 May. MS: FC. Hitherto unpbd.

1. Extinct Indian tribe of Paraguay and Argentina. For the books alluded to, see TC to JF, 12 May.

2. Adam Gottlob Oehlenschläger (1779–1850), Danish poet and dramatist, *Oehlenschlägers Levnet, fortalt af ham selv,* 2 vols. (Copenhagen, 1830–31). No articles on the *Autobiography* have been traced before one by George Levine, *Dublin Review* 17 (1844).

3. TC never wrote on Oehlenschläger, although he does mention a tragedy by him in "Early Kings of Norway," *Works* 30:222.

TC-[CD], 18 May. MS: NLS 1808.118. Hitherto unpbd. Most probably addressed to Dickens, who was involved in an "Association for the Protection of Literature" and who had written to Charles Babbage, 27 April, that, though opposed to John Robertson's Society of Authors, he believed that "Authors and Publishers must unite" and that "the Longmans and Murray have been with me in proposing such an association" (*DL* 3:477–78). Dickens chaired the first meeting, 17 May, at Longmans', which resolved to "form an Association of Authors, Publishers, Printers, Stationers, and others," to protect copyrights and fight piracy. Dickens and Bulwer were on the committee, and among subscribers were John Forster, Lockhart, and Chapman & Hall (printed account of resolutions and "proposed objects" in Princeton Univ. Lib.). There were so many printers and publishers involved, that the printed account could have been in TC's hands by next day.

1. TC is probably commenting on the printed account and favorably contrasting it with Robertson's Society of Authors, whose second meeting, 8 April, Dickens had chaired before refusing further involvement (*DL* 3:477–78).

lead to some third thing better still. It is urgently desirable that "Authors," or Persons who lead the Public Mind whatever title they may bear, should gradually form some kind of Brotherhood with one another, and become an organised Corporation, as far less important bodies of man have done: and in the present state of Authorship, perhaps the bringing of Authors together into a room, that they may occasionally look on one another and grow accustomed to one another, is almost all that can be done for that unfortunate class. I shall wish you heartily success in this adventure.

As for myself, I am so circumstanced in various respects I have found it unadvisable hitherto to become a member of any Club, reunion or general Assemblage of men whatsoever; my necessity is rather to live in the utmost quiet and solitude that is possible for me here. On other men, meanwhile, other duties are laid. For me too, better health, and other changes, may by and by make new habits eligible. I will wish you again all manner of success; and remain, as a spectator for the present,

Very Sincerely Yours / T. Carlyle

TC TO ALEXANDER CARLYLE

Chelsea, 19 May, 1843–

My dear Brother,

I have waited this good while for some leisure moment, wherein I could write to you deliberately; but there seems none such to lie near me yet: so I must write in haste, rather than not at all. I must at least pay you the Tobacco Merchant's account; that is a plain matter! Here is an order for two sovereigns which I procured yesterday: what residue there is over, after satisfying the Tobacconist, you are to divide equally between Tom and Jane,[1] as a gift from their "Uncle in London." And so, many thanks for your care in this matter, dear Brother. The tobacco is excellent; and came in good stead to me here, the old supplies being out or nearly so. I have begun heartily smoking it now.

I forget your Leith Wine & Spirit Merchant's name.[2] We are nearly thro' our Brandy here; and can take a little more Wine from him too. We will say *two dozen and a half* of Port, two dozen of Sherry, and three gallons of Brandy; that will make six dozen bottles in all, and will perhaps be sufficient for one Box. Let the Account come along

TC-AC, 19 May. Addr: Ecclefechan. MS: MUL. Pbd: Marrs 552–54.

1. The two oldest children, Jane Welsh (1831–84) and Thomas (1833–1921).
2. Hutchison & Bowe; see 14:37.

with the Articles, and it shall be paid when they arrive. There is no special *immediate* haste, if the people have not a set of articles they can recommend at the moment: the *last* were found to be satisfactory, and if they stand at the old price and quality we may deal satisfactorily again. I daresay you will give the necessary orders for all this, and set it in motion for me, with great readiness. And so no more of it at present.

Many a time, in these days, do I think of Whitsunday, and the important resolutions and inquiries my Brother must have in his mind at present! You are certainly wise to have done with Ecclefechan at any rate. What is to follow next may be obscure and doubtful enough; but it cannot easily be worse than the certainty was there. Alas, dear Brother, I can do nothing for you at this stage of the business; but be very sorry, very anxious for you,—yet still with good hope. If it please God, a better day *shall* yet come! Let us press on, nothing daunted: if we can grow *wiser* by our past errors, they too will not have been in vain! Of the son of Adam there cannot in this world be more required, on the whole, than that he do grow wiser by past mistakes; and be always learning while in this School of Life. It is not in one of us to direct his steps; but in all things we fail and err continually.

You will have a *roup* [auction] I fancy in about a week; all will be bustle round you already. The Dr, I suppose, has given you all his ideas: do not adopt them, if they seem unwise to you; the great thing is that your own inner heart went along with the undertaking whatever that were. His reports about you are more cheering than I expected. May God turn it all to good, my dear Brother; may God direct you towards what *is* wisest, best, and strengthen you to do that however difficult it be! I will not continue farther,—even if I had more paper and time. I send my heart's blessing to all of you; and wait with anxiety to hear the result. Ever your affectionate Brother

T. Carlyle

TC TO BASIL MONTAGU

Chelsea, 19 May, 1843—

Dear Mr Montague,

My knowledge of this embryo "Authors' Society" is all but altogether exactly on a par with your own. Several weeks ago, after much solicitation, I attended once, for ten minutes, in a room of the British Hôtel, a meeting of some twenty or thirty extremely ugly men,

TC-BM, 19 May. MS: Duke. Hitherto unpbd.

only some three of whom were even by face known to me; I admitted in a whisper, in answer to the Secretary's whisper, that [several words cut away] Sir Lytton Bulwer had been saying was of a reasonable nature; and thereupon took my hat and walked away.[1] Bulwer himself, I think, withdrew about the same time. This was the "motioning" and "seconding of the motion"; this, and on my part nothing more than this. I have since directed with all due distinctness that my name, if it were on their List, should be entirely obliterated.

Authors ought to unite, and will, I have no doubt; but not till they *cease* to be "animals of prey": this, curiously enough, was precisely my remark to Secretary Robertson in regard to the Authors' Society.

With many kind regards from both of us to Mrs Montague,[2]

[signature cut away]

TC TO [ROBERT WHITE]

5 Cheyne Road, Chelsea
19 May 1843.

Dear Sir

Accept my thanks for your two Poems,[1] which I received last night. I have read them over; which fact, if you knew my habits with respect to that class of compositions in these times, might itself, mean something for you.

I can with great sincerity bear testimony to the existence of a vigorous, genial and truly valuable endowment in the writer of these verses; for which endowment, I should say, the right concern or species of utterance had by no means yet been discovered;—but was likely such seemed his honesty and energy, to discover itself better and better to him, as he unconsciously struggled along his way. And so what can I do but commit you to your own good genius, to whatso-

1. The meeting had been held 25 March; see TC to MR, [14 March]. Sir Edward George Lytton Bulwer (1803–73; *DNB;* see 11:61); was a member of the society and on the provisional committee; see Walter Besant, *Essays and Historiettes* 284–85.

2. Anna Dorothea Montagu, b. Benson; see 2:451 and *Reminiscences* 240, 249–51.

TC-[RW], 19 May. Longhand copy of MS: Humanities Research Lib., Univ. of Texas at Austin. Hitherto unpbd. On the same page of the copy of TC's letter is a copy of one by Thomas De Quincey (1783–1859; *DNB*), presumably meant for the same addressee. With this is a letter signed by Robert White, dated from Newcastle-on-Tyne, 13 Nov. 1863, stating that he is enclosing "copies of the Notes of Carlyle and De Quincey." Robert White (1802–74; *DNB*), antiquary; pbd. works on Scottish border legends and ballads, poetry, and other writings.

1. Unidentified.

ever of good and striving is in yourself; and to all good influences from without which fail not at any time to wait upon that.

With many kind wishes and good hopes

I remain / Very sincerely Yours
T. Carlyle.

TC TO RICHARD MONCKTON MILNES

Chelsea, 19 May, 1843–

"Cid mio [My Lord], in good hour hast thou returned!"[1] The impatience of the public was fast mounting towards anxiety. Everybody said, We cannot want our Milnes!

I am here on Sunday Morning entirely free;—and if you came before one o'clock, we could fly out into the Lanes, and escape the *profanum vulgus* [rabble]. I am also at home, I think, every evg till Tuesday. Thirdly, I will call at Pall Mall N*o* 26,[2] the first day I pass within wind of it. And so let us meet *quam primum* [as soon as possible]. Yours ever

T. Carlyle

TC TO JAMES DODDS

London, *20th May,* 1843.

My Dear Sir,—Several weeks ago I duly received your letter, and read it, as I always do your letters, when they bring such news of you, with welcome and pleasure. It has been in my mind ever since to write to you with a certain expansion in some hour of leisure, but as that hour does not arrive, and, alas! gives no promise yet of arriving, I must content myself with this swift and brief acknowledgement, rather than with none at all, which is the other branch of the alternative.

You are an enthusiastic man, and look at all things through magnifying lenses, productive, too, of beautiful prismatic tints brighter than nature; nevertheless, I find your image of the object sharply distinct, and just, too, though exaggerated on a larger scale than usual.

TC-RMM, 19 May. MS: Trinity. Pbd: Reid, *RMM* 1:290. Richard Monckton Milnes (1809–85; *DNB*), politician, author, and bon vivant; TC's friend since 1836; see 9:8.

1. Milnes had spent the winter travelling in Greece, Turkey, and Egypt.
2. Milnes's house.

TC-JD, 20 May. Pbd: Rev. James Dodds, "Memoir of James Dodds," in James Dodds, *Lays of the Covenanters* (Edinburgh, 1880) 58–60. James Dodds (1813–73; *DNB*), poet, lawyer, and lecturer; see 12:30.

The *scale* is not mathematically important; the distinctness and the justness are alone important. On the whole, I like that mood of mind very well; a true portrait and a gigantic one, done with haloes and tints of the rainbow; there are worse kinds than that.

It gives me great pleasure to find you persevere so manfully, "following your star," where, except the star itself occasionally beaming in the distance, there can be little to cheer you by the way. Persevere, persevere; that is the strength of a man. I will promise you all manner of good if you persevere. You shall have victory, more conquest perhaps than perhaps you yet believe; you shall have heroic battle, which is the noblest conquest of all.[1]

It is far from my advice that you should relax in your law studies, in any of your studies, which I honor you for prosecuting in a strenuous silence. Nevertheless, it strikes me that you might be gradually attempting something in the way of writing too. You have, doubtless, hours now and then which, by thrifty assiduity, you might devote with advantage to trials in that kind. I speak with reluctance about writing, whither, I know, all your ambition tends, opposed by all your virtue and philosophy. But I fancy you are getting stronger on that latter side, and can afford a little excursion there by a time. Writing as well as law requires to be *learned;* and to writing, as I can predict, you, amid all your law, or after all your law, will pretty certainly come at last. A solid man knows how to combine the ideal with the practical; to do the *obligato* [that which one is obliged to do] better than another, and combine with it the *voluntario* [that which one wishes to do], which others think not of. May a good Genius guide you always.

To Gordon,[2] who likes you well, I send many kind regards, and with good hopes and good wishes, I am, yours most truly,

T. Carlyle

1. For TC's advice to Dodds, see 13:58–59.

2. John Gordon (1797–1882), sec. of the General Assembly's education committee since 1825; ed. of the *New Statistical Account for Scotland,* 1834–45; gen. sec. of Univ. of Edinburgh, 1833–43 (see 6:168–69, 177); apptd. as the second inspector of schools, 1844 (see also 12:129). Dodds wrote of him: "He is a true-hearted man, and one of the best friends I have in Edinburgh. He is, like myself, an *eremite;* when we get together in his snug library, we sit talking metaphysics, when all the other grave citizens are drawing on their night-caps. . . . He is what Carlyle calls 'a true man' " (Dodds 60).

TC TO SAMUEL GRIDLEY HOWE AND JULIA WARD HOWE

5 Cheyne Row, Chelsea, May 20, 1843

[Contents unknown but probably inviting the Howes to come to tea on Monday, 22 May, instead of Sunday.[1]]

JWC TO JEANNIE WELSH

Saturday [20? May 1843]

My dear Babbie

I am sure with all his scribbling he will make no sensible story of it— I sat up till after midnight the night before last to write to you—and yesterday such was my hurry and stupefaction that I quite forgot to send off the letter—your note this morning was the first thing to remind me of it—

I am very hurried to day, writing letters about my German governess—whom I hope at last to have found a situation for[1]—and my

TC-SGH & JWH, 20 May. MS: sold at auction, 20 Dec. 1917, Anderson Galleries, New York City. Dr. Samuel Gridley Howe (1801–76), American humanitarian (see 15:142), m., late April 1843, Julia Ward (1819–1910), humanitarian and poet.

1. The Howes were spending their honeymoon in London, staying at 31 Upper Baker St. Howe had a leg injury and was confined to the house. The couple thus sent off their letters of intro. to various persons "and were soon favored with the calls of the lettered" (*Letters and Journals of Samuel Gridley Howe* [Boston, 1909] 2:127–28). "Thomas Carlyle . . . was one of our earliest visitors. . . . Before taking leave of us he invited us to take tea with him on the following Sunday [21 May]" (Julia Ward Howe, *Reminiscences 1819–1899* [Boston and New York, 1899] 96). Though she implied that the visit took place on Sun., JWC to JW [28 May] makes clear that the party was on Mon.

JWC-JW, [20? May]. Addr: 20 Maryland Street / Liverpool. PM: 19 May 1843. Hitherto unpbd. Enclosed in the same envelope was a note by John Robertson, also dated "Saturday." Since 20 May was a Sat., either JWC and Robertson both mistook the day of the week or the date of the PM is an error; JWC's letter of "the night before last" (now lost) was apparently not posted on Fri., 19 May, either.

1. Amalie Charlotte Elise Mariana Bölte (1811–91), German writer and governess. Da. of a cultivated Mecklenburg family, she became a governess, 1828; came to England, 1839, and met the Carlyles, 1841. See intro. to her *Briefe aus England an Varnhagen von Ense 1844–1858*, ed. W. Fischer and A. Behrens (Düsseldorf, 1955). Espinasse says that she was "a clever German lady (Jewess, I think)" who in Berlin "had been a friend of Rahel, and remained a friend of Rahel's husband, Varnhagen von Ense . . . , letters from whom . . . she used to bring with her and read aloud at Chelsea. Governessing was her main occupation, but she wrote among other things novels, chiefly sentimental, which appear to have had some vogue in Germany. Carlyle tolerated her as a correspondent of Varnhagen, and Mrs. Carlyle befriended her as a clever lone woman in a foreign

headaches—and Oh I do so wish that Robertson the writer of your letter would go away[2]—

TC TO ALEXANDER CARLYLE

Chelsea, Friday Evg / 26 May, 1843—

My dear Brother,

Yesterday I had a Letter from the Doctor, who had seen you as he passed thro' Ecclefechan; you need not doubt but the news he gave me was interesting! You have now finished the Sale of your effects in Ecclefechan, this very day you must have been removing from your house, into some other temporary abode; and in a short time, it appears, you are to make a much farther removal, and try the new Country over the Sea. My dear Brother, it is a great and painful enterprise; but, I trust in Heaven, it may be a blessed one. My thoughts have been with you constantly in these days; ever and anon the image of poor Ecclefechan, and my good Brother closing his sorrowful battle there, has risen on me strangely thro' whatever I might be looking at here. Courage, my Brother! You will get thro' all these pains and confusions; you will cut your way, like a brave man, into new battleground, and rise into victory yet, if it please God! Few sights I have looked on have been painfuller to me than that of a man with your energies and qualities struggling in such a scene, under such galling impediments, as yours have long been. I have a clear hope that better times, and a more generous fight, are appointed for you in that new home. You will have no miserable Laird or other Fellow-mortal whatever, to ask leave of there; you will, at least, appeal direct to the Great Powers, and ask

land, and was successful in getting her situations" (Espinasse 233). In this instance JWC was to find her a position in the home of Charles and Isabella Buller.

2. John Robertson wrote: "Know all people that on earth do dwell and Miss Jane Welsh that Mrs Carlyle of No 5 Great Cheyne Row Chelsea has opened a bureau for young women destitute of situations to the suspension of her ordinary business of supplying the wants of young ladies destitute only of Epistles. The abovementioned Mrs Carlyle also carries on a considerable business in the upholstery line in sofa covers chair covers &c which she carries on so intently sometimes that she forgets to post even the few epistles not professional which she does write. Otherwise be it known to all whom it may concern that the said Mrs. Carlyle is as well as can be expected for the Sole Manager of the New Gratis Bureau for providing situations for Destitute Young Ladies. In absolute despair of being able to accomplish the correspondence of her office this day Mrs Carlyle has employed the pen of a ready writer to indite this placard and supplied him with a thousand and one penny stamps that the facts it contains may be duly transmitted to a portion of the young ladies suffering great distress from a mournful destitution of Epistles" (MS: NLS 1891.289).

TC-AC, 26 May. MS: MUL. Pbd: A. Carlyle, *NL* 286–92; Marrs 554–57.

them where[1] you deserve to prosper or not. It seems to me a most blessed change; worthy of being purchased at a very great cost of pain.

The report John gives us of your present mood of mind is very satisfactory. He rather complains that you have not yielded to his scheme of going out to Canada first, and looking at it: this surely was kindly intended on his part; but on the whole both Jane and I are of opinion that your own resolution, for your own behoof, is the wise one.[2] It will be a confused forbidding aspect that the new country offers you; but under that first look, which you will not let dishearten you, there will lie a *second* look, there will lie all manner of possibilities, which to the brave man will become more and more productive. On the whole, is it not better that you buckle to it, as you mean to do, resolutely, with your whole heart, *at once?* "There is a puddle at every town-end," says the Proverb:[3] it is better to get *thro'* that, perhaps, without looking at it farther. I anticipate great things for you in that new way of life;—first of all far better health than you have had lately; healthy honest *field*-work, far better for the body; and then still more, the awakening of a generous manful hope in your heart and mind, such as has long been absent in these late sorrowful times.

Your parting with us all will be painful; yes, dear Brother, it will be a cruel sorrow; but on the whole this too must be borne. Nay you are not to think it a *final* leave you are taking of any of us: Canada, by Steam and other means, is coming daily closer to Britain; for my share, I see not but it is likelier the whole of them may have to go out to *you* if times do not mend. There is positively no existence for an industrious tiller of the soil in this country in our day; and the view I have of the days that are coming often makes me shudder! To struggle out one's own life in such a Country is dreary; but to leave a quantity of children in such a scene, which grows yearly more unmanageable, is frightful. No; rather consider yourself as the harbinger and pioneer of the others, than as one cut off from them: the blessing of God *does* rest upon the brave man, who with a sincere wise heart goes forth in the name of God.

I remember well, at this moment, the last look I got of Jamie and

1. Probably a slip for "whether."

2. John Carlyle wrote from Dumfries, 19 May, that "Alick 'sees no use in looking at Canada beforehand'" and from Scotsbrig, 23 May: "He seems now really determined to go with his family at once to Canada, & has an air of being relieved from painful uncertainty. . . . Last week I repeated to him more strongly than before all the reasons that had weighed on my mind in favour of his first going to see the country; but they appear to have produced no impression."

3. Scots proverb; cf. 7:129.

you, as I went off in the Steamer towards this place some eight years ago.[4] I felt that I was gone from you; but that I had been bound and compelled to go;—that, in the name of Heaven, I must now do and struggle! In the midst of pain, a better feeling rises: it is good for a man that he be cast, from time to time, forth from his old refuges, and made to try what his relation with the great seen and unseen Realities is!— I hope yet to see you in Canada some day; and sit by your hearth on ground that belongs to yourself and the Maker alone!—

Jack talks of £300 as a sum that you would have a fair chance with, were it lying ready for you on your landing on the other side. I can only say that I will right heartily go halves with him in any such sum that may be considered fittest; and it will be a true tho' small relief to my mind to do so. I know [not][5] whether I should have spoken to you about this at all; for perhaps he has not yet mentioned it to you, and the consultation may be still incomplete: but I could not help signifying my readiness even before the time.

Our poor dear Mother will suffer sore; but you, of course, will do all that is in you to spare her true heart any sorrow that is not inevitable. The good old heart of a Mother! She is the saddest and the tenderest sight we have in this world; one could weep floods of tears, were there not something in it of a sacredness that led one beyond tears. It was the Most High God that made Mothers and the sacred affection of children's hearts: yes, it was He;—and shall it not, in the end, be *all well,* under His management? It shall be *all well;* on this side of death, or beyond death. We will pray once more, from our inmost heart if we can, "Our Father which art in Heaven, *thy* will be done!"—

My dear Brother, I am scribbling here to give some utterance to myself on this occasion; and yet I feel that I have no utterance; that all I can say is but dumb half-utterance;—that in fact I ought to end and hold my peace, and leave you to conceive what it is that I am meaning. You know well enough what I mean! I pray with my whole soul all blessings to be upon you. I bid you be of courage, and quit yourself like a man; I prophesy all good, spiritual and temporal, to you if you do. And so let me not speak another word.

You need not answer this at present; you will have enough to do otherwise in these days.—

Last week you would receive a Post-office order (or was it the beginning of this week) for two pounds.[6] I think it was not specifically

4. Nine years: TC left for London on 8 May 1834; see 7:146, 161.
5. Word omitted.
6. See TC to AC, 19 May.

mentioned that one of the pounds was a gift to the poor little Lassie who has just arrived, and is lying asleep on its Mothers' knee, little conscious of all this bustle![7] I hope there will be something for *snaps* [gingerbread biscuits] to Jane and Tom besides.— I expect to hear very soon from the Doctor again. I send my blessing to you all; and am ever

Your affectionate Brother / T. Carlyle

JWC TO JEANNIE WELSH

[27 May 1843]

Private

My darling

I have been dissipated all this week—extremely dissipated *on programme;* not settling myself to anything—writing to Babbie included!

The fact is, a *sublime absurdity* occurred to me the other day, and threw me into a sort of nervous flurry which I saw more likelihood to get rid of in everybody's or anybody's company rather than tete a tete with myself. My goodness! surely the mantle of *Ninon de l'Enclos* has fallen upon me![1] One might have thought that in this year of grace I was pretty safe from having my tranquillity assailed by the *grandes passions* of *young* gentlemen! But as the old Countess of Essex said when asked *at eighty* by a young jackanapes; "when does a woman have done with love"—?— "Ask some one older than me"![2]

Be all that as it may I have *done* a deal of company this week—and talked— Oh good heavens—*such* a quantity! *You* would have been perfectly *terrified* at my *liveliness* had you been by—but those, who have had the benefit of it, have seen in it, the simple souls, only a most sudden return to good health and good spirits—on which they cannot sufficiently compliment and congratulate me! At a dinner party at the Wedgwoods[3] on Tuesday Miss Darwin,[4] who was there, said to me

7. TC thought the new baby was a girl. John Carlyle wrote, 12 June: "Alick's youngest child is a *boy* & Mr. Tait is to be here to-day to christen him *Alexander* & Jamie's girl *Jenny.*"

JWC-JW, [27 May]. Addr: 20 Maryland Street / Liverpool. PM: Liverpool, 28 May [1843]. MS: NLS 1891.292. Pbd: Huxley, *JWCLF* 126–29 inc., where dated 28 May; Bliss *JWC* 117–19 inc.

1. Ninon de Lenclos (1620–1705), beautiful and witty Frenchwoman who had many celebrities as lovers and whose salon was frequented by famous men of letters.

2. Untraced, possibly Harriet, countess of Essex, 2d wife of 4th earl of Essex, widowed 1799, d. 1821, aged 86.

3. Hensleigh and Frances.

4. Erasmus Darwin had four sisters, two unmarried: Susan Elizabeth (1803–66) and Emily Catherine (1810–66).

before I came away—"*Mrs* Scott[5] and I have just been remarking to one-another that everybody that has sat next *you* thro the evening has been one after another in incessant fits of laughter!— What a comfort it must be to have the consciousness of being so entertaining"! An immense comfort to be sure! especially when one has the additional comfort of having just made a person one likes and wishes well to, extremely miserable (for *the time* being) in the abstract cause of *virtue*

Well! John Sterling has given me a German novel by Tiek—*Vittoria Accorombona*—which contains a woman he said "exactly after my own heart" I was curious to see *his* ideal of a woman after *my* heart—and so far as I have gone which is but some eighty pages I find he has made a wonderfully good hit![6] Poor John! he has recovered his spirits with a rapidity! "You will see," says Helen while clearing away the breakfast things the other morning "that M*r* John Sterling will very soon be married again!—but indeed I dont, for *my* part, think there is any *love* in the world now a-days like what used to long ago!— If one hears of it at all it is just *momentary and away! There* was *No 4* how soon *she* got over the death of *her* lover!— And Mr Brimlecombe, the milkman was married seven months after *his* wife's death![7]— But I I[8] do think" she resumed after some interruption of dusting "that M*r* Carlyle *will be* (admire the tense!) a very *desultory widow!* he is so *easily put about*—and seems to take no pleasure *in new females"!*— Yes! there is one *new female* in whom he takes a vast of pleasure, Lady Harriet Bahring[9]

I have always ommitted to tell you how marvellously that *liason* has gone on. Geraldine seemed horribly *jealous* about it—nay almost "*scandalized*"—while she was here—for my part, I am singularly inac-

5. Ann Scott, b. Ker (d. 1888), wife of Alexander Scott; see 10:31.

6. Ludwig Tieck (1773–1853), *Vittoria Accorombona* (Breslau, 1840), about a highly intellectual woman married to a nonentity but later, after his murder, able to marry the man she loves. After Sterling's return to Falmouth, Caroline Fox noted, 29 May, that "he dwelt with delight on Mrs. Carlyle's character—such hearty sympathy in the background, and such brilliant talent in front; if it were merely 'eternal smart' with her, it would be very tiresome, but she is a woman as well as a clever person. She and her husband, though admiring each other very much, do not in all things thoroughly sympathise; he does not pay that attention to little things on which so much of a woman's comfort depends" (Fox 181).

7. Nextdoor neighbor at 4 Cheyne Row. William Brimlecombe, dairyman, 26 Laurence St., Chelsea, is presumably the young man who m. Mrs. Wright, the "large Dairywoman," and who was supposedly inconsolable when she d., Nov. 1842; see 15:190.

8. Thus in MS.

9. Spelling probably intentional as the name was often pronounced with the broad "a."

cessable to jealousy, and am pleased rather that he has found *one* agreeable house to which he likes to go and goes regularly—one evening in the week at least—and then he visits them at their "Farm" on Sundays. and their[10] are flights of charming little notes always coming to create a pleasing titillation of the philosophic Spirit!— M*rs* Buller in her graceful quizzical way insisted I should "see a little into the thing with my own eyes," and promised to give me notice the first time she knew beforehand of the Intellectual Circe's coming to her house— And accordingly M*r* Buller came last Monday[11] to ask me to meet her that evening at tea at seven oclock— She is in *delicate health* you may remember and not up to parties or late hours— I said at once yes—and appointed him to bring the carriage for me at half after six— He was not long gone—when it flashed thro my mind that a whole bevy of Americans male and female were coming *here* to tea by invitation at seven— —D*r* Howe the man who puts souls into people blind and deaf and dumb—you would read about him and his Laura B[r]idgman in *Dicken's Notes*[12]—his wife—a M*r* Mann and *his* wife and a Miss *Peabody*[13]— What to do?—I posted off to Chester Place to explain the necessity of my giving up the Lady Harriet for that time. But the Bullers would not hear of it—"it was my husband not *me* all these Americans were coming to stare at— I would simply pour out the tea for them—and if I spilled it or committed any awkwardness they would go home and *put it in a book*"!—there was truth in these suggestions[14] and finally it was agreed that M*r* Buller should still bring the carriage for me, and unless Carlyle made violent resistance, should snatch me away like Proserpine out of the American environment! C was at first quite furious at the project—but I got the better of him by saying "Well then there will be nothing for it but to let M*r* Buller when he

10. Thus in the MS; "ommitted" and "liason" also thus. The farm was Addiscombe.

11. 22 May. Charles Buller lived at 2 Chester Pl.; his parents were staying with him.

12. Letter omitted. For Dr. S. G. Howe's education of the blind deaf-mute Laura Bridgman (1829–89) and Dickens's account of it in *American Notes,* see 15:142.

13. Horace Mann (1796–1859), educator, had m., 1 May, his 2d wife, Mary Peabody (1806–87), educator and author. They had sailed for England on the *Britannia* in early May with the Howes and Mrs. Howe's youngest sister, Annie Ward. JWC was not clear about the relationship and perhaps thought that she was Mrs. Mann's sister, Elizabeth Peabody, mentioned by Emerson in his letter of 29 April, in which he also spoke of Mann as "little known to me, but greatly valued as a philanthropist in this state." Emerson gave Mann a letter of intro. to TC, 30 April, and asked him to deliver a copy of *The Dial* (Slater, *CEC* 343–44).

14. As by Catherine M. Sedgwick in her comments on the Carlyles; see 13:250, 252.

comes *stay here*"—the idea of *that*—the deafness & the trumpet was worse than anything—so he told me "in Heaven's name to do anything rather than introduce such an element into the concern"—

Happily M*r* B came first—and off I went in cold blood—leaving C to pour out the tea himself and make what excuses of me he pleased![15]— I do not remember when I did such a spirited thing or one which I so little repent of doing— *I* have no reason to study politeness with the Americans.— But Lady Harriet!— I liked her on the whole—she is immensely *large*—might easily have been one of the *ugliest* women living—but *is* almost beautiful—simply thro the intelligence and cordiality of her expression— I saw nothing of the impertinence and hauteur which people impute to her—only a certain *brusquerie* of manner which seemed to me to proceed from exuberant spirits and absence of all affectation— She is unquestionably very clever—just the wittiest woman I have seen—but with many aristocratic prejudices—which I wonder *Carlyle* should have got over so completely as he seems to have done—in a word I take her to be a very loveable spoilt Child of Fortune—that a little *whipping*, judiciously administered would have made into a first rate woman—we staid till eleven and as there were no other strangers, I had ample opportunity of estimating the amount of her seductions— — What *she* thought of *me* I should rather like to know—she took prodigious looks at me from time to time— In the *last* note to Carlyle inviting him to Addiscombe for next Sunday she says— "I meditate paying my respects to M*rs* Carlyle—so soon as I am again making visits— She is *a reality* whom you have hitherto *quite suppressed.*"

15. Julia Ward Howe wrote of the visit: "my husband was kept at home by a severe headache, but Mr. and Mrs. Mann, my sister, and myself drove out to Chelsea. . . . In receiving us he apologized for his wife, who was also suffering from headache and could not appear. In her absence I was requested to pour tea. . . . As I filled and refilled his cup, I thought that his chronic dyspepsia was not to be wondered at. . . . The conversation was mostly a monologue. Mr. Carlyle spoke with a strong Scottish accent, and his talk sounded to me like pages of his writings. He had recently been annoyed by some movement tending to the disestablishment of the Scottish Church. . . . 'That auld Kirk of Scotland! To think that a man like Johnny Graham [Sir James Graham, home sec.], should be able to wipe it out with a flirt of his pen!' Charles Sumner was spoken of, and Mr. Carlyle said, 'Oh yes; Mr. Sumner was a vera dull man, but he did not offend people, and he got on in society here.' Carlyle's hair was dark, shaggy, and rather unkempt; his complexion was sallow, with a slight glow of red on the cheek; his eye was full of fire. . . . Mr. Mann expressed great disappointment with our visit. He did not feel . . . that we had seen the real Carlyle at all. I insisted that we had" (*Reminiscences 1819–1899* 96–97). Mann was to say afterward that he was pleased with "the genuine, boyish, unrestrained heartiness of his [TC's] laugh" (Mary P. Mann, *Life of Horace Mann* [Boston, 1888] 180). Charles Sumner (1811–74; see 10:29) was a friend of S. G. Howe.

Mazzini is all in a worry about a concert he is getting up for the Italian school[16]—indeed he has been of late so over head and ears in what Richard Milnes would call "beastly little businesses" that I get next to no good of him— I never saw a mortal man who so completely made himself into "minced meat for the universe!

Your letter came since I began to write—my poor Uncle— I do wish to heaven that the weather would mend for him— I am excessively glad that Maggie's neck is healing—these things are sometimes very difficult to get over—why *will* young ladies be m[eddli?]g and mending at *themselves*— I could tell you a story about a *pimple* if I had time and paper which would make your blood run cold—(if that were not superfluous)

Bless you my love— Remember me to all

Your own J C

I will exert myself about the picture frame M*r* Hick was off to Liverpool again before I received your letter— What a good innocent soul he looks[17]

TC TO JOHN A. CARLYLE

Chelsea, Monday, 29 May, 1843

Dear Brother,

Your Letter from Dumfries,[1] as you will have inferred, came safe to hand; but there has no second arrived hitherto, so that I am partly in the dark as to your address in these hours. I write to Dumfries as the likeliest.

On Saturday, hard upon five o'clock, in a very hasty, half-wet and wearied, muddy condition, I wrote, on the Counter of a Stationer in Pimlico,[2] a word of announcement to you that the Cigar-box (the smaller, a very light one) and the Canadian Book[3] were under way: I had just been depositing them with the Strand Booksellers,[4] and

16. The evening school for poor Italian boys; see 15:119–20. For the previous concerts, see 15:183–84, 187–88.

17. A Liverpool artist; see 15:200, when JWC asked Jeannie to send him to visit her.

TC-JAC, 29 May. MS: NLS 512.4. Hitherto unpbd.

1. He had written from Dumfries, 19 May, and then from Scotsbrig, 23 May, when he said he would probably write next "from Dumfries."

2. Between Chelsea and Westminster.

3. By J. S. Buckingham; see TC to [JSB], 16 May. John Carlyle had asked TC, 23 May, to send it and the cigars.

4. Chapman & Hall.

then attending a Yearly Meeting of the London Library,[5] and doing manifold *etceteras;* the Packet, I suppose, will be in Edinburgh, at least in Leith Roads, tonight; and as "speed" also was written on it, probably it may arrive at James Aitken's by Coach on Wednesday. The Book is of no moment to me, if you can turn it to any account whatever.

What you say of Alick is naturally very interesting to me. On the whole, it may be admitted that, if he is resolved to go to Canada, he is wise in his circumstances to get thro' it at once, and not to spend another season in reconnoitring: it will all be a confusion, when once practically begun, after never so much reconnoitring. I have good hopes of Alick yet; and am heartily sad of heart about him,—if sadness availed anything. It is the best chance I see anywhere open for him, this of Canada; a new free field, where many of his talents will come into wholesome play, and a fresh purpose and hope will arise in him again, after so long and sad an abeyance. You speak of £300 to lie ready for him when he reaches the new Country:[6] is that enough, the *fittest* sum one could afford him? Whatever sum you find, on investigation, to be best, I will cheerfully go halves with you in it. On Friday or Saturday I wrote to Alick himself to that effect. I shall be anxious now to learn what he is doing since Wednesday last, and how the matter shapes itself for him and those interested. Does he mean to bend towards Brantford and our Brother John? Or will he not go by Canandaigua, and Clow and Greig?[7] I had an American Mr Colman,[8] an agricultural missionary of some distinction, sent hither to me by Greig on Saturday night last: I could write to Greig freely if Alick liked it. Canandaigua, they all say, is a beautiful place; but I think there is said to be some *aguish* ground about it: this is one of the

5. After a committee meeting TC had attended the annual gen. meeting, at which were reported an addition of 4,000 vols. to the library, an increasing membership, and a balance of £230 after spending £1,538.

6. John Carlyle said, 23 May, that Alexander "will have money enough . . . left to pay all his debts at Ecclefechan & his passage out. Some three Hundred Pounds more remitted to Canada will give him a fair trial." His stock was sold, 24 May, for between £80 and £100, leaving "only some very trifling debts to pay" (JAC to TC, [31 May]).

7. Alexander Carlyle went first to Canandaigua, then to Brantford, where their half-brother, John Carlyle, lived. For this and Robert Clow, see next letter. John Greig (1779–1858), lawyer and banker, Grace Welsh's old friend, had emigrated, 1797; see 8:297.

8. Henry Colman (1785–1849), American unitarian minister and agricultural writer; went to England, April 1843, and spent three and a half years studying agricultural conditions of Britain; on Continent, 1846–48, also studying agriculture; author of *European Agriculture and Rural Economy from Personal Observation,* 2 vols. (1844–48) and *Agriculture and Rural Economy in France, Belgium, Holland and Switzerland* (1848).

prime things to be *avoided* at all rates.— My poor Mother, she will need all your support at present; for her imagination too will greatly aggravate the matter: it is now no such business going to America; America is in very fact *nearer* to us at present than London was fifty years ago. O be kind to our good old Mother,—and say all that is kind to her good ever-loving heart: no Mother has deserved better of children than she of us. Are you sure this driving up and down, in such weather (if your weather be like ours) is not too much for her?[9]— I reconcile myself to her arrangement about Scotsbrig for another year. She might have a Cottage made out of that old wrecked House, if she liked to live at Ecclefechan. It could all be made neat and trim; built fronting into the garden; divided from the others by a wall. If Jenny were with her, she might do very well. I do not think Jenny will ever get more good of Hanning;—but she too must be convinced of that by better evidence first.[10] I long to hear from you what turn all things take in poor Annandale, with the good souls that are still there for us.

That blue Letter came from Varnhagen last week: there are others besides, but they are not worth stuffing in. Today there has one come from Cavaignac, one from Thomas Spedding, which latter I may send to you, when once I am sure of your address. *Hat* WENIG *zu bedeuten* [It matters little].

On Wednesday night I did go to Bunsen's: he stood at the stair's head, red as the Northwest Moon, an assiduous hospitable man; his soiree was laid out according to the first-rate style of Art, his rooms luminous as the summer sun, and "all the world and his wife"[11] parading gallantly there. There were whole regiments of quality ladies young and old, they came floating and flocking on towards the music room, literally whole shoals of peeresses in esse or posse [actually or potentially]; a tremendous Turk also was there, in full costume; and in short *everybody*,—from Henry Chorley up to the Duchess of Suther-

9. John Carlyle had been driving his mother back and forth between the Gill and Dumfries (staying overnight), and Ecclefechan and Scotsbrig. He wrote, 19 May: "Our mother is better for the movement." Mary Austin, at the Gill, had just had another da., and Jean Aitken, at Dumfries, had just moved house.

10. John wrote, 19 May: "There are two good rooms at the Gill which Mary is anxious they should occupy, & Jamie wishes our mother to remain at Scotsbrig getting one of Mary's girls when Jenny was away to remain with her. I suppose Jenny has hardly given up hopes of her absurd husband & that introduces an element of unrest which is difficult to manage." On 23 May he confirmed that their mother was "averse to Dumfries, & inclined to pass the winter here," at Scotsbrig, and "the summer at the Gill," as "the old house in Ecclefechan" was "a total wreck" and "irreparable."

11. Swift, *Polite Conversation,* Dialogue 3. John had encouraged TC, 13 May, to "go & see Bunsen. You will find more in him than you expect."

land! It was at last a perfect squeeze; and the music (Mendelsohn's *Antigone*),[12] which seemed very beautiful, could no more be heard than if you had sung it in the inside of a carding-mill. I saw a good many people whom it was pleasant to salute and speak a little with; and towards midnight, at the very crown of the game, I hustled on my *Tweed*, and walked home, smoking a cheeroot under the peaceable stars. I mean to call for Mrs Bunsen in due course. No *Rask* has yet arrived: and now Brandis[13] undertakes to write "to Koopenhagen" for a Danish one. Brandis has only been once here for the last fortnight, owing to influenza: he is decidedly *fabulous;* a pleasant enough, but rather indifferently conditioned man.— Our Library Meeting, in the close foul air, was a real oppression to me; I left it half done.

Jean got two Newspapers from me, which contained insignificant reviews of *Past and Present*. If you *are* at Dumfries, remember me affectionately to them all;—and ask for the N*o* of their new House.[14] I would have written to my Mother; but fancying you always beside her, this seems *hers* as well as yours. It was right good, that kindness to Mary![15]— My love to one and all

Your affectionate / T. Carlyle

TC TO ALEXANDER CARLYLE

Chelsea, 31 May, 1843—

My dear Brother,

Your Letter which arrived yesterday (Tuesday) is very sorrowful; yet at the same time resolute, sincere, and on the whole ought to be of good omen to us. A new Note from me can do nothing more than express anew my deep fellow-feeling with you; my exhortation and encouragement to go on bravely, and in this your difficult position to quit you like a man! We have often sore afflictions laid on us, which turn out to be the highest blessings when the results of them are summed

12. Henry Fothergill Chorley (1808–72; *DNB*); see 9:330. Harriet Elizabeth Georgiana (1806–68; *DNB*), duchess of Sutherland; see 12:160. Felix Mendelssohn-Bartholdy (1809–47) composed incidental music to Sophocles' *Antigone* (1841).

13. Possibly Christian August Brandis (1790–1867), German classical philologist and historian of philosophy, a friend of Bunsen's, on a visit from Bonn, where he was prof. of philosophy.

14. The Aitkens had moved, 18 May, to Assembly St., which John said, 19 May, was "much more comfortable than the other in English Street."

15. John Carlyle had given the Austins "two bushels of corn & a good cart load of clover hay which were much wanted for the horses" (23 May).

TC-AC, 31 May. MS: MUL. Pbd: Marrs 557–58.

up. You have had a dreary time of it for many years;[1] and things without and things within have gone far awry: you are now called as it were to make a revolution, a radical reform; and that is no easy business! But by Heaven's favour it may be a most blessed one. I say often I have known no man so wasted, fettered, and sunk in deep imprisonments as my poor Brother Alick; one of the bravest of men too;—but deficient in *patience,* in candor of self-examination; too *violent,* on the whole, for making his way thro' quagmires, and rough boggy ground! My dear Brother, it will be the joyfullest thing that can befal me to hear that you have gained new life and virtue, in these sore trials; that you have risen into victory at last, after all this fighting. It is a change not to be effected without pain, without agony of heart; but it is cheap at any price of pain; it is great and blessed, if it happened in the lowest cottage in Earth; it is a thing well-pleasing in the sight of God and man, and is *sure* of its exceeding great reward! I forbear to *speak* farther; for I have often felt that my silence was more eloquent than anything I could say.

Canada is very vague to you; and unluckily I can throw no practical light on it. If John do not write, did it never strike you to look in by Clow, who I think is in New-York State,—perhaps not far from the road to Hamilton?[2] I could give you a good Letter to Greig, tho' I think the last failed of an answer. It is represented as a pleasant region (one ought to see also, whether wholesome or not), and more cultivated and settled than upper Canada. But a man that *can* till the Earth, what has he to dread when there is free Earth offered him to cultivate, and God's sky and blessing spread over his head? There is something manful and heroic in taking one's stand on that Ground; saying, "I will appeal to nobody, but to the Maker over me; *He* will prosper me, if I do follow His appointments!" I flatter myself with thinking that all your qualities and talents will come out in this new

1. A. Carlyle wrote in his "Jottings": "There was no prospect of his ever making with his utmost energy more than a bare living out of his business, in such a small village. Some years before this he had lost most of his small patrimony in farming Craigenputtock, which was in those days rented far too dear and had to be lowered to a considerable extent for the succeeding tenant. It was in those days, and is now, mainly a sheep farm, only a few small patches of it being cultivatable. . . . After leaving Craigenputtock my Father tried various other things, among them one or two of the best of the farms then offered; but nothing could be made of them; so as a last resort he went to Ecclefechan" (MS: NLS 739).

2. Robert Clow, Janet Carlyle's cousin, had emigrated, 1837, and rented a farm belonging to John Greig at Alton, N.Y., 30 mi. E of Rochester and ca. 15 mi. N of the road to Hamilton. Alexander and his family stayed there from 30 July to March 1844, when they moved to nr. Brantford, Ontario, where John Carlyle had settled.

employment far better than they have ever hitherto done. Your children, your little Jane, will be a great treasure to you, yearly growing more *valuable* in every sense of the word;—how different from the case of children here, in this country which seems *doomed*. Courage, my dear Brother; stand up to the task, and you *will* find it *doable:* "all tasks are like swimming"; the water threatens to drown one; yet dash fearlessly abroad in it, it does not drown you![3] I augur much good, as the fruit of all these sufferings. Men are not *made anew,* and reformed into health and life of soul again, without terrible sufferings! Your Brother's affection, his remembrance of your affection to him, remains to you (know this always) while he continues on this Earth.— And so I will say no more,—if I have not even already said too much.

The Tobacco, I begin to imagine, was *half* a stone, not a *quarter*? In that case, I owe the little Baby a sovereign still for a frock to her. God's blessing be on you all. Your affectionate,

T. Carlyle

TC TO [HENRY DRUMMOND]

5. Cheyne Row, Chelsea / 3 june, 1843—

My dear Sir,

Thanks for your kind renewal of the invitation to Albury.[1] I am very weakly, indeed unwell, or possibly you might have heard of me sooner. At present I wait daily for some symptom of steady weather to run off to the coast of Glamorganshire, where a friend[2] has provided some hut or altogether solitary lodging for me, that I may collect myself again a little, in conversation with the mere Winds and Seas. These always tell a true story to one, if a somewhat indistinct one!

I shall hope to look towards Guil[d]ford[3] again on some happier occasion; and in the meanwhile do very sincerely wish all blessings to you and yours there.

With many thanks, with much regard, I remain always,

Truly yours, / T. Carlyle

3. Cf. *Wilhelm Meister's Travels, Works* 24:321.

TC-[HD], 3 June. MS: EUL. Hitherto unpbd. Addressee identified by the invitation to Albury, where Drummond lived.

1. See TC to [HD], 20 Jan. and 26 Jan.
2. Charles Redwood.
3. Letter omitted. Albury is nr. Guildford.

TC TO JOHN JOHNSTONE

5. Cheyne Row, Chelsea / 4 june, 1843–

My dear Sir,

"The British Authors Society," I much fear, is little other than a devout imagination. My own knowledge of it, tho' I find my name circulating as seconder of motions &c, is about as good as none at all: I attended once for ten minutes, in a Tavern at Charing Cross,[1] a company of some thirty very ugly men, not above three of whom were known to me; I did admit in a whisper, in answer to the "Hon. Secretary's" whisper, That thing Sir L. Bulwer[2] said appeared to have reason in it;—and thereupon, little edified by the physiognomy of the business, I took my hat and glided away, without intention to return. Since that, about a month ago, I formally declined putting my name among the members,[3] and have heard nothing of it farther.

My decided idea is that "Authors" will associate, and become a most stupendous Body Corporate, one day, and the Chief of all Bodies Corporate: but it will be, I think, as indeed I have written somewhere, "when they *cease* to be a *Canaille*"; not while they continue one, does it seem very possible! Hunt merely for pudding or praise, we have, like all animals of *prey*, to do it in a solitary manner. Solitude and hunting are two things that go together.— "Authors," it seems to me, are somewhat difficult to lay hold of, and define, in these days: not all who talk with Printer's Types are *Authors* now! On the whole, I will not recommend my brave Mrs Johnstone to disturb herself with this affair, unless it assume some other aspect than the present one.[4]

We are very glad to exchange a salutation once more with you and her, tho' only on this "imagination." I remember you both, with the liveliest distinctness, with the utmost good will; and always shall, I believe. My Wife joins heartily with me in all kind regards and wishes. "Success!— Courage, with or without success!"

Yours very sincerely / T. Carlyle

TC-JJ, 4 June. Addr: 12. Comely Bank / Edinburgh. MS: NLS 1796.63. Pbd: *Glasgow Herald*, 16 Nov. 1912, p. 10. John Johnstone, Edinburgh ed. and printer; see 7:163.

1. British Hotel, Cockspur St., 25 March.
2. Sir Edward Lytton Bulwer.
3. See TC to [JR], 1 May.
4. Christian Isobel Johnstone (1781–1857; *DNB*), novelist and ed. of *Tait's Edinburgh Magazine*, where *Past and Present* was reviewed in the June number, pp. 339–48, signed "B" (J. S. Blackie).

JWC TO JEAN CARLYLE AITKEN

[early summer 1843]

the Liberty of looking at for nothing—but a woman started from behind them to demand "3 pence each"—"she rented them from the Proprietor"— There is nothing that certain Proprietors will not make money of—if they can!

What you say of my coming to Scotland is very kind—Isabella too has sent me the heartiest invitations—and I should like so well to see you all again— But when I try to fancy myself on the road—to fancy myself *there*—every thing the same for me *there* as it used to be, and beyond nothing of all that used to be—I feel so sick at heart, and so afraid of encountering the pain that seeing all those places again and going about like a gohst in them would cause me—that I can do no otherwise but say I will not go. It looks very cowardly to you—this? perhaps too, unkind and ungrateful towards the living—but try to fancy yourself in my place—looking out on hills at the back of which there had so lately lain a little loving *home* for you—where your mother had ran to meet you with such joy—and now nothing for you there but the silence of Death— If you do not feel that you would be just as weak at least you will understand how I might be so without unkindness— If I were going beside your Mother and all of you, I should think myself bound to be cheerful and to look as if I were happy among you— and until I know myself *up* to that is it not right to stay away? at present it seems to me I could do nothing in Scotsbrig or Dumfries but cry from morning till night— All this is excessively weak— I am quite aware of that—and if anybody will show me a way of being stronger I will follow it to my best ability—but merely telling me or telling myself to be stronger is of no use— Ever your affectionate

Jane Carlyle

JWC TO JEANNIE WELSH

[8 June 1843]

So! young Lady! You must have been *living fast*—since you have been so slow to write!— As Harriet Martineau says of me I am "dreadful at

JWC-JCA, [early summer]. MS: NLS 602.99 inc.; longhand copy with TC's notes: Berg inc. Pbd: Froude, *LM* 1:185–86 inc. On the MS TC later noted: "(early sum̄er 1843)." On the copy he wrote: "To Mrs. Aitken Dumfries," "Chelsea," "Frag*t* (very mournful), first small half of it lost"; and he also made some minor corrections of the copy, not noted.

JWC-JW, [8 June]. Addr: 20 Maryland Street / Liverpool—. PM: 8 June 1843. MS: NLS 1892.1. Pbd: Huxley, *JWCLF* 129–31 inc., where dated 9 June.

drawing inferences"!— You *have* written at last however—and you will say perhaps it was not your turn—that I owed you a letter— Bah, Debtor-and-creditor-accounts between you and me are a thing not to be spoken of— Had you been in your "normal state" my silence would only have been an additional reason for your writing to me. you would have felt a *besoin* to know why I did not write— Well!—I did not write because literally I *could not*— I took into the doing of good works like Mazzini one day—rushed about from two in the forenoon till near eight at night—without having eaten from eight in the morning—*verifying* a case of extreme misery[1]—preparatory to exerting myself for its alleviation—and the result—"virtues reward" as usual was a severe attack of rheumatism in the head and shoulders which kept me lying several days on the flat of my back—and which is not entirely removed even now—for I am still obliged to move myself *all of a piece*—and my head feels as if it had been pounded in a mortar— Mazzini too has been and is very ill—an abscess inside his cheek—headach of several days standing and fever— I am very unquiet about him for in that accursed Tancioni establishment there is no help for a person who is incapacitated from helping himself— He persists too in declining to send for a Dr— But I have written to that Dr Toynbee who has shewn himself so friendly towards him[2]—stating his melancholy predicament—and urging him to lose no time in going to his assistance— Mazzini will be angry at me for this but no matter—if he be the sooner recovered.

In fact it has been all going ill for the last week—the only consolation a letter from Cavaignac—to Carlyle—but containing some precious words for *me*— He is not coming—cannot come—has to go to Africa his brother's health making him *"inquiete de nouveau"* [uneasy again] and being besides "pauvre comme Job" [poor as Job]—but he says *"je voudrais bien vous voir; voir madame, bonne et noble àme s'il en fut!"*[3]—and Madame is almost as content as if he had come!— And the letter ends with "Adieu, chère dame, je declare que de vous on peut dire *bien!* toute mortelle que vous soyez. je me suis dit plus d'une fois, depuis que je [v]ous ai quitée: par le ciel, il n'y a pas sur cette terre trois femmes comme celle-la! adieu tous deux—Madame une lettre![4]—now

1. That of the Mudies; see JWC to JW, [15 June].

2. Joseph Toynbee (1815–66; *DNB*), aural surgeon, currently surgeon to the St. James's and St. George's Dispensary, living at 12 Argyll Pl.; an early supporter of the Italian Free School.

3. "I should like very much to see you; to see Madame, good and noble soul if it could be." Col. Louis Eugène Cavaignac (1802–57; see 9:91), Godefroy's brother, was serving in Algeria.

4. "Farewell, dear lady, I declare that one can say of you *excellent*, mortal though you be. I have said to myself more than once since I left you: by heaven,

such words from any other man might be mere *words*—and I should not care rigmaree for them—but from *him!*— Ah c'est autre chose [Ah that's something else]! *he* never praises except as it were *on compulsion.* If it were not for this confounded stiff neck and aching shoulder I would tell you my case of distress, which moved me to such energetic doings ending in sufferings—but it is long—and I should not like to curtail it for the exigence of the occasion so I leave it for a future letter— If you do not hear from me for some days do not fancy me worse—but only that I am working at *that*—for I *must* raise a hundred pounds or so for this starving family—who seem to me to have quite as good a claim on the public as many who are getting what is called "*Testimonials*" to the extent of thousands of pounds.[5]

Poor dear Maggie! she seems to be as stupid as—myself! give her six kisses from me. if they might but be of any comfort to her! My love to all the rest—also to Walter—pray tell him that I should have written to him ere now but for these "ills that flesh is heir to"[6]—tell him also that the *shag* tobacco he sent to Carlyle is the best he ever had—but he has a great many different kinds on hand at present and will not need more for a good while

Your own
[no signature]

TC TO JOHN FORSTER

[ca. 10 June 1843]

Dear Forster,—I blush for myself; I did mean to write to you, however, and should have done it, in about an hour hence. Patience and shuffle the cards![1]

---

there are not three women on earth like that one! Farewell to you both—Madame a letter!" JWC wrote "jous" for "vous."

5. A "Testimonial of Esteem" for Harriet Martineau in appreciation of her "valuable public services" and "exalted motives" had been advertised, 3 June, in the *Athenaeum.* Darwin, W. E. Hickson, Robertson, and Wedgwood were among those listed as receiving contributions (which came to over £1,358) to be "left entirely to the disposal of Miss Martineau." A testimonial in the form of a piece of silver plate valued at £500 was presented to W. C. Macready, 19 June, to honor his efforts "to elevate the National Drama."

6. Cf. *Hamlet* 3.1.

TC-JF, [ca. 10 June]. MS: FC. Hitherto unpbd. Dated by TC's promise to give Forster his MS for the article on Dr. Francia "within the next ten days," i.e., roughly 20 June, about four days before the *Foreign Quarterly Review,* in which TC's essay appeared (31 [July 1843]:544–89) and of which Forster was ed., went to press.

1. *Don Quixote* 2, ch. 23.

It will be shameful to write on Dr Francia, when one really *has* and can have nothing but a kind of *balderdash* to write about him:—and yet, on the other hand, after all this higgling and hanging off and on, it will be very shameful *not* to write about him![2] Yesterday, after some painful reflexion, I decided that the *latter* shame was the greater; and accordingly here I am this morning, probing for some footway thro' endless quagmires,—in fact actually writing (and *blotting*, so it must go for a time) about 'Dr F.' or 'S. America,' or Heaven knows what: about *something* I will give you from 16 to 20 pages within the next ten days: I have said it,—for my sins and yours! And so adieu, and say not a word of it!

Ever yours (in great affliction)
T. Carlyle

TC TO CHAPMAN & HALL

To Messrs Chapman & Hall.

The purport of the Order, which it seems your man has lost, was for a Copy of Dr M'Cormac's *Methodus Medendi* from the Messrs Longman.[1] The Doctor was here, and wrote it out for me.

T. Carlyle

Chelsea, 13 june, 1843—

JWC TO HENRY COLMAN

[14 June 1843]

My dear Mr Colman

No! I would not alter you even to the extent of introducing a new letter into your name! As the Duke of Wellington "found the English Constitution so perfect that he should despair of making any improve-

2. See TC to JF, 12 May and 17 May. On 5 June TC borrowed from the London Lib. Charles M. de La Condamine, *Relation abrégée d'un Voyage fait dans l'Intérieur de l'Amérique méridionale . . . en descendant la Rivière des Amazones* (Maestricht, 1778), cited "Dr. Francia," *Works* 29:279.

TC-C&H, 13 June. MS: Yale. Hitherto unpbd. Someone, possibly TC, has written "30/—" at the bottom of the letter.

1. Henry M'Cormac (1800–86; *DNB*), Belfast physician; graduated M.D. at Edinburgh, 1824, two years before John Carlyle; *Methodus Medendi; or, the Description and Treatment of the Principal Diseases Incident to the Human Frame* (1842), pbd. by Longman, Brown, Green and Longmans.

JWC-HC, [14 June]. MS: Strouse. Hitherto unpbd. Dated by TC to AC, 17 June, in which TC, writing on Sat., tells that Colman had been to Cheyne Row "last night," i.e., the "Friday evening" for which JWC here invites him.

ment on it."[1]—the *'e'* was a quite *"unconst[itu]ion[al]"*[2] piece of presumption on my part—

For the rest, will you come here on Friday evening?—the Mackintoshes have offered themselves for "any evening this week" and I have just written to them appointing Friday[3]—deferring "the good the Gods have provided me"[4] thus long to give myself the better chance of having it increased by a provision of my own viz: *you*—

Now dont be going to a lecture!

Affectionately yours
Jane Carlyle

5 Cheyne Row
Wednesday Morning

TC TO ALEXANDER CARLYLE

Chelsea, Wednesday Evg [14 June 1843]

Dear Brother,

I have written to you at the "Post-Office, Liverpool," today; but I find, on computing, that the Money Order must go off tonight also, or you will not get it in time for Friday,—perhaps. I will take it up into the region of the General Post tonight.— As £500 is the sum agreed on, I here send you my full half of it (£250) according to original intention. May it be a blessing where it is going!

Unless there be some great haste, you had better let me speak to Colman before you dispose of it thro' any Bank. Colman is the American from Canadaigua.[1]

I have written to Mr Adamson of the Irish Street Bank,[2] that he is

1. The Duke of Wellington had said to the House of Lords, 2 Nov. 1830, that he "was fully convinced that the country possessed at the present moment a legislature which answered all the good purposes of legislation, and this to a greater degree than any legislature ever had answered in any country whatever (*laughter on the left of the house*)" (*Times*, 4 Nov., 1830).

2. Letters omitted.

3. Probably Robert James Mackintosh (1806–64), Mary Rich's half-brother and Frances Wedgwood's brother (see 10:238), and his wife, Mary (1813–89; see 13:159).

4. Cf. Dryden, "Alexander's Feast" 106.

TC-AC, [14 June]. MS: MUL. Pbd: Marrs 569, where tentatively dated 21 June. Dated by the proposal to talk to Henry Colman about money matters "on Friday Evening," which TC reports having done "last night" (Fri.) in TC to AC, 17 June.

1. Thus in MS. TC regularly but not invariably misspells Canandaigua.

2. Robert Adamson (d. 1861), manager of the Dumfries branch of the British Linen Bank; see 10:23.

not to pay the money to any but *yourself,* to avoid mistakes.— I will lose no time in seeing Colman. Probably on Friday Evening. You will in that case hear the result by Saturdays Post.

I ought also to take care of not missing the Post for America! I will buy that "shilling book" you talked of,[3] this very night at the Post-Office, if they have it.

My affectionate regards to Jean and her Household; my blessings to all.

Ever your affectionate / T. Carlyle

JWC TO JEANNIE WELSH

[15 June 1843]

Here is half a sheet of *pretended* foreign paper for you Dearest—the other half is gone *only yesterday* to Cavaignac— You may think what a worry I have been in, since I have not answered even *his* pressing demand for a letter sooner!— The Devil has been in the wind for me these two or three weeks—every kind of thing that could be imagined in the shape of business and interruption has come to trouble me at one time. My *business* is still at the thickest but I may anticipate some alleviation from the interruptions—one fertile source of these embarked in a steamboat for Scotland last night—not to return these two years god willing I think I mentioned to you that Bishop Terrot was here—but you could hardly attach all the sad importance to the fact which it deserved— The man is mad I think—when I admired him long ago as *the clever man* of the place he scarcely showed any preference for me—now that I admire him no longer but on the contrary regard him as what Mazzini would call a *"self-constituted imposter"*—and have hardly patience to be reasonably civil to him for old acquaintance's sake; he seems to have *constituted me* into his *Santa Maria!*—has been coming during his stay in London at a rate which it is almost *fearful* to look back upon—staying each time three mortal hours at the least—making me all sorts of extraordinary confidences—never seeing Carlyle who *hated* him, and kept himself determinedly out of his way—and in short keeping me I will not say *in hot water*—but in a sort of *lukewarm* water even more detestable—Thank heaven he is gone at last—with his bits of black leggings and shovel-hat—and *shovel-heart and soul!* In all the arguments we had—and they were many—it seemed to me that it

3. Probably an emigrants' handbook.

JWC-JW [15 June]. Addr: 20 Mary Land Street / Liverpool. PM: Chelsea, 15 June 1843. MS: NLS 1892.5. Pbd: Huxley, *JWCLF* 131–34.

was *I* always who defended the *religious* side of the question, and he the worldly—the devil's side— —and he *dares* to go about in black leggings and call himself Bishop![1]— Bah!

Then that *german romance*—which I spoke of[2]—I am still in the third volume of it—and the *interest* (to use Godwins curious phrase) is "rather exquisite"[3]—with all my remarkable foresight I cannot predict the catastrophe—but certainly George Sand in her most impassioned moments never *wrote* any thing equal to it—you understand me?— But the engrossing business of all—my poor family[4]—Heaven and Earth! what *am* I to do with them?— I will enclose you some thing that was printed about the Father at the time of his death—about a year ago—so that I need not speak of *him*—(send me back the paper) But the family's history has been this—briefly; for it would take hours to tell it with all the *details* I know—The widow and five children, all daughters except one, a boy of fourteen—"a very bright boy" (the poor mother called him) was left quite destitute—a small subscription was raised among those they were known to which just sufficed to pay *the Undertaker's bill* of 30£—and some such like bills— Their rent was still unpaid—the Landlord put an execution in the house—and all their furniture books &c were sold for an old song— They removed into one wretched appartment for which they paid 5 shillings a-week and subsisted—or rather starved on what they could earn by sewing "slop-shirts" at a *penny-farthing a* piece—and *stitching five stays* for EIGHTPENCE! With hardship of one sort and another the Mother fell ill of Typhus fever—she recovered—but the boy—the one boy—her hope in life—caught it—lingered six weeks—died!—*another burial to pay for!* and then—a chandler with whom they had accumulated an account of 5£ during this agonizing period seized the mother—and before her

1. Charles Hughes Terrot (1790–1872; *DNB*), bishop of Edinburgh in the Episcopal Church of Scotland, 1841–72; educ. Cambridge, where he was a friend of Thomas Wilson (8:196); pastor of Haddington, 1829–33; junior minister, 1833, then rector of St. Paul's, Edinburgh, 1839; m., 1818, Sarah Ingram, b. Wood, with whom he had fourteen children. See 13:178–79, where JWC also ridiculed his hat in July 1841. "Shovel hat" signifies a clergyman; cf. 13:115.

2. Tieck's *Vittoria Accorombona;* see JWC to JW, [27 May].

3. Not traced; presumably William Godwin (1756–1836), philosopher and novelist; see 5:337.

4. The family of Robert Mudie (1777–1842), misc. writer; schoolmaster, ca. 1801–20, in Inverness and Dundee, where he took part in reform politics; moved to London, 1820, to work as a journalist; failed in a publishing venture in Winchester, ca. 1838; returned to London, ill and poor, and d. 29 April 1842, leaving his widow, son, and four das. destitute. TC thought him "a literary adventurer," his widow "foolish," and their case "abundantly piteous" but "hopeless" (Froude, *LM* 1:263).

first tears were dried for her only son—threw her into prison—*for 5£!* She lay there three weeks—desperate it would seem for she appealed to no one—a stranger a *Russian* heard tell of her case and set her free, another stranger gave her 5£ more for immediate need—and this was her situation when I first heard tell of her—

She thought that if thirty pounds were given her she could start a small school—being an educated woman—a woman that has herself written things for journals—and that by this together with needlework she and her daughters might make an independent livelihood—she talked like a *practical* wellmeaning woman—I though[t][5] one should get her *a hundred* pounds—to give her a fair start—too little would only be flung away in an impossible attempt— And I seemed in a fair way of getting it till there arose certain insinuations that she had been *improvident* in her better times—nay that she had indulged too much in stimulants—all that by the minutest investigation I have been able to ascertain to her disadvantage amounts to no more than what would be quite easily pardoned in any body but in *one who is asking help*—in matters of charity however peoples consciences are *extremely* nice! and so because in her hard labours of writing to her husband's dictation from morning till night for fifteen years—and being often very savagely used by him—and educating at the same time all her children herself—because thus situated, she *may* have been tempted to take more drink than was Lady-like— —the subscription I am told must be abandoned—can only at least be carried on among private well-wishers—and where are they? except myself and Professor Gillespie of St Andrews[6]—I know of none that trouble their heads about her— I must move heaven and earth to find situations for the girls—such of them as are fit for situations—and then they if they are good for any thing will be able to assist their Mother— Geraldine who has continued like the wonderful being she is to write me twice or thrice a week—the longest letters—without ever getting a word of answer—wrote last week to beg that I *would* send one line at least to say if I were ill—so I wrote that I was occupied—with a family in great economical affliction on this small notice she writes instantly again proposing—

Enter people— / no more time / Your own

Jane Carlyle

5. Letter omitted.

6. Thomas Gillespie (1777–1844; *DNB*), b. at Closeburn, Dumfriesshire; prof. of humanity at St. Andrews Univ. since 1835. His first wife was Elizabeth (d. 1821), da. of Dr. John Hunter, his predecessor as prof. of humanity, and an aunt of Susan Stirling (see 8:160). JWC's cousin Thomas Gillespie, of Ardarchy nr. Fort Augustus, was wrongly identified as this Thomas Gillespie at 2:279.

JWC TO JOHN STERLING

[16? June 1843]

My dear John

Thank you *passionately* for giving me *Vittoria Accorombona*—and thank you even more for knowing before hand that I should like her. Your presentiment that this was "a woman exactly after my own heart" *so* pleases *my own heart!*—proves that I am not *universally* "*a woman misunderstood*"!— But you said nothing of *the* MAN AFTER *my own heart* so that Bracciano took me by surprise, and has nearly turned my head![1] My very *beau ideal* of manhood is that Paul Giordano; could I hear of the like of him existing anywhere in these degenerate days; I would—even at this late stage of the business—send him— —my picture! and an offer of my heart and hand, for the next world—since they are already disposed of in this— Ah what a man that must be who can strangle his young beautiful wife with his own hands, and—bating one moment of conventional horror—inspire not the slightest feeling of aversion or distrust! When a man strangles his wife nowa-days he does it brutally—in drink, or in passion, or in revenge: to transact such a work coolly, nobly, on the loftiest principles—to *strangle with dignity,* because the woman "was unworthy of him"—*that* indeed is a triumph of *character,* which places this Bracciano above all the Heros of ancient or modern times! which makes me almost weep that I was not born two centuries earlier that I might have been—his mistress—*not* his *wife*![2]

But what think you befell? In the simplicity of my heart I lent the book to a friend—a *man* of course—whose hitherto-version of me has born a considerable resemblance to the *Santa Maria*—lent it too with all my marginal marks—(as Carlyle would say) "significative of much"!—and when the man brought it back he could neither look at me nor speak to me; but *blushed* and stammered as if he were in the presence of a new Godess of Reason![3] Disliking all that sort of thing I asked him plain out what ailed him? "The truth is," said he, "Mrs

JWC-JS, [16? June]. MS: NLS 602.100. Pbd: Froude, *LM* 1:192–94. Dated after 15 June, when JWC had not finished vol. 3 of *Vittoria Accorombona;* see JWC to JW, [15 June].

1. Paulo Giordano Orsini, duke of Bracciano, with whom the married Vittoria is in love, kills his wife and Vittoria's husband and later marries Vittoria.

2. The ninth edn. of the *Encyclopaedia Britannica* (New York, 1890) notes that Tieck's novel "is probably best known to English readers by Mrs Carlyle's half-earnest half-mocking admiration of the hero . . . and her wish that she could have lived two hundred years before, 'to have been—his mistress, not his wife' " (23:382).

3. Charles Terrot. JWC first wrote "Passion," then overwrote "Reason."

Carlyle—that book (looking at it askance) has—confused me! May I ask who recommended to you that Book"? "A clergyman" said I—for the first, and probably the last time in my life, recognising your sacred vocation— "John Sterling gave it to me"— "The *son*"? "Yes to be sure *the son.*" and *then* I laughed outright—and the man looked at me with a mingled expression of pity and alarm—and—changed the subject!—

I am over head and ears at present in what Carlyle anathematises as "an unfathomable puddlement of *Mudieism,*" into which I have flung myself with *my usual impetuosity,* and am *perfectly certain* to be swallowed up"— Not so the Prophet of evil! I have no fancy for playing Curtius in so obscure a cause![4] But I would fain save if possible without absolute self-sacrifice, a woman of the name of Mudie and her four daughters from committing simultaneous suicide, or dying of simultaneous starvation. You have heard perhaps of a self-taught author or artist Mudie who migrated hither from Scotland some twenty years ago and within that period wrote upwards of a hundred volumes better or worse—*Modern Athens Babylon the Great* &c &c[5]— Well he died a year ago—leaving his family destitute—a wife and five children— —they struggled on a while, sewing what is called *slop-shirts* at a penny-farthing each—and stitching fine stays at eightpence a pair! But the Mother fell ill of Typhus fever—and the son—the only son—caught it from her—lingered six weeks and died—an account of *five pounds* was accumulated during his sickness for the necessaries of life— Their furniture, books, every thing had been seized and sold for rent long before—so they seized the Mother herself—no matter that her only son was just dead—and flung her into jail—for 5£! a gentlewoman—educated—and sewing shirts at a penny-farthing a piece!— She lay in prison three weeks—quite desperate it would seem—appealing to no one—at length a stranger—a Russian—who chanced to hear the facts gave the 5£ and she was set free—to what?—an old Lady gave her five pounds more for her immediate want,—and it was at this point of her history that I heard tell of her for the first time in my life— *Esprit de corps* with the backing it is to be hoped of some natural benevolence sent me immediately in quest of her and she and her daughters have lain on my heart like so many millstones ever since. In the beginning I set about organizing a public subscription to enable her to realize her

4. Marcus Curtius, legendary Roman hero of the fourth cent., B.C., who in full armor and on horseback leapt into a chasm in the Roman Forum caused by an earthquake and thereby closed the fissure, believing that the oracle's call for the sacrifice of Rome's "chief treasure" meant that of a brave warrior.

5. *The Modern Athens* (1824), a description of Edinburgh; *Babylon the Great, A Dissection and Demonstration of Men and Things in the British Capital,* 2 vols. (1825).

utmost ambition the taking up of a little school— But alas: it comes out in the course of my investigations that she was "an improvident woman" in her better days—and still worse—that she has been *suspected*—only *suspected* observe—of paying a little secret worship to the God—that shall be nameless— All this makes no difference in my zeal to help her—but people in general have such delicate *consciences* in matters of charity— They can only give *conscientiously* to those who have led immaculate lives— This womans life has been so very hard that one may well I think abate a little from ones requisition of immaculateness—,for fifteen years together she wrote to her husbands dictation—and was savagely used by him for her pains—besides having educated all her children herself— *That* would be cried up as virtue in a woman that could still give dinners but it goes for nothing in one that needs a dinner— Oh dear dear I am bewildered what to do— The girls at all events cannot be charged with improvidence poor things, will nobody relieve one of them? Do *you* want a needle woman?—or a nurse-maid?— I have a moonbeam hope of getting one placed in Liverpool—but—in short I am in a mess of *Mudieism* and must pray your excuse for disturbing your contentment with Providence by this long tragical story— God bless you ever your affectionate Jane

TC TO JOHN GREIG AND JWC TO ALEXANDER CARLYLE

[17 June 1843]

I write at present to request a very special favour. A Brother of mine, Alexander by name, whom I love much, and am very sad indeed to part with, is about emigrating to America. He is a farmer, of the race of farmers; a man in no wise destitute of due specialties for farming; who nevertheless, like so many others, finds it a too unprosperous enterprise in this heavy-laden country; and so, after many years of hesitation, decides at length that he must go and try the business under new conditions, on your side of the sea. He has a wife and family of young children; he is still in the vigour of life (two years younger than myself); a man of short stature, but of robust force of muscle, impetuous energy of character, exceedingly expert, shifty and adroit in all kinds of rural and miscellanious labour; he will have I understand,

TC-JG and JWC-AC, [17 June]. JWC's copy of TC's MS followed by her postscript: MUL. At the top TC wrote: "Copy of the Letter to Mr Greig 17 june, 1843—" and "The first paragraph is about Mr Colman &c." Pbd: A. Carlyle, *NL* 1:292–94 inc.; Marrs 559–61 inc. This copy and the next three letters to Alexander Carlyle were mailed together.

some £500 clear money when he reaches your coasts: with these capabilities and the impartial sky over him, and the impartial earth under him, he must do the best he can! I believe I may venture to add that he is a man of real integrity and veracity; of deep affections, true-hearted honourable spirit;—intrinsically a bit of good Annandale stuff, with perhaps far more of faculty in him than has ever been developed, or in this world is ever likely to be developed now. But your neighbour Mr Clow[1] knows him well, and can give a more impartial account, tho' he also is related to him, being cousin of his wife.

My Brothers first aim was towards Upper Canada, but I have advised him to take Canadagua by the way, and pause till he have examined there. Mr Colman, whom I have consulted on the subject, votes emphatically to the same effect: my Brother determines to do so. He hopes to sail by the *Ashburton* line ship in a few days, and may reach New York probably within a month after this letter. In three days more I suppose he may be in Canadagua. He is writing by this Steamer to Mr Clow; will hope to find a letter from him lying in the Post office at New York. I will give him a Note of your address with my signature to it, in his pocket. If there be any furtherance, guidance, or honest help you can yield this Brother of mine in the present trying state of his affairs,—I only say it will be about as true a service done to me as one man can do another. There are few wishes more ardent in me than for a blessing on this Pilgrim and his wayfaring!—Mr Colman fancies he might find some temporary occupation, lease of a farm, charge of a farm, or other convenient means of duly investigating Canadagua for a year or so till he saw where to settle. This also seems to be my Brothers own notion. But I have already said enough. If there be any opportunity of helping, you on the spot will know best what opportunity,—and on various grounds I persuade myself, you will not be slow to use it. And so &c

---

My dear Alick I pray heaven that the above letter will make your difficult way somewhat smoother for you—I am sure that Mr Greig is a most kind-hearted man, and for old affections sake will feel strongly disposed to serve you. Nevertheless, in this world one's best help must lie always in oneself—as you and I and every one of our standing, with any grain of sense in his head, cannot have missed to perceive— — God go with you, and bless you wheresoever you go— I might say many things—sad, and encouraging both—but all that I might say is best

1. Robert Clow.

summed up in those three words God bless you. I will always think of you with affection and hope that you will do the same by me.

Jane Carlyle

TC TO ALEXANDER CARLYLE

Chelsea, Saturday 17 june, 1843—

My dear Brother,

We saw Mr Colman, the Canadaigua American, last night, and had a great deal of talk with him. He is a highly sensible, good-natured, well-bred man; and likely to understand this business specially well, being direct from the spot, and sent hither I believe to inquire about farm matters as a Secretary of some Agricultural society; that being his business when at home.[1]

He is clear that the Canadaigua region greatly excels the Hamilton or Upper Canada one: it is a pleasant, fertile and settled country in a higher degree than the other; it is peopled generally with farmers of a much better character (the Hamilton men being given to drink &c); it has plenty of schools, of mills, markets, is crossed both by a canal and a railway,—has plenty of cross roads too, which are hard and firm with ice in winter, with drought in summer, and "only in a slushy state for about a fortnight in autumn and some four weeks in the thaw of spring." Many of the settlers are Scotch. Farms that touch on the railway or canal have a free market for their butter, poultry &c; and all farms are within reach of a mill and miller, who buys the grain (not without competition) at a fair price. The main white-crop grown is wheat. The land generally is fertile; some of it very fertile. It seems to be in the hands partly of small farmer-proprietors; and then there are, besides Mr Greig and a "Mr Wadsworth" whom he spoke of,[2] some who have large spaces of land, which they subdivide into farms, and let in various ways, or cultivate by agents of their own. Farms, he says, are let usually from year to year; and they are to be had at all times of the year,—some of these large proprietors having always farms on hand, which they are very willing to dispose of to a tenant, rather than keep cultivating by themselves or servants. A common way (I think he said, the general way) of letting, is that the landlord furnishes his tenant with all manner of stock &c (which is valued

TC-AC, 17 June. MS: MUL. Pbd: Marrs 561–64.

1. Henry Colman had been agricultural commissioner of the state of Massachusetts; TC refers to this or some other post.

2. James Wadsworth (1768–1844) or his brother William, owners of and agents for large tracts of land in western N.Y. state since 1790.

in money, by judges appointed, at the entrance on the business); the tenant binds himself to give his landlord a certain *proportion of the produce; half* of the produce, he seemed to say, was very common; but on worse soils, it is as low as a *third:* the tenant cultivates in this way for one or more years; and then at the end has to *return* an equal value of stock, or make it up according to the finding of judges. The farms have, almost all, a portion left in wood; that being the only fuel,—I suppose, the only building material too, that lies convenient: the rest of the ground is *all* arable, and takes its due rotation: wheat, potatoes &c. You can *hire* the ploughing of your land, if you have not horses of your own; Farmers' sons and such like are willing to make a little money by doing it for you. It is very common also that a man skilled in farming and with a good character gets a place as manager (what I called "agent" above): the proprietor, living at a distance, gives him a house and provision for himself and family: I think he said, a man and wife with perhaps only one young child would get 300 dollars (£60) a-year beside their keep,—or perhaps it was "with five young children"? I am not clear; but think it is as stated. On the whole, he represented it as decidedly easy for a skilful farming man to find some one or other of these positions for himself; and so to wait for a while, and look about him before purchasing land. My brother and his family, he said, might at any rate, failing all else, board very comfortably for about a guinea a week the whole of them,—I suppose, in some public boarding-house, as the Americans often do: that was the way he himself with his wife had lived while there. The climate he persisted in describing as good and wholesome,—no ague known, except perhaps in some "indiscreet reckless person": a wholesome good climate he again and again called it,—tho' children take something of a *rush fevever*[3] (no, that was not exactly the name!), and other kinds of fever for grown people were by no means unknown. But it is a pleasant airy green country, he says; with "*swift* streams" (whether they are *all* swift or not?); and broken into knolls and moderate hills. Fifty years ago, it was all a wood; and belonged to the State of Connecticut.[4] There was never much, or perhaps any, *pine* on it; hickory

3. Thus in MS.

4. Western N.Y. had belonged to the Mass. Colony. After commissioners from both states met in 1786 to settle their rival claims, Mass. retained its title W of Seneca Lake, though N. Y. had political sovereignty. They sold much, in its undeveloped state, to land speculators, including Phelps and Gorham Purchase, who bought the rights to six million acres and opened one of the first land offices at Canandaigua. The confusion may have arisen from the fact that Jeremiah Wadsworth (who had holdings in Phelps and Gorham and was responsible for his nephews, James and William, going to the area) and Oliver Phelps both came from Connecticut.

and hard wood.— This is nearly all I can recollect, dear Alick; and I tried to state it faithfully,—but it rather seemed to me, as if my informant, tho' evidently a most truthful man, was a little sanguine of temper; so you must make abatement and allowance! The price of land to purchase is not a thing I can state now, tho' he did try to make a guess: my impression rather is that it seemed unexpectedly high for America.

The way to *get* to Canadaigua was altogether simple: directly on landing at New York, either at morning or at evening, you would find a Steamer up the Hudson River to Albany, some 10 hours,—the fare, I think, a dollar and a half (6 shillings) per head, children half price: from Albany there was a railway; in 18 hours more (including very frequent stoppages of 15 minutes) you were at Canadaigua, and the fare not very high. Or you might go by canal,—or by a few stages of railway (which carry you over a hilly country where there are many *lochs*) and *then* by canal in three days,—still cheaper. The railway he tho*t* would be best; for it also was not dear.

I write you down all this, my dear Brother, because naturally you will like to know even the vague figure of it: but our good Colman undertook to write it all down on paper himself very shortly, and in that shape so soon as I have read it, you shall have it to keep and study. Colman undertakes farther to answer pointedly any question you may put; he will write you Letters of Introduction to this person and to that (over many parts of the Union), if they were necessary: but he kept repeating that "Mr Greig could do it all"; that you should certainly stop at Canadaigua, and examine *it* well. As to remitting of money; he supposed it would naturally be by Draft on some Bank at New York,—and you need not take the real *money* with you even from New York (if you got your Draft *accepted* and indorsed there, it might save time), but Greig, who did bank-business too, could manage it all at Canadaigua. We were to take care that the Draft *were on a good Bank* at New York: but that, I suppose, the Scotch Bankers take care of, and are themselves responsible for.— You were by no means, on your passage to Canadaigua or the like, to bargain with any private party "to take you all the way for a certain sum"; they would weary you out with waiting.— This is all I will say of Colman.

This morning also I have written to Greig; and Jane has added a Post-script. She is making a Copy of the thing for you.[5]—Tell me, or bid Jack tell me whether you have a right map of New York State, and especially of that part of it; that if not, I may send you one.—— Dear

5. See previous letter.

Brother, I did not sleep at all last night (what has not happened with me for years), and now it is about ten o'clock, and I am going to try it again. The Letters are all ready now, let me be asleep or not. You may judge that I have a million of things to say, which *this* is not the good time for saying! In fact I am very stupid; and in hopes that I shall get some sleep. May God's blessing go with you, my dear Brother!

Amen.—T. Carlyle

TC TO ALEXANDER CARLYLE

Chelsea, Monday Morning
19 june [1843]

My dear Brother,

At going to sleep, as specified in the foregoing paper,[1] I left the Letters for America (Mr Greig's Letter, and another of small consequence) in charge to Jane to put into the Post-Office; all sealed and ready: the Letter for yourself was left also all ready only not sealed. Jane omitted to take your Letter; so here it still lies,—and I now today add this little Postscript before sealing.

I went to bed, as stated, about 11 o'clock; by degrees fell sound asleep, and awoke in great astonishment about seven in the evening! Your Letter still lay here unsealed; but the American Letters had been most punctually put into the Post-Office in good time. Well, I thought it was all right; I went out and walked in the twilight &c: but just at going to bed I incidentally learned that poor Jane had *put in* the American Letters indeed, but never dreamed of paying the shilling apiece for them! There they were therefore, lying hard and fast in the Dead Letter Office, the Post-Office sealed till Monday morning, and the Mail Steamer sure to sail from Liverpool *without* them! I hardly remember a more provoking circumstance; poor Jane was in despair: we knew not what to do. I got a reasonable sleep in the night, however; and next morning early sallied forth, in one direction after another, to see whether something could not still be done. After several fruitless attempts, I went at last to one Mr Baring one of Peel's Ministry (whom John knows about);[2] he undertook, if I would write *another* Letter, to get it still sent off that night by the Government Bag, which was to depart in the evening and still be in time for the Steamer. I directly wrote another Letter to Mr Greig, explaining the mischance,

TC-AC, 19 June. MS: MUL. Pbd: Marrs 565–66. In the upper left-hand corner TC has written: "No 2. read the other papers *before* this."

1. TC to AC, 17 June.

2. W. B. Baring was sec. to the board of control in Peel's second ministry, 1841–45.

referring him to Clow for the particulars of your situation, promising *the* Letter itself by the next Steamer (*4th* of july), and in the meanwhile recommending you to his furtherance with all emphasis. This I have good reason to hope is already in the Steamer at Liverpool, and travelling on by the side of a Letter of your own to Clow. The other I will today recover from the Dead Letter Office and get forwarded by the swiftest route,—at latest by the *4th* july Steamer; whereby even it, I suppose, may arrive before the *Ashburton:* and so again, we hope, it is all right; at least much better than we once expected!

I have slept *both* nights since that bad adventure; and am now for a heavy day's work at my *Article* (a most beggarly piece of work, which I repent a thousand times having engaged in!)[3]— I will write very shortly to some of you again; probably I shall hear from some of you today; and so, with my blessings and heart-affectionate regards, I conclude. Ever your Brother

T. Carlyle—

TC TO ALEXANDER CARLYLE

W. Hamilton's 127. Cheapside
Monday 2½ o'clock [19 June 1843]—

My dear Brother,

The instant John's Letter came to hand, I set about fulfilling what it ordered. I have written the Letter he spoke of to our half-brother's old address in Canada (Brantford, Hamilton, Upper Canada), and put it into the Post-Office; I have *recovered* the Letter to Greig from the Dead L*r* Office, paid it and sent it off— Still in time they tell me! All which is well.

As to remitting of money, I find I shall be at any rate too late,—yet I come hither to Hamilton's to ask about it: Hamilton is not in London; nothing but Laurie here (the Doctor knows all these people)—and from Laurie is no light at all to be got.[1]— The Dr will indeed have already decided: so it is no matter, at bottom. Colman did not seem to know much of it. I should have considered a Letter or Bill or something of that sort on John Greig himself the safest of all ways. But I suppose the Bank people know several ways safe enough.—

You are going far sooner than I expected! My head is in a whirl,

3. "Dr. Francia."

TC-AC, [19 June]. MS: MUL. Pbd: Marrs 566–67. In the upper left-hand corner TC has written "N*o* 3, to be read *last* of all."

1. William Hamilton's partner Laurie not further identified.

and I am writing with the noise as of Babel rolling by me.— I will write again certainly,—and have it left for you at "Mr Welsh's 20. Maryland street,"—unless you write from Ecclefechan (or Jack do), and appoint me another address. I have several things to send you, I have so many thousand things to say, dear Brother! Adieu. Courage, Courage! God's blessing on you forevermore.

Your affectionate Brother
T. Carlyle

TC TO ALEXANDER CARLYLE

Chelsea, Monday Evg
(19 June [1843])

My dear Brother,

Here, by the last Post of the day, has come a packet of letters from Mr Colman: if despatched directly they will still reach you in Ecclefechan on Monday morning.[1]

Colman's directions about your journey seem very precise, and may be of use as you go along. His Letters of Introduction were not expressly solicited by me, and are the kinder on his part; they may do you some good,—at lowest they can do you no harm. When you are to deliver any of them, you enclose it in a sealed cover, address it, and go with it. I believe they are honest well-disposed people in those parts, many of them; and of course they have fashions of their own,—which you will gradually learn.

If the Dr have not yet *got* the Bill of Exchange, I should think it would be very safe to have it drawn upon that New-York House, for which Colman gives you a Letter, and which is the owner of the Ashburton. But if the Bankers have already given you a Bill on some House which *they* can vouch for,—probably that too is perfectly good. I suppose Liverpool would be the place to get a choice of Bills;—but I have as you may perceive next to no experience in that sort of affairs.

The Dr does not say whether he means to go with you to Liverpool; but I hope he does. He will have it in his power to help you there, I should think, in many little ways. As to me I have been thinking daily whether I should not run up to Liverpool, and see you all before you went: Do *you* wish it, my dear Brother? I have got into the ugliest evil of hurry here, about a piece of insignificant writing, which I *needed* not have bound myself to; and I am yet but quite in the middle of it;—

TC-AC, 19 June. MS: MUL. Pbd: Marrs 567–69.

1. Presumably TC meant to write "Wednesday morning," when they did arrive.

but I will fling it away, if you express any wish to see me: on the whole, I will be guided by that, and by the time you have to stay in Liverpool.

My dear Brother, it does seem to me, looking at the state and prospects of this country, that the whole farming kindred of us, our good Mother at our head, might all yet have to follow you, if you did well in that new Country! Consider yourself as a pioneer sent out before the rest; to make the way smoother for the rest. It is clearly the voice of Providence, one would say, that bids you go. In the midst of my sorrow, something whispers to me that my brave Brother will become a new man, and find a new and worthier career open for him there. It is the sweetest consolation that could come into my heart.— I will talk of these things no more. God is near us all, if we with faithfulness draw near to Him, follow His eternal Laws.——

I wrote to John[2] in Canada today, as I told you. There are now probably *two* Letters on the way to Canadaigua. Write to me whether you find a good map of New York State in Liverpool; that I may send you one, if not. Buy that Book, mentioned by Colman, when you get to New York.[3] Probably I shall hear from John[4] tomorrow or next day. The daylight is gone for the present. Adieu for this night.— Yours ever,
T. Carlyle

TC TO [HENRY COLMAN]

Chelsea, Wednesday [21 June 1843]—

My dear Sir,

It will be impossible for anybody to be totally a bore, if you escort him. Pray bring us your white-oak Professor,[1] and let us see whether there is no promise of red wood in him! Till Monday Evening, I am incessantly occupied; but *then*—at the old hour, if you can.

A Mr and Mrs Orville Dewey, from New York, send me down a Note from Emerson, with a request to know when they are to call,—

2. Their half-brother.

3. There were works such as S. Buller, *The Emigrant's Handbook of Facts,* reviewed in the *Athenaeum,* 8 July, as containing "much useful information" about Canada and not raising "expectations too high."

4. Their brother.

TC-[HC], [21 June]. MS: Hist. Soc. of Pa. Quot: Slater, *CEC* 336n. Addressee identified and letter dated by TC's reference to Colman's letters of intro. for Alexander Carlyle, sent 19 June; see previous letter. John Carlyle acknowledged their arrival, 21 June.

1. Unidentified; probably a fellow agronomist.

but have omitted to add any address of their own![2] I wish you could find them, and bring them down with you on Monday evening,—or at least make known to them my embarrassment.

Your letters were a most kind gift; and may be very useful to my Brother. Nay they *are* already useful to him; casting a ray of friendly hope and help over what otherwise, no doubt, looks dark and hostile enough in his notions of it. My good old Mother, to whose affectionate imagination "America" seems a great devouring gulph, would see (this morning, I think), that it is not so; that there are kind brother souls and various good men in America! I owe you many thanks. I know not yet what day my Brother goes, but fancy it must be very soon.

—On Monday Evening; with or without the Deweys!

Yours always truly / T. Carlyle

I have read your farm sermon;[3] and answered all along "Hear, Hear!"—

JWC TO JEANNIE WELSH

[21 June 1843]

Darling

I am afraid you will get no good of me until the Mudie concern is off my hands either as a success or a failure—I have just been writing a long letter to Jeffrey about them till my head is all in a mash—yesterday *ditto*—to Geraldine!—that unwearied girl has fairly *conquered* me into a hot correspondence with her again after all—by taking up this matter I have so much at heart with an enthusiasm—even surpassing my own!— I cannot but feel grateful to her at least for what she has done and is in the way of doing—nay *at times* I am almost over-persuaded back into my old illusion that she *has* some sort of strange, passionate—incomprehensible *attraction* towards me that leads her thro what is even more repugnant to natural feeling than "fire and water"—thro *the miry puddle*—of tearying and *begging*—to do me

2. Orville Dewey (1794–1882), unitarian minister of N.Y. City, m., 1820, Emerson's cousin Louisa Farnham. They were in Europe, Oct. 1841 to Aug. In his letter to TC, 26 Feb., from Staten Island, N.Y., Emerson had said of Dewey: "You will find him well acquainted with the most noted of our people, as I believe he already is with many of the most eminent of yours."

3. Probably one of Colman's many agricultural addresses; possibly *Improvement of Agriculture as an Art and a Profession* (Rochester, 1842) or *Agriculture of the United States* (Boston, 1841).

JWC-JW, [21 June]. Addr: 20 Maryland Street / Liverpool. PM: 21 June 1843. MS: NLS 1892.10. Pbd: Huxley, *JWCLF* 134–35 inc.

pleasure—Whatever be her *motive* her *results* are worthy of admiration—and lay me under a considerable debt of toleration towards her—

Then here has been Carlyle fretting himself—and family— —that is, me and Helen—to fiddlestrings—having two incompatible worries acting on him at once—the thought of his Brothers departure to America with all the *practical* work *that* brings with it—such as writing of recommendatory letters—gathering of all sorts of information for his guidance &c &c— And on the other hand an *article* for Forster's review which *must* be finished by Saturday night;[1] if he would not run the risk of Forster's hanging himself. And so—we have sleepless nights—terrific explosions at breakfast—and all the et ceteras you can figure!

You speak of fine weather it has only reached *us* this morning—so all our dreams of the Country have been kept in abeyance— *Now* it looks as if it *would* be summer at last—So when the article is finished there will be some movement surely—or at least emphatic enough *speech* about movement—but it will be time enough to speak of *our* plans when they have assumed the slightest appearance of certainty—One thing seems pretty clear—that my uncle will be gone before I can come—and so—I must keep Liverpool *in prospect*—for I *must* find *the people* as well as *the house* when I come—having none of John Carlyles preference for the mere *shelter* which is got by visiting—Blame me and not Gambardella *now* about the pictures until you get them[2]— Have patience [with][3] me in every way and love me always—

Your own bedevilled / Jane Carlyle

TC TO WILLIAM BAXTER

5. Cheyne Row, Chelsea
22 june, 1843—

Dear Sir,

There can be no possible objection to your dedicating your Book to me,[1] if you determine to do me that honour. I regret that it can be

1. "Dr. Francia" for the *Foreign Quarterly Review,* which was to go to the printer, Sat., 24 June.

2. Gambardella's portraits of JWC and Jeannie Welsh; there had been a delay in framing JWC's (see JWC to JW, [18 April]). Gambardella had finally given them to JWC when she was most involved with the Mudies (see JWC to JW, [30 June]).

3. Word omitted.

TC-WB, 22 June. Addr: Mr W. Baxter / Mr John M'Callums / 37. Buchanan Street / Glasgow. MS: NLS 3823.111. Hitherto unpbd. William Baxter, author of *Love, and Other Poems* (Glasgow, 1843), *The Land Question: Whose is the* of no benefit to the Book; but my side of the business is not to look thitherward, but to thank you for all your goodwill towards me.

With true wishes in return / Yours very sincerely

T. Carlyle

TC TO ALEXANDER CARLYLE

Chelsea, Friday Afternoon
[23 June 1843]

My dear Brother,

John's Letter came to me this morning;[1] I had been looking every night and morning for it: the news of it fell on my heart like a heavy stone. My dear Brother,—it is very touching what John says, that you went thro' the business "like a right brave man"; that "all your old energy, alacrity and clearness of mind shewed itself again in you in these hours!" Yes, my dear Alick,—when I think and hope that perhaps it is God's *merciful* ordering, this very sore trial, to bring you back again out of fatal declivities, into a true path; and make you yet even yet the victorious *man* you were meant to be—that is the only thing that sweetens this bitter sorrow to me.—

But why do I talk in that dialect? The truth is, I am worn down with writing day and night, and in a very weak sorrowful humour; I never in all my life was so busy. But it will end on Sunday;—it *must* end, for the thing has then to be printed.— It is most absurd that this too should have intervened to aggravate us.

Tell me truly if you would *wish* to see me; if it would not be rather a sorrow for you? I promise and assure myself that I *will* come yet, and see you in that new Home,—to which may God Himself give

---

Land? A Dialogue. By W. Welsh [*pseud.*] (Glasgow, 1870), and *Thoughts on the Land Question and the Right Way to Settle It* (Glasgow, 1881); probably the William Baxter listed in the Glasgow P.O. Directory, 1845–71, as variously draper, hosier, and proprietor of a lace warehouse, 442 Argyll St.; apparently working before that for John M'Callum, silk mercer to Her Majesty for Scotland.

1. His dedication made clear that it did not come from ever having met TC, but from his admiring TC "as a gifted literary man," whose books Baxter had read with "much pleasure and profit." He was "one of the 'self-taught,' " and writing the poem had been "a pleasant employment after the business of the day." He speaks of the dedication as "a slight but sincere token of my esteem for you as an author; of my admiration of the doctrines you teach; of your excellent talents; of the noble use to which you apply them."

TC-AC, [23 June]. MS: MUL. Pbd: Marrs 571–72. Under the heading TC later wrote: "(about the 20*th* june 1843) This Letter went to the Post-office Liverpool; but my Brother Alexander, just on his way to America, did not get it; and it came back to me at Llandough, july 12!"

1. From Scotsbrig, dated 21 June.

a blessing! There has no solicitation yet from all America that had any strength at all upon me like this.— In God's name, let us look up then; and take Hope and Courage for a loadstar. I will engage not to write another weak word to you,—not even in such a whirl of haste as I write in at present.

Tell me exactly on what day you expect to sail. I will not bid you call at Maryland Street; but call again at the Post-Office, if there be again any chance.

Your Letter to the Owners of the Ashburton will perhaps do you good with the Captain. You carry a Letter to one Mr M'Connel,[2] John says, at Canadaigua. We knew his Wife; an excellent kind creature, Jane thinks her. My American Colman in describing the population of Canadiagua spoke of one "M'Connel" or "O'Connel," as a kind of questionable man,—you will keep this in your mind, but of course *entirely* secret; and look at your man with your own eyes, when there. Greig will be able to do you your Money-bill; he if there were even no other.—— Jamie is coming over,[3] they tell me; which is a great comfort Adieu dear Brother. Fear nothing; my brave brother's courage once roused, there is nothing in the Earth or under it that shall daunt him. God be with you. I will surely hope to write again. Write you a word,—one word if you can! / T. C.

TC TO MARGARET A. CARLYLE

Chelsea, Friday Evening
23 june, 1843—

My dear Mother,

John's second Letter of today has just come.[1] The first arrived at 11 o'clock; tho' I had been expecting the tidings, and had nothing else

2. Robert Adamson's relation and John Greig's friend, according to John Carlyle, 21 June.

3. James Carlyle went to Liverpool, Sat., 24 June, to see Alexander and his family off "on sunday morning . . . quite safely & in good spirits," returning to Annan, Tues. morning, 27 June (John Carlyle to TC, 27 June).

TC-MAC, 23 June. MS: NLS 521.13. Pbd: A. Carlyle, *NL* 1:295–96 inc.

1. John Carlyle wrote, 21 June, that Alick was to sail from Annan that evening and as he left Ecclefechan, "Our mother . . . stood through the parting like a true christian though she had cried bitterly when I first saw her early in the morning. Alick too behaved like a brave man, & seemed both last night & this morning to have all the energy & dispatch of his best days again. At least a third of the inhabitants of the village were collected at his door many of them crying as if he had been their own brother. . . . Alick has about eighty pounds to take with him & I suppose the whole journey will not cost more than forty pounds or so. He got your American's letters of introduction & information about the journey this morning but hardly had time to read them properly." John Carlyle wrote,

to expect, it fell upon my heart like a heavy stone!— He says you bore your great sorrow with the firmness we have known in you, "like a Christian and a brave woman." It is what I had to expect also,—thank Heaven for it! You have had much to suffer, dear Mother, and are grown old in this valley of Tears; but you say always as all of us should say, "Have we not many mercies too?" Is there not above all, and in all, a *Father* watching over us; thro' whom all sorrows *shall* yet work together for good?— Yes, it is even so. Let us try to hold by that as an anchor both sure and steadfast.[2]

What John says of Alick was highly affecting and consolatory to me. "He had recovered all his old energy and manful activity":—yes, poor fellow, by God's blessing he will yet recover all, and be himself again, in that new Home. I reflect always that it seems to be by far the best chance this world held out to him of that: where he *was*, and as he was, there could no good be. He will rally himself for a new onslaught; the very solitude of his sea-voyage will do good to him: he will step into a new scene of activity, with added years and wisdom, and see that it says everywhere to him, "As thou art wise in me, so shalt thou prosper!" Even I, who am not much given to hope, have a real expectation that this will be the saving of our poor Alick. May God grant it. A brave man, and a true; but borne down, and torn away by this thing and by that, as I have hardly seen any man.

You may depend on it, dear Mother, it is, as compared with ours, a *good* Country he has gone to. There are friends there in very fact who will be ready to welcome him. Nay, as I say often, What good hope is there for a working industrious man anywhere if it be not in America, as times go with us? If the course of things here do not alter beyond my expectation, I think the whole kindred of us had better go and quit such a country as it will ere long be! You at the head of us,—for you are a good sailor, and a brave Mother! Courage, my dear Mother; courage, the saddest-looking is sometimes the joyfullest when we see the real end of it! If Alick prosper in that new Country, he may be a real blessing to his whole kindred,—and a double blessing to himself that will be.

I wrote to him today before dinner "Post-Office Liverpool." It is a comfort to me that Jamie is going over. I hope to write him another word before the ship sail.

In a short time, dear Mother, I think I shall see you too. I long al-

---

22 June: "Alick & all his family got off quite safely by the Victoria last night between seven & eight. Jamie returned with the gig about eleven. Our mother has slept well."

2. Cf. Heb. 6:19.

ways to go and see you; and soon I shall probably be able,—and if able, surely I should. More about this in a day or two.

At present and till tomorrow night late, I am the busiest mortal I ever before in my days was. I write all day and all night (till near mid-night),—running against time, at a a[3] very useless "Article" which I had undertaken; which must be finished, being undertaken. I could have liked it better at another time! On saturday night, however, it has to go to press,—the whole Review Number has to be *out* on the first of July. I shall soon now have room to consider myself,—with a sharp fight still in the interim, however!

It is now near tea; I have my scrawls of Manuscript to look over; and make ready for the "three pages more" before bed time. My sleep is good enough again. We are all well. A terrible quantity of Americans &c here! I have three or four Notes daily to answer beside my other writing.— That Note for John[4] came this morning.

Adieu, my dear Mother: do I not hope to see you soon? Ever your affectionate

T. Carlyle

TC TO JOHN FORSTER

[23? June 1843]

'Dr Francia,' or *'Dr Francia and South America'* (for I have been obliged to babble far too much about the *adjuncts* of the man, not knowing the *man* to any right extent at all!) The latter will be *truer,*— preferable therefore?

The Famulus may have some twenty pages even now,—and shall? No: tomorrow will be better!

—In breakneck haste,

T.C.

3. Thus in MS.
4. Presumably enclosed.

TC-JF, [23? June]. MS: FC. Hitherto unpbd. Approximately dated by the offer of "some twenty pages even now" or "tomorrow," which was apparently 24 June (see TC to MAC, 23 June).

TC TO W. E. FORSTER

Chelsea, 23 june, 1843–

My dear Sir,

Your kind invitation to Craven[1] is far too good to be rejected at once; nor do I so reject it; far from that. But I am in such an unutterable whirlpool of haste, confusion, and hard work at present, I can think of nothing extraneous whatever; and must beg to *postpone* my answer till a freer time, which I hope will soon arrive[2]– That is the meaning of my writing to you tonight,–past the hour of midnight when all *canny* things are in bed!– Good sleep to both of us!

Yours very truly always,
T. Carlyle

There is no haste at all about the Greg Pamphlet,[3] so it do come certainly at last. Take your own time with it.

JWC TO JEANNIE WELSH

[ca. 26 June 1843]

My good darling

You must not lose heart. Easy to say! but when it comes to *doing!*– Well–no one knows better than I do the immense difference betwixt saying and doing; Still I am not ashamed to *say* to you you must not lose heart, because I really see good cause why you should not;–setting aside all *moral obligation* in the matter.

Amid all your present troubles, whatsoever they be, you have a ground of comfort which *I* have not, which so many have not!–

You are young–very young–with *youth* on one's side depend on it one has *the odds* on one's side against the sorest trials. One may not

TC-WEF, 23 June. MS: Scripps College. Hitherto unpbd.

1. A district of striking landscape in the western dales, W Riding, Yorks. Forster lived in Bradford, also in W Riding.

2. Forster replied, 7 July: "Relying on your note of the 23*rd*, from which I gather that the pleasure of a visit from you is not altogether hopeless, I write to tell you that Mr & Mrs Charles Fox their daughter & myself purpose setting forth on a few days tour in Craven about the middle of next week. . . . I do really hope you will be able to join us." Sarah (1801–82) and Charles Fox (1797–1878; *DNB*), scientific writer; Caroline Fox's uncle and currently partner in and manager of the family firm, the Perran Foundry Co., at Perranarworthal, Cornwall.

3. Probably one of the 1842 pamphlets on the Corn Laws or farming by Robert Hyde Greg (1795–1875; *DNB*), economist and antiquary.

JCW-JW, [ca. 26 June]. MS: NLS 1892.13. Pbd: Huxley, *JWCLF* 135–36 inc., where dated [before 30 June]. Approximately dated by TC's plans to visit Charles Redwood, arranged in TC to CR, 28 June.

feel this at the time—nay, one may find the prospect of a long life to come only aggravation of one's suffering— But in the long life to come lie so many glorious possibilities! And some fine morning, without knowing precisely how, one awakes to a recognition of these, and can smile over the despairing past as over a bad dream! I can only *guess* at what ails you— I may or may not be near the truth—but of this I am *certain* as I live—that *whatever you* are suffering—*I* have suffered, and under more terrible conditions than can in your case be possible— And see—after all, I am here *alive*, speaking *hope* to my Babbie! Not very *gay* certainly—not *"happy"*—who in a world like this, that has any more reflection than the Brutes can be what they call *happy* at my age?—but I am better than happy in having learned to *do without happiness*— and I have this knowledge to communicate to you, drawn from my own life-experience; that the heart even of *a woman* can stand an infinite deal more breaking without being broken than one can form the smallest conception of at five and twenty. There is a beautiful proverb and it is as true as beautiful that "the darkest hour of the night is nearest the dawn." So have I found it, and so will you too find it—*Wait*, and hope for the dawn in patient faith— There is no use in tormenting oneself into *got-up* good spirits. That is, as it were, to light a parcel of farthing candles and call *that* "the dawn"! a sort of beggarly brightness that serves only to make the darkness visible[1] to show one how *very* miserable one is!— But *wait*—Mazzini you remember did not like that word—nevertheless it is a good word—and one which if *he* had better appreciated he would not have lain under the reproach of having been turned back from revolutionizing Italy "by a toll-bar"![2] and under many other consequences sad to think of! Wait—not in sloth indeed—but in inward prayer—with *your face towards the East*— till the *true* God-sent brightness comes—and pours itself afresh over all your world and into the depths of your soul—you know not how— but no matter *how* so it be there! Oh *that* is joy! such as one knew not of BEFORE having suffered!—when one feels oneself *awake—alive*—no longer a gohst among the living and the loving—but living and loving like a newborn creature, in a newborn world!— My darling! if I had you here I could *make* you believe that all will be well with you in good time I could *kiss* the belief into you—I am sure that I could!— But the things that are in ones heart to say grow so cold on the

1. *Paradise Lost* 1:63.

2. TC's phrase (see JWC to JW, [27 Jan. 1844]), probably referring to the chaotic and unsuccessful invasion of Savoy, in Piedmont, 1–2 Feb. 1834, which Mazzini helped to plan and during which he collapsed.

paper!— Well the practical inference from all that is, that we must speedily meet— A lingering cold—and castor oil are things to be put down by some vigorous measure without loss of time— The continued coldness of the weather is keeping back the fruits of Carlyles numerous projects as well as "the fruits of the season"—but if he do not decide on what is to be done thro the summer in the course of a week or two we (you & I) must get up a small seperate decision for ourselves. He *talks* at present of going into Glenmorganshire[3] to the Welshman's for bathing—"almost immediately" (but one knows what *his "almost immediatelys"* mean) and leaving me here to keep the house during that *first* part of the programme—(*the house* having become since the thieves[4] a really serious difficulty—) then the Liverpool coast is to be investigated after—but if he *do* Glenmorganshire, I do not think it at all likely that he will seek for any seabathing quarters elsewhere—it will end probably in his going for a short time into Annandale and leaving me with you on the way—or in his going nowhere—in which case I should go to Liverpool alone in the first instance and take my "country air"—afterwards at Troston— In that case—if I am not to get to you for a good while yet, the best of all possible *solutions* would be for you to come here and be with me till I *can* get away to Liverpool— Would there be any hindrance to this arrangement on *your* side—I do not mean on your *individual* side—should it look to me when I see more clearly into his scheme of movement to be the best thing to do?—My own babbie I wish that your head *were* "on my shoulder"*—it* would be good for us both—

—Tell my uncle that I know nothing whatever of Grace Welsh[5]— God forgive me I had utterly forgotten her existence! I had a long kind letter from M*rs* Russel this morning in answer to one I sent her with a copy of C's book— I am sorry I cannot forward it to you—Carlyle having stupidly *burnt it*—because it had set me a crying—

You are to tell my uncle also that if he feels interested in Icelandic matters there are several books about Iceland which Carlyle strongly recommends to his perusal— He has written the names on an old

3. Thus in MS, for Glamorganshire.
4. Who broke into the house, summer 1842; see 15:96.
5. One of JWC's three paternal aunts in Edinburgh. They were "women of deep, severe piety, and considerable force of character . . . . They kept up a correspondence with Mrs. Carlyle, and she occasionally visited them, but she did not fall in readily with their religious views and habits. Mr. Carlyle had a great regard for them . . . . Grace, by much the youngest, a pretty and attractive woman, died soon after Mrs. Carlyle . . . . The other two, Elizabeth and Ann, died within a few days of each other, and were buried together" (David Davidson, *Memories of a Long Life* [Edinburgh, 1890] 326).

envelope—which it is easier to send than copy them— They are put down in the order of their respective worth[6]—

I wonder if Walter Macgregor's *heart* is in this marriage? I cannot help feeling great misgivings on the subject— He left London one of the most *wretched* looking men I ever tried to comfort and suddenly he blooms up in Liverpool into a happy accepted Lover!— If he found a letter from the Lady awaiting him in Liverpool—with an almost despaired of *Yes*—then the inconsistency is explained—but if nothing had altered in his circumstances from the time of his leaving London—if the Yes had been given *before she sailed* (as one would suppose) then I declare myself entirely at a loss what to make of him!— Nor was the letter he wrote to *me* like the letter of a *happy* man— Is it with me or with others that he is acting a part?— All this of course is strictly *private*— God bless you my child your own

JC.

TC TO CHARLES REDWOOD

Chelsea, 28 june, 1843

My dear Sir,

I have been waiting all this while for some summer; but none comes. I determine therefore to come without much summer! My aim at present is for the beginning of next week; I have to pause at Clifton,[1] but it cannot be for long; neither can I linger as long as I once hoped in Glamorganshire: but I will come and see you and it, that is now fixed! Pray let me know by return of Post whether you are at home. If you say, Yes, my next Letter will probably bear the date of Clifton, and appoint our time of meeting at Cardiff.

I have some thoughts of getting up to Carmarthen (where the Bishop is[2]), nay of going thro' Wales all the way, to Chester, to Liver-

6. Possibly the travel books TC mentions in TC to KAVE, 1 May; see also 12:32–35.

TC-CR, 28 June. Addr: Llandough / Cowbridge / S. Wales. MS: NLS Acc. 9294. Pbd: Faulkner 153–54.

1. To visit Julia Strachey. Her youngest son, George, quotes from JWC's letters to Julia (whereabouts now unknown) before the visit about "the subject of his wants and habits. To the question, 'How was he to be made comfortable?' Mrs. Carlyle replied that 'she had never been able to find out that, and could only say, as his own mother did, "he's gey hard to deal with:"' he must smoke a long clay pipe after breakfast, and that not in the garden but in the house. And then a question—poultry were to him *anathema maranatha*—had we any cocks or hens? No 'demon-fowls' existed, and the tobacco problem received a similar solution" (G. Strachey, *CRG* 478–79).

2. Connop Thirlwall (1797–1875; *DNB*), bishop of St. David's since 1840; see 11:132–33 and 12:221.

pool, witherward and across the Solway I am ultimately bound. But all this we will discuss on meeting,—if *Rebecca*[3] and the Fates permit!

Yours always truly,
T. Carlyle

I fear the *horse* is sold! We will speak of that too nevertheless—

TC TO [JOHN EDMUND READE]

5. Cheyne Row, Chelsea
30 june, 1843—

My dear Sir,

I received some days ago a second Copy of your *Sacred Poems;*[1] a copy was already in my hands, and I had been reading in it with interest, but in a great press of occupation had delayed to acknowledge it. I now beg your acceptance of many thanks for both; the succedaneous copy, which it is not fair for me to keep, I shall know how to dispose of with advantage if you allow me.

I wish you would write me a good *prose* book withal, such as you are *well able* for. You will think it sad heresy; but I do infinitely prefer prose to poetry in these earnest days. It is the nature of the beast!

In poetry or prose I remain always, / Yours with true goodwishes
T. Carlyle

TC TO JOHN FORSTER

Chelsea, Friday morning
[30 June 1843].

Dear Forster,

Now that the hurlyburly's done,[1] could you induce your assiduous Printers to send me *three* separate copies of that *Dr Francia,* one of them to keep here, two to send by post? If their types are already all gone to *pie* again,[2] the thing wanted will be procurable out of the "waste" so-called,—tho' in that case the contiguous pages will adhere

3. Figures in woman's attire who led the rioters to demolish the toll gates in S Wales, 1843–44; in allusion to Gen. 24:60.

TC-[JER], 30 June. MS: Huntington Lib. Hitherto unpbd. John Edmund Reade (1800–79; *DNB*), poetaster and novelist; imitator of Byron.
1. *Sacred Poems, from Subjects in the Old Testament* (1843), advertised in the *Athenaeum,* 17 June, as "Now ready."

TC-JF, [30 June]. MS: FC. Hitherto unpbd. Dated by TC's finishing "Dr. Francia," 24 June.
1. *Macbeth* 1.1.
2. Been broken up and disarranged.

to *Francia;* which is not so pretty a method. One stitch of packthread will hold him together.

I am going off for Wales on Monday: I have a sort of half-mad appetite for being left alone, in green places, within sound of the Sea! My Wife is to remain here, at least for a week or two. Shall I not see you?

In terrible haste!

T. Carlyle

JWC TO JEANNIE WELSH

[30 June 1843]

First of all, Dearest, what of Walter Macgregor? He has not dawned on *my* horizon—so I cannot believe him here—but I should like to know whether he be coming at present— Those pictures begin to torment my conscience—they were finally consigned to me when I was driven from post to pillar betwixt *Mudieism* and rheumatism— You may think it required no great effort of kindness to get them packed and carry them to the rail-way station (for I absolutely durst not trust them to our monster of a carrier who flings boxes out of his cart on the street as if they were blocks of granite) but I assure you the effort required was under all the circumstances *so* great as to be well nigh impossible—then when I *could* have gone, a speculation had arisen of a box to be sent to Alick (my Brother in law at Liverpool) nay Carlyle spoke at one time of *making a run* to Liverpool himself to bid Alick farewell— And with my usual stupid turn for economy I thought your parcel might as well be sent by *that opportunity*— But Carlyle was so hunted here with printer's devils that not only the *run* to Liverpool but the box to Liverpool remained a devout imagination—and just when I had again made up my mind for a journey to Euston Square[1] came your intimation that Walter might probably be here within two weeks— If he be still coming, I may as well keep them for him—having kept them so long—but if not I will send them immediately under the care of Providence— I wish Gambardella had *packed* them himself—I should then have cared less as to their manner of going—

I do wish you were *settled* one way or other—I know no state which it is so difficult to lead a rational—never to say a *contented* life under as that state of hanging in the wind— —God knows *I* have had enough of it in my time but even custom never reconciled me to it the least in

JWC-JW, [30 June]. Addr: 20 Maryland Street / Liverpool. PM: 30 June 1843. MS: NLS 1892.17. Pbd: Huxley, *JWCLF* 137–38 inc.

1. To Euston railway station.

the world— Carlyle has finally determined on starting for Wales on Monday or Tuesday— We have just been emptying the portmanteauful of books which *you* packed[2]—to replace them with the necessary clothes—so I suppose he is *really* in earnest this time— He had no idea how long he will stay or whether he will come straight back or go round by—Scotland! or the Moon!— He "hopes that *I* will go *somewhere* during his absence"—and then the next minute agrees to the necessity of my staying to take charge of the house until at least I can find some safe person to put into it besides Helen— Then half a minute after asks if I am not going down next week to the Isle of Wight?— —I have an invitation to go to John Sterling there—and of course a most pressing invitation to Troston— But the confounded house—and the scattering in Liverpool confuse my mind beyond all power of scheming even.— When *He* is fairly out of the way—and the ceilings whitened and the carpets beaten and *some* painting done—even if I should do it out of my own pin-money—then I will *try* to "go somewhere"

Meanwhile I shall not be lonely—never fear for that—I have always visitors enough and to spare—when I am *single*—and when a domestic earthquake is going on there is no leisure for *feeling* lonely suppose no one came near me— I hope to get the Mudies put into some sort of small line of business in a week or two—thanks chiefly to the active exertions of Geraldine!—and then I *must* positively wash my hands of them—for they take up far more of my time and thought than is at all reasonable— I believe if I had sat down at once and written a *novel* in three volumes—and given them the procedes[3] it would have been easier work for me than the writing of all the *letters* I have had to write on their account. and all the talking and walking besides.

My head is aching very badly today—so you must put up with a mere apology for a letter— I have been rather ailing for some days from *natural causes,* and made worse by the dreadful quantity of human speech I have had to transact with a scotch lady that has been on a two-days visit to me—a M*rs* Sterling ci devant Susan Hunter[4] (Helen[5] will remember her by that name—and her faculty of speech) she is a good warmhearted woman and was very kind to us in Edin*r* before others had discovered our merits—

Poor Mazzini is again very ill with his cheek—the swelling has ended in an immense tumour outside—which is fearful to look at and think of— I went to see him yesterday the one side of his face looked

2. During her visit in 1842.
3. Thus in MS.
4. Susan Stirling, b. Hunter (1799–1877; corrected birth date); see 8:159–61.
5. Welsh.

as sweet and placid as if nothing ailed the other—but the other!—made me absolutely sick—with apprehension chiefly.— I wish I could bring him here and nurse him—he is very illcared for where he is— In fact we are all of us *you* included in a badish way—love to my Uncle and the rest Tell me particularly how is Maggie?—I know I have forgotten a hundred things but better this than nothing Your own

Jane C

TC TO [HENRY COLMAN?]

Chelsea, 30 June 1843

I am mediating a sally into Wales and farther. . . . Your Professor is a wiry adroit New Englander, and will ferret out many a thing with that 'proboscis' of his, if I mistake not!

TC TO CHARLES REDWOOD

Chelsea, 1 july, 1843—

My dear Sir,

I am for Clifton, if all go well, on Monday;[1] I will write to you from that. I am terribly bilious; and shall require to be set on horseback, and well let alone!

To meet at Cardiff,

Yours ever truly / T. Carlyle

Your Letter come; thanks, as always.

TC TO JOHN FORSTER

Chelsea, Monday Morning [3 July 1843]—

Dear Forster,

I am about getting off, hitherto without accident. The process of Packing is frightful! You have to get into such a state of *clairvoyance*, and prophesy everything!—

TC-[HC?], 30 June. MS: sold at auction, Swann Galleries, N. Y. City, 3 Feb. 1966, lot 694. Addressee tentatively identified by "your Professor," who may be the "white-oak Professor" in TC to HC, [21 June].

TC-CR, 1 July. Addr: Llandough / Cowbridge / S. Wales. MS: NLS Acc. 9294. Pbd: Faulkner 154.

1. 3 July.

TC-JF, [3 July]. MS: FC. Hitherto unpbd. Dated by TC's departure for Clifton, 3 July.

The three *Francias* came. Any farther "message" there may be about that business, pray leave it with my Wife, who is instructed how to dispose of it.

The last *Chuzzlewit* on Yankeedoodledodom is capital.[1] We read it here with loud assent, loud cachinnatory approval! You may tell Dickens if you like.

And now Westward Ho! And may the Heavens be good to you all, and to Forster in especial, till I come back!

T. Carlyle

JWC TO TC

[3 July 1843][1]

Dearest

It is two o'clock—and nothing has *happened* yet of any moment—I send all the letters that came—except the receipt from Leith[2]— I have been very sick and *queer* ever since you went—but I will now go out and walk. and subside into my normal state—if possible—

I have written a note to Miss Maurice—ditto to M*rs* G. Rennie[3] and a "rather weak" letter to Jeffrey—

I wish Pearson[4] would come—

Remember me to M*rs* Strachey— I will *send* the Crawfurds address tomorrow if I can get it by then[5]—

God keep you— Of course I *cannot* write *just now*— I am all castaway so to speak—

Your / JC

1. In ch. 15 (June) of *Martin Chuzzlewit,* "The Burden Whereof is Hail Columbia!," the young Chuzzlewit lands in N.Y.

JWC-TC, [3 July]. MS: NLS 602.101. Hitherto unpbd.

1. TC has later written "Chelsea, Monday 3 july / 1843."
2. From Hutchison & Bowe, wine merchants.
3. Probably Priscilla Maurice (1810–54), one of four surviving sisters of Frederick Denison Maurice (1805–72; *DNB*), who had kept house for him before his marriage and who with her brother had attended some of TC's lectures in 1840; but possibly Esther, who m., 1844, the Rev. Julius Hare. Mrs. George Rennie, b. Cockerell; see 7:253, 328.
4. The carpenter.
5. Probably John Crawfurd (1783–1868; *DNB*), orientalist (see 7:340), and his wife, staying at Blackbrook House, Monmouthshire, ca. 8 mi. NW of Monmouth.

TC TO CHARLES REDWOOD

2. Lower Terrace, Clifton
Tuesday Morning [4 July 1843]—

My dear Sir,

I yesternight arrived here safe, and am bent now towards Llandough with all my industry. My intelligence about the Welsh Posts and conveyances is none of the best; but I find there is a Steamer for Cardiff daily, which seems to sail on Thursday at a convenient hour, and also that there will probably be time for this Letter to arrive at a due distance before it. For tomorrow (Wednesday) there would not, or there might not; else perhaps I should have preferred Wednesday.— I decide accordingly to sail on Thursday morning, about 11 o'clock (if that, as I dimly gather from the Newspaper Advertisement, do prove to be the hour): the time of our arrival at Cardiff, which is left to the Fates, you can yourself guess at. The Boat's name, I find by the *Bristol Mercury*, is "Prince of Wales." You were once hospitable enough to speak of meeting me at Cardiff: this of course would be a great pleasure; nevertheless I will not take you away from any engagement or business you may have; with or without your escort I shall get along; and hope to find myself under your roof at Llandough that same evening.

Today is wet; but in old trowsers and a water-proof blanket coat (*Tweed* I think they call it) and other *un*injurable apparatus, I mean to perambulate Bristol nevertheless: tomorrow, if there be nothing better, I think of sailing up to Chepstow to look at Harry Martin's Dungeon and the other notabilities in that quarter.[1]

The breath of new hay and green fields for so many hours has, in spite of much injury otherwise, done me good. I beg to be recommended very kindly to your good Mother, whose acquaintance I may hope to make before long.

Yours always truly / T. Carlyle

TC-CR, [4 July]. Addr: Llandough / Cowbridge / Glamorganshire. MS: NLS Acc. 9294. Pbd: Faulkner 154–55.

1. Henry Marten (1602–80), regicide; after the Restoration imprisoned for life, much of the time in Chepstow Castle, Monmouthshire; "a tight little fellow, though of somewhat loose life" (*Cromwell, Works* 8:4).

TC TO JEAN CARLYLE AITKEN

Clifton, Bristol, 4 july
(Tuesday) 1843—

Dear Sister Jean,

Accept from me the shortest Note you ever got in the world. I arrived here yesterday, on my way to Wales, to my Welsh Attorney, to rest for a week or two, and see what farther! Your Letter has followed me. I left Jane well: I am myself well, *except* biliary fret and misery produced by the London whirlpool and too hard work there. I am staying at Mrs Stracheys. I go across a kind of frith into Wales, like crossing to Maryport,[1] in a Steamer on Thursday morning: my address after that will be, "Care of Charles Redwood Esq Llandough, *Cowbridge,* S. Wales": but I will write to you from that. I design to see Scotland before I return to London.

This is a huge smoky City this Bristol,—yet not above half the size of Liverpool, nor half the ugliness. The Country all round it, in a gentle *lukewarm Scotch Mist* is of the greenest and beautifullest.

Thanks to my fair Panegyrist at Dumfries![2] She is very highflown, but I suppose not without a sincere heart in her way.— I have been almost put to death with *Yankees* buzzing round me in London, and feel a kind of blessedness in the fact that they *cannot* get at me here.

Poor Alick, he will be bounding away over the far seas in these hours. God go with him. Jack has a new *article* of mine,[3] or my Mother has, which I will bid them shew you.

Ever your affectionate / T. Carlyle

TC TO JWC

Clifton, Tuesday, 4 july / 1843—

Dearest,

Your Packet of Letters was handed in duly at breakfast; I send you back certain of them, to try if the contents will amuse you even a little. The young lady at Dumfries with her verses is very grand;—evidently one of those who "flatter me too much": I must carry my head under it if I can.

You will go, I think, with Sterling? If it promise to yield you a few

TC-JCA, 4 July. MS: NLS 512.6. Hitherto unpbd.
1. 22 mi. across Solway Firth from Port Annan.
2. Unidentified.
3. "Dr. Francia."

TC-JWC, 4 July. MS: NLS 611.123. Quot: Froude, *Carlyle* 3:298–99.

days of recreation, go surely. The old Stimabile will be best out of the way as the young one suggests.[1]

Yesterday I got along successfully enough. I was landed at the Paddington Station half an hour before my time; got with some difficulty (from defect of Porters and excess of Passengers) my arrangements completed; set to reading in my first-class and indeed *first-rate* vehicle, and whirled off so soon and so swiftly as the apparatus pleased. I had a side of the thing to myself; an insignificant well-mannered Cockney-tourist Mother and her little girl sitting opposite; the other *compartment* of the vehicle (for it is of breadth to carry *four* on each side, and is divided by a door with sliding window which can be shut or opened at pleasure) was occupied by a comfortable very stupid-looking man and wife with two units of offspring,—the father bought the *Morning Post* for his studies, and I noticed the Mother at one time pour herself out into a glass without foot a considerable dram of cognac: peace be with them,—our side had shut the door before that. Our Weather was hot for more than half the way. Accoromboni (poor Holcroft being exhausted)[2] was ready whenever we got into the bottom of *cuts;* atop again I preferred looking out into the blessed ocean of green, with human figures making hay: "I feel the gales that from you blow" &c &c.[3] At Reading I scanned the wrecks of the old Abbey, nearly hidden now by a gorgeous Poor-Law Bastille;[4] I looked out for the duel island of Henry of Essex;[5] and admired the immensely shrunk dimensions of the Thames. Not very far westward of this, the sky overcast itself, grew ever greyer, till towards three o'clock we got into incipient Scotch mist: at Bristol it turned out to have been a wet day, as *this* again is. But on the other hand the country grew ever rockier without losing of its greenness;—really beautiful to look at. Bath built of white stone, in trim streets, enclosed amid gnarled beautifully green and feathered hills, looked altogether princely, after these poor brick towns,—like an

1. John Sterling had written JWC from Ventnor, 2 July: "On Tuesday I leave this for Falmouth whence I hope to return within a week. Then I shall go to London for a few days I hope to bring you back with me hither While Carlyle visits Wales & I hope meets rather with Shakspere's Fluellen than Gray's Bard. . . . I think my Father will project to come here with you Prevent this."

2. Referring to Tieck's novel *Vittoria Accorombona* and a pamphlet presumably by Thomas Holcroft (d. 1852; see 6:50); see TC to JAC, 8 July.

3. Untraced.

4. The ruins of a magnificent Benedictine abbey, founded 1121 by Henry I, nr. which was a workhouse.

5. Henry de Essex, hereditary standard-bearer of England, was accused of treason by Robert de Montfort, who offered to prove his accusation by combat. The two fought a duel on an island in the Thames, 1158, in the presence of Henry II. Essex was defeated, his estates were confiscated, and he became a monk at Reading Abbey. See *Past and Present, Works* 10:106–10.

ancient *decayed* Prince, for it was smoke-soiled, dingy and lonely-looking; yet in the chimney-tops and gables, of a certain polite fantasticality, and all ranked in straight short streets, which ran in every direction on every variety of level, as if they had all been *marching* and drilling in that rough hollow place, each in the road that suited him best,—there was something in all this that reminded one of Beau Nash and Smollett's Lady of Quality.[6] My Cockney tourist Lady pronounced it to be a City built of stone, and of considerable extent; facts both.

It was not till after five that I got dragged thro' the muddy narrow streets of Bristol, and landed (by the aid of a Porter ultimately) at N*o* 2 here. My welcome was of the kindest; but how much simpler would Accoromboni by itself have been for the evening! Ah me, we had Montague the mad Captain-Parson, and a certain Dr Symons to tea for the evening:[7] I was heartily glad to get to my bedroom,—tho' with poison in the inner man of me! At five o'clock the "*Swee-ep!*" awoke me, to inquire if I had any foul chimneys: I had been dreaming—of you, you fool! By the aid of a spunk I smoked a pipe; did after 7 fall asleep again; at 8 was awakened again, and finally succeeded in getting breakfast about half past 9. The air in spite of all things has done me real good.

I have written to my Welshman that I will meet him at Cardiff on Thursday. The Boat sails at 11,—so there will still be time for Letters from *you.* I should have preferred Wednesday (tomorrow), but there seemed no certainty that my Host in that case could have due warning to meet me at Cardiff. Tomorrow I think of sailing to Chepstow in a Steamer that there is, and returning by the same at night. This evening we have to go to a Party at Mrs —— (Miss Strachey's that was).[8] My head, my head! Dr Symons, a far too flattering man, asked me to dinner: *Ach Gott, nein, tausentmal nein* [Oh, Lord, no, a thousand times no]."

This day as I said is Scotch-misty, occasionally it rains: I put on old trowsers and my blanket coat, and sally forth almost rejoicing. This is a dingy region of reek and industrial confusion; but with some-

6. Richard (Beau) Nash (1674–1761) established the Assembly Rooms and a code of etiquette and dress at Bath. Frances Anne, Viscountess Vane (1713–88), infamous for her gambling and profligacy at Bath, contrib. ch. 81, "Memoirs of a Lady of Quality," to Smollett's novel *Peregrine Pickle* (1751).

7. Horatio Montagu (1796–1862), naval officer and clergyman; see 11:130. John Addington Symonds (1807–71; *DNB*), physician in Bristol since 1831. TC speaks of him as the "skilful and ingenious Dr. Symonds," Sterling's "physician as well as friend" (*Life of Sterling, Works* 11:184). Symonds's da. Mary Isabella (1836–83) was Edward Strachey's 2d wife, m., 1857.

8. Jane (d. 1886), da. of Edward and Julia Strachey, m., 1842, John Hare of Hare & Co., Temple Gate, Bristol, floor cloth and color manufacturers.

thing antique and respectable in the air of it,—not merely so lath-and-plaster like as much of Liverpool is. I passed thro' a massive old Town-gate yesterday: on one of the Quays too as we drove along, I read "SOUTHEY: Grocery and Tea Establishment."— It was in this very street that Sterling lived, a N*o* or two from ours.[9]

Adieu dear Bairn: there is no end to my clatter if I did not *put* an end to it. I send thee a thousand blessings. Wales and quiet are within sight almost. Westward ho!

Ever your affectionate
T. Carlyle

If you get no Letter tomorrow, consider me *gone* to Chepstow.

JWC TO TC

Tuesday [4 July 1843]

Dearest

The first night is over and we are neither robbed nor murdered. I must confess, however, that I observed last night, for the first time, with what tremendous facility a thief—with the average thief-agility—might swing himself, by laying hold of the spout, off the garden wall right into my dressing closet!—leaving me no time to spring my rattle or even unsheath my dagger— I must have Pearson to put some screw in the window when he comes tomorrow—

I awoke this morning to sleep no more at four o'clock. a sudden thought having struck me in my sleep that I had *de grandes choses à faire!*[1] But now that I have had a cup of washy *tea* (for I took blue-pill last night by way of clearing my faculties) I see "nothing pushing"— I have only "to pree-pare the criminal (your room) for execution" (Pearson is to come tommorow at six)—and to drive to Greenwich and *sit some time under a tree* with old Sterling— He came yesterday

9. Reminding TC of the poet Robert Southey (1774–1843), b. at Bristol, who had d. 21 March. 2 Lower Terrace, Clifton Pl.

JWC-TC, [4 July]. Addr: Care of Mrs Strachey / Lower Crescent / Clifton / Bristol. PM: 3 July 1843; Bristol, 4 July 1843. MS: NLS 602.103; longhand copy with TC's notes: Berg. Pbd: A. Carlyle, *NLM* 1:106–8 inc.; quot: Froude, *LM* 1:194. On the envelope TC has written: "1 & 2 july 1843 / (I *just* gone to Clifton: *in*)." Apparently JWC used an envelope prepaid and postmarked 3 July, and posted Tues. morning to reach Bristol by afternoon.

1. " 'Rise M. le Comte, you have great things to do,' so said M. de Sa[?] Simon (not the Louis-Quatorze one, but his miserable windbag of a descend*t*, the Père de l'Humanité, new Messias &c of Paris in those years), and immediately got out of bed" (TC's note); see 7:192.

just after I went out—and was told by Helen my first direction was to the Postoffice so presently in walking up Church Street towards Pearson's—I heard a horse and wheels *pirring* [running quickly] after me which I understood by the sound of it somehow—without turning my head—to be in chase of *me.*— He drove me to Pearson's, then to take the air on foot—or rather the dust—for it was blowing a perfect torpedo of dust—on Battersea bridge—where I spoke to Helps going forth on his ride[2]—then to the dyers[3]—and set me out in Kings road having "important business in town"—viz: having to eat mutton chops at the Carlton—

Juliet Mudie did not appear last night—instead came the Irish woman with a rigmarole of a letter from the Mother which I answered peremptorily enough— If she chose I told her to send Juliet to the dressmaker I would complete the necessary sum and find her some cloathes—if not I would give her at once the £5 contributed by the only people who knew any thing whatever of M*r*.-Mudie—and the rest—received from my own friends—*because I had asked it*—and because I had represented her case as very distressing—and given on the understanding that *I* should see it usefully employed—*that* part of the money I would either keep till I saw some effectual thing to be done with it for her family or—I would return it to those from whom it had come— As I considered *her* scheme of taking up house on such a limited sum entirely unfeasable—I was very angry—it is so selfish in her—wanting to appropriate the money and it was so provoking that Julia had not been let come to go to M*rs* Tagart after all the botheration I had in recommending her[4]— Besides Helen told me yesterday that she had heard from the irish woman that if her Mistress could get a comfortable house to sit down in, she intended writing a novel!!

Elizabeth Pepoli came in the evening—nobody else—she invited me to go tonight when Carlo would be out at dinner; but Greenwich will be *distraction* enough for one day!

The poor little Umbrella is not come yet[5]— I will go to see about it

2. Arthur Helps (1813–75; *DNB*), later govt. clerk and historian; see 12:101. A commissioner of French, Spanish, and Danish claims, 1838–41, he had pbd. *Essays Written in the Intervals of Business* (1841) and was now devoting himself to literary work, including his historical dramas *Catherine Douglas* (1843) and *King Henry the Second* (1843). He lived in Chester Sq., Pimlico.

3. Probably John Newman, 1 Strongs Pl., Brompton.

4. Probably Helen Tagart, b. Bourn (1791–1871), widow of Thomas Martineau, Harriet's eldest brother, m., 1828, Edward Tagart (1804–58; *DNB*), unitarian minister, of 233 Porchester Terrace. Julia and Juliet Mudie are the same.

5. " 'Mudie'—'Pearson' umbrella" (TC's note). Before leaving for Wales TC had bought JWC an umbrella for her birthday, 14 July, at a shop in Oxford St., which failed to deliver it.

tomorrow if there be not time today—never mind the failure of your little strategem—it is only the more affecting for me from its failure.

—No letters today except one from Jeannie—

Here is Sterling come for me already—so farewell— Write instantly

Your affectionate unfortunate—goody

JWC TO TC

[5 July 1843]

Dearest

The earth-quake is commenced—awfully grand I assure you—and the heat too is awfully grand—I was up at six—and had a pitcherful of water poured on me the first thing—

The time I have been reading the letters is the only time I have sat still since I rose (*irish*)—Miss Bölte has been here but I absolutely refused to go down to her— She was here yesterday also while I was at Greenwich—Greenwich methinks is an extremely *"nasty"* place—but we had good cold chicken and strawberries— Little Mr Cowan came while I was away to offer me his boat for the Regatta[1]— —but I should not have gone having no idea of losing my one life at a sailing match—Darwin also came—and Elizabeth—but I missed the whole—I should like to be "well let alone" for I have *grandes choses a faire* [great things to do]—

For your comfort under any noises that may wake you what think you *roused me* this morning? *the buzzing of flies!*

Here is a note requesting for the King of Prussia the same extraordinary piece of information which Mazzini applied to you for the other day—the Devil fly away with that foolish *double!*[2]— What a

JWC-TC, [5 July]. Addr: Mrs. Strachey's / 2 Lower Terrace / Clifton—Bristol. PM: 5 July 1843. MS: NLS 602.104; longhand copy with TC's notes: Berg. The copy records as an enclosure JWC's letter to TC of 3 July; at the top of the copy of the enclosure TC has written: "*Enclosure,* written day before.—I just gone to Clifton." At the top of the MS JWC has written, as promised in JWC to TC, [3 July]: "Mrs Crafurd Blackbrook / Monmouth." On the envelope TC wrote: "5 july 1843 (going to Redwood's) / (in)." Pbd: A. Carlyle, *NLM* 1: 108–9; quot: Froude, *LM* 1:194–95.

1. Cowan unidentified but probably the same as mentioned at 14:159. "Have quite forgotten him" (TC's note). The Thames Regatta, the first of its kind, with races for watermen and gentlemen, was 3–5 July, attended by "shoals of small boats, and a large display of steamers" (*Times,* 5 July).

2. The letter, 4 July, was from C. K. J. Bunsen, about the advocate Thomas Carlyle (1803–55; *DNB*), apostle of the Catholic Apostolic Church (see 6:132); see TC to CKJB, 7 July. Frederick William IV (1795–1861; reigned 1840–61), to whom TC had been presented in 1842.

pen!—also an invitation from the Bishop of St Davids[3]—I send them on without delay tho I am not sure they will overtake you at Clifton—

You do not tell me how you like my beautiful *Vittoria* do please condescend to particulars— Krasinski[4] has sent me a long list of Icelandic books—shall I send it—

"You must excuse us the day."[5] I am in a complete mess and my pen refuses almost to mark—I shall be in complete mess for a time and half a time— I will perhaps go a few days to the Isle of Wight for breathing in the midst of it—but I shall not be done with my work this month to come— You see—you do so hate commotions that this house gets no *peridodical cleanup* like other people's and one must make the most of your absence— Do not curse this writing I will try to get some pens mended for next time— your affectionate

J C

TC TO JWC

Wednesday [5 July 1843], Midnight—

My Bairn,

I have been at Chepstow; in all kinds of weather, in rain, in glowing heat, and then home thro' the heart of thunderstorms: I am totally wearied; and have just got up to my sleeping place, which seems tolerably quiet: I must not spend above a minute or two in *writing*. But tomorrow at 11 o'clock, I have to be on board the Cardiff steamer; there will not then be any Letter for perhaps two days,—as, I believe, a day is *lost* somewhere between Wales and this by all Letters: take my kind goodnight therefore dear Goody, and thanks for the punctual most welcome despatch which I found lying on my table on returning today. You are very good. Write always. Write to the new address: "Cha*s* Redwood Esq, Llandough Cowbridge S. Wales"; except thro' your Letters I am at present disunited with all the Earth.

Chepstow is beautiful; the rocks of the Avon at Clifton on the road thither by steam excel all things I have seen,—even I the most deter-

3. Connop Thirlwall.

4. Walerjan Skorobohaty Krasinski (1780–1855), Polish nobleman, writer, and political exile; lived in London, 1830–50, and in Edinburgh, 1850–55; author of *Historical Sketch . . . of the Reformation in Poland,* 2 vols. (1838–40); *Poland,* 4 pts. (1855), and other works. "Amiable, mild gentleman, Polish exile; utterly poor; died in Edinburgh ten years afterwards" (TC's note in Froude, *LM* 1:348).

5. Coterie speech; see 7:199.

TC-JWC, [5 and 6 July]. MS: NLS 611.124. Pbd: Froude, *Carlyle* 3:299–300 inc.

mined *Anti*-viewhunter[1] find them worthy of a word. I have passed the day perhaps not ill,—tho' in laborious idleness: who knows? Yesternight we had a soiree at Mrs Hare's: one or two intelligent persons; the Doctor Symons, a hectic clergyman, a Mr Frippe (I think) very deep in business, all decided Carlyleans—ach Gott. There was also a tremendous artist-fiddler and piano-player, and certain pretty young women sat speechless.[2]

I will to sleep, I will to sleep!

The Scoundrel umbrella-vender! He is the *first* below Darwin's entry on the same side, as you proceed towards the Quadrant: send the Stimabile in his Brougham to *thunder* eight-ninths of the wretched tailor-life out of him for his sin![3]

Adieu, and thousand goodnights. You have done quite right about the Mudies.— Ever your affectionate

T. C.

Thursday morning [*6 July*] *7½ o'clock.*— The best good morning to thee, Dearest! I have got the third of my nights put behind me, not so badly after all; and am now up, waiting for hot water, then for packing, then for breakfast, then for Cardiff at 11 o'clock. There is a brisk cold wind, which will brighten up to drought and brightness I think. My longing to be in some kind of quietude is considerable.—

Perhaps there will a Letter come from you yet this morning? If so, I will mark a *pencil stroke* on the outside of the cover; for at present I must seal. Adieu, my Dearest! I hope thou hast slept, and art soon to have some coffee!

The hot water is here. Off!—

Affectionately ever / T. C.

1. Cf. "Characteristics," *Works* 28:24, and Harrold, *Sartor* 151–52.

2. George Strachey has described TC's talk with the clergyman (probably one of the many Fripps in the Bristol area): "Although Carlyle was devoid of the aesthetic sensibilities, he was taken to a party at the house of my married sister, where despite his recorded contempt for the portion of mankind that listened to Paganini, he attended with propriety to some solos executed by that great violinist H. C. Cooper. During the pause for supper, the hero of the evening was buttonholed by a local clerical magnate, whose attitude towards the new philosophy, if not that of a proselyte of righteousness, was that of a proselyte of the gate. They got into a warm controversy on matters of faith, and when Carlyle said, 'If a man's maker bid him go to the bottomless pit, he should go,' the clergyman asked, 'What do you mean by the bottomless pit?' The answer was: 'Sir, I mean the pit of love and despair; and now, sir, we will go back to the fiddlers.' Saying which Carlyle triumphantly returned to the drawing-room" (G. Strachey, *CRG* 400). The violinist was Henry Christopher Cooper (1819–81).

3. The Quadrant: the curved part of Regent St. leading N from Piccadilly Circus. Edward Sterling, nicknamed both *Stimabile* (Estimable; see 8:224) and "the Thunderer" (see 8:144).

TC TO JWC

Llandough, Cowbridge
Thursday Night—[6] july, 1843

Dearest,

The Post goes tomorrow at nine o'clock; wherefore tho' very tired I will write thee a word: it will have to lie at Bristol all day, and you will not get it till Saturday morning, as I find, at any rate. A brief word must suffice.

Your precious little billet came to me at breakfast,—for breakfast did at last come, tho' my patience was well nigh worn out waiting for it in vain. A pencil stroke on the cover would indicate the fact, according to agreement.

I got down in good time to my Cardiff Steamer; a brisk breezy morning promising well: and again after endless ringing of bells and loading of hampers, and bullying and jumbling, in which I took part only as a distant onlooker, we got off down the muddy Avon once more. I passed a most silent day, remembrances of all kinds and these only my occupation. On the Somersetshire shore we passed a bathing-establishment; hapless Mothers of families sitting on folding-stools by the beach of muddy tide-streams,—ach Gott! It is a solitary Sea the Severn one;[1] we passed near only one ship, and in that there lay a cabin boy sound asleep amid ropes, and a black-visaged sailor had raised his shock-head only half a-wake, thro' the hatches, to see what we were: they lay there waiting for a wind. I smoked 2 cigars and a half; I hummed all manner of tunes, sang even portions of Psalms in a humming tone for my own behoof, reclining on my elbow; and so the day wore on, and at three o'clock we got into Cardiff Dock; and I, sharp on the outlook, descried the good Redwood waiting there. He had a *tub-gig*, a most indescribable thin-bodied semi-articulate but altogether helpful kind of factotum man-servant, who stept on board for my luggage, and so in few minutes, after giving a glance at Cardiff Castle,[2] and buying a few cigars, we got eagerly to the road, and not long after five, had done our twelve miles and were safe here. It was the beautifullest day; a green pleasant country full of shrubby knolls and white thatched cottages: altogether a very reasonable drive. Unexpectedly in a totally solitary spot I was bidden dismount, and looking to the right, saw close by the Redwood Mansion. A house about the

TC-JWC, [6 and 7] July. MS: NLS 611.125. Pbd: Froude, *Carlyle* 3:300–1 inc.; Bliss, *TC* 161–63 inc.

1. Bristol is approx. 8 mi. inland from the Bristol Channel, and is linked to it by the Avon, a tributary of the Severn.

2. Dating from 1080.

capacity of Craigenputtoch tho' in Welsh Style, all trim-shaven, covered with roses, hedged off from the Parish-road by invisible fences and a pa[t]ch[3] of very pretty lawn. The old Lady an innocent native old Quakeress[4] received me with much kind simplicity, asked for *you* &c: our dinner which she had carefully cooked, and kept hot for an hour and a half consisted—of VEAL![5] Nay I heard of a veal-pie for future use; I suppose they have killed a fatted calf for me, knowing my tastes! There was good *ham* and a dish of good boiled peas and a pudding: I did very well. And then we have been to *walk* since; and the place on the whole is the loveliest and most *silent* in all the Earth, and I think I shall learn to do very well. But here in the meanwhile are tidings of a *dish of hot milk:* I must off, dearest, with brief salutations. Perhaps I shall again find time tomorrow for a word. Adieu, adieu!—Sleep well, and dream of me. / T. C.

Friday morning [7 *July*] *half past 7.*— Being on my feet again too early, I will add a word till there be some likelihood of breakfast, or at lowest of *shaving*. All is still, here, as in a hermitage of La Trappe;[6] but one dirty little yelp of a dog was sufficient to awaken me a while ago,—a *messin* [small dog] is as good as a lion! I am tolerably well nevertheless; and shall get better if I had broken my fast, I hope.

Things are not arranged in a very artistic way, I fear in this establishment of mine, and the servant maid seems much of a blockhead; but we will hope better things tho' we thus speak.[7] The *simplicity* of my kind hosts verges also a little on the inane; and conversing with them does not promise to be a treat. Perhaps they will let me well alone. We shall see,—and if they do not, take our departure all the sooner!

I am come away out of the region of the Crawfords; and my Bishop is still some sixty miles inland: I know not whether I shall get to either, nor indeed what my capabilities yet are. Nor have I yet got any tidings about the *independent lodging* on the sea-coast; I rather think Redwood indicated last night that he had given up that place. On monday morning, you will hear farther and more distinctly about all manner of things.

This morning still if I can, at all events on Sunday (for Monday's

3. Letter omitted.
4. Elizabeth Redwood.
5. Which TC found indigestible.
6. Home monastery of the Cistercian order of monks, noted for strict observance of silence; see 6:432.
7. Coterie speech; cf. 11:94.

Post) I will write to Bunsen: he is a provoking blockhead that double of mine![8]

You need not send K[r]asinski's[9] Iceland List into this region.— I will now set to *Accoromboni,* of which I have not yet read a hundred pages, promising as the whole matter looked. O dear Duckie, I wish I were near thee with thy hot coffeepot at this moment! But I could not stay there when I was so.— I will end, and go and shave at present.

Has that accursed Chimera of a Cockney not sent the umbrella yet? I could see him trailed thrice thro' the Thames for his scoundrel conduct: no man knows what breaking of his word will do for the general injury!— Adieu Dearest. I will write again by the next post, with more specific news. A thousand blessings!

T. C.

TC TO C. K. J. BUNSEN

Llandough, Cowbridge, S. Wales
7 july, 1843—

My dear Sir,

There is or lately was a Thomas Carlyle, once an Advocate in Edinburgh, but who quitted that profession for some form of religious Fanaticism ("Irvingism" is the name of it); who preaches accordingly, as an "Angel" so-called, at Albury in Surrey, under the wing of Henry Drummond the rich Banker, a Patron of that sect, and perhaps an "Archangel" in it. This Thomas Carlyle, besides his Angel-work at Albury, goes now and then to Germany, as I have understood, and specially to Berlin, for the purpose of converting your benighted people to his Doctrine; with what success I cannot conjecture. He is the man, I imagine, who must have written this Book on the German Nobility; and thought it so profound as to deserve the King of Prussia's perusal![1]

8. Thomas Carlyle the apostle; see TC to CKJB, 7 July.
9. Letter omitted.

TC-CKJB, 7 July. MS: Yale. Hitherto unpbd.
1. Bunsen wrote to TC, 4 July: "I am asked: who is Mr Thomas Carlyle, who lately being in Berlin sent to His Majesty a Memoir intitled:/On the position & prospects of the German nobility,/ and then returned to England & Scotland by Hamburg? Now I never knew there existed a *double* of yourself, and I know that you have not been at Berlin. . . . Perhaps you can say something to explain this mysterious circumstance." As an apostle of the Catholic Apostolic Church, Carlyle (see 10:160) became known as "The Apostle for North Germany," with Prussia and N Germany as his special province. He often resided in Germany, where he superintended congregations of converts. Within the next few years he came to know Bunsen, who introduced him to King Frederick William IV.

Another friend[2] was already inquiring of me on the same subject; to whom I made answer that I never wrote, or designed to write, or had heard even in dreams of the writing of such a Book;—and this, all except the *last* clause of it, may stand for a response in the present case too.

T. Carlyle the Angel has more than once got me into scrapes of a similar kind. He is, I believe, a zealous, very well-intentioned man; but narrow, headlong, dim, and probably not without a dash of the [word illegible]—he is an "Angel" at Albury, in short; and I am no Angel anywhere! There is in fact nothing common to us but the Name, and general descent from Adam. Me, I have heard, he considers to be a man of some ability, but "possessed with *a Devil*": I shall very specially request of you to assure all persons high and low who may inquire of you, that we have "*no* concern with the other house".[3]

It was yesterday that I arrived here: a most solitary green region, very rainy too at present;—in which I feel hitherto very much like a man fallen out of the Moon. The people speak inarticulate Welsh or *Kauderwälsch* [gibberish], and they, and the whole world, except the rain-clouds, seems to be asleep or nearly so. I have Tieck's *Vittoria Accorombona,* and care for no weather today!

With many kind regards and wishes / Yours ever truly

T. Carlyle

JWC TO JEANNIE WELSH

[7 July 1843]

Oh Babbi! —would thou wert here to do my hair!— Words cannot paint it Babbie! *Infernal?*—that is too mild an epithet by far, for the "hubbub wild and dire dismay" which I am now actually in the midst of! In the Lobby—close at my ear there is a noise as of the tumbling down of continuous cart-loads of hard-ware—diversified by snatches of wild strains—the youth is there scrubbing the wainscot with pumice-stone preparatory to painting and is cheering his soul under the discordant task by singing bits of "the Red cross Knights"—Evelyn's Bower &c &c—,[1] in a voice almost as unmusical as the pumice-stone itself—this part of the operation had already lasted two days—it is impossible to hear oneself or anyone else talk thro it—yet this is the only

2. Mazzini; see JWC to TC, [5 July].
3. Trade statement, disclaiming connection with another firm.

JWC-JW, [7 July]. Addr: 20 Maryland Street / Liverpool. PM: 7 July 1843. MS: NLS 1892.29. Pbd: Huxley, *JWCLF* 140–42 inc.

1. Popular songs.

room left tenable—yesterday M*rs* Chadwick came—Robertson was here at the same time[2]—and no sooner had the lady seated herself on the sofa beside me and begun to utter the usual civilities—when bang, bang, crash, screetch, came the pumice stone over the room door to the tune of "Oh rest thee my darling," in a way that made us all with one accord start from our seats and utter a loud simultaneous scream—which was followed by fits of laughter— "It was too ridiculous *for anything*" Then ev[e]ry[3] time one ventures up stairs one is bespattered with whitewash—and the smell in this hot weather!— Oh upon *my* honour it is awfully grand!

For my plan of reformation this time is on a very extended scale—I am whitewashing all the ceilings—design to have that closet taken away which gives the library the look of a person with one eye—to paint and paper that room and paint the passages and staircase—not before they needed it—Carlyle said I might lay out ten pounds—my estimate is for fifteen—but if he *grudges* the additional five when he sees it all done—why I can pay it out of my own pocket thank goodness!—Then I am making with my own hands new slips for the furniture—and shall have a tough job at window curtains when they come from the dyer. and if you take (to use the Dumfries Courier's favourite expression) "a birds-eye view" of all this—and then reflect on the extraordinary attentions which the public thinks it proper to pay me always, when I am alone—and *the letter* to be written to *him* every day—with so many other letters that his absence involves me in answer[in]g, you will not wonder that I say oh that you were here to do my hair!

I awake regular[l]y every morning at *four* to sleep no no more— —get up at six when the workmen come—with a vague feeling that I have "*grandes choses à faire*" The night before last indeed I felt in such a press of things that I could not sleep *at* all—but sat in my shift at the open window looking at the sultry rain-drops falling on the sleeping grass and trees—and then I cannot *eat* anything to speak of—yesterday I went entirely without dinner and almost without breakfast also and felt the better for "wanting" them— Most days however, you will be glad to hear, that Sterling brings his carriage and drives me wheresoever I please— I have him in perfect subjection at present— On Wednesday I dined there to meet Charles Barton poor M*rs* John Sterlings brother[4]— He told me that Sterling's phrase of invita-

2. Rachel Chadwick; John Robertson.
3. Letters omitted here and later.
4. Thomas Charles Barton (1805–56); educ. Corpus Christi College, Cambridge, 1826; B.A., 1830; M.A., 1833; see also 8:140; settled at Bonn, Germany. JWC met him on 5 July.

tion to him had been "Will you come to me at half after five—that Angel dines with me today—that Angel of consolation and mercy"—!!!— Last evening I had a quiet walk in Battersea fields. with Plattnauer—the only good hour I have passed since Carlyle went away—we talked of "*that sweet girl*"[5] as we often do—that young man improves under my "*angelic ministrations*"—there is an *earnestness* a something of *noble* of *self-sacrificing* in him now which gives him about the same amount of resemblance to Cavaignac *spiritually* which I used to find in him *externally*—it is not very *striking*—but still something to be glad of—

Mazzini is still confined to the house with his face but he *professes* to be quite well otherwise—I have not seen him for a week— It always puts me into such a bad humour going there—to see the *mess* in which these wretched Tanceonis keep him. and the silly way in which he submits to be made their *prey* as it were—that I never go except in case of necessity—and last day the sight of his face was a sight to make one dream bad dreams of him for a week after— Had he taken care after the first abatement of the swelling it would have been all well—but he went fussing out day after day on the business of the Italian school and got more cold in it—and then the tumour came outside and burst and had to be lanced—and heaven knows when his face will look as it did—but what cares *he* how it looks? I wish you would write him a little note of enquiry—he needs all the kind attentions possible from without, his consolations at home are so few!— And now what of *your*self—after all this about *my*self—are the rest gone? I hope so—for the getting of certain persons fa[i]rly off is a devil of a business, as I was fully sensible the last Sunday and Monday morning— I have no paper—so be thankful for the backs of old notes—love to all that are at home and to Walter[6]—I hope he will soon seek me in my chaos— Bless thee darling of my heart—

Your own J C

JWC TO TC

[7 and 8 July 1843]

Dearest

I *take time by the pig-tail*[1] and write at night—*after* post-hours—during the day there is such an infernal noise of *pumice-stone*—diversi-

5. I.e., Jeannie.
6. Macgregor.

JWC-TC, [7 and 8 July]. MS: NLS 602.105–6; longhand copy with TC's notes: Berg. Pbd: Froude, *LM* 1:202–8 inc., where dated 18 July; A. Carlyle, *NLM* 1:110–12 inc. On a slip of paper, now bound with the MS, TC wrote: "?/ july, 1843 (*before* going to Ryde." On the copy he gives "12 july" as the date.
1. A play on the saying to "take time by the forelock."

fied with snatches of "wild strains"—the youth who is scraping the walls, (—as if it were a hundred knife-grinders melted into one)—consoling himself under the hideous task by striking up every two minutes *"the Red-cross Knights—"* or *Evelyn's Bower"* or some such plaintive melody, which after a brief attempt to render itself predominant "dies away into an unintelligible whimper[2]— Yesterday forenoon M*rs* Chadwick came—and had just seated herself on the sofa beside me and was beginning to set forth amiabilities; when bang, bang, crash, screech, came the pumice-stone over the room-door—to the tune of "Oh rest thee my darling

Thy sire is a Knight &c &"

making us both start to our feet with a little scream—and then fall back again in fits of laughter— Then the stairs are all flowing with white-wash—"and altogether" when I fancy *you* here "in the midst of it," I do not know whether to laugh, or to cry, or to shriek— But it will be a clean pretty house for you to come home to—and should you find that I have exceeded by *a few pounds* your modest allowance for painting and papering; you will find that I have *not* been *thoughtless* nevertheless, when I show you a document from M*r* Morgan[3] promising to "idemnify us for the same in the undisturbed possession of our house for five years"!—a piece of paper in fact equivalent to a lease of the house for five years "with the receprocity all on one side"[4]—binding him and leaving us free—"such a thing" old Sterling said who attended me to *Popes head ahoy* "as no woman but myself would have had the impudence to ask," nor any *law*yer *in his senses* the folly to grant"— I do not see but we might get a lease of the house after all for as long as we pleased—if *I* went about it, instead of the voluptuous Perry[5]— M*r* Morgan said he rather thought *he* had the first claim on the property himself and that "it was a pity but he had *seen me* sooner"—at all events as it stands at present—should the woman die tomorrow they cannot raise the rent on us or turn us out without remunerating us for our outlay—and *that* was really as much as I could in my conscience insist on—seeing that we have the house so very cheap—and that M*r*

2. "My father's acc*t* of a Precentor who lost his tune, desperately tried sev*l* others, and then 'died away into an &c' " (TC's note).

3. "Lawyer in the city; virtual proprietor here" (TC's note on MS); of William & James Morgan, stockbrokers, 3 Pope's Head Alley, Cornhill.

4. Coterie speech.

5. "Pedant Carpent*r* and House Ag*t* here; characterised unthrift of the poor by that adjective" (TC's note on MS). Presumably John Perry, carpenter and builder, 29 Lawrence St. On the copy TC has crossed out the "tu" in "voluptuous" and added "chi" above the line. Froude, *LM* prints "volup*chious.*" JWC writes "Pope's head ahoy" twice, presumably as an unexplained joke.

Morgan had been *till he saw me* quite indifferent whether we kept it, at the present rent, or not— But this was one of those remarkable instances of *fascination* which I exercise over gentlemen of "a certain age." before I had spoken six words to him it was plain to the meanest capacity that he had fallen over head and ears in love with me—and if he put off time in writing me the promise I required, it was plainly only because he could not bear the idea of my going away again!—no wonder!—probably no such beatific vision as that of a *real, live woman,* in a silk bonnet and muslin gown, ever irradiated that dingy dusty law-chamber of his and sat there on a three-feet-high stool—since he had held a pen behind his ear—and most certainly never before had either man or woman in that place addressed him as a human-being—not as a lawyer—or he would not have looked so struck dumb with admiration when *I* did so.— For respectability's sake I said in taking leave that "my husband was out of town or he would have come himself"— "Better as it is" said the old gentleman "do you think I would have written to your *husband's* dictation as I have done to *yours*"?— He asked if your name were John or William—plainly he had lodged an angel unawares[6]— By the way—that other *angel*[7] is becoming a bore—Charles Barton with whom I dined at Sterlings in returning from Popes head a-hoy—told me that he had been making quite a sensation in Berlin and been invited to a great many places on the strength of *The French Revolution*— He (Chales B) was asked to dine with him—that is, "with Thomas Carlyle author of the French Revolution," at the Marquis of Westmorland's[8]— "Is *he* here" said Charles—"I shall be delighted to see him I know him quite well"—and accordingly on the appointed day he "almost ran into the arms of the announced Thomas Carlyle—*and then retreated with consternation.*" It was so far good that he had opportunity to disabuse *these* people at least—by declaring "THAT was not Thomas Carlyle at all"! But is it not a shame in the creature to encourage the delusion, and let himself be fêted as a Man of Genius when he is only a "crack-brained enthusiastic."[9] Charles walked home with me and told me of a great many domestic grievances—amongst the rest that the poor Maurices have lost *the whole* of Annie's fortune by America![10]— This is a secret however—another thing

6. Heb. 13:2.

7. "'T. Carlyle' of the Irvingite Church,—long a double-ganger of mine" (TC's note).

8. John Fane (1784–1859; *DNB*), 11th earl of Westmoreland, resident minister at Berlin.

9. "My Father's epithet for Mrs. Carruthers, long ago" (TC's note).

10. Presumably by a bad investment in American securities. Maurice's biographers make no mention of it. Anna Maurice (1810–45) m., 1837, F. D. Maurice.

about the Maurice's affected me strangely—the new baby is perfectly healthy and well formed[11]—but it never ceases from *sobbing and sighing*—not like a baby but like a grown person!—the D*r* imputes it to the Mother's suppressed grief[12]—and says the habit will *wear off*—

I have awoke at four every morning since you went away—and the night before last I slept just *half an hour* in all—it is always the effect of finding myself *in a new position*— When the work people come at six I get up, which makes a prodigiously long day—but I do not weary—having so many mechanical things to do—this morning I took—or rather failed to take the showerbath— —I pulled with concentrated courage and nothing would come—determined not to be quite baffled however, I made Helen pour a pitcherful of water on me instead—

Forster writes today that he will probably call for me tomorrow evening—if not tomorrow; on Wednesday—moreover that I must *dine* with him in your absence and he will get M*rs* Macready[13] for decency's sake—*"never Sir"!*[14]—I sent the note to *Krasinski* as it chiefly concerned *him*—

Mazzini came this forenoon for the first time—very pale and weak—but his face pretty well mended— He was horribly out of spirits, and no wonder— They have brought out the British & Foreign Review *without* his article!![15] a most untimely contretemps for him in an economical point of view—and besides very mortifying to him *morally*—as he is "sure it is merely because of his being a foreigner that he is so ill used"— I was strongly advising him to—run away!—to hide himself from all people—friends and *creditors* and disciples, in Switzerland or some cheap, quiet place. And I should not wonder if he did some such thing in the end—a man cannot live "in a state of crisis" (as he calls it) forever—

The umbrella?—not yet!—they themselves are going to keep it I think till the 14*th*[16]— Sterling was to take me in returning from M*r* Mor-

---

Her money would have been inherited either from her father, Lt.-Gen. Charles Barton of Waterfoot (1760–1819), or her mother's family, the Johnstons of Bordeaux, wine merchants.

11. Charles Edmund Maurice (29 June 1843–1926). Their other child was John Frederick (1841–1912).

12. "On her Sister's death in April last" (TC's note). Anna's sister, Susannah Sterling, had d. 18 April.

13. "The famous Actor's wife: well liked here" (TC's note).

14. Coterie speech.

15. "The Works of Thomas Carlyle," trans. Geraldine Jewsbury, *British and Foreign Review* 16 (1844, pbd. Oct. 1843):262–93, on *Heroes* and *Sartor*, sent to John Mitchell Kemble, 6 July 1841, with a para. added on *Past and Present* (see 13:171); not paid for till Feb. 1844.

16. TC's note on this is largely illegible: " 'Umbrella' I had ordered before

gan's—but as with my usual negligence—I started with no other address except *Pope's head Alley*—it was a work of time and difficulty to find it—and then I kept him so long waiting *outside* Mr Morgans dais—that all the way home he was in the sulks—declaring that Charles Barton would be come—and so would not go a yard out of the straight road—yesterday he was at the christening of William Coninghams child[17]—(they *have* christened it!) and I was too weary after my sleepless night to go up to town on my own foundation— Today I was *obliged* to write to Jeannie—and a final letter about the Mudies to Geraldine, and then Elizabeth came and I was made too late—tomorrow I *will* go or the Devil is in it You made me "heir you said to *all* your *note paper* and *writing paper*" and when I went to enter on possession of my anticipated *rich* legacy I found—a tiny slip—*four* sheets—of note paper—and devil a morsel of any other!—except the foolscap So I had to purchase almost immediately—and as you see by the foregoing sheets have got more than the average proportion of plaster of Paris— By the way Mazzini has heard from Paris that *the book*[18] was *for certain* delivered *into Cavaignac's hands.*—so it is very stupid of *him* to have sent no newspaper— I think I have told you every thing I have to tell—except that I was mighty glad of your letter— — I do not see how I am to get to the Isle of Wight— I cannot leave the house with work people coming and going—and Helen declars naturally—that "without *me* she could not stay a night in the house for the whole world"— But I dare say I am quite as content here studious of household good[19] as I should be, dragged about to look at picturesque views at the Isle of Wight—or anywhere else that "fool creturs go for *diversion*"[20] If I disliked London heat it would be different the preservation of one's health is *duty* not *diversion*—but London be it e'er so hot its ne'er too hot for me![21]— Today we have had the beautifulest soft rain—to make all fresh again and on the whole the weather is charming and I never go into the dusty streets on foot—good night—

---

leaving Town . . . with [instructions?] that it was to be deliver*d* . . . before the 14th. . . . Promise *broken.*"

17. The son b. 14 March.

18. Presumably *Past and Present.*

19. *Paradise Lost* 9:233.

20. "Her Grandf*r* John's definit*n* of poetry, 'Pack o' lies, that fuil craitures write for, &c' " (TC's note).

21. "Mrs. Siddons, replying to her host, apologetic for his salt fish: 'Fish, be it ne'er so salt,' &c" (TC's note). Sarah Siddons (1755–1831), actress; see 9:170, where the phrase was untraced and JWC applied it to Fanny Kemble, Mrs. Siddons' niece.

Saturday [8 July 1843]

When one gets up at six and "is always *virtuous*"; it *does* look so long till post-time!— But I have your letter, now, and have been to Regent Street too—altho it is still but one oclock. and a regular rainy day!— Sterling came to ask if I wanted any thing, on his way early to the club—so I told him to take me up—and *drop himself at the club*—and I would fetch the carriage home—acceded to—in spite of the discontents occasioned by Popes head alley!— Well the beast of an Umbrella-man simpered and bowed and told endless great lies, and, plainly had—utterly *forgotten* the whole transaction! I recalled it to his mind "emphatically enough" especially the fact of his having received payment for an article which he had failed to send and seemed to be never intending to send— He promised for tonight and I left him with a look—"significative of much"![22] Never mind dearest—the poor little umbrella is only the more precious to me for the difficulty of getting it—

If you have not that sea-bathing lodging I am afraid these good lean people will soon weary you— Well! you cannot come back here just now at all rates—*that* is flat— What think you of going to this Forster— Here indeed you would not *"come out strong"* under the existing circumstances—it is only *I* who can be *"jolly"*[23] in such a mess of noise—dirt, and wild dismay! I said to the Lad in the lobby this morning who was filling the whole house with *"Loves young dream"*—"how *happy* you must feel—that can sing thro' that horrible noise you are making"!—"Yes, *thank you mam*" says he—"I am happy enough *so far as I knows* but I's always a-singing anyhow!—it sounds pleasant to sing at one's work—does'nt it Mam?" "Oh very pleasant" said I quite conquered by his simplicity "but it would be still pleasanter, for *me* at least, if you would sing a song from beginning to end—instead of bits here and there"— *"Thank you* Mam" says he again—"I will try"!—but he does not succeed—

I have the most extraordinary letter from Terrot which I would send only that it would cost *2d* of itself— He writes to tell me that he "did not like his reception" that "often as he came and long as he staid I treated him indeed with *perfect civility*—did not yawn—or appear to be suppressing a yawn—but I seemed to *labour under a continual feeling of opression* (!) and to be thinking all the while of something else (!)" What did I see to offend me in him"? he asks with great humility—"from what he heard of my preferences and saw of my so-

22. "Quiz on me" (TC's note).
23. Cf. Mark Tapley's observations in Dickens, *Martin Chuzzlewit* ch. 5.

ciety, he was inclined to suppose that what I objected to in *him* must be the want of *that first great requisite earnestness*—"! But he begged to assure me &c &c—in short that he had as much earnestness "as he could bear"!!— A letter from a man calling himself Bishop to a woman whom *he* calls infidel—and pleading guilty to her of want of earnestness— Bah! I wish I could snort like Cavaignac

There now I *must* stop I dare say I have wearied you— God keep you Dear Be quite at ease about *me*

Ever your J C

TC TO JOHN A. CARLYLE

Llandough, Cowbridge,
Glamorganshire
8 july (Saturday), 1843—

My dear Brother,

You would find by the hurried word I wrote in the cover of Holcroft's Pamphlet whither I was bound on Thursday morning. We set off at the due hour towards Cardiff by a tract of sea which, I think, is partly known to you: the day was windy, but dry and moderately pleasant; so after an insignificant voyage of four hours we got safe into Cardiff harbour; and there I found my good Attorney in waiting, with a rough "tub-gig," and one of the strangest old grey Welsh servants I ever saw,—a melancholy semi-articulate man, not entirely unlike "Cutty Wright" the Tailor[1] changed into a mixture of ploughman and servant in grey livery: this artist whirled us along in our tub at a moderate rate over the twelve miles to Cowbridge, a village seemingly comparable to Lockerby,[2] but of which I saw only the end, for we there turned off by a narrow precipitous country road, or track between two hedges, and did the other mile and half to Llandough without passing thro' the Cowbridge concern. A modest trim house, of about the capacity of a Minister's Manse, stood suddenly disclosed with roses and a little shaven lawn in front, in a pot amid little bushy hills of which the whole country seems to consist: this was Redwoods house; there did his old Mother in black Quaker bonnet and grey gown, an innocent simple old woman who seems to spend her whole day in reading the New Testament, receive us,—and instantly produce dinner, "which had been waiting for near two hours." As it consisted solely of *roast veal,* it might as well have *continued* waiting, for my share of it!— The vil-

TC-JAC, 8 July. MS: NLS 524.45. Hitherto unpbd.
1. Presumably of Annandale.
2. About 13 mi. NE of Dumfries.

lage of Llandough, if village it may be called which is hardly half the size of Middlebie,[3] and the stillest place I ever saw in my life inhabited by man, lies on the other side of the hillock behind Redwood's house, and was hardly visible, except some chimney-tops if they happened to be pointed out.

I have now been here two nights; but have not yet recovered my clearness of discrimination, so strange is all to me, so still and dreamlike;—add to which that I have slept but indifferently, and only today for the first time have begun to look about me with some composure, in a silent state. Besides it has rained almost incessantly, or at least in successions of lengthy showers. This morning I have sat, till it is now one o'clock, reading a Novel of Tieck's in the porch of the house, the rain falling round me, but all silent otherwise without and within;—a truly *Mährchenhaft* [fairy story] kind of outlook and position. The people of the house seem to have intercourse with absolutely nobody: they are as *good* as possible; considerably inclined to the *wearisome,* but have decided to leave me much in silence, which is all I want. The rain has ceased for the present, but will begin again soon. I have a horse standing ready, if I like to venture out; but I hardly shall, preferring Tieck and Nothingness in these circumstances. Redwood is over at his office in Cowbridge till 4 o'clock, which is the dinner-hour; I gave him to know yesterday that I had pressing need of silence: he, the hospitablest of men, requires only to know what it *is* that I want. He took me yesterday to the shore at St Donat's, some four or five miles off, thro' indescribably rough country road-tracks: there we found a drab-coloured sea, moaning hoarsely towards high limestone cliffs over endless expanses of smooth lime-stone boulders, no sand discoverable, a place *ill* adapted for bathing, unless you either plunged out into the deep water and swam, or sat down (as I did) at knee-depth, and *let* the waves break over you and bathe you. St Donat's is a small sleepy village like the others, with a strange old Castle, now patched into a farm establishment; the village lies sprinkled about in a kind of *gill* or hollow green chasm; very poor, very lazy, all over with odd pebbles, broken cart-shafts and unswept litter; dead-*asleep,* you would say, as I think all the hamlets here are. Over the water we looked thro' the scudding showers to your old region of Linton and Ilfracombe[4] a pleasant outlook: something like the Lothians from Fife: the distinct localities, specific names of hills &c, no mortal on this coast

3. Small village ca. 15 mi. E of Dumfries.
4. Lynton and Ilfracombe are small towns on the N coast of Devon (across the Bristol Channel from St. Donat's) which John Carlyle had visited with William Ogilby; see 12:307.

seems to know. We are all a limestone country, all a *somnolent* country:—and I begin to ask myself, without yet answering distinctly, How I am to get out of it best! Unless I could learn to sleep in it too?

Bishop Thirlwall asks me towards Carmarthen to see him there: this my present host will not hear of till we have been "up three days among the hills," about Merthyr Tidvill[5] I suppose. Thirlwall, however, I have a notion to go and see. He is some sixty miles off this; in the direct course towards Aberystwith:[6] if I could calculate on getting a Coach to Aberystwith and then a steamer from that to Liverpool, I should at once fix on that as the route. But nobody can tell me precisely here: I think however, that is my likeliest way. Failing that, I do discover that there is a steamer from Swansea to Liverpool: I can turn back from Carmarthen and embark at Swansea as a *pis aller* [last resort],—or *mieux aller* [better way]: land-route to Liverpool I think there is not any without going back to Bristol and beginning there.— Well, dear Brother, this is all I can say at present till I have learned farther. Thirlwall cannot receive me till after the eleventh, and with him I may stop perhaps a couple of days: then for Aberystwith or for Swansea,—for Liverpool by some route or other! I could like right well to meet you somewhere, at Aberystwith, in Anglesey,[7] in Liverpool at farthest. But how can I *bid* you travel? You are still and anchored where you are![8]— At lowest write to me instantly by return of post. I shall be here till your Letter come; in any case, it would be forwarded. If Redwood can learn nothing about Aberystwith for me, I think of writing to Alick Welsh at Liverpool. I have brought *your* portmanteau with me, shifting the Books into a trunk as I have no drawers allowed me here (so oblivious the good old Quakeress!) I find it a great convenience. The Coat you gave me ("Tweed" so-called) is a kind of factotum to me, beyond price in these climates! I brought a quite *thin* new one, made to measure, for wearing in hot bright weather: but there is no need of that yet.——

Bunsen's Note I have answered; my "Double," I conclude to be the indefatigable Irvingite *Angel* of Albury; with a murrain to him! Thirlwall's Letter I have not yet answered. The Post is expected in these minutes; but he will bring nothing from you; only news from Jane perhaps, which if they are all right I may indicate by two strokes.— Did you write to Alick? My heart follows him over the waters, in these

5. Carmarthen, a river port, SW Wales. Merthyr Tydfil, the center of iron manufacture, 22 mi. N of Cardiff.

6. Aberystwyth, coastal town, W Wales.

7. Island off N Wales where John had also stayed with Ogilby; see 12:289.

8. At Scotsbrig.

lonely hours, almost incessantly. My blessings on *you* dear Good Mother! Blessings with one and all

Your affectionate / T. Carlyle

The Postman is come; and there are no Letters good or bad. I heard from Jane the morning I left Clifton; busy painting the house &c. Write you soon! A Dr Symons whom I saw at Clifton recommended himself to you; one of John Sterling's friends.— Take care of my Mother!—

TC TO JWC

Llandough, 8 july, 1843—

My Dearest,

It is Saturday night, getting late; and tho' there is nothing very new to be said, I cannot rightly rest till I have written down that nothing and told thee how it goes with me.

Yesterday and today have been showery, unfavourable for excursions or making acquaintance with a new country; neither have I slept well, or till today got anything but *veal to dine on:* nevertheless I get along tolerably well, and shall make out my visit, I think, in a reasonable manner. There is a horse to ride, there is Accorombona to read; I have tobacco, and the people do let me pretty well alone. The simple *inanity* of my kind friends and environment does not diminish, increases rather; but they are very kind to me, very quiet with me: the whole country is of a totally *somnolent* nature, not ill fitted for a man that has come out to see if he can find any sleep!

Yesterday, the breezy morning soon settled down into dim showers of rain: Redwood, at his fixed hour (for he goes like an eightday clock) returned duly from his office at Cowbridge, and took me off to the St Donat's shores for a bathe, and dinner in his lodging at that village. He had a most lively cantering pony for me: he seems to keep a kind of farm, and has several horses and non-descript serving men not a few. Our road was an inextricable series of lanes, with which the whole country seems to be covered; some two yards wide, of precipitous steepness and the *worst* macadamization I ever experienced in this Planet. My brave pony however did not stumble at all; nay seem[1] entirely indifferent to road, and gallops much at its ease over mere stone-heaps mud-gullies or wherever the direction may be. We passed thro' several hamlets, all littery, unswept, bestrewn with chance stones

TC-JWC, 8 [and 9] July. Addr: 5. Cheyne Row, Chelsea / London. MS: NLS 611.126. Pbd: Bliss, *TC* 163–65 inc.

1. Thus in MS.

and pieces of old carts; yet whitened, slated on the *ends,* or well thatched—an air of picturesqueness and sluttish beauty about them; *laziness* and sleep their chief feature. Old castles were not wanting; all grown with ivy, patched sometimes into a kind of farm houses; the people, tho' there were many houses, did not appear anywhere: perhaps they were asleep. Devonshire hills lay across the sea, somewhat as Lothian does from Fife. The sea itself when we arrived at it was moaning hoarse, loud and far, over an endless *cairn* of big boulder stones, without a bit of sand or flat ground visible anywhere: a baddish outlook for bathing, unless you meant to play the Leander there![2] I did step cautiously in, however; then knelt and the big wave, of a respectable drab-colour swashed satisfactorily over me, and again over me (filling my very mouth that second time), whereupon I withdrew. My clothes were in a cavern screened from the rain; there, after dressing, I sat perfectly dry, and smoked a cigar not without comfort. One ship was visible in the distance, making out for Ilfracombe or God knows whither; living creature or trace of living creature was none: one of the loneliest wast[e]s[3] in all her Majesty's dominions. Thro' rain we picked our way up again over the cliffs; got into R's lodgings and found spread out for dinner—the prophecied *veal-pie* and nothing more! I ate some of it, under spoken protest, and drank three glasses of excellent wine. This and the gallop home again jumbled me considerably; and today I have had to go upon diet, pill-box and teetotalism. No more veal will be presented me here.

Today, being well let alone, I sat down in the Porch with Accorombona, read most pleasantly at two feet distance from the rain, till near two o'clock, when I became terribly impatient for the Postman and Letters from Goody. The Postman came; but the Letters from Goody—*ay de mi!*[4] Well, I said, it might have been worse: *bad* news might have come! I took a walk over the height in front of us, in the interval of showers: beautiful green country, rising up northward into insignificant hills, all a cluster of limestone knolls near us, many of them feathered with trees on the top, and a rim of rich meadow always at the base. *Llans* (that is *churches*)[5] without number rise all round: I have been in the inside of this at Llandough; Troston is a Cathedral to it. But the outlook from the door itself there as I sit in the Porch and read; nothing can suit me better: A steep hill covered with wood rises within few yards, and at a gunshot to the left another ditto ditto: these

2. Leander swam the Hellespont to meet Hero, his beloved.
3. Letter omitted.
4. See 6:241.
5. *Llan* could also mean an enclosure or village.

two hills and the bit of meadow between them and the bit of sky over them are all of Nature or of Art that you have anything to do with there. Nay a *road* goes between you and the near hill, but it is so deep that you merely see the *hats* of the people (when any pass) over R's small lawn, and then the people themselves appear farther up on the hill as if they had mounted like exhalations out of invisibility: very queer looking bodies many of them, especially the bits of women. To-day and yesterday I heard a low sound, unlike any other in the whole world; a kind of murmur as of a Psalm-tune sung placidly thro'—Good Heavens!—thro' a part of the body never elsewhere employed in that service! My amazement was great: but today I discovered the perpetrator: a poor ideot, it seems, son of the late Parson here. He looked very happy; and his fundamental base[6] is a not inharmonious feature of our scenery here!—

But enough, O Heavens enough! I ought to tell you what my plans and outlooks are, if any. Thirlwall I do design to visit, if I can; but R. will not hear of it till I try this place a week or so. I must write to his R*t* Reverence, at least; tomorrow, I suppose. To Bunsen I write by this post.[7]— There will be no way for Liverpool, except by Steam from Swansea near this: or better from Aberystwith (if there *be* any steam there), which would take in Carmarthen and the Bishop very neatly by the way. Nobody can tell me the least tidings about it here. I think of writing to Liverpool to ask Alick Welsh. You may ask if you like: Any Steam from ABERYSTWITH, and when?— O my own Dear, I will end this clatter, which perhaps excels all that I ever did in the world before;—which means at least, O good Jeannie, I trust in thee, and love to tell thee all things, my good little Jeannie! Well, here is news of the "hot milk ready Sir": I must down stairs without delay; and so God bless thee Darling, and may there be a Letter tomorrow, and good news! Thine ever

T. Carlyle

Sunday morning [9 July]. Bright weather again, which perhaps may grow to rain again. All well; a better sleep than before: no breakfast as yet,—*there*fore not a word more!

T. C.

6. A pun, on "fundament" (lower part of the body) and "bass" (deep singing voice); that is, the person was singing the psalm employing an unusual part of the body.
7. Presumably TC to CKJB, 7 July.

TC TO W. E. FORSTER

Llandough, Cowbridge
S. Wales, 9 july, 1843—

My dear Sir,

A few days ago I escaped hither, and am got into sea-bathing and rambling in this solitary region; tending, more or less slowly, towards Liverpool the while. Of course Craven for this time is out of the question.[1] Once arrived at Liverpool, I expect to find a Brother, Dr C., perhaps waiting for me; and what possibilities may then have turned up there is no saying with any accuracy as yet. If any likelihood of meeting you in any point of your orbit do present itself, I will not fail to write and investigate.

This is my post-night; a terribly busy one!

With many kind remembrances to Mr and Mrs Fox,[2] with many thanks and regards to yourself,

Yours always truly / T. Carlyle

TC TO CONNOP THIRLWALL

Llandough, Cowbridge / 9 july, 1843—

Dear Bishop Thirlwall,

You are very kind to invite me to your house: your house, Bishop's-palace or whatever the name and nature of it be, is a place I think I might contrive to feel at home in: accordingly I do mean to try, if the Destinies and Possibilities will be so kind to me.[1]

Till some days after the *11th* I am as good as fixed here, or on the neighbouring coast of St Donat's, the total solitude of which is greatly to my mind at present. My aim, after that, is towards Liverpool. If there be a mail coach from Carmarthen to Aberystwith, and then a Steamer to the Mersey,[2] that would be my route, and you lie precisely on it. Perhaps you can enlighten me as to some of these points? For the Aberystwith Steamer I have written to inquire at Liverpool itself;

TC-WEF, 9 July. MS: Pierpont Morgan Lib. Hitherto unpbd.

1. See TC to WEF, 23 June. He is here responding to Forster's letter of 7 July.

2. Charles and Sarah Fox.

TC-CT, 9 July. MS: Yale. Hitherto unpbd.

1. Thirlwall had written to Milnes, 3 July, anticipating TC's acceptance: "I have very little doubt that the people here . . . will believe Carlyle to be the celebrated atheist [Richard Carlile (1790–10 Feb. 1843); see 1:206], an opinion which he will probably confirm by his demeanour. Could you contrive to get Spedding to join him?" (Reid, *RMM* 1:302).

2. Liverpool is on the river Mersey.

the question of the Mail is probably soluble at Carmarthen. Nobody here has ever turned his thoughts in that direction.— Failing everything I know there is a Liverpool Steamer at Swansea; and it were but turning back from the Bishop's House a score of miles to get securely into that:—an audacity I feel almost equal to, if the times and other circumstances will agree.

Pray inform me a little how you are as to engagements about the end of this week and beginning of next;[3] and when I could best intercalate two days of myself into your leisure. I will do it if I can.

The Address is, "Care of Charles Redwood Esq," superadded to the date given above.

With much kind regard, and hope of soon meeting,

Yours very sincerely / T. Carlyle

TC TO JWC

Llandough, 9 july, 1843—(Sunday Evening late).

My Dearest,

I sat today on a board stool among trees at the end of the house on an elevated level, reading *Accorombona* vol 2 (a dreadful piece of work on Tieck's part!)—smoking at due intervals, and looking out into my silent bits of wood and meadow, under the grey lukewarm sky: one of the stillest Sunday mornings I ever spent or figured. The public road, within few yards of distance, was altogther hidden, cut into the side of the the rising ground, so that I merely *heard* Welsh voices, at times, and then all again grew still as Hades. Redwood was at his office: ach Himmel [O Heaven], he returned at 2 o'clock; set me on horseback, galloped me over precipitous roads, bathed me in stony seas, made me drink two glasses of champagne (it being Sunday), in short, bored me, the good man, till I had enough of it and more! No tea is procurable till near *five* hours after dinner here. Tea done, I have fled up stairs to a kind of closet nearly insupportable with *back-smoke*,[1] and have there written Letters to all people ever since! To Thirlwall (half accepting),—to Richardson, to Nickisson with the sonnet, to Bradford Forster,[2]—and now to my own Goody. Blessings on her: the big Letter

3. TC is writing on Sun.

TC-JWC, 9 July. MS: NLS 611.127. Pbd: Bliss, *TC* 165–66 inc.

1. Smoke in the room caused by a badly drawing chimney.

2. Probably David Lester Richardson (1801–65; *DNB;* see 9:372), who was in London on a visit from India and had written a note, 24 June, to say that he would call on the Carlyles, Mon., 26 June. George William Nickisson, publisher and ed. of *Fraser's Magazine;* see 13:282. W. E. Forster, of Bradford.

which Redwood brought me today was a cheap price for all his dulness afterwards: it is the blithest thing I have seen since I came hither. A thousand thanks to thee! The sealed Letter inclosed (why did not you open it?) was an invitation[3] to dine with the Chevalier and Madame Bunsen for Saturday, including John if he were present!

The infatuated R. kindest and most wearisome of men, insists on making me quite happy tomorrow; and so will have me down to St. Donat's and spend the whole day upon the coast: what an outlook! He has three days more of riding among the mountains; he is a curious man. A kind of Henry Taylor without the genius! Solemn mouthing and emphasis in speech; regularity as of machinery in meal-times, shower-bathings &c, diligent land-practice with plenty of cash, and seemingly total isolation from all men; a curious character;—most worthy, most courteous, kind and good, were he not such a *terrible* bore! I will stand him as long as I can; till towards the end of this week at least. The lodging at St. Donat's will not do: clay floors, desolation, savagery, neither market nor post,—and not even independent after all; for I do not see how R. could be quitted in that way without cutting him to the heart. Let us be quiet, then; let us learn to stand boring too: a man cannot have blessed green fields, kind welcome and board and lodging for nothing!— Enough of all that.

The wretched crotchet of a *Cuittikins* Bishop![4] Let him rest under his ecclesiastic shovel;[5] *he* has missed the meaning of life, or we know nothing of it. There is something tolerable in such a man, something pitiable even praiseworthy,—but it ought to be at a distance chiefly!

Worse, far worse, what is this I hear about your sleeping! Are you going to get into your old watchful state again? I pray you despatch those pumice stones about their business if they tend that way. We cannot have houses painted, at the expense of Goodies!— I do entreat thee, endeavour to sleep. And do not say endeavouring will do nothing. Endeavouring will do much, *if you begin it far enough off*. Send me better news of that; and I will praise thee more for Pope's Head Ahoy[6] and all the rest of it!

John talks of coming on to London, as you see. We could put him into the house. But I suppose he and I will meet at Liverpool first.

Poor Mazzini! He ought really to go to Switzerland, or into Wales, or somewhere altogether *lose* himself for a space of twelve months. I

3. Dated 7 July.
4. C. H. Terrot; see TC's note to JWC to TC, [20 July].
5. Hat.
6. JWC's joke for Alley; see JWC to TC, [7 and 8 July].

noticed the want of his Article in the Review Advertisement[7] with real regret for him.

Thomas Carlyle of Berlin is really what they call there a *sonderbaver* [strangely wonderful] *Christ*. To pass himself off for a man that has a devil: it is too bad! Let him be doing nevertheless; it will all come right for both of us by and by; and for me it is not far wrong even as it is.—

Poor old Mrs Redwood, *she* is still up in the lower story (I hear), and possibly I am keeping her up. R. has gone by to bed some time ago. The poor old Dame, a most excellent simple Quakeress, of few words, and few ideas I must cease; and send thee a kiss in tho*t;*—a "puir revenge."[8]—— Such a Letter as todays I cannot hope for above once in a week; write, write what thou canst.

Ever affectionately / T. Carlyle

TC TO JEAN CARLYLE AITKEN

Llandough, Cowbridge, South Wales
10 july, 1843—

My dear Jean,

You had a small Note from me at Bristol, announcing my journey hitherward, and promising you a fuller detail so soon as I should arrive here. On Thursday morning, as appointed, I left Bristol in a Cardiff Steamer; nearly half full of cabbages, carrot-hampers and other vegetable stores superintended by little busy angry-looking Welshwomen in men's hats: what could be the meaning of exporting cabbages *from* Bristol, the Liverpool of the South? I ascertained that they were all for Merthyr Tydvill, a huge iron work in this side of the world, and that it was a regular trade these Welshes had established for themselves. Poor little bodies— After four hours sailing, first down the Avon river, a most muddy stream enclosed in high precipitous banks of limestone mountain for a part of the way; and then across the Severn Sea, Bristol Channel or whatever they call it (as from Arbigland over to Workington,[1] only muddier a little, and with far *blunter* hills on each side),— we got into Cardiff harbour, as I was finishing my last cigar, all safe, about three in the afternoon. My Welshman was in waiting, the hospitable man. An ancient lean very queer-looking Welsh servant jumped

7. *British and Foreign Review;* see JWC to TC, [7 and 8 July].
8. Coterie speech; see 9:85.

TC-JCA, 10 July. MS: NLS 512.5. Pbd: A. Carlyle, *NL* 1:296–98 inc.
1. I.e., across Solway Firth.

on board for my luggage, a venerable *tub-gig* and able horse were standing near; we all jumped in, and rolled off thro' Cardiff, a flat stupid-looking town half the size of Dumfries,—forward twelve miles westward to Cowbridge, a place not unlike Lockerby, only cleaner and airier-looking among the green knolls; and then, turning off abruptly to the South for about a mile thro' green woody knolls with spaces of fat meadow intervening, we finally arrived here at this clean-trimmed, lonely establishment,—standing on the slope of just such a meadow as the others are, with two woody knolls rising near in front, and the one in the rear looking into our very chimney-pots, the feeblest *clachan* in the world (*Llandough* by name) just showing its poor gable-ends over another part of the same height, two fields farther to the left. An ancient douce-looking Quakeress, the Mother Redwood received us, with great kindness,—and a gentle statement that the dinner was somewhat injured by waiting. As the dinner consisted of *veal*, which I never eat of, this was a small matter! Here in this loneliest of all civilized establishments, I have been ever since; not ill off at all; enjoying the profound silence and *soughing* of the winds considerably; contented even with the wet weather when we have it, for I sit there in the porch and read, not without due tobacco-pipes, and look out into the rain, and green bit of meadow and rustling woods. The people, Redwood and his good Mother, are not witches for wit;—but they let me pretty well alone, and are heartily kind to me. The good man has horses; on which we have ridden twice to the Sea, five or six miles off,—thro' truly awful roads, for they are steep as *scaurs* [precipices], about a yard and a half broad, all made of rough limestone *cobbles* as slippery as polished iron, and rough of level, as if no spade or pick had ever been used upon them: down and up these the little fiery quadrupeds take the greatest delight to *gallop* as if that were the only conceivable pace for a horse of *speeret!* The shore itself is greatly lonelier than Priestside,[2] but far beautifuller too: high limestone cliffs broken sheer down, then a wilderness of sleek big boulder-stones (all lime too), from a hundred weight to half-a-ton each, tumbled together like a pavement of disorderly giants; and farther out, the great hoarse Sea moaning, and singing "Alone, alone!" on this hand and on that. The first day, showers were ruffling it, and one ship was visible: I sat smoking a cigar in a cave where I had dressed after bathing; dry amid heavy rain: living sight or sound was none other. Across the Channel you see Devonshire piled up, heavy and blunt-looking, but of considerable height: it is "the English hills"; nobody knows or cares about it

2. Priestside Bank, a shoal N of Solway Firth, 3 mi. S of Annan.

farther.— Old ruined castles all grown with ivy are abundant; and straggling most disorderly little villages, whitewashed but sluttish, all hanging by the bank of some small rivulet, or by the skirts of some old Church on the knoll-top,—the houses all sprinkled about as if you had shaken them out of a pepper-box. They are a lazy people, good and kindly I suppose, but in a "very backward state of figures."[3] Great part of their ground is in grass, which they are getting up into hay just now,—all *natural*-grass hay, which horses are very fond of: the farming seems very bad; but the rents are cheap and the soil good.

Well, dear Jean, you did not expect to read a description of Wales, did you? I will say no more of it at least! Our Household itself is sufficiently strange. My "honest Lawyer," for I think he deserves that name, is a man about as tall as myself and perhaps twice as *lean*, somewhat younger, tho' he looks older; a person truly worth giving a glance at. He appears to associate with no Son of Adam; tho' he has great work as an Attorney at Cowbridge and I believe three men in his office, and indeed seems to have already become rich: he *screws* his voice into dreadful emphasis when he says anything, which is but rarely: he rises, goes to bed, eats, drinks, bathes, writes, and does all things with a rigour of *method* which no eight-day clock can surpass;—looks out with long innocent nose, with thin sunk cheeks and *clasped* lips, into life, with a kind of mournful affectionate smile! Good Redwood, he is dreadfully *un*entertaining for a *crack;* but he goes away, the instant you hint such a thing, and leaves you alone: what could man do more! I believe I shall grow to like him yet. His Mother is a most douce quiet person in black quaker bonnet and drab-brown shawl; reads all day "good books," or looks a little after the dinner. Our house for most part, as at present, is silent as if inhabited by ghosts. I lounge about all day, with books, under trees, lying on the grass: I have not at all grown tired of it yet. As the weather is delightful, perhaps I may still make out almost a week. I have then two days (if I can manage it) to spend with the Bishop of St David's (a brave man tho' a Bishop!) at Carmarthen some sixty miles off: after that I think of making towards the Coast and getting into a Steamer for Liverpool. Brother Jack will perhaps come and meet me, then or sooner: we are in communication already.— Jane is in a tumult like the sack of Cities, at Chelsea, with Painters &c thoroughly revising the house there, in my absence: I think I must bring her up to Liverpool, were all that over; she might stay there for a while.

This, dear Sister Jean, is all my history at present. If you write

3. Untraced.

again, if it be not *instantly,* address "care of John Welsh Esq 20. Maryland Street, Liverpool": I shall there get it sooner or later. You I will apprise some way or other when I am about coming home.—That poor deaf little boy;[4] that poor Brother Alick tossing over the far Deep at present! I remember *all* things here. Adieu, Dear Sister!

T. Carlyle

TC TO JWC

Llandough, 11 july, 1843—

My Dearest,

Did you get the little slip of paper insinuated, yesterday morning, after the Letter had been sealed? It struck me at breakfast that I had forgotten to explain the mystery of that horrid Basil-Montague "disappointment" in the Shower-bath,[1] analagous to the muskets all refusing to go off in case of a battle! To meet every accident I will repeat it. Helen pulls the showerbath *too high up;* an inch too high will do it; the ropes, running a little oblique, catch as you will see, in that case, the *ends* of the cylinder which holds the water; wherefore it declines to turn: let it down an inch, it swashes off. By terrible experiments oft repeated, and by reflexion grounded on these, I made out the mystery. The little red carpenter was to blame. Shew it to Pearson, he will at once understand it:—he ought to, if not mend it, at least nail a bit of wood on the ceiling to *prevent* the machine from getting up too high: Helen will never learn to hold her hand, except by accident, till it is held for her. And now, you yourself, if you attend to me, can always secure a good splashing to your white shoulders, and the proper general submission under the shower-cataract,—you little cutty [mischievous girl]!— It was also a real distress and surprise to me that my legacy of Paper turned out so inconsiderable! Did you look in the red painted box? Certainly there was more there than you describe! If not,—alas, I was a fool, and had taken no heed.

From this Temple of Inanity you can expect no news; nevertheless I keep writing. Today no Letter has gone; but I have taken Time not by the pigtail, and there is to be a full sheet tomorrow ready for me. It is now past one o'clock: who knows but at half past two there may be another little missive from yourself after the Sunday vacancy. I

4. Jean's son Tom.

TC-JWC, 11 July. MS: NLS 611.128. Quot: Froude, *Carlyle* 3:303; Bliss, *TC* 167.

1. See JWC to TC, [7 and 8 July]. The showerbath had been installed in 1842; see 14:191. Montagu's disappointment is unexplained.

shall at least know, and say, before I seal. Nobody less deserves a letter; for my replies, as I often confess, are by the nature of them *zero* in more words or fewer.

Yesterday, with a rational exertion of ill-nature, I briefly declined going for an Arcadian ramble to the coast all day, or indeed going anywhither; indicating that I preferred the green grass, sunshine and solitude among the trees and winds. The good R. in an instant cheerfully surrendered, cheerfully went off to his Attorney-office, and left me totally alone till dinner. I have not for long had a peaceabler day. The old black cobweb coat was warm enough for the temperature; I lay upon the grass on the brae-side, under shadow if I liked; read the critique on Accorombona[2] (alas, Accorombona itself was done); read the Examiner; smoked my pipe, and looked out upon the waving woods, and felt their great deep melancholy *sough* a real blessing to me. At dinner and after it was different! However, I got away by myself upon the Pony and galloped thro' multifarious lanes, not without jumbling myself. The worst of all however is that you can get no tea here till towards nine at night, *five* hours after dinner; and then it is dreadful stewed tea, with blue milk,—and these three nights I have kept myself awake with it till I came in sight almost of three o'clock and the *Un*delectable! I decide now that I will take no tea more, if I cannot get some about three hours earlier,—which perhaps indeed I shall not try, so solemnly methodic is the arrangement of all things here. Stoicism and a draught of hot water will be supportable for a day or two. I have not yet got Thirlwall's answer, nor indeed do I expect it till tomorrow: but very probably, I think, about the end of this week or beginning of next, I shall make off thitherward. The "expedition into the Hills" with my good dull R. looks very questionable at present.

In fact this kind Host of mine is an extremely good man: can he help it if he is a wearisome one? He would so gladly be the most entertaining of men, did it lie with *him!* A most modest, timid, truly courteous man; with a certain *wish* to be king over all movements of men and things round him,—but who instantly desists, and withdraws into invisibility if you indicate never so faintly that he is like to bore you! I have nowhere seen a more perfect Piece of Mechanism, not even old Mr Bradfute;[3] the history of his Day here might be written down in Almanacks the year before. From the hour when he issues, lean and gaunt but full of hope, thro' this *window* of the little reeky "study"

2. No pbd. critique has been traced prior to "Tieck's Vittoria Accorombona," *Fraser's Magazine* 36 (Nov. 1847):567–75.

3. John Bradfute (1764–1837), Edinburgh bookseller; see 1:204.

so-called, and stalks along in flannel dressing-gown into the Shower-bath,—till as the clock strikes eleven, he snatches his little candlestick and vanishes,—it is all marked out in rigorous stages and courses of method, not to be varied from without pain. After showerbath, he walks "seven minutes," on a scant path which he has hewn out for himself on the hill-side amid the trees and bushes: to go and to come takes "seven minutes." He strips and dresses from the very skin and outwards four times every day. The arrangements of our household *Hydrastisy*[4] (in which he loves to linger) would fill you with amazement. And then that mournful serenity of cheerfulness, like Arctic sunshine on the edge of eternal Winter, that long innocent nose, those lips *smacked* together, hiding as in a smith's-vice—almost nothing! And the screwed-up emphasis of what small unimportant speech there is:—a Henry Taylor without the genius! I could often almost laugh in the worthy man's face,—and yet on the whole how can I but esteem him; almost begin to like him, so good is he, so unweariedly polite and kind to me. At bottom, I believe the solution is that I ought to go about my business, as soon as convenient. It is unfair to stay as a man's guest whom you are like to laugh at: I feel it hourly a kind of treachery. I think I shall be off in the end of the week.

Accorombona is far the pleasantest thing I have yet fallen in with since I left you. A very gorgeous composition,—but somewhat too shewy, in diamonds, Bristol-diamonds,[5] tinsel and the precious metals, for my taste! One finds it to be untrue, almost as an Opera: yet much is true, genial-warm and very grand. Vittoria herself is about the best of all Opera-heroines, a right divine stage goddess. Bracciano too is clearly her mate, as you said;—yet I could not but *abhor* that murder he did of the poor frivolous trembling creature: it is detestable. The sublime Song-of-Solomon passages did also somewhat transcend me. In fact, it is a grand thing, but *Bristol* diamond not a little of it. A thousand thanks to Tieck and the Coadjutor[6] for such a gift in these latitudes. Alas, this morning I am reduced to *Lyell's Geology,* a twaddling circumfused *ill*-writing man; I seem to hear his uninspired voice all along, and see the clear-*leaden* twinkle of his small bead-eyes![7] However, I must persist a little.

Yesternight in my gallop I came, about a mile to the west or north west of this, upon a beautiful little hamlet or village, all hanging in a

4. A neologism; literally, "water standing-place," i.e., a showerbath.
5. Rock crystals found in the limestone nr. Bristol and used in ornaments.
6. I.e., JWC.
7. Charles Lyell, *Principles of Geology,* 3 vols. (1830–33) or his *Elements of Geology* (1838). TC had attended his lectures in March.

straggle on the two sides of a green chasm or ravine, with a white Church-tower atop: the name of it Llanblethian: here, as R. cursorily informed after my return, "a Mr St*ar*ling once lived, who wrote afterwards, as was said, in the *Times!*" By Heaven, I believe it is a fact; for John Sterling once described the place of his boyhood to me exactly as this is![8] A new interest is added to Llanblethian; I will go and see *it* another time before all is done.—— But now two o'clock being near, I will smoke and wait for Letters. A bathe I suppose comes next. The weather is grey but warm tho' windy. *Before* dinner I will ride, not after. Adieu Dearest, with ten kisses.

---

11 at night. No letter from thee: only this from Alick Welsh, which cuts off the hope of Aberystwith. Unless there be some hope, from Carmarthen, of Coaches inland, I must go by Swansea; which will be, as it were, turning back.— I rode before dinner, did not bathe, and with great care, by means of a hint, got *all* the teas transferred to about 7 o'clock. The old Mother, I doubt, would suffer most, for R. seldom takes almost any tea.— My Dearest, how art thou going to sleep? Tell me, tell me! Directly after post tomorrow, we are off for the sea-side. Country evening is delicious. I had a walk thro' hay fields, and heard the *corncraik.* Good night! / T.C.

JWC TO TC

[11 July 1843]

Dearest

I have no time to write a letter today—but *a line* you *must have* to keep you easy— It is has been such a morning as you cannot figure—a painter filling the house with terrific smell, the white-washer still white-washing—Pearson and men tearing out the closet—and the boy always grinding with pumice-stone!— Having been taught politeness to one's neighbours by living next door to Mr Chambers[1] I wrote a

8. See *Life of Sterling, Works* 11:15–22; see also 11:179. Llanbethian is between Cowbridge and Llandough.

JWC-TC, [11 July]. Addr: care of—Redwood Esq*r* / Landough / Cowbridge / S— Wales—. PM: 11 July 1843. MS: NLS 602.107; longhand copy with TC's notes: Berg. Pbd: A. Carlyle, *NLM* 112–14; quot: Froude, *LM* 1:195. On the copy TC wrote: "Charl*s* Redwood, 'the Honest Lawyer,' a silently deep friend of mine, and of all good men and things was, at pres*t*,—and twice after on diff*t* occas*ns*, My Host at Llandough. He was not entertaining to me, but I much [re]spected him, and felt his kindness and fidelity." On the envelope TC wrote: "11 july 1843."

1. At no. 4.

note to M*r* Lambert N*o* 6—regretting that his and family's slumbers were probably curtailed by my operations—and promising that the nuisance would have a only a brief term— This brought in M*r* Lambert upon me ("virtue ever it's own reward &c") who staid for an hour talking you know how— Then came Perry[2] trying to look a suff[er]ing injured Angel, but absolutely *white* with concentrated rage at my having employed another— He came for his rent—and got it— Then before he was out—Elizabeth—anxious to know what ailed me as she had not seen me for some time—and poor Elizabeth herself was full of troubles—more money to be lifted![3]—and so "altogether"[4] you may fancy whether I am in favourable circumstances for writing. For God'sake do not let John[5] plump in upon me in my present puddlement there wants only him or the like of him constantly running out and in—interfering with every thing and needing to be attended to, to make my discomfort complete— The bare idea of it makes me like to scream!— There are no more letters come for you. Arthur Helps paid me a visit on Sunday forenoon and found on the table a new legitimate drama!![6]—actually another come!—but what is far more extraordinary I have read it from beginning to end with considerable pleasure! which was a little abated however when I found that you had to pay four shillings for it—*Launcelot of the Lake* by one J. Riethmüller[7]—is he a german *par hazard* [by chance]?— He writes the best english rythm of the whole bunch of them— And you do not like my beautiful Vittoria!— Oh what want of taste!—the umbrella is come and awaiting Friday— Bless you dear try not to get excessively *dull*

I am getting into my sleep again I rise always at six—of course—but I go to bed between ten & eleven[8]—

[no signature]

2. "'Perry,' a greedy pragmatical master-Carpenter of the neighb*d*, Landlord's manager; of whom, for 9 years, there had been experience suffic*t*, as it appears" (TC's note).

3. TC copies out "Eliz*th*, money to be *lifted*" in his notes but does not annotate it.

4. "Macdiamid of the *Dumfries Courier's* wearisomely recurring phrase" (TC's note on the copy).

5. Carlyle.

6. See 13:46.

7. Christopher James Riethmüller (d. 1895), English writer, *Launcelot of the Lake, a Tragedy in Five Acts* (1843); a friend of Frederick Lucas since they attended Univ. College, London; in his short life of *Frederick Lucas* (1862) he said that Lucas always spoke of his visits to TC "with delight and enthusiasm, which were nowise abated by the radical differences between himself and his host" (76). TC had promised to buy a copy (see TC to JWC, 13 July) and was listed by Chapman & Hall as a subscriber to *Launcelot*.

8. "No room for signature; last paragr*h* crowded in on inverted top of page first" (TC's note).

TC TO JWC

Llandough, 12 july 1843
(Wednesday Night, late)—

Dearest,

I have been at that St Donat's, "the day" requisite; I have just got home thro' rain and precipitous rough roads at a gallop which after tea and dinner has jumbled me all to pieces: Devil take all "days" of that sort! I had just got your Letter when I went away; I went happy, I return *meeser*-able,—fly up into my sooty "study" to be at least alone for a while. How happy I was over Quarterly Reviews, peace, silence and my Goody's Letter,—and now!—

Well one good thing I got was this smallest of small memorials of the *14th*,[1] which, as the umbrella all went aback, you must accept with resignation. I have worn it all day in my pocket; this and its *foreign* nature, as decidedly Welsh, from the main Shop of Cowbridge, must give it some worth.

I enclose Thirlwall's answer to my Letter which also came today. I have not yet decided what day I shall appoint him: but judge it may be some day in the early half of next week. He is sixty or seventy miles off me: how I go next is not in the least plain.— Jack has no intention of coming down to Chelsea just now, or perhaps at all. Here is his Letter of today. Poor Alick did *not* get my Letter; it comes to me *here*:[2] pray lock it by for me somewhere. Often in these days and nights the image of his Ship far out on the waters comes to me almost like a flash of actual vision,—infinitely sad, as Death and as all Parting is. Adieu Dearest! I am right glad to hear of the sleep; I too am improving. Good night!

T. C.

JWC TO TC

[12 July 1843]

Not a line from you today Dear!—*that* is stupid— I, in the midst of my bit earthquake, am excusable for missing plenty of posts—but

TC-JWC 12 July. Addr: 5. Cheyne Row. Chelsea / London. MS: NLS 611. 129. Quot: Froude, *Carlyle* 3:302.
1. A ribbon for JWC's birthday.
2. See TC to AC, [23 June].

JWC-TC, [12 July]. Addr: care of—Redwood, Esq / Landough / Cowbridge / South Wales. PM: Chelsea, 12 July 1843. MS: NLS 602.110; longhand copy with TC's notes: Berg. Pbd: Froude, *LM* 1:195–97 inc. On the envelope TC has written: "13 july 1843? *in*."

you in the midst of a "simplicity verging on the inane"—with "conversation which does not promise to be a treat"—you, for your own sake, ought to write *every day*—better or worse— If you had seen me last night asleep—you would have seen a pretty sight! The paint was *smelling* of course—one cannot make a household's revolution any more than a state one with rose-water—and so this house did not smell of rose-water I can assure you— Old Sterling had said so much about its "costing me *my life*"—and the "absolute necessity" of my at least *sleeping* at his house—that I did begin to think it might cause me—a head-ach!—so I took all wise precautions against it—kept my room door carefully shut all the day—and slept with *both* my windows wide open—so that I really suffered very little inconvenience from the smell— But just when I was going to bed it occured to me that in this open state of things, with several *ladders* lying quite handy underneath the windows—"heavy bodies" might (as Helen phrased it last year) "drop in" and be at my pillow before I heard them—so *"feeling it my duty"* to neglect no proper precaution, I laid my dagger and the great Policeman's-rattle on *the spare pillow,* and went to sleep quite peaceably without any more thought about thieves! M*r* Lambert told me yesterday that *he* sleeps in the back room of the ground floor "for protection's sake"—and has always "besides his dog a loaded gun at his side"— I was on the point of asking him what on earth he had *to protect* that was worth so much trouble— When he took his leave he hoped that I would "apply to him if he could be of any use to me in my husbands absence"—"whatever *protection* (in the *virtuous* sense of the word of course) *he* could afford me &c &c" I thought to myself that a man who slept on the ground floor with a loaded gun was more in a condition to *receive* protection than to lend it to a woman who slept with open *windows* and *ladders. Darley* brought back your book[1]—last night stuttering forth infinite approbation—

I have got such a pretty writing-establishment—a sort of Gipsy's tent which I have mounted in the garden *with my own hands*[2]—constructed out of the clothesropes and posts and the crumb cloth of the Library! I sit under its "brown shadd"[3]—the macready of "natur"![4]—

1. "George (still remembered) a most amiable, intellig*t* stuttering Irish*n*, whom we both liked. The 'Book,' I suppose, might be Past and Pres*t*" (TC's note). George Darley (1795–1846; *DNB*), poet and dramatist; see 13:50.

2. Coterie speech; Edward Irving's phrase.

3. " 'Dark-brown shade' was, to both of us, infinitely ridicul*s* in this place, tho' the spirit of it is now fled irrevocable. Old Dr Ritchie, Divinity Professor in Edin*r*, was a worthy, earnest, but somewhat too pompous and consciously eloqu*t* old gent*n*,—gone quite into the state of antique, and curiosity fit for museums. He

an arm chair and the little round table with my writing materials—and my watch to keep me in mind that I am in a time-world"—a piece of carpet under-foot—and a footstool—behold all that is necessary for my modest garden-house!—woman wants but little here below[5]—an old crumb-cloth[6]—but one has "no credit in being jolly in such a pretty bower—by and by I shall have to return indoors to "come out *strong*"— You see I am out of paper again—this is the back of an invitation from that Chimera Swinfin Jervis[7]— I shall answer it so do not trouble yourself—and now I have to write to Betty and Mary Miles[8]—some better thing according to old use and wont—for my birth-day—

Your descriptions of your quietude give me what Terrot complained of "a sense of oppression"—I feel as if you were living in an exhausted receiver— — God help you— You have credit in keeping pretty jolly— But if you do not write to me every day you will turn into a vegetable!

ever your Jane Pen[9]

JWC TO MARY RUSSELL

[12 July 1843]

My dearest M*rs* Russel

I have no leisure today—and, what is still stupider, no *paper*— But a minute, and this little pink sheet will suffice for saying the *needful*— and the rest will keep for another time— The 14*th* is my birth-day—

---

had no teeth, a great deal of white hair, spoke in a sonorous rumbling voice, with much proud almost minatory wagging of the head & to a rhythm all his own, wh*h* loved to end always with an emphatic syllable, with victorious grave accent, and a kind of 'uh!' or 'h!' superadded.— For confutation of Gibbon his principal argument, the only one that I can recollect, was, That G*n*, in his latter years, grown rich, famous &c &c, 'confessed that the end of life to him was involved *in a dark brown shade*—uh!' " (TC's note). On the copy itself TC changes "brown shade" to "dark-brown shadd," thereby restoring JWC's spelling. For William Ritchie (ca. 1748–1830), see 1:97.

4. Unexplained.

5. Cf. Goldsmith, *The Vicar of Wakefield* ch. 8.

6. "Mainly for [word illegible]" (TC's note).

7. Swynfen Stevens Jervis (1797–1867; see 12:159) had written, 11 July, inviting both Carlyles to dinner on 20 July presided over by his da. Agnes, "Mrs G. H. Lewes," as his wife, Anne (see 12:138), was in France. TC wrote on the letter: "(we didn't go;—a worthless fellow) / (1868)."

8. Betty Braid (see 2:306) had written to JWC from Edinburgh, 10 July. Presumably Mary Mills.

9. JWC's old pet name; see 2:92.

JWC-MR, [12 July]. MS: NLS 602.109. Pbd: A. Carlyle, *NLM* 1:114–15 inc. Dated "12 july 1843" by TC on MS.

and timeless and paperless tho' I be, I must send by this post, or Margaret and old Mary[1] will not be put in mind of me on my birth-day.— I dare say you think me full of odd fancies—but I cannot help it— I feel my *fancies* to be more a part of myself than my *reasons*— I am in the thick of what I call *a house-hold* earthquake—have been and will be for days to come—my husband is gone into Wales—and I am taking the opportunity of his absence to do a deal of painting and papering and cleaning &c that was become absolutely needed— He will never suffer the least commotion when he is at home—so one is obliged to concentrate the whole horrors of such operations into the rare periods of his absence— I believe he is going from Wales to Annandale— I do hope he will go to see you— For me I know not where to go—now that I *cannot* go to Scotland all places look alike undesirable— I am better in health however—and do not dislike London in the summer as C. does— I send a little parcel for Margaret to your care and shall enclose a post-office order (when I have got it) for a pound of tea to Mary— Would Mary be the better of any old clothes? She used to have such quantities,—but if she need any now I could so easily give her some?— Love to your Husband and Father[2] ever your affectionate / Jane Carlyle

JWC TO JEANNIE WELSH

[12 July 1843]

Dearest Babbie

The sympathy between us continues to be perfect in all respects—both materially and morally—to a degree unprecedented I really believe except in the case of the *Siamese twins!*[1] Unfortunately it is not oftenest sympathy in bliss! at this moment?— Oh Good Heavens, after all!— The unspeakable is going on in this house!— Every morning at six of the clock a legion of devils rush in under the forms of Carpenters, Painters, whitewashers, and non-descript apprentice-lads who grind grind, grind, with pumice-stones—and saunter up and down the stairs

1. Hiddlestone and Mills. In 1842 JWC began sending them something on her birthday; see 14:219.
2. The Rev. Edward Dobbie (1773–1857); see 14:65.

JWC-JW, [12 July]. Addr: 20 Maryland Street / Liverpool. PM: Chelsea, 12 July 1843. MS: NLS 1892.34. Pbd: Huxley, *JWCLF* 142–43 inc.
1. Chang and Eng (1811–74), twins joined at the waist; b. in Siam of Chinese parents but became naturalized Americans surnamed Bunker after being taken to Boston, 1829; m., April 1843, two sisters and had nineteen children; exhibited in U.S. and Europe.

whistling and singing as if I had hired them to keep me in *music!*— At the first sound of this *Legion* spreading itself over the premises, I spring out of bed—dash down stairs, and "in wera desperation"[2] take a shower-bath!— After which I feel more up to standing the noise—and smell, and hideous discomfort! I am oil-painting the staircase and passages and the wood of the Library— So you may conceive the smell in this warm weather! Sterling predicts my *death* in consequence— various persons remonstrate against my staying—above all sleeping—in it—but what can I do if I were not here to look after what is a-doing I can see that there would be fifty blunders made—and to leave Helen alone during the night—or to bring any stranger in to keep her company while the house is in such disorder would be equally inexpedient—"*death*" indeed were to be avoided on any terms and if I saw *that* likely to ensue I would accept a sleeping room in Sterlings house—but by keeping my bed-room door always closed and sleeping with the two windows wide open I do not feel the smell very bad thro the night— "And *the thieves* Cousin"? two wide-open windows and plenty of ladders lying quite handy in the court underneath them"?— My dear, when one is painting and papering one's house, one has no time to think of thieves!— It did occur to me last night in lying down, that "heavy bodies"[3] might drop in thro the night—and be at my pillows before I heard them—but my nerves are pretty strong at present—I took the precaution to lay the Policeman's rattle on the spare pillow— and went to sleep without thinking more about them—a curious contrast to M*r* Lambert next door—father of the young pianists—who sleeps in the back room of the ground floor—"for protection to his house"—he told me—and besides his quick-eared dog has ever in readiness a loaded gun—pistols he says are "worth nothing in such cases"—I told him that rather than pass my life in such a state of armed defence; I would adopt Darwins plan of leaving all the plate &c every night on the lobby table—I told him also of your screams of delight in seeing "a small cannon" carried into his house last year—and thinking what an unexpected reception the next thieving party was likely to encounter— He laughed himself till the tears ran down but told me "the small cannon" was a small steamengine— He seems to be some sort of military engineer— All this passed between us yesterday morning when in return for an amiable Note of regrets about the noise &c which I had felt it polite to write to him, he came himself to assure me "he had never heard the noise"—and to *offer me "his protection"*—(in the vir-

2. Coterie speech.
3. Helen Mitchell's phrase.

tuous sense of the word of course)—from all he said, he left me with the idea that HE stood much more in need of *my* protection than I did of *his*—

Carlyle writes to me almost daily—*dullish* letters to say the truth—I fancy him very *sleepy* in Wales—and why not? it was just for that he went so far!—"the simplicity of his kind hosts verges on the *inane*" "their conversation does not promise to be a treat to him"!— Well—I suppose he will leave that region the end of this week—and where will he go then? neither he nor I can tell yet!— *Here* sure enough he cannot return so probably he will go on to Annandale John talks of meeting him in Liverpool and "coming on to London" being dead-weary of the country— There justs wants John here to make my actual position perfectly hideous—and tho he find the whole house in a state of wreck and nobody with a moments leisure to attend to him he will not for that, dream of taking a lodging—if I can get a room ready for him with ever so much inconvenience— I cannot tell you how this prospect of his return "exactly at the wrong time" puts me out of humour— Mazzini is better considerable—his face almost quite restored to its original beauty—he and Plattnauer walked with me to Knightsbridge yesterday—for furniture-print![4]— As we returned I took Plattnauer into Gambardella's to see his picture of Brougham—Mazzini had had to send him (Gambardella) a note requesting that he would either pay his subscription for the Italian school or withdraw his name from the list—he had received *no answer*—so under these delicate circumstances he could not go in but waited for us outside—whether Gambardella had seen him from the window—and felt sore at the notion of his having perhaps told *me* about the unpaid subscription I do not know—certainly *something* had jarred the music of his soul for he was quite as rude to *me* his "perfect woman," as I ever heard tell of his being to other people— I am not exactly the person to put up with rudeness from *a man* especially—and the first rudeness from him would have been the last he would ever have had *opportunity* to exhibit—had it not been for the thought of you, my Babbie, and your picture! To have quarrelled with him would have laid me under the same necessity which he has imposed on so many other people to return him both your likeness and my own—and I *could* not do any thing so cruel to both you and myself—so I pretend not to see his impertinence—and do you not say a word of this when you see him as you will shortly—he is returning to Liverpool next week to "live there *for ever*"!—till he tires again!— Plainly *all* things must have been going awry with him here—

4. Presumably a printed fabric for slip-covers and the like.

—he quarrells so incessantly with those who wish to serve him— He said he would take the picture and the frame himself "there was no use in sending them by Walter[5] now even if he did come"

You tell me *our Walter*[6] was to meet my Uncle and the others at *Greenwich!!* In that case had not I better go to?—but perhaps you meant Greenock my Dear?[7] Bless you love perhaps even in your *material earthquake* you will find more time to write to me than when they were all at home in the usual routine— your own / J C

TC TO JWC

Llandough, 13 july, 1843—

My Dearest,

There being no Tea to be had this night apparently till towards nine o'clock (when by Heaven's blessing I shall hope to decline it), let me write to you in my dry state, with at least daylight round me. You had a most short scrape of a pen last night: I was tired and sick; I could do no more. Today your Letter accuses me for not writing "better or worse"; better therefore not being altogether roadready, I give you a chance of worse. No great burden to me, if it be none to you!

Your Letter and Newspaper have been almost the only event of the day: thanks for the gardenhouse, and what comes from it! Do not torment yourself with "thieves"; no thief will meddle with you. Lambert is an ass, and *needs* protection as you say. I sleep here with the window gaping as wide as it will go; ten yards from the highway of the parish, nothing but the hill-sides and stars, and general conscience and cowardice of the Welsh population watching over me. Fear nothing of thieves. But get done with the painting too;—I fancy you will need no bidding to do that!

This day here has been as close dim and sultry as day need be; thunder rumbling on all sides of the horizon ever since morning; very loud just lately over to the east about Cardiff. I have read several articles in the *Quarterly Review*, kept aloof from *Lyell* hitherto,[1] de-

5. Macgregor.
6. Welsh, coming from Auchtertool.
7. Greenwich is on the S bank of the Thames, SE of London; Greenock is on the S shore of the Firth of Clyde, 22 mi. NW of Glasgow, opp. Helensburgh, where the Welshes were going to stay.

TC-JWC, 13 July. Addr: 5. Cheyne Row, Chelsea / London. MS: NLS 611. 130. Quot: Froude, *Carlyle* 3:303–4.

1. Lyell's *Geology;* see TC to JWC, 11 July. Presumably the most recent issue of the *Quarterly*, May (vol. 72).

clined to ride, walked out a little way,—in short sauntered in the idlest manner. Till dinner arrive I am always very comfortable. But then—breaks in the reign of hollow Nothingness, the *tea*less reign of the Inane! That is the labour, that is the work.

However, I have written to Thirlwall that I leave this on Monday; and so we see the *end*. A coach goes thro' Cowbridge about noon: some sixty miles I believe it is to Carmarthen: after that I must pick my way northward as I can. The one possibility still remains to me of faring on to Milford Haven,[2] and getting the Steamer for Liverpool there. How long I may stay with Thirlwall is not perfectly clear: "two days" was the time I talked of; but if all prospered exceedingly, it might extend to three. I shall get no *rest* in any of these places: and it may as well be in a *plenum* [fullness] as in a *vacuum* in that case.—R. knows that I must go on Monday; regrets &c &c, but reconciles himself like a polite man.

Tomorrow I believe he meditates a new excursion to St Donat's: I think I shall wait for Letters, and then go. The sea-side yields at least a bathe, and one weariness is appointed here equally as there. The high lime-stone cliffs and great solitary sea: there is something that *blunts* the poignancy of boring in all that! We are to stay all night too: I will not gallop again after dinner in that fashion—for any man's pay.

Today I was out near Llanblethian (Sterling's place). In Llandough close at hand here over the knoll-top, I saw certain of the population in the street as I passed along: little flabby figures, brown as a berry, fat, squat, wide-flowing, their clothes of almost *no* colour (such is the prevalence of *lime* and poverty) hung round them, as if "thrown on with a pitchfork": very noteworthy little fellows (of both sexes) indeed! They saluted kindly as I passed. Llandough consists of some 9 houses, or huts most of them, built in a row, on elevated ground, and looking blank (the greater part of them) into the back wall of Redwood's garden, which back wall is on the very crown of the height. The common well lies down below in the hollow on our side, and indeed is our well too. An old squire something lives in a Llandough Castle close at hand, a little behind the village: poor fellow the grave of his old Wife is the newest in Llandough Churchyard, and he sits solitary, R. says, and "scolds his servants, being a *proud* man."—— ——I will have a pipe now; and not finish this till towards bedtime. Adieu, Dearest. There *is* rest—for the just, is there not?[3]

2. Pembrokeshire, SW Wales.
3. Cf. Isa. 48:22.

10 p.m. I drank hot water at my usual time of tea, and then at 9 o'clock went out walking, with a notice that I should not be in again to tea. I virtuously de[c]lined the article![4]— The evening walks are altogether beautiful: the silent silver sky, the green universe, and sound of *corncraiks* and milldams!

Reitmüller, I suppose, is the son of a German; some German Music-master, it is like. He is the "young man of genius" whom Lucas recommended to me. He now costs me four shillings;—I promised to pay it; but did not think the demand would be made so soon![5] I am glad his legitimate drammar has any worth at all.

Thanks for answering the Chimera Jervis. He is certainly the most perseverant man in asking and still again asking us. Without result. "O for a lodge in some vast wilderness" &c![6]

John and I can as yet make no bargain for meeting in the North. I still think he may as well go back with me into Annandale. He does not seem yet to have shaped any plan for himself; and, unless he end by going with Lady Clare, I do not see that he is very likely at present to do it,—poor Jack! It is a horribly difficult thing to do; *all at once*, especially!

I sometimes have a thought of Forster at Bradford; but doubt it will not at all do. They are a terrible set of fellows those open-mouthed wondering *gawpies* [silly fellows], who lodge you for the sake of looking at you! It is horrible.

Our thunder is all away; and the stillest serene night come instead: the great old Elm-trees looking in at this poor Study-window with the sky thro' them, in a truly sublime manner; every Elm-tree lost *beyond the window-lintel,* of infinite height therefore, and motionless as if every leaf of it were enchanted,—as if the whole were a cerulean petrifaction; and I some poor Devil jailed in the middle of it; which perhaps is the fact! O my dear, this universe is great, most great; enough to strike one dumb.

And now suppose thou were to take a little drop of something hot (porridge I fear there is none), and then go quietly to bed? For the protection of Lambert and other purposes! My poor little Bairn, a sound sleep to thee, and right pleasant dreams if any. Will not some Great God gather all the widely-separated together again! It is a hope that will never die, that one. Adieu, adieu

T. C.

4. Letter omitted. Coterie speech; see 4:316.
5. See JWC to TC, [11 July].
6. Cowper, *The Task* 2:1.

TC TO JOHN A. CARLYLE

Llandough, 13 july, 1843—

My dear Brother,

Your Letter arrived yesterday, fully as soon as I had expected; the other came the day after mine had gone away. I wish I were able at once to point out what my plan of travel is; but I can only give it you so far as it is yet matured, which indeed is as far as there yet exists knowledge for maturing it. A Steamer, it would appear, sails weekly from Swansea for Liverpool on Wednesday at some hour or other, and touches at Milford Haven, and nowhere else. This you do not commend as a conveyance. On the other hand, Alick Welsh apprises me that there is now no Liverpool Steamer from Abe[r]ystwith,[1] and the Bishop gives evidence that there is no coach *to* that place. I can prefigure nothing till I have got to Carmarthen, and consulted men of knowledge!

The Bishop again invites me very kindly; and I have written today to him, agreeing to come thither on Monday. The Coach goes thro' Cowbridge about noon; and I fancy it must be some sixty miles. I talked once of staying "two days" with the Bishop; it is not likely that my stay in such an establishment can be long: but it may be a day or so more than the "two," if things prove inviting there, if I sleep well &c. You had better address your next Letter, "Care of The Lord Bishop of St David's, Carmarthen": it will find me on Monday, Tuesday, Wednesday, or be sent after me at worst. I will write to you from Carmarthen (or Abergwili, a country place near Carmarthen, which seems to be the precise spot), so soon as I have decided what way to go. Going back to Swansea or Milford is of course always a do-no-better possibility. But I should like well to take a glance at the Mountains; a sight of Snowdon, Plynlimmon &c would do me good, even from the distance;[2] and you seem to say there is all requisite convenience for travelling in the North region of Wales. Whatever accurate knowledge of that business you may have will be instructive to me at Carmarthen.

I should like very well to meet you somewhere on the road, anywhere, and carry you about, or be carried about, and if possible bring you back to Annandale with me! At Liverpool, Alick Welsh writes to me his Father is off with two of the girls Helen and another to Glas-

TC-JAC, 13 July. MS: NLS 524.46. Hitherto unpbd.

1. Letter omitted.

2. Snowdon is the highest mountain (3,493 ft.) in Wales and England, 7 mi. SW of Caernarvon. Plynlimmon (2,468 ft.) is in mid-Wales.

gow or Helensburgh;[3] Cousin Jeannie is there, and the House almost empty. You will see by one of the inclosed Notes that a certain W.E. Forster would be very glad of us at Bradford in Yorkshire: he is a very good young man, a manufacturer come up thither from the Quaker circles of Falmouth: I have of course declined his "Craven" expedition, but promised to think if there were any farther possibility. You now see all my engagements, chances and outlooks, just as they lie before myself. Your Annan Steamer sails on the 19*th,* 22*nd* and 28*th:* the 22*nd* seems your likeliest day; but it is at 6 in the morning. If I could find somewhere in Wales, at the Menai Bridge,[4] or farther down, it would be a merry enough thing!—

On the whole I do very well here, tho' my worthy host's conversation is by no means the most exhilarating part of the phenomenon! He has a smart galloping pony, however; thro' all the forenoon from ten till four he leaves me totally alone; and I have got two or three good dips in nice sea-water: nothing can exceed the kindliness or real innocent worth of the good man. We shall be well content till Monday.[5]— Jane writes to me from the middle of painters, joiners and loud confusion. Here are two other Letters from Bunsen;[6] which, as I had already answered the former, did not now require any answer.

Poor Alick did not get my Letter then! Poor fellow, I think of him daily and hourly, with sadness yet with hope. My Mother's articulate remembrance was precious to me. Give her my love, my hope of soon being there. Blessings on all of you.

Your affectionate / T. Carlyle

JWC TO TC

14*th* [July 1843]

Dearest

Even if I had not received your pathetic little packet,[1] for which I send you a dozen kisses; I meant to have written a *long* letter today—

3. Town on N shore of Firth of Clyde, ca. 24 mi. NW of Glasgow.
4. Connecting Anglesey and the mainland.
5. 17 July.
6. Of 4 and 7 July, the latter inviting TC and John Carlyle to dinner to meet Wilhelm von Willisen, "a distinguished Prussian officer who has brought a letter to Mr. Carlyle," which was from Varnhagen von Ense. For Willisen, see JWC to TC [28 July].

JWC-TC, 14 [July]. Addr: Care of—Redwood Esq / Landough / Cowbridge / S. Wales. PM: Missent to Kingston; Kingston, 14 July 1843. MS: NLS 602.114; longhand copy with TC's notes: Berg. Pbd: A. Carlyle, *NLM* 1:115–18 inc. On the envelope TC wrote: "(14? july, 1843) / (Kitty Kirk*k* visits) / *in.*"

1. The ribbon for her birthday; see TC to JWC, 12 July.

but there is one from Geraldine requiring answer by return of post—and it has taken so much writing to answer it that I am not only weary, but have little time left— Geraldine is like the broomstick that was let to carry water[2]—she threatens in spite of all I can say to the contrary to keep me in a deluge of Mudieism to the end of the chapter— Then has *she* been writing herself to the woman[3]—reproaching her (for she sends me a copy of the letter) with her "folly, ingratitude, and exceeding stupidity" and ordering her to come and implore me not to throw up my charge of her family—this was indiscreet to say the least—without having asked my leave but it must be allowed she has made great exertions for them and has some right to be provoked at the idea of these being all thrown away. She has collected £14.12 first and last and writes to day of a place ready for Juliet— But will she take it?—we can lead the horse to the water—but not make it drink— It would be good still could one save the girl or both the girls from the streets their only open field—let come of of[4] the Mother what likes—

Yesterday evening I received a most unexpected visit from—Kitty Kirkpatrick!![5] A Lady sent in her card and asked if I would see her—*Mrs James Phillips*—I supposed it must be some connection of Kitty's and sent word "surely—if the Lady could stand the smell of the paint"—and in walked Kitty looking as tho' it were the naturalest thing in the world!— When I expressed my surprise at her sudden return she merely said that "she had found coming up before so easy"! there was something rather *dandaical* in that answer for I suppose the fact was she had come up to her Cousin's marriage[6]— Oh my dear she is anything but goodlooking! very sweet however and says such flattering things— She told me that two friends of hers a M*rs* Hermitage (or Hemorrhage) and a M*rs* Daniel ("wife of *the* great east-india merchant") were "dying to know ME (?)[7]—they had seen I think she said some of my—*letters!* (ach gott!) and had heard of me from so many people and lastly from our Rector M*r* Kingsly[8] (! wolf in sheeps clothing that I am!) that I was "quite an angel"—and of course the thing to be done with an angel was to ask her to a seven o'clock dinner—at Fulham—where she Kitty was staying with M*rs* Daniel—and for this

2. See Goethe, *Der Zauberlehrling* [The Sorcerer's Apprentice].
3. Mrs. Mudie.
4. Thus in MS.
5. Catherine Aurora Phillipps, b. Kirkpatrick (1802–89); see 3:166.
6. Unidentified. The cousins the Carlyles knew were the Bullers and the Stracheys, none of whom were married this summer.
7. Mrs. Hermitage unidentified. Mrs. Daniel, possibly the wife of Daniell, of Daniell, Dickinson & Co., E India agents, 6 Gt. Winchester St.
8. Charles Kingsley (1781–1860), rector of St. Luke's, Chelsea; see 14:9.

day— Impossible—I said—too late—too far and you absent &c &c— "But said Kitty, what *can* I say to them?—they will take no refusal, and I *promised* they should make your acquaintance—in fact they are now in the carriage at the door"!—a shudder ran thro my veins—the fine Ladies—the dismantled house—the wet paint—good heavens what should I do?—a sudden thought struck me—my courage rose superior to the horrors of my situation— "Well I said—I will go, if you wish it, and make their acquaintance *in the carriage"!* "Oh how obliging of you! if you *would* be so good"!— I jumped up instantly lest my enthusiasm of desperation should evaporate, walked along the passage under the fire of all the enemies eyes—peremptorily signaled to a blue-and silver footman to let down the steps—and to the astonishment of the four fine Ladies inside, and my own, mounted into their coach and told them here I was!—to be made acquaintance with in such manner as the sad circumstances would admit of!— Kitty stood outside meanwhile throwing in gentle words—and the whole thing went off well enough. I should not know one of these women again— I saw nothing but a profusion of blond and flowers and feathers—it was an action equal to jumping singlehanded into a hostile citadel— I had no leisure to notice the details—mercifully—as it happened—I had *dressed* myself just half an hour before—and rather *elegantly*—from a feeling of reaction against the untidy state in which I had been *cinderellaing* all the day—so as Grace Macdonald[9] said when she broke her arm and did *not* break the glass of her watch—"there has been *some* mercy shewn for a wonder"!

The evening before, instead of Forster who again puts off till Saturday, I had little Mr Hugh Ross and your disciple Mr Espinasse—a painful youth—whose "conversation does not promise to be a treat" I gave him some tea and what comfort I could—but I question if he were capable of receiving any.[10]

9. "Our first Craig*h* servant" (TC's note).

10. Espinasse, an "Edin*r* semi-Frenchman; since Journalist &c" (TC's note); Ross not further identified, though Edinburgh Univ. lists record two Hugh Rosses contemporary with Espinasse, one from Bengal, who read literature, 1837–38, and the other from Rossshire, starting with literature, 1838, then law, 1839–42. Francis Espinasse (1823–1912), journalist and man of letters (see 13:227); last recorded in the univ. lists as reading literature, 1842. He now worked as an asst. to the keeper of printed books, British Museum. He records in detail this first meeting with JWC when taken to Cheyne Row one evening "by a Scotch friend": "Conversation was soon in full flow, for she knew something of one's Edinburgh belongings, and this was never, in her husband's absence, a silent hostess. The first of her peculiarities which struck me was her Scotch accent . . . as marked as . . . her husband's . . ." (63–64). Espinasse had seen the procession of ministers from the General Assembly leaving to found the Free Church "for conscience' sake. . . . Mrs. Carlyle declared that if she had been there she would

Tell John when you write that M*r* William Ogilby has left his card for him— Jeannie with a kind letter and a pretty pincushion sends me word today that I will receive from my Uncle a tasting of some new Madera he has been bottling—I will not drink it *all* before you come—see what a deal I have written after all— Again bless you for your thoughts for me—the Umbrella was *no* failure however[11]—do not think that—

Ever your affectionate / J Carlyle

TC TO JWC

Llandough, 15 july (Saturday), 1843—

My Dearest,

About the time when you read this on Monday (that is, towards noon), I shall, it may be hoped, be getting myself planted on the outside of the mail for Carmarthen, about to bid adieu to these *inania regna* [inane realms]. The distance before me is some sixty miles: the direction as you may see by turning up the Maps of Wales in that Atlas of mine, is north by West; we are to get thither it seems about nine o'clock at night; the Bishop's place, Abergwili, seems to be some mile or two farther. You will bid me good speed! You will have a Letter swiftly under way for me "Care of the Lord Bishop of St David's, Carmarthen": will you not? Swift, swift! I will write you next day from that place; that is to say, on Tuesday, and you will get it on Thursday. Most probably you will again have of me, yet once, from this locality. I write today, early, little past noon yet, tho' it cannot go till tomorrow morning;—being uncertain of my possibilities at a later hour; for we are going off to St. Donat's *this* day, having avoided it yesterday to no purpose: *niemand entgeht seinern Schicksal* [no one escapes his fate]! We go to St Donat's; and may or may not return tonight: so I make this ready in case of extremity: if I do return tonight, I will burst up the cover again, and add a word. R. is at Cowbridge waiting for me, "at one o'clock." I hope to find a Letter there from you, my day promises few other "good joys."[1]— But it is impossible to refuse this worthy man: one cannot say to him "Let thy house be mine, and do thou in

---

have cried." JWC gave an "amusing account" of Terrot's visit and told that TC was in Wales visiting "some simple-minded admirer." She gave "the impression of a very clever and agreeable woman, with a vein in her both of satire and sentiment" (Espinasse 65–66).

11. The umbrella for her birthday had finally arrived by 11 July.

TC-JWC, 15 July. MS: NLS 611.131. Pbd: Froude, *Carlyle* 3:304–5 inc.; Bliss, *TC*, 167–69 inc.

1. Coterie speech; see 10:167.

the interim—disappear!" He really does so to a respectable extent. A good man;—and his good old Mother intent on cooking excellent puddings, on darning tablecloths, and reading *Yearly Monitors*[2] or *Lives* of Quaker Saints, I like her too very much, and shall long remember her still existence in this hollow of the green hills.

Nothing can be better than my mornings, perfectly alone under the shade of big trees, looking out over the Earth, seeing "Nature budding, Percy!",[3]—and a few Welsh bodies of both sexes, in brown discoloured and indeed quite ruinous hats and costumes, stradding about assiduous at haymaking. I read even *Lyell* with the "same relish!"[4] But then indeed comes the afternoon and dinner, or some St Donat's or the like:—such a life is too good to last forever.

Yesterday passed as the brightest beautifullest day in the whole year might do in these circumstances. I had an excellent four hours till two o'clock; then an excellent solitary gallop to the solitary sea-shore, a dip in the eternal element there, and gallop back again. The world was all bright as a jewel set in polished silver and sunshine; the sky so purified by the past day's thunder. The little hamlet of Aberddaw, a poor grey *clachan* [village] crouched under the shelter of a kind of knoll the half of which was eaten sheer off by the sea,—"poor Aberdaw!" I said to myself, "thou sittest there ill enough bested; God help thee!"— The bits of Welsh women with their cuddies [donkeys], lugging small merchandise about, a very scrubby kind of figures, seemed highly praiseworthy, humanely pitiable to me. The wor[l]d[5] is so beautiful, when you see it from the knoll-tops, soft, green, yet shaggy and bushy, and sunshine kisses all things: and the upper moors themselves (dull blunt hilly regions) look sapphire in the distance,—and I am *not* to go thither with R.!

Poor R. At my return to dinner, he produced instead of port, a bottle of excellent claret, and said we must "drink Mrs Carlyle's health, as it was her birthday!" This fact he had gathered from seeing me purchase the bit of a ribband for a band to the said Mrs C.! Well, the feat accordingly was done; and even the ancient Quaker Mother had her glass filled, and wished "many happy years to Jane Carlyle," for which I duly returned thanks. The day had no other *public* event in it. R. made me sit with him till we *finished* the bottle and, as we had copious tea realized about *seven* o'clock, the affair did me no harm at

2. *The Annual Monitor,* pbd. in York, contained obituaries of the members of the Society of Friends.
3. Untraced.
4. Coterie speech; see 5:331.
5. Letter omitted.

all, rather good.— How strange is it that one should come upon the traces of James Spedding here! The Romillys, it seems, have an estate not far from this: Spedding was on a visit to them; then he winded up with a visit to an old Bury Schoolmaster of his, settled here at Cowbridge his native place in his old age; and Redwood lent them a horse for the riding purposes of Spedding.[6] We are strangely shuffled together in this world.

My malison on this glazed paper, on this detestable *leather* pen! The world gets ever madder, with its choppings and changings, and never-ending innovations *not* for the better! My collars too are all on a new principle: O for one hour of Dr Francia!— But here comes our great stalking Maid, an immensely tall woman: "The 'oss is *out*, Sir!" I must instantly be off. Will there be any letter from thee?

Adieu, Dearest, with my heart's blessing.
T. Carlyle

Saturday night. 10 o'clock.— Home from St Donat's; thro' a grey foggy evening; not the worse for the ride, as we came slow and only at a *trotting* pace. The good R. gives me half a glass of sherry, in spite of all protestings, to "settle me." The misty dim vacant sea, with nothing but a Cork Steamer visible in it; the hoarse moan far and wide against the stones and cliffs; the poor distracted-looking hamlet of St Donat's with nothing but asses, geese, and Welshmen tattered and torn: all this I have witnessed once more. Devonshire lay across like a dim dream. *Vida es sueño,* Life is all a Dream.[7]— No Letter from you, you cutty [worthless woman]; nothing but those ugly newspapers! Well, I suppose you have concentrated yourself on Saturday; and a Letter from you *is* actually on the way to Bristol *this* night. I will write to you, one other word from this place tomorrow: do you deserve it? Yes! Sleep sound, and dream of me if you like: the respect due to genius. Ever your affectionate / T. C.

6. Edward Romilly (1804–78), a commissioner since 1836 for auditing public accounts and later chairman of the board; of Porthkerry, on the coast SE of Cowbridge; educ. at the grammar school, Bury St. Edmunds (which Spedding also attended) and Cambridge, 1823–27, overlapping with Spedding at Trinity, 1827. Schoolmaster unidentified.

7. A play by the Spanish playwright Pedro Calderón de la Barca (1600–1681).

JWC TO JEANNIE WELSH

[16 July 1843]

Pins! dearest Babbie—you cannot mean that I should stick common earthly pins in that love of a cushion— I thought it was to lay diamond rings on or something of that sort— I could not find in my heart to bore little holes in it!—and the beautiful cuffs!—take twenty kisses dearest such as imagination *can* take for the little gleam of sunlight which your letter and gifts shed in upon my most solitary and all too earthquaky Birthday[1]—

—What a difference from the exceptional dinner, and strawberry-feast, and ball of long ago was yesterdays *one ill fried whiting*—and for company; painters and singing apprentice-boys who begin to drive me mad with their dawdling and stupidity! when the hamper came—as it did in the evening—I considered whether it would not be good sense to break into it at once and drink *a bottle* of the wine. and rid myself of all sense of the *actual* in the untried pleasures of being dead-drunk— But one cannot hope to get to the end of one's existence as an indulged only child— All *that* is behind—behind!—and one must forward—as one can!—

Pray when you write—in case it should be before me—tell my Uncle that I am very "*proud* of his kindess" as Helen judiciously phrases it—but I will write myself the first quiet hour.— I have a note from Helen this morning[2]—meant to have come Yesterday I dare say—with little perfume papers—and with the best news of their health and locality—You are all dear *children*—and *so* good to me—

But I must not *expatiate* any at present— My superintendence is very much wanted in the staircase where they are making horrible botching (from the complicacy of the carved work) every time I turn my back— God bless thee Babbie love to Mary and the boys ever your own

Jane Carlyle

JWC-JW, [16 July]. Addr: 20 Maryland Street / Liverpool. PM: 16 July 1843. MS: NLS 1892.40. Hitherto unpbd.

1. Jeannie's letter, [12 or 13 July], unlike most of her letters, was preserved because JWC sent it to TC, 14 [July]. TC wrote on it: "from 'Cousin Jeannie' to *Her*."

2. The first Helen is Helen Mitchell, the second Helen Welsh. John Welsh was sending JWC a case of Madeira.

TC TO JWC

Llandough, 16 july 1843
(Sunday night, 10 o'clock)

Yet a few last words before quitting this place! I have had, as usual, a divine forenoon, lying under shady trees in the most exquisite summer atmosphere; and then a most *laborious* afternoon, bathing, galloping, dining, talking; till now when I ought to proceed to pack and arrange—if I did not prefer scribbling to Goody, still a word or two.

Your Letter of Today ought, as I find, to have been a Letter of Yesterday: "missent to Kingston" is on the back of it, and the date "14 july." All the welcomer when it does come! It is the last I shall get here; for there *can* be none tomorrow.

Did you write a word of response to Miss Wilson?[1] If not, or still better, *at any rate*, go and see her: I will try to write from Carmarthen; the smallest Note from a Bishop's will have a certain smack in it for her.— I can hardly make out poor Betty's Letter;[2] but it means, "I do heartily love you, and rejoice in my simple heart to learn that you are well!" Poor Betty, she always does make that clearly and credibly understood. The Liverpool anticipation of me was somewhat of the suddenest: but tell Jeannie I shall gradually approach, and if all go right, arrive; and should it be in a household earthquake, they are never to mind. I am bent on not staying long in any *Town* till I return to Cockneydom again. You should really get these Mudies done: the placing of the two girls if it be possible is palpably the right course; if impossible, the project I think should be with all despatch renounced and finished off. Mudiedom, one has reason to apprehend, is a bottomless quagmire of gin confusion and falsity, on the brink of which it is not pleasant to linger— — *Did* Fuz[3] come on Saturday? He is the old fellow; great cry, and a *reasonable* stock of wool.[4]

But I must not scribble and babble in this manner; at such an hour. Tomorrow at noon I have to be on the roof of the Mail at Cowbridge. A day of hot travel. I shall certainly not again be lodged so quietly anywhere. There will be rapid spiritual conversation in the Bishop's; and no green tree with Book and Tobacco to lodge under. One must

TC-JWC, 16 July. Addr: 5. Cheyne Row, Chelsea / London. MS: NLS 611. 132. Quot: Froude, *Carlyle* 3:305–6; Bliss, *TC* 169.

1. JWC had forwarded Jane Wilson's letter of ca. 12 July asking TC to visit. TC noted on it: "(Miss Wilson to Her)," though in fact it was to him.
2. Betty Braid's letter of 10 July is very hard to read. TC wrote on it: "from poor dear 'Betty' to *Her* (july 1843)."
3. Nickname for John Forster.
4. Cf. "Great cry and little wool," Scots proverb.

take the good and the evil. I find this Redwood a really excellent man; honest, true to the heart, I should think, and with a proud and pure character hidden under his simplicity and timidity. He has been entirely hospitable to me; is sorry that I should go; speculates on my coming back &c as a proximate event: ah me! The old Mother too is very venerable to me. Poor old woman, with her *yearly Monitors,* with her suet dumplings, and all her innocent household good!—

My packing will not be difficult: I have never had any *drawer* here, not one, and my few *Coats* &c have had to lie folded on a chair: the servant is a rustic *gearpole,* and my bedroom is without bell. After a day or two I reconciled myself to the arrangements, but never approved of them!—— Tomorrow I shall probably carry this Letter to the Post-Office myself; and its com[ing][5] safe without accompaniment must be considered a sign that I have got off safe. On Wednesday you get nothing. On Thursday? Yes, if possible. Bless thee.

T. C.

JWC TO TC

Monday before posttime
[17 July 1843]

Dearest

Tout va bien [all goes well][1]—the work goes well and myself goes well— The early-rising, and the shower-bathing, and the having something to look after agrees with me wonderfully—the degree of heat also is exactly suited to my needs— This and the other person drops in and asks if I do not feel very lonely—it is odd what notions men seem to have of the scantiness of a womans resources—they do not find it anything out of nature that *they* should be able to exist by themselves—but a woman—must always be born about on somebods shoulders and

5. Letters omitted.

JWC-TC, [17 July]. Addr: Care of The Lord Bishop / of St. Davids / Carmarthen. PM: 17 July 1843. MS: NLS 602.115; longhand copy with TC's notes: Berg. Pbd: Froude, *LM* 1:197 inc.; A. Carlyle, *NLM* 1:118–21 inc. At the top of the first page of the MS, beneath JWC's dating, TC wrote "17 july, 1843," and on the envelope he noted "Chelsea, 17 july 1843." At the head of the copy TC noted: "From Llandough and C. Redwood I went to B*p* Thirlwall and Abergwilly (Laud's old Palace), staid 3 days with this esteemed Thirlwall, riding in the rain, dialoguing in the big empty 'Palace,' &c.; mournful in my tho*ts,* but kindly, and entitled to respect, these 3 days and their B*p* & his life. Returned as by Glo'ster; went thence, I suppose, to Annandale? No, by L*r*pool, and thence with Br*r* John to Wales,—top of Snowdon in mist &c &c." William Laud (1573–1645), archbishop of Canterbury, had been bishop of St. David's, 1621–26.

1. Coterie speech; see 7:272.

dandled and chirped to or it is supposed she will fall into the blackest melan*cho*ly. When I answered that question from Arthur Helps yesterday in the negative—"Why should I feel lonely?—I have plenty to do—and can see human beings whenever I choose to look out at the window"—he looked at me as if I had uttered some magnanimity worthy to have place in a Legitimate drama and said "Well—really—you *are* a model of a wife!"— Again that young man yesterday![2] He said that "as he was *passing to*—I dont remember where—he thought he might as well *look in*"— —decidedly that young man is *in love* with me—and quite hopelessly I am afraid!— When people tell one they were *passing* at any rate; it means always that they are *ashamed* of coming and could not help themselves—moreover he begins to grow *stupid* and to look on the carpet— Poor little soul, I dare say he finds an infinite charm in the *perfect opposite* of his own little beauty at home![3]— Darwin also called yesterday he had been absent all the week—first at Mrs Marsh's[4] and then *"lounging about all the great mourning shops in London"* equipping the Wedgwoods with mournings for Mr Wedgwood's father![5]— Good God—how some people take these things!— The wedgwoods were to have gone to Mair the beginning of the week— "Oh what a pity I said that they had not gone the week before—that they might have been in time *to* see their Father"— "Why no, said he it was much better as it is—for it is much more convenient for them being all here to get their mournings before going—there are such a quantity needed so many children—servants and all that—*they are quite spending their life* in Jay's in Regent Street![6]—" It made me quite sick to hear of a Father gone out of the world and no other care felt about the matter exept that of getting mournings— Darwin was very much out of humour yesterday about Harriet Martineau! and applied to *me* for approbation and comfort under "a rather *brutal* thing" which Wedgwood and he had felt it their duty to do to her— Did I tell you before— She wrote to them last week desiring that from the thirteen hundred pounds collected there should be first and foremost bought £100 worth of—plate!!! She had Cox the great Jewllers list sent to her by Mrs Reid[7] and had marked off various articles silver

2. "*viz.* Helps" (TC's note).
3. Elizabeth (Bessy) Helps, b. Fuller; m. 1836; they had a son, 18 May.
4. Probably Anne Marsh (1791–1874; *DNB*), novelist; see 9:134.
5. Josiah Wedgwood (1769–1843), d. 12 July at Maer Hall, Staffordshire; second son of the famous potter, Josiah (1730–95); father of seven surviving children, including Hensleigh; maternal uncle of Erasmus Darwin.
6. Jay & Co., The London General Mourning Warehouse, 247–51 Regent St.
7. Elizabeth Jesser Reid (1794–1866), women's educationalist; see 14:237–38. Thomas Cox Savory, silversmith, 47 Cornhill, London.

tea-pot &c £45! &c &c Darwin "thought at first she must be gone mad"—then he fancied she wished, in spending the rest of the money, to preserve this much of it in shape of a *testimonial!*—then that she wished to leave it in a legacy to her Brother James![8]— Any how, after some days deliberation Mr Wedgwood and he who were required to do this thing in *their official capacity*—wrote to Mrs Reid that they, in their *official capacity* peremptorily declined it—if Miss Martineau chose to buy a hundred pounds worth of plate she must do it herself after she entered on possession of the money—as they had expressly stated the *money* not *plate* was to be given to her— Certainly Harriet is going all to nonsense with her vanities—now she will probably be quite angry at these men who have done so much for her—because they refuse to comply with her whim[9]—

After post

Here is your letter dearest—and all is well—only that I do not comprehend how you should have failed of getting mine of the 14*th*— I wrote on Friday—took it to the post office myself and paid twopence for it—there was a note from Miss Wilson along with my letter and a letter from Jeannie & Betty— —I think it was the same day I sent the "three ugly newspapers"—which makes the delay of my letter the more mystairous[10]— But you will have got it by this time surely— I would not for any thing have missed a post—in sending you a kiss for the dear little band— I wrote five minutes after receiving it—

The hamper of Maidera arrived from Liverpool that night[11]—and I was feeling so dreary that night in spite of all your and so many other peoples kindness to me and in spite of all that I could repeat to myself, that it was distraction to regret that I could not pass to the end of existence as an indulged fêted only child—that I felt almost tempted to break into the hamper and lose all sense of the actual in the unknown pleasures of being dead-drunk—but of course I did not do it—

8. The Rev. James Martineau (1805–1900; *DNB*), unitarian minister at Paradise St. Chapel, Liverpool, 1832–57; prof. of mental and moral philosophy and political economy, Manchester New College, 1840–57; author of many works on philosophy and religion.

9. The testimonial fund (see JWC to JW, [8 June]) had been advertised as at Martineau's disposal, with no mention of money or plate; but she wanted to commemorate the testimonial and her gratitude, and wrote to Darwin, [23 July], after he and Wedgwood had apparently agreed to order the plate, of which there were to be seventeen items, costing £104 12s. 8d.: "I think you and he are quite right in your scruple, and I hope now all will be well" (*Harriet Martineau's Letters to Fanny Wedgwood*, ed. E. S. Arbuckle [Stanford, 1983] 57; see pp. 57–65 for further details).

10. "Servant Helen's phrase" (TC's note).

11. "Her *birthnight*, note" (TC's note).

— I called for Miss Wilson that she might not think you impolite—which was a real *great* action on my part—she was mighty civil—Forster came on Saturday forenoon with "great Gods"[12] enough to blow up a steam vessel—he gave me a check for fifty pounds which I have *not* left on the floor of the china-closet[13]— His dinner invitation I gracefully but peremptorily declined— I have a long history to tell you of the wretched Mudies—plenty of long histories to tell you but they will keep—and today I have no more time Tell me if you have got the other letter I am sure I addressed it right— Ever your affectionate

Goody

Please give my compliments to Thirlwall

TC TO JWC

Abergwili, Carmarthen, 18 july, 1843—

My Dearest,

I have been in many "new positions";[1] but this of finding myself in a Bishop's Palace so-called, and close by the Chapel founded by old Scarecrow LAUD of famous memory, is one of the newest! Expect no connected account of the thing, nor of anything whatever today: I have not yet learned the *airts* [directions] of the place in the least; and it is a morning of pouring rain; and in one hour (at noon) the brave Bishop, be the weather what it may, decides on riding with me "four hours and a half" thro' the wildest scenery of the country, that *it* may not suffer by the tempestuous nature of the elements. The Post will be gone before I return. Take one word therefore, to assure thee that I am alive, comparatively speaking *well;* and that I think of thee here,—here very especially where all is so foreign to me. Heavens, do but think, I was awoke before seven o'clock, after short sleep, by a lackey coming in haste, to indicate that I must come and say my prayers in Laud's Chapel of St John! I did go accordingly, and looked at it and at myself with wonder and amazement.[2]— Besides my table *shakes;*—and I have a word to write to John.

Yesterday at noon I had got handsomely away from Llandough,—

12. One of John Forster's favorite phrases.

13. "For the Article, *Francia, Fn Quarty Review,* I suppose. 'Floor of the China-closet' was an actual accid*t* that happened once,—and bro*t* some quizzing" (TC's note).

TC-JWC, 18 July. MS: NLS 611.133. Pbd: Froude, *Carlyle* 3:307–9 inc.; Bliss, *TC* 168–71 inc.

1. Coterie speech; see 8:127.
2. Coterie speech; see 5:217.

the good old Dame,[3] desired me "Thou please to give my regards to Mrs Carlyle": I was taken in the "tub" to Cowbridge, and there the Mail came up: full all but one inside seat! I had to take that seat such as it was; the rather as it turned out that there was to be a vacancy on the roof in some 17 miles farther. It was very hot and disagreable inside; a huge grazier fast asleep; a destestable-looking parson with yellow skin and jet black tattery wig; and old burgher of the Town of Neath, very talkative, very innocent: to this latter I chiefly attached myself. Neath at last came, the end of the 17 miles, and I got out and had a cigar, and saw undeniably clear around me the face of Heaven and Earth. An Earth very tolerable; sandstone coal-country now, green sharp hills with wood enough, green fields ill-ploughed and cultivated, with ditto; houses plastered with whitewash; ridiculous Welsh bodies, all the women of them now with men's hats,—a great proportion of them looking very hungry and ragged. Swansea, enveloped in thick poisonous copper-fumes, and stretching out in winged desolation (for the copper-forges are of the last degree of squalor, low huts with forests of chimneys, and great mountains of red dross which *never* changes into soil), is a very strange and very ugly place: we dined there (on next to nothing except ham,—for I would not eat lamb); and then bowled along into the hills of the interior: no great shakes of *hills,* but as the road goes over the *top* of them all it makes them somewhat impressive. About 7 in the evening we plunged down by a steep winding way into the "valley of the Towy," a dim enough looking valley—for there was a windy Scotch mist by that time,—with a river of some breadth and of muddy colour running thro it; and a little farther up, a strange *bleared* mountain city hanging in a disconsolate manner on the farther bank and steep declivity: Carmarthen at last! No *Bishop's* carriage was waiting for me: ah no, I hired a gig and flunkey, for which to this distance of *two miles* I paid 5/ and 1/6, 6/6 in all: there is a way of doing business!

Abergwili is a village of pitiful dimension, all daubed as usual with whitewash and yellow-ochre; it is built however like a common village, on both sides of the public road: at the farther end of it, you come to solemn large closed gates of wood; on your shout they open, and you enter upon a considerable glebe-land *pleasance,* with the usual trees, turf, walks, peacocks &c, and see at fifty yards distance, a long irregular (perhaps *cross* shaped) edifice, the porch of it surmounted by a stone *mitre:* ach Gott— I was warmly welcomed; tho' my Bishop did seem a little uneasy too, but how could he help it! I got with much pomp an extremely bad and late dish of tea; then

3. Elizabeth Redwood.

plenty of good talk till midnight, and a room at the farther wing of the house, still as the heart of wildernesses, where after some smoking &c, I did at last sink into sleep till awakened as aforesaid. We have had an excellent cup of tea to breakfast; and I feel ready for a bit of the world's fortune once more.— My Bishop, I can discern, is a right solid honest-hearted man, full of knowledge and sense; excessively *delicate* withal, and in spite of his positive temper almost *timid;* no wonder he is a little embarrassed with me, till he feel gradually that I have not come here to eat him, or make scenes in his still house! But We are getting, or as good as got, out of that; and shall for our brief time do admirably well. Here is medicine for the soul, if the body fare worse in such sumptuosities; precisely the converse of Llandough! It is wholly an element of rigid decently elegant *Forms* that we live in; very wholesome for the like of me to dip for a day or two into that: is it not? For the rest, I have got two other Novels of Tieck, of which the admiring Bishop possesses a whole stock.[4]

O Duckie, I do hope thou will write to me this day! I feel as if a little friendly speech even "about time and space"[5] with my poor Goody would be highly consolatory to me. Tonight I shall sleep better; tomorrow I shall be more at home; and the next day—? There is nothing yet settled about the next day. This morning however I have given out all my shirts to be washed (five of them now accumulated).

Coaches it seems and some kind of straggling chances and possibilities of conveyance, do exist till one get within wind of Liverpool: I think of persisting by this route; the mountains lie all upon it, which one is bound to "see."— O my dear, how much richer am I than many a man with £3000 a-year if I but knew it! What is the worth of Goody herself, thinkest thou? God bless thee.

T. Carlyle—

TC TO JOHN A. CARLYLE

Abergwili Carmarthen
18 july 1843 (Tuesday)

My dear Brother,

I got along yesterday to the "Bishop's Palace" here; but am yet so confused in my new locality that nothing but the desire to give you my promptest news could excuse me for writing today. Add to all things

4. Thirlwall was an admirer of Tieck and had trans. some of his works; see 12:120.

5. Coterie speech; see JWC to TC, [31 Aug.].

TC-JAC, 18 July. MS: NLS 524.47. Hitherto unpbd.

that it is raining, and I am to go out in *fifteen* minutes for a *four hours ride* with the magnanimous Bishop! He fears no weather.— This is the house old Laud inhabited; I was summoned this morning to say my prayers in the very chapel of the old Chimera. I went but did not try to pray much,—at least not in *his* dialect.

My route hither you probably know: By Neath, Swansea &c. I have seen no such place as Swansea for horrid deformity produced by labour of man. The copper dross is ugly as Golgotha; the Welsh bodies too, men and women, are *duddy* [ragged], dirty, all in hats the womankind, and look extremely queer. We passed successively thro' four tollbars demolished by Rebecca. The gates were sawed off close by the ground,—great thick posts; and had then been burnt or carried away. The tollhouse was totally demolished; the roof rolled up within the ruined walls of it, seemingly by long levers, and left there in a mass. No toll was asked, no person was there. The nocturnal riots, we are told, have not ended; but one sees nothing of it by day, and nobody seems to mind it at all.[1]— There is a bell tinkling for something or other! I must be brief.

Perhaps this afternoon there will be a Letter from you at five o'clock? I will write in deliberate answer to that; nay probably tomorrow at any rate.— I still persist in making my way thro' by Aberystwith, and onwards to Menai perhaps or Bangor[2] or wherever the conveniences are. As no regular coaches are to be heard of, I cannot prophecy my *times:* two or three days here, that is the last *appointed* pause I make. Cannot you if you like to meet me, and stroll about a little, get over straightway to Liverpool, and there appoint *me* place and time, at Bangor or elsewhere? Or perhaps you do not care to tourify in Wales any more at present. I cannot ask you to come, for what have I to give you? Only it would be pleasant enough to meet! I will therefore continue to prophesy my motives as near as I can.— Jane informs me Mr Ogilvy called for you at Chelsea; only left a card, I think. Jane is well, still painting, painting! *Nichts zu bedeuten* [nothing of importance] otherwise.

My dear good Mother—O I wish I could write a volume to tell all

1. At the time TC placed little importance on it, but he wrote in his Journal, 2 Oct.: "'Rebecca' (the Gatebreaker) was in the very quarter of Wales where I passed (Carmarthen &c), but except the sight of her broken gates she amounted to little; nobody seemed to regard her much: she is grown more impressive since. Wales seemed to me not worth going to see." Milnes on his visit to Thirlwall in Sept. reported: "This Country is on the brink of becoming as bad as Ireland. The serious fun of breaking the turnpike gates has ended in fire and bloodshed" (Reid, *RMM* 1:304).
2. Coastal town, NW Wales.

I think about her and the rest of you. I shall see you all soon if it please Heaven. I sent a Newspaper to Jean, to Mary, and to my Mother; flung in yesterday as I passed thro' Carmarthen, in hopes the Post-office people would *stamp* them. Mary, I think, unless you have explained to her would hardly know what to make of it. Adieu, dear Brother. God's blessing on you all. Poor Alick too!—

Ever your affectionate T. Carlyle

I go always in the *Tweed*,—one of the best of coats!—

JWC TO JOHN STERLING

[18 July 1843]

D'abord [first of all], I am glad that you do not come just now—I should have grudged to see you go back without me—and to have gone with you would have been a base desertion of my post.

Ever since my husband saved himself in Wales, this house has afforded the liveliest image of a sacked City!—has been a house possessed with seven devils!—two carpenters—a painter—a paperhanger—a nondescript apprentice lad and "*a spy*"—the latter hardly taller than your boot—the master's son, placed there to see that every man did his duty—such hurrying and scurrying—"up stairs down stairs, in my lady's chamber"[1]—such a smell of paint—such an infernal noise, such perfection of material discomfort: it would need the pen of a Dante to give you an adequate idea of it! Ach Gott!—but this household earthquake was greatly needed—and *no* sort of revolution can get itself accomplished with rosewater— There will be a clean, bright house for my husband to come home to. and I shall get—PERHAPS—*a little praise*—and if not; why I shall have virtue's own reward.—"*Die Tugend* &c. &c.—"[2] you remember? Meanwhile I am dreadfully falled out of the sphere of the Ideal—am a sort of possible practical *T[h]eresa*[3] at present— I go about scolding my work-people and, cutting out furniture-print—and suggesting improved methods of doing things. Even the Apprentice Lad's singing I take cognizance of—always in grinding with the pumice-stone this Devil of a boy *will* sing—snatches of wild strains—as if *the Redcross Knight—Joclyn's bower* &c. &c. were fitting

JWC-JS, [18 July]. Addr: Ventnor / Isle of Wight. PM: 18 July 1843. MS: NLS 602.117 inc. Hitherto unpbd. On the envelope TC noted: "(18 july 1843)."

1. From the nursery rhyme "Goosey Goosey Gander."

2. "*Die Tugend findet ihren Lohn in sich selbst* [Virtue is its own reward]"; proverbial.

3. TC has added the "h." A character in *Wilhelm Meister's Apprenticeship* (bk. 7, ch. 6) who maintained that a wife who properly conducted her household economy could be sure that her husband would return; see *Works* 24:41.

accompaniments for the hideous noise he is making— the day Mrs Chadwick called for me—had just seated herself on the sofa and was beginning to utter—insipidities; when crash, screech came the pumice-stone over the room door to the tune of

"Oh rest thee my darling!
Thy Sire is a Knight! &c

making the poor Lady start to her feet and utter a little scream— I said to him at last grimly, but with an awkward calm—"how happy you must be that you *can* sing at such unmusical work—!"

"Oh thank you Mam" says he quite unconscious that I was in a bad humour "I's quite happy—*so far as I knows*—(beautiful illustration of C's doctrine of unconsciousness![4]) but I's always a-singing any how—it sounds pleasant at work, do'snt it Mam"? "Oh *very* pleasant said I! but if you *would* sing a song from beginning to end it would be still pleasanter—for *me*." "Thank you Mam—I will try"! But he does not succeed—. At six in the morning so soon as I hear the hubbub commence, I jump out of bed and "in wera desperation" take the shower bath," then I have such a long day before me!— "How charming to inhale the morning air when one has been always virtuous"! Sometimes I am seized with a passion for rural life—and then with *my own hands* I construct a gipsey-tent in the garden, out of clothes-lines—long poles—and an old brown crumb cloth!—within which I establish myself with the indispensabilities of life, a chair, a table, a bit of carpet—and the implements for writing and sewing—Woman wants but little here below! This retreat has only one drawback; it is too much the envy of surrounding nations[5]—from every window in the row heads peer out to penetrate my meaning! If I had a speaking trumpet I would address them once for all: "Ladies and gentlemen! I am not here to enter my individual protest against the progress of civilization—nor yet to mock you with the sight [of][6] an arcadian felicity, which you have neither the taste nor the ingenuity to make your own!— I am here simply to enjoy nature according to ability—and to escape from the poisonous atmosphere within doors! Retire I pray you—and leave me unobserved to pursue my innocent labours"!— But at night? I cannot sleep in my tent? and as your father said "God Almighty Mrs Carlyle if you sleep in that stew of new-paint *you will awake dead*"! No—I take all proper precautions I sleep with my two windows wide open—"and plenty of *ladders* lying underneath so that the thieves need only walk in

4. See "Characteristics," *Works* 28:1, 16.
5. Cf. *Richard II* 2.1.
6. Omitted by JWC.

JWC TO JOHN WELSH

[18 July 1843]

Dearest, dear, only Uncle of me!

I would give a crown that you could see me at this moment, thro a powerful telescope! you would laugh for the next twelve hours—I am *doing the rural* after a fashion so entirely my own! To escape from the abominable paint-smell and the infernal noise within doors; I have erected *with my own hands* a gipsey-tent in the garden, constructed with clothes-lines—long poles and an old brown floor-cloth!—under which remarkable shade I sit in an arm-chair, at a small round table—with a hearth rug for carpet under my feet—writing materials sewing materials—and a mind superior to Fate!— The only drawback to this retreat, is its being exposed to "the envy of surrounding nations"—so many heads peer out on me from all the windows of *the Row*—eager to penetrate my meaning!— If I had a speaking-trumpet I would address them once for all—"Ladies & gentlemen, I am not here to enter my individual protest against the progress of civilization!—nor yet to mock you with an Arcadian felicity which you have neither the taste nor the ingenuity to make your own!—but simply to *enjoy nature* according to ability, and to get out of the smell of new paint! So pray you, leave me to pursue my innocent avocations, in the modest seclusion which I covet"!

—Not to represent my contrivance as too perfect, I must also tell you that a strong puff of wind is apt to blow down the poles and then the whole tent falls down on my head!—this has happened once already since I began to write—but an instant puts it all to rights again—Indeed without counteracting the indoors-influences by all lawful means I could not stay here at present without injury to my health which is at no time of the strongest—our house has for a fortnight back been a house possessed with seven devils!— A painter, two carpenters a paper-hanger, two non-descript apprentice-lads and "*a spy*"—all playing the devil to the utmost of their powers—hurrying and scurrying "up stairs down stairs and in my Lady's chamber"! affording the liveliest image of a sacked City! When they rush in at six of the morning and spread themselves over the premises, I instantly jump out of bed and "in wera desperation" take a shower-bath. Then such a long day to be virtuous in! I make a chair and sofa covers—write letters to my friends—scold the work people, and suggest improved methods of doing things—and

JWC-JW, [18 July]. Addr: The Baths / Helensborough / N.B. PM: 18 July 1843. MS: NLS 602.116. Pbd: Froude, *LM* 1:198–201 inc.; Bliss, *JWC* 121–23 inc.

when I go to bed at night I have to leave both windows of my room wide open—(and plenty of ladders lying quite handy underneath) that I may not as old Sterling predicted "awake dead" of the paint— The first night that I lay down in this open state of things, I recollected Jeannies house-breaker-adventure last year, and not wishing that all the thieves who *might* walk in at my open windows should take me quite unprepared, I laid my policeman's-rattle and my dagger on the spare pillow—and then I went to sleep quite secure— But it is to be confidently expected that in a week more things will begin to subside into their normal state—and meanwhile it were absurd to expect that any sort of *Revolution* can be accomplished with *rose-water*

There!—the tent has been down on the top of me again but it has only upset the ink—

Jeannie appears to be earthquaking with like energy in Maryland Street—but finds time to write me nice long letters nevertheless, and even to make me the loveliest pincushion for my birthday—and my birthday was celebrated also with the arrival of a hamper into which I have not yet penetrated. Accept kisses *ad infinitum* for your kind thought of me dearest Uncle. I hope to drink your health many times in the Maidera when I have Carlyle with me again to give an air of *respectability* to the act— Nay on that evening when it came to hand, I was feeling so sad and dreary over the contrast between this 14*th* of July—alone—in a house like a sacked city—and other 14*ths* that I can never forget—that I hesitated whether or no to get myself out a bottle of the Maidera there and then—and try for once in my life the hitherto unknown comfort of being dead-drunk But my sense of the respectable overcame the temptation— I am so thankful to hear such comfortable accounts of you from Helen—whom you are to kiss one dozen of times and thank in my name for her welcome letter—I will write to herself very speedily—

My husband has now left his Welchman and is gone for a little while to visit the Bishop of St Davids Then he purposes crossing over somehow to Liverpool—and after a brief benediction to Jeannie passing into Annandale— He has suffered unutterable things in Wales from the want of any adequate supply—of tea! the *Spooney!* For the rest his visit appears to have been pretty successful—plenty of seabathing—plenty of riding on horseback—and of *lying under trees!*— I wonder it never enters his head to lie under the walnut tree here at home—*it is a tree!*—leaves as green as any leaves can be even in South Wales!—but it were too *easy* to repose under that— —if one had to travel a long journey by railway to it—then indeed it might be worth while!

But I have no more time for scribbling just now—besides my pen is positively declining to act— So God bless you Dear and all of them— Ever your affectionate / Jane Carlyle

TC TO JWC

Abergwili, 19 july 1843 (Wednesday)

My dearest,

I am very consciencious in writing to you! Here, for example, I have missed viewing the City of Carmarthen for your sake, having by candid computation when I got hither to my own room, found that I could not write to you if I went. What a favour! you will say. Yes, you gipsey; and a favour to myself too!— Your Letter of last night was a real consolation to me. I have lost my *liberty*, I have lost my sleep; I am in a baddish way here: but it will soon be done. From *vacuum* I have got into *plenum* with a vengeance: what with chapel-duty, riding to see views, talking with the brave Bishop, late dining, limited tobacco and flunkies awakening you at seven in the morning (the very terror of whom awakens you at six), it is a business one needs to be trained to; and that is not worth while at present.

We sallied out yesterday in the midst of thick rain, on two horses,—mine was the highest I ever rode; bigger fully than Darwin's Cab-horse. We rode for four mortal hours; no trotting permitted, except when I contrary to all politeness, burst off into a *voluntario* [willfully fast pace], and then had soon to lie-to for my Host, who rides somewhat ecclesiastically. What was worse too, my high horse was in the fiercest humour for riding, and I longed immensely to take the temper out of him; but no; we plodded along, and saw a circle of views. Views very good; vallies, scrubby or woody hills, old churches, and ragged Welsh characters in torn hats: all very good; but tho' the rain abated, and finally subsided into mud, and soapy dimness, I was glad enough to get home! And today again, while the weather is bright we are to renew the operation at 3 o'clock. Well,—and yet I am very glad I came in by this establishment, even at the expense of sleep. Nothing similar had ever before fallen in my way; and it was worth seeing once. Do but think of a wretched scarecrow face of Laud looking down on us, from Laud's own house that once was, as we sit at meat! And there is much good in all that I see; a *perfection* of *Form*, which is not without its value. With the Bishop himself I, keeping a strict guard on my mode of utterance, not mode of thinking, get on extremely well; find him a right solid, simplehearted, robust man, very strangely *swathed;*

TC-JWC, 19 July. Addr: 5. Cheyne Row, Chelsea / London. MS: NLS 611. 134. Pbd: Froude, *Carlyle* 3:310–12 inc.; Bliss, *TC* 171–73 inc.

on the whole right good company; and so we fare along, in all manner of discourse, and even laugh a good deal together. Could I but sleep;—but then I never can! I had according to the original program decided to be off tomorrow morning: but the worthy host insists with such an earnestness, that I by way of handsome finish shall be obliged to put off till Friday morning, and see two other *sleeps* still before me. Then however it *is* up; I see my route, and am off!

By the maturest calculation, it seems my far best route will be Northeastward thro' Brecknockshire and Monmouthshire to Glo'ster, Wor'ster, Birmingham and Liverpool. A coach passes us here to Glo'ster in one day; the rest of it is railway. I *could* have gone to the Crawfords; and now, alas, I cannot! You did send me their address; but tho' I rigorously kept every scrap of your writing, that individual Note seems to have gone to ruin somehow or somewhere in my chaotic *drawer*less state; and tho' I have read and re-read all your Letters three times, I cannot now find it at all. "Ross" is all I remember; and we go thro' Ross: there I might have staid all night. But perhaps it is just as well! I am about done with my capacity of visiting for this heat; I shall like about as well to take my ease at my inn. Spending the night at Glo'ster, I shall view the City in the morning: a Cromwellian place that I wanted this long while to see.[1] Then Wor'ster in like manner;[2] till the new railway train come that will take me on to Birmingham and Liverpool: that will be the best. On Saturday night, I think I shall be there.— John it seems is arriving there from Annandale tomorrow morning. He is to see Arbuckle &c: then perhaps we may take another little stroll in Wales; in the Northern or Hill part of it. That will all do, as we like it to do: and so *dabei bleib' es* [it is settled].

Forster has paid very handsomely.[3] Give Darwin his checque to change into cash for you; and you may send five pounds of it on to me by the Post Office to Maryland Street Liverpool. There is no haste about that; for one of my five-pound Notes is still unchanged: but the *expense* of these visitings is very great; dearer I think than moderate board at an inn would be. Never mind!— If a Letter come today, *and* another tomorrow even, I shall rejoice. But I must not bid you write hither any more. Write to Liverpool; that will be the best; and I shall get it on Saturday night. Write at large, my Duckie; I too have a kind

1. For the siege of Gloucester, Aug. 1643, see *Cromwell, Works* 6:165. Cromwell had addressed his troops in Gloucester, 8 May 1648, on his way to subdue Wales; see *Works* 6:320.

2. Worcester, about 25 mi. N of Gloucester and 25 mi. SSW of Birmingham, was the site of the battle, 3 Sept. 1651, in which Cromwell routed Charles II and his Scottish army; see *Cromwell, Works* 7:325–34.

3. For "Dr. Francia."

of admiration of thy letters, especially of those to myself!— I will write a word, if I anywhere can, by the road: once more at any rate you shall hear from me before Sunday.

That of Harriet Martineau is flat distraction: I am more and more content that we had nothing whatever to do with it.[4] Alas, it is a very sad business that of setting up to be "one and somewhat."[5] Let us pity the poor white woman,[6]—and take care of ourselves!

I find here a Letter from Mrs Mudie which has had written on the outside of it "send this back." Here it comes accordingly,—tho' I have just the one stamp left for it! I am writing far too much. I will end now.

What a blessed rustle among these green trees, on that sunny lawn, with woods and fields and hills in the distance! How happy could I be, would all the world, except one small cooks-assistant, *fall asleep;* and leave me alone with Tieck's *Vogelscheuche* [*The Scarecrow*]![7] We are an excellent building: long galleries, spacious quiet rooms, all softly carpeted, furnished; room enough for the biggest Duke. The *mitre* does not exclude soft carpeting, good cheer, or any contrivance for comfort to the outer man.— A dreadful "chaplain" is here, tho' a good-humoured entirely polite one.[8] A man à la Terrot, without Terrot's sense; Drinks well, eats well, toadies as far as permitted; turned of forty; lean and yellow; has boiled big eyes; a neck head and nose giving you a notion of a gigantic human snipe. Is not that a beauty? I have had to look into about a thousand Books: the good Bishop is simple as a child, as a College recluse. We are alone all but this Sucker-Chaplain or Snipe. Tomorrow there is talk of a Judge dining with us:—hang it perhaps that is one of the reasons why I am to be kept here!

O Goody I send thee a hundred kisses; I have much need to be kissed myself—by a Goody's lips!— Is there no hope for Helps then, thinkest thou? Never! Poor Helps, his fate with that small beauty[9] is rather painful.

Adieu Dearest, adieu! Ever affectionate

T. Carlyle

4. The testimonial for Harriet Martineau.
5. Coterie speech.
6. Coterie speech; see 3:390.
7. (1834), subtitled "a fairy-tale novelle in five acts."
8. Unidentified further.
9. Bessy Helps.

TC TO JOHN A. CARLYLE

Abergwili, Carmarthen, 19 july, 1843—

My dear Brother,

I wrote to you yesterday; but it was to Scotsbrig, and you will not now receive it, I find. In these hours you are driving (or rather you have driven for it is now three o'clock) from Dumfries towards Annan; and have left our good Mother at Gill: a scene very lively to me, and very curious as I paint it out here!— Yesterday I could decide on nothing as to roads, and was still thinking of struggling thro' by Aberystwith, and some uncertain intermittent conveyances there are: but seeing you now at Liverpool I decide another way. We have a Coach to Glos'ter; and that, with railways, will be it. It is a mail, goes well thro' pleasant country; reaches Glo'ster about 8 at night. Tomorrow morning I meant to be off; but the Bishop will not let me, I perceive: he is very good, this brave Bishop, and we do extremely well together. But on Friday morning I set out. At Glos'ter I survey the town, pass the night; take an early train for Wor'ster, see that town; and then get on for Birmingham and Liverpool that same night. Pray tell Cousin Jeannie that this is the way. And so on Saturday evening, by the late or latest train very probably, I shall hope to see you.

If after we have looked about us in Liverpool, you will embark on a small foot excursion into Welshland, by Bangor or otherwise, I shall be very willing to entertain the project. We shall see,—we shall see, about that, and all things!

You did well to write to Alick; poor fellow, he sticks nearly constant in my head at present: but I have never got him written to at all. If it please Heaven, there is a time coming. That little *frustrated* farewell[1] was very sad to me at Llandough.

Today I will write half a line also to my Mother. I think I have told *you* all that was essential; and as my time is in the strictest sense limited, I will cease. My kind regards to all at Maryland Street, and to the good Arbuckle withal. Hoping for Saturday night,

Your affectionate / T. Carlyle

I meant to visit the Crawfurds somewhere about Ross; but that is now off, and no matter. George Johnston at Glo'ster I shall remember kindly, but not mean to visit.[2]— Our weather is broken, but very bright occasionally. I have the prospect in twenty minutes time, of *three*

TC-JAC, 19 July. MS: NLS 512.7. Hitherto unpbd.

1. The failure of TC's letter to reach Alexander before his sailing.

2. Dr. George Johnston, originally from Ecclefechan, then Liverpool and finally Gloucester; see 15:202–3.

hours riding "for views" with the Bishop. Yesterday, in rain, I had four hours of it,—*ach Gott!*

TC TO MARGARET A. CARLYLE

Abergwili, Carmarthen, South Wales
19 july (Wednesday), 1843—

My dear Mother,

Yesterday came John's Letter; and by it I learn that today about this time (3 o'clock), you are probably set down at Gill, and the Doctor gone off towards Liverpool. I *see* it all *here* in this strange City and Bishop's House; and cannot but send you dear Mother a half word of salutation, tho' I have hardly half a minute of time! I already sent you a Newspaper the day before yesterday (and another to Gill), and a Letter to John yesterday; but both these would go to Scotsbrig, and you will have yet no news of me.

I got here safe on Monday evening; was and still am safe lodged with the Bishop,—in a grand mansion, which it is not easy to get at home in all at once! A much smaller one would serve *me*. Abergwili is a poor village little bigger than Middlebie, some two miles from Carmarthen, which is a straggling *blae*[bluish-grey]-looking old Welsh City about the size of Dumfries or smaller. Our Bishop's House and Park is the foundation of Abergwili; a sovereign palace for that little hamlet. The Bishop himself is a man I like well;—tho' were he *not* a Bishop I could like him far better! There is but one thing more I will add: *this* was Archbishop Laud's House! the portrait of that miserable chimera still hangs here; and we go every morning soon after seven o'clock to do our devotions in a Chapel established by him. The present Bishop knows how I hate *him*, and does not disapprove much. I attend at the "morning service" out of politeness and to avoid scandal,—but cannot boast that I pray much there. It will "do thee neither ill ne' guid!"[1]—

However, I will *tell* you about all that, dear Mother; for I hope we are soon to meet. I have just written to the Doctor to say that I expect to meet him in Liverpool on *Saturday evening* first. I leave this on Friday morning; stay all night at a place called Glo'ster (Gloucester), a town I wanted to see, then get into railways, to Birmingham, and finally to Liverpool, by a very easy route. I had some more visits; but give them up since John is come. The most part of Mr Welsh's people, as he himself is, are absent about Glasgow or west of that at sea-

TC-MAC, 19 July. MS: NLS 521.15. Hitherto unpbd.
1. Coterie speech; see 4:369.

bathing: "there will be the more room for you," says our little cousin.[2] After a little pause at Liverpool I propose to Jack that we go over, and have a few days walking among the hills in North Wales. I will write to you how we get on,—if I know correctly where you are! Jenny or some of them may write a word. Stay where you are, dear Mother, and bathe quietly; you are quite safe of me for some time yet,—say two weeks almost; not till after the tides are done!

But I have to go out and ride with my Bishop; I must cease. Jane is well and cheery, still engaged among painters. I send my affectionate regards to all at Gill, Jamie, Mary, Jenny, and all the small ones: Good be with them all. Hoping soon to meet once again by God's great goodness, I bid my dear Mother farewell for this day. Dear good Mother!—T. Carlyle

JWC TO TC

Thursday [20 July 1843]

Dearest

I quite fretted last night at your having been cheated out of your letter—*d'abord,* I had a headach but that was not the reason. for it was not an evendown headach under which no woman can write. I *could* have written—better or worse, but I put off, thinking always I should get into "a freer and clearer state" (John's favorite phrase) before the post left— And, as the copy line says, "procrastination is the Root of all evil"[1]—from two till four I had visitors—and not of the free and easy sort who could be told to go away and return at a more convenient season—first M*rs* Prior, Sterlings[2] Sister—and her companion Miss Allan—the prim̄est[3] pair! but meaning well, and making me a long *first* visit of ceremony in testimony of M*rs* Prior's sense of my "goodness to her poor Brother." By the way I really believe that I have been the instrument under Providence of saving old Sterlings life—I told you how D*r* Ferguson[4] seemed to me to be ruining him with recommendation

2. Jeannie.

JWC-TC, [20 July]. Addr: Care of the Lord Bishop of St. Davids / Carmarthen. PM: 20 July 1843; Carmarthen, 21 July 1843. MS: NLS 602.118; longhand copy with TC's notes: Berg. Pbd: Froude, *LM* 1:208–12 inc.

1. JWC combines two maxims.

2. On the MS TC added "old" before "Sterlings." Mrs. Prior, presumably a widow, lived in Brighton.

3. TC added a dash above the "m" to indicate double "m." Miss Allan not further identified.

4. Possibly Robert Ferguson (1799–1865; *DNB*), physician of 9 Queen St., Mayfair; M.D., Edinburgh; moved to London, 1823, where he met many literary people through Lockhart's intro. of him to John Murray; became resident medical officer of Marylebone Inst., where he learned "many of those strange resources and

to "a plentiful use of porter, wine, and other stimulants to *restore the tone of his nervous system*(!)" Then he recommended to him vapour baths!— I saw him after his first bath—all scarlet as a lobster and pale as milk by turns—and shivering and burning by turns— I had an uncomfortable feeling about him all the evening—was not sure whether I ought not to write to John[5]—he looked to me so much in danger of some sudden stroke— Two days after he came and told me he had been twice cupped![6] He had been so ill that he had himself proposed the thing to Ferguson who approved— Now this was quite enough to show what sort of Jackass thi[s] Ferguson must be—feeding a man up with porter and wine and cupping him at the same time— I told Sterling most seriously that he looked to me in a very critical state—and that if he did not go home and send at once for Old Morrah[7] who was no quack and had never flattered his tastes, I would not answer for his living another week— He was furious at my suspicion of Ferguson—but on the way home thought better of it and did send for Morrah who immediately proceeded to scour him with the most potent medicines—Morrah called for me two days ago, and said that he did not believe he could have gone on another week under Fergusons system without a stroke of apoplexy—that his pulse was a hundred and thirty and his tongue quite black—now he is sleeping well—and much better everyway— After M*rs* Prior came the Dundee Sterlings and the Sister who is going to India.[8] I liked the big bald forehead and kind eyes of Stirling very much indeed—he looks a right good fellow— They are to return to Dundee in a few days— But the most unexpected, the most stroke-of thunder visitor I have had—was—Chutikins!!![9]— I de-

---

prescriptions on which to the surprise of many of his contemporaries" he was "wont to rely" (William Munk, *Roll of the Royal College of Physicians of London* [1878] 3:296). Though he now specialized in obstetrics, he became a general consultant about 1857.

5. Sterling, the son.

6. For blood.

7. "'Old Morrah' or Murrough, was an Irish Surgeon, of much sense and merit, well-accepted by the Sterlings and us" (TC's note). James Morrah, 62 Sloane St.; see 9:178. JWC omits letter in "this."

8. James Stirling (d. 1876), civil engineer, and his wife, Susan. Her youngest sister (who may have lived with them; see 13:12), Jessie Haddow Buist, b. Hunter (1818–45), had presumably recently m. George Buist (1804–60; *DNB*), ed. of the *Bombay Times,* 1840–58; she died in India.

9. "'Cuittikens'" (old Scotch word for spatterdashes, 'Cuits' signifying feet) means Mr Terrot, now become 'Bishop' so-called 'of Edin*r*' (title, we used to think, analogous to *Great-Mogul of London?*),—in whose episcopal uniform, unsuitable to the little bandy-legged man, the *spats* were a promin*t* item. Indefinable man of talent and veracity, tho' not of much devoutness, of considerable worldliness rather and greatly composed [of?] conceit,—gone now, ridiculously, into the figure of a 'bandy-legged Black Beetle,' as was tho*t* by some!" (TC's note).

clare when Helen told me he was below I almost sprang *the rattle*[10]—

I had not answered his letter[11]—had made up my mind not to answer it at all—a man puts one in quite a false position who demands explanation of ones *coldness*—coldness belongs to the great sphere of *Silence*—all speech about it can only make bad worse— Was he come there—because like Kitty Kirkpatrick he "had found it so easy"—to ask me for an answer?—was the small chimera gone out of his wits?— When I came down to him tho' outwardly quite calm even indifferent—I was in a serious trouble—he put me speedily at ease however by telling me that he had been sent for express to see his Aunt[12] who had thought herself dying (and from whom he has expectations) she was now recovering and he hoped to be able to go back in a few days— I hope so too— I *said* that I had not answered his letter—because it seemed to me *that* was the best way of counteracting *the indiscretion of his having written it*—that "altho as a man much older than myself and a dignitary of the church he ought to be wiser than me, I could not help telling him that I had learned a thing or two which he seemed to be still in ignorance of—among the rest that *warmth of affection* could not be brought about by *force of logic*"— He said, "I was right and he did not design to bore me this time" and so we parted with polite mutual toleration— But you may figure the shock of having that little black Cutikins descend upon me out of the blue so suddenly when I was relying on seeing no more of him for three years!

Only think what human wickedness is capable of— Some devils broke into Pearson's work-shop the night before last and stole all the men's *tools!* the poor creatures are running about quite lost; their occupation gone.[13]—they have never any money laid by—so they cannot buy new tools—till they make money—and they cannot make money till they get tools!—it is the cruelest of thefts a man's tools! Last night six or seven pounds worth of glass was cut out of a new-house—out of the windows that is to say—.

I have got a very good situation in Manchester for Juliet Mudie[14]—she is to go to it on Monday fortnight I will get her clothes myself

10. "The police*n's* 'rattle' was a thing she actually had on her night-table at the time" (TC's note).

11. See JWC to TC, [7 and 8 July].

12. Unidentified.

13. Cf. *Othello* 3.3.

14. "Those wretched 'Mudies,' ab*t* whom a great deal of pains was taken (one of whom I remember as living here some time) came all ultimately to the ruin overhanging their folly and them. Some months after this, one day in Piccadilly, amid the crowd of the White-Horse Cellar I was shocked to notice our last quondam guest (Juliet, most probably) in a dress and with an air & face, wh*h* too plainly indicated what her now profess*n* was!—" (TC's note).

and take her myself to the rail way—if one trusted her with the money she would have it all taken from her— This however will be one of them saved from the Devil if she like to be saved— She has now a free field to make herself GELTAN [worth something]—what more has any of us a right to look for—

Your letter is just come,—I thank you for never neglecting me— Yesterday looked such a blank day—*no* letters came—as if in sympathy with your silence— You must feel something of a *self-constituted Impostor* in your present location— I have a good many little things to do—and an engagement with M*rs* Prior who is to come to take me a drive at two oclock— Oh if you could mend me some pens!— Bless you dearest— — Here is Juliet Mudie too about her outfitting Your own J C

JWC TO JEANNIE WELSH

Thursday / night [20 July 1843]

My own Babbie

Is it credible, possible conceivable that Gambardella can be gone off to Liverpool without coming to bid me goodby and to take the pictures? I passed his house this evening and saw all the blinds removed—and Wednesday being the day he spoke of when I saw him. I actually incline to believe the strange mortal has taken this french leave of me! I said that day; "if I passed in a carriage I would *bring* the pictures" "Why that?" said he, as of course I will come to see you *just before* I go, and will take them then"?— His conduct is very prepostrous—but whom does he *not* tire of and behave ill to— You, be sure of it, will have your turn of his displeasure— What sort of reason he can give to his own mind for quarrelling with *me* I have not the faintest idea, unless it be that he mixes me up with Mazzini—who must have made him furious by writing him a second letter about his subscription to the school, when the first remained unanswered—the second had no better fate— But why try to account for the behaviour of a man who with all his talent and kind impulses is *really* hardly within the pale of rationality? The kind fates that are merciful "to *women, drunk people,* and *fools*"[1] watch over him, go where he likes!

The same Fates watch over you and me (under the first of these categories)—at this trying epoch of our household history *My* trial may be said to have reached its crisis yesterday

Yesterday morning the man proceeded to put on the paper on the

JWC-JW, [20 July]. Addr: 20 Maryland Street / Liverpool. PM: 21 July 1843. MS: NLS 1892.43. Hitherto unpbd.

1. An anon. epigram with many variations.

Library having spent many days in preparing the canvass &c—the paper realized my beau-ideal of paper—a bright crimson flock—much dearer than beseemed my modest means. Well I went into the room to see how he was getting on and conceive my dismay in finding this man who had hitherto seemed to thoroughly understand his work smearing and *tearing* the paper as if he had suddenly been possessed with a Devil!— I remonstrated—and he cut off little bits and stuck them on the tears!! The paper moreover exhibited numberless dark stains of the batter and every piece that he put on made the matter worse— The room was in the fair way of being completely spoiled after all my trouble and outlay— I sent off for Pearson in an agony—(Pearson was doing the whole thing for me by estimate) and it was two oclock before he arrived—you may judge of my situation in the meanwhile seeing the destruction going on unable to put a stop to it— When Pearson at last came he said at once that all that [had][2] been put up (two whole pieces) must be torn off again—and the man was sent home to his master with this news—and there seemed every chance that my library would have to lie in that horrible unfinished state, till a law suit was settled between the paper-maker and Pearson!—

This morning however the paper-hanger returned in a calm state—declared that he perfectly understood his trade but that the whole lot of paper (9 pieces) which had been made on purpose for me—was bad—had been made too thin—*could* not be put up—that he was now there by his masters orders to tear it all down again!—if I still insisted on the same pattern I must wait eight days (!) till a new lot was made— There was something magnamon[3] in the man having taken all my scolding without laying the fault on the paper until he had his master's leave!— To wait eight days was impossible besides I was pretty well disgusted with my crimson flock after walking up to the ancles in the tatters of it—so I went up to the Papermakers and chose another which I think I shall like better after all—and that the man is putting up rapidly a[n]d perfectly well—his distracting manner of working yesterday having been caused apparently by the consciousness that he had got an impossible task—

I had the discretion moreover to go to the paper shop in a fine yellow chariot with bright blue liveries—not hired for the occasion but taken the advantage of—and it is wonderful, I have observed, how business is smoothed for people when they go about it in *style*—this convenient equipage belonged to M*rs* Prior old Sterlings sister who is at present on a visit to him, and who came to take me to Knightsbridge

2. Word omitted.
3. Thus in MS for "magnanimous."

to an early dinner— She is a good kind woman as *still* and simple as her brother is tumultuous and *complicated*—the strangest contrast! She besought me *with tears*—(for she looks on me as a sort of relict of her sister in law of whom she was very fond) to come to visit her at Brighton and I think I will go sometime—*sometime*

I had a visit from my old Doctor the other day[4]— Sterling had told him that I was living in a smell of new paint—would not take a room at *his* house, and the kind old man drove down to remonstrate with me— But he found me sitting in the garden in *a tent* which I put up with my own hands—of the gipsey sort—and which has only one disadvantage that if a strong puff of wind comes the poles on which it rests blow over and the whole thing flaps down on the top of me— This happened *twice* the other day while I was writing to my uncle!—it played its part well however during Morrah's visit, and I seemed to be enjoying such rural felicity *out* of the smell of new paint; that he fell away from his intended remonstrance— He said I looked better but he "wished I would grow a little fatter—only I fear you are not one of the fat kind"— Alas no! if I were I should be much better natured— Sterling says that he (Morrah) has since told him that he "believed me to be seriously ill but it was of no use telling me so as I would never do anything for myself." Curious if I am "seriously ill" without knowing it!!

I heard from Carlyle today out of a Bishops palace!—certainly no suitable place for such a hater of every thing connected with the Shovel hat!— He seemed to be liking his new quarters however.— Thirwall is a different sort of talker from poor Redwood! I suppose you will have a *glimpse* of him shortly—do not tell him of my paper trouble—or any of my *troubles* I wish him to get all the result without having it spoiled by mental contemplation of the unlovely means!

I write this at night—my mornings are so busy—for besides the looking after the peoples work and doing a deal of virtuous needlework (chair covers &c—) I have to write always to him—and so very often to Geraldine about these eternal Mudies—and so many incidental letters besides—

Would to Heaven I could wish myself onto your sofa or you onto mine to have a right good talk, and plenty of good Babbie-kisses! One would fall to work again with so much better heart— Tell me of your new Cook for godsake—how you are pestered with these servants— Is Walter coming? Is our Walter going to get a church?[5]—is Alick still

4. James Morrah.
5. The first is Macgregor, the second Welsh.

loving Topsy[6] like "melted sugar candy" Reveal me most affectionately to her Mother and her—and to Marychen and the boys[7]— Your own / J C

TC TO JWC

Abergwili, 20 july 1843 (Thursday)

Dearest,

It is late, 11 o'clock or after; I have ridden *about forty miles,* to look at nonsense of views &c; and have to be off tomorrow morning on the coach roof at eight: I therefore will not write a word here; I will carry the sheet on with me, and try to despatch it from Gloucester if I get happily there.

We had our grand dinner *last* night: a Judge called Baron Rolfe,[1] and about 20 advocates; a dreadful explosion of dulness, champagne, and ennui; which however I took little hand in, being empowered by His Reverence[2] to "go out and smoke whenever I found it dull." Rolfe, first fiddle on this occasion, was a man I had seen at Stanley's[3] (or some such place) playing fourth or fifth fiddle. The Advocates generally filled me with a kind of shudder—to think that had I once had £200 I should perhaps have been that![4] One of them named Vaughan pleased me not a little.[5] They went all off soon,—and then I had a long questionable bout of *prints* to front! Sound sleep for a few hours, and a lackey to awaken you at half past six. It is over now, all that lackeying, thank God!

The Bishop received your compliments (did I tell you) with much modesty and gratitude; mumbled something about *you* being here, how happy &c &c.

He has been most kind to me. Poor fellow, think of a solid Bishop

6. Sophy Martin.
7. Mary Welsh and the Welsh boys.

TC-JWC, 20 July. MS: NLS 611.135. Pbd: Froude, *Carlyle* 3:312 inc.; Bliss, *TC* 173–74 inc.

1. Sir Robert Monsey Rolfe (1790–1868; *DNB*), knighted, 1837; a baron of the exchequer and judge since 1839; created Baron Cranworth, 1850; lord chancellor, 1852–58, 1865–66.
2. Thirlwall.
3. Edward John Stanley (1802–69; *DNB*), politician, husband of Henrietta Maria (1807–95; *DNB*); see 12:59.
4. See 1:231–32.
5. Henry Halford Vaughan (1811–85; *DNB*), clerk of assize on S Wales circuit since 1841; apptd., 1843, temp. asst. to the poor law commission to inquire into the employment of women and children in agriculture; prof. of modern history, Oxford, 1848–58.

riding post as we had to do today! It was literally altogether very good. Our talk has been extensive; rather interesting occasionally; always worth its wind or nearly so. Peace be with Abergwili,—and may it be a while before I run athwart such a mask of *forms* again, requiring such a curb-bridle on your liberties to observe them rightly.[6] For what we have received Lord make us thankful. Today handling the Tinder-box, I *found* your Letter in a pocket of the Tweed, and Crawfurds Address there![7] It is Monmouth, and would not have done.—

Adieu, adieu, dear Jeannie; wish me a good ride to Glo'ster;—and sleep sound, my Bairn. Thine ever—

T. C.

Gloucester. Friday Evg near 8 o'clock (waiting for dinner). I am arrived here safe, thro' the pleasantest country, some 120 miles gone over at full gallop. I am hungry, wasted, weary woebegone; but waiting *for dinner*. Uncertain whether I shall not go on to Wor'ster this very night; for this house is swarming with *assize* people. Dinner here!

Adieu Dearest, ach Gott, adieu. I wish I wish I were with thee!

T.C.

JWC TO TC

Library South Place [22 July 1843]

Dearest

I write to you in a new position—and one of tolerable comfort— I have for the present this room—and indeed this whole house all to myself[1]— I have made them put on a good fire, the day being wet—have

6. Thirlwall wrote to Milnes, 21 July, that TC had "gone this morning. . . . He stayed here 3 days, on one of which he enjoyed the appropriate felicity of meeting the Judge of Assize, lawyers, justices of the peace, peace-preserving warriors, and a host of equally congenial people. . . . I mounted him upon a high strong horse, and we scoured the country together, he with a cigar in his mouth and arrayed in a 'gray savagery of three sacks with a hem!' expressing much compassion for all mankind, but particularly for the poor inarticulate little Welsh creatures who could only smile when he asked them the way. The sights of the gates and houses lately demolished by Rebecca did not appear to distress him in the least" (Reid, *RMM* 1:302–3).

7. See JWC to TC, [5 July].

JWC-TC, [22 July]. Addr: Care of Miss J. Welsh / 20 Maryland Street / Liverpool. PM: 22 July 1843. MS: NLS 602.119; longhand copy with TC's notes: Berg. Pbd: A. Carlyle, *NLM* 1:112–24 inc. On the envelope TC noted: "22 july 1843 / (*after* Abergwilly: *in*)."

1. " 'Livrpool' indicates that I have met Brr John there, in view of the Welsh Tour,—wh*h* did not prove a very interestg or successful one. 'South Place' is the Sterlings' residence, in Knightsbridge" (TC's note).

ordered the dinner—have strengthened my mind with an adequate supply of bread and butter and sherry—and now sit down, within a yard of the fire, to send you a blessing on your wayfarings and thanks for your letter which I had before I left home— Sterling came with the carriage early to fetch me up here—for no special reason—"*just for diversion*"[2] (as my Penfillan Grandfather[3] said he eat cheese and bread in the forenoons)—and I consented, because the day being wet and myself somewhat *low*—I thought *a change* (Helens favourite prescription) might be of service—particularly as he held out the prospect of my being left alone while he went to call for Charles Barton and to do some "indispensible business"—one benefit resulting from the "change" you will gratefully acknowledge viz: the *better pens* I have to act with—it is not the pen's fault if my writing be illegible today— M*rs* Prior and Miss Allan went off this morning to Tunbridge[4]—M*rs* Prior "came out strong" on this occasion. I have never before the smallest idea what a good kindhearted woman she was. At parting she held me in her arms as if I had belonged to her—and prayed me *with tears* (not of her Brother's sort) to come and visit her some time at Brighton—one would have said she regarded me as a legacy left her by Mrs Sterling—for she never used to be able to tolerate me before for my "irreligion" and unconventionalities— Besides the melancholy appearance of the house here she had been sadly shocked at the broken down state of old Sterling and at the communication he made to her about his income having been curtailed by his children—Anthony especially who was the mover of the arrangement has lost I fancy more by disgusting this Aunt than he has gained by taking three hundred pounds a year from his old Father— She has thirty thousand pounds to leave—and Anthony I fancy will not now succeed to a farthing of it. He deserves it the shabby gigman that he is! Whatever stupid uses his Father might have put the money to; will he put it to better?— One thing I was told that made me absolutely sick—of the funeral expenses there was *twelve* pounds which Anthony as the heir was not *liable* to pay—it was for the part of the burial ground which the old man had reserved for himself beside his wife—and Anthony kept that back—his Father was applied to to pay down the twelve pounds—in advance as it were for his own funeral!!! Oh my dear let us be thankful to God that *we* are not money-lovers! how hard of heart that rage for gain does make people!

Poor Pearson has lost his old Mother and is gone to the country to

2. Cf. JWC to TC, [7 and 8 July].
3. John Welsh (b. 1757), paternal grandfather; see 2:369.
4. Tunbridge Wells, spa town in Kent, 29 mi. SSE of London.

bury her— You would have been wae [sad] to see the iron looking man yesterday going about quite flushed and with tears in his eyes. He told me he was sitting writing a letter to her to say he would come and pay her visit, when he received the accounts of her death—she was turned of ninety— I gave him a glass of wine and shook hands with him when he went away on his sad errand—I felt so sisterly towards him—

I have nothing to tell you today—I have seen nobody since I wrote last except Mazzini who seemed in the fair way of having another tumour in his cheek— I have asked Geraldine to translate his article[5] for payment—and she agrees—Forster begged me to find a translator for it "as he really wished to print it for the poor fellow"—and I could think of no likelier person than Geraldine— He is to go to Lady Harriet[6] on Wednesday— John Mill leaving him no rest on that subject[7]—

—And now I will tell you a political secret—but for gods sake speak not a syllable of it—there is "a movement" in Italy projected in two months!!—contrary to Mazzini advice who thinks two months *rather soon*—but if the leaders insist he will evidently *take part in it!*[8]—! ———!—

John Ruffini writes that he has read Carlyl's[9] past and Present—and has seen many persons "who by the reading of it have recovered their *souls*—or had not till now been sensible that they ever had any"—

Kiss Babbie[10] for me— She will be very glad to see you, the dear child—though her *mess* at present seems to be the counterpart of my own—

M*rs* & Miss Kingsley called for me yesterday while I was at dinner[11] Helen in the desperation of the moment—my dinner being too

5. "Dante Allighieri," *Foreign Quarterly Review* 33 (April 1844):1–30.

6. "Baring, aft*ds* Lady Ashburton" (TC's note).

7. Mill had been friendly with Lady Harriet for some time, possibly having met her on a visit to her father-in-law's house at Buckenham (see Greville, *Memoirs* 2:52). Greville wrote in 1857 that Mill was "sentimentally attached to her" and later resented "her indifference" (7:286–87). But F. A. Hayek says that, as in the case of his relations with TC, his later dislike arose from his loyalty to Harriet Taylor (*John Stuart Mill and Harriet Taylor* [1951] 90).

8. Mazzini thought the simultaneous uprisings in the Roman states and Naples inopportune and counselled Nicola Fabrizi and his Legion of Italy to postpone any action. In Aug. a revolt in Savigno failed miserably, and Mazzini was blamed unfairly.

9. Letter omitted. Giovanni Ruffini (1807–81; see 12:74), member of Young Italy; in Paris since 1841 (see 13:67–68).

10. "Cousin Jeannie " (TC's note).

11. Mary Kingsley, b. Lucas (1788?–1873), wife of Charles Kingsley, Sr. Charlotte Kingsley (1828–82), their da., who later m. John Mill Chanter, vicar of Ilfracombe, and wrote novels. The copy reads "Mr. and Miss Kingsley," and TC noted "Rector and Daughter in this Parish."

laughable—said I was "not at home" tant mieux [so much the better]—
If you see M*rs* Paulet do not let her seduce you— God keep you dear

Your affectionate / Jane Carlyle

I send the money-order[12]

TC TO JWC

Liverpool, 23 july, 1843—

Dearest,

Last night, about half past seven, I arrived here safe at Maryland-Street, and my weary pilgrimings have again for a day or two terminated!

The Letter despatched from Glo'ster would give you at the end of it a faint shadow of my desperate situation there. It was like a section of Bedlam that Bell Inn. Sound of harps and stringed instruments; ruffing [foot-stamping] of applausive barristers over table-oratory heard from the distance; waiters running about in a distracted state; hapless bagmen sitting round one, either preparing to go off "by mail,"[1] or else swallowing punch in the hope to escape from their wretchedness by getting drunk. I had felt thankful and hap-hap-happy in the morning; but then I was mees-erable. I fled out into the streets, where indeed my duty lay, and there I wandered till late in the bright summer twilight; returning to my Inn, found it madder than ever; then called for my glass of brandy and hot-water too, and took it up to my bedroom, where, once I had locked the door, a kind of noble defiance came over me, and I went to sleep in the middle of the tumult, saying to it, What have I to do with thee? No gladder sight since I went on my travels than that of the railway omnibus next morning that was to take me out of the Bell Inn for all time and all eternity! The dirty scrub of a waiter grumbled about his allowance which I reckoned liberal; I added sixpence to it, and produced a bow which I was near rewarding with a kick,—accursed be the race of flunkies!—the Boots then clambered to the omnibus to say that he also had been hardly dealt with; I thought, As we are never to meet more thro' all Eternity, thou too shalt have another sixpence;—and so at last by God's blessing we did get away, and embarked thro' the verdant *Carse* or plain of Severn, and could look abroad in peace over God's handiworks, and man's

12. Which TC asked for in TC to JWC, 19 July.

TC-JWC, 23 July. MS: NLS 611.136. Pbd: Froude, *Carlyle* 3:313–14 inc.; Bliss, *TC* 174–76 inc.

1. I.e., on the mail coach.

*un*flunkeyish industry, and in particular descry the hills (not entirely without emotion) where the Glo'ster Puritans in their strait siege saw Essex's signal fires blaze up, and notice to them in spite of the bad weather that help was nigh.[2] Thank*s* Heaven![3]— We saw only the roofs and steeples of Cheltenham;[4] quite enough for me. The country was lovely even under the grey blustery sky; I rode in the "second class,"—much the best class in such circumstances as mine. Wor'ster was three miles off the Station, westward of the station; I rode thither smoking, by the London road; duly noticed Malvern[5] &c, duly honoured every thing, and then was set down at some Crown Inn, quite vacant of customers, to a most blessed breakfast of coffee and ham and accompaniments about eleven o'clock; a considerable Christian comf*ort*.[6] Before breakfast ceased, the Sky began pouring rain; I purchased a cotton umbrella; cleared up the distracting mysteries of my future railway course (for they have no "time bills" in those countries), and set rapidly out to explore the City. From Severn Bridge I could see the *ground* of Oliver's battle;[7] it was a most brief survey: a poor labourer whom I consulted "had *hee*rd of sitch a thing," wished to God "we had another Oliver, Sir; times is dreadful bad!" I spoke with the poor man a while; a shrewd well-conditioned fellow;—left a shilling with him, about the only good deed I did all day. In the railway train (second class still) and on the road to the train, I had adventures of a small evil kind: two men to quench, who attempted (partly by mistake) to use me ill; they proved quenchable without difficulty,—for indeed I myself was in somewhat sulphurous condition, not handy to quarrel with. One of them, my fellow-passenger in the railway, took it into his head to smile visibly when I laid off my white broadbrim and suddenly produced out of my pocket my grey glengarry. He seemed of the mercantile head-clerk species, and had been tempted to his impropriety by a foolish-looking pampered young lady in tiger-skin mantle whom he seemed to have charge of. I looked straight into his smiling face and eyes, a look which I suppose inquired of him, "Miserable ninth part of the fraction of a tailor, art thou sure thou hast a right to laugh at me?" the smile instantly died into another expression of emotion. When a man is just come out of a section of bedlam, and has still a long confused journey, in bad weather in the second class train, that

2. See *Cromwell, Works* 6:165.
3. Coterie speech, variant of Mazzini's "thanks God."
4. Gloucestershire, 7 mi. NE of Gloucester and 42 mi. S of Birmingham.
5. In Worcestershire, where Jane and Thomas Wilson often stayed (see 15:224).
6. Coterie speech; see 3:412–13.
7. See *Cromwell, Works* 7:326.

is the time for getting himself treated with the respect due to genius! At Birmingham I had to take the first-class, there being no second without waiting; and we whirled along hitherward,—poor Goody's Letter within a few yards of me, but unattainable till the morrow; a curious reflexion for me at the moment. Foolish young women nearly sta[r]ved[8] us with bad air, and windows closed for the rain; but it was beautiful to get along *without* either flunkeyism or disorder; and when the ready porter at the Station here seized hold of my luggage, and toiled with it till he was all in a sweat to get me some conveyance, and did at last get me a foot porter, I could not but thank the man with real gratitude real respect.— At Maryland-Street, where they still sat at wine, with Jack here, and a certain Miss Baird (I think) from Ross-shire,[9] I was welcomed with open arms: I felt and feel comparatively as if I had got *home;* and having kept pretty well last night, and received Goody's Letter this morning, it is now all right; in spite of the headache, the showery weather and all the rest of it. I did kiss Babbie for you; showing her my Letter for credential! But you must not give me any more such commissions; they are too delicate to transact before company. Poor little Jeannie, I was right glad to see her blithe bonny face again: she seems to me looking well, and is Mistress of the house here and bound to care for all.

The money order I will get cashed tomorrow; I had but 18/ left. I have spent all this morning talking to John; and now they are home from Church, and wait till I finish my Letter. I have to write to my Mother also.— John is of course totally planless, wavers between a journey on foot into Wales, and one by sea into the United States! The weather too is bad and broken. Nothing can be settled, except that we must stay here "for a day or two," and see. The two young damsels, John apprises me, are for being off to Helensburgh (the news from that are good); Alick will be left in the house himself. You, I suppose, would not at all like Liverpool in *these* circumstances! Jack is lodged at a place called "the Feathers"; seems to dine here pretty often. We are going to see the Paulets, the Chorleys,[10] the—who all and the what all? I will "fall in love" with nobody. I will also write no more to *thee* today for one.

Adieu with blessings and kisses, / T. C.

8. Letter omitted.
9. Agnes Baird, a friend of the Welshes.
10. See TC to JWC, 24 [25] July.

TC TO CHARLES REDWOOD

20. Maryland Street, Liverpool
24 july 1843—

My Dear Sir,

As, most likely, your hospitable imagination has sometimes followed me northward on my progress from your quiet kindly regions, it seems proper I should send you an authentic specification from this resting place I have now got to.

The outer seat at Bridgend, that morning, turned out to have been bespoken by another, a fellow sufferer in the interior; who accordingly took possession of it there; I remaining in confinement as far as Neath. There however there was deliverance into the sunshine, into the smoke of Morriston and Swansea;[1] into all the *etceteras*, none of them very disagreeable, none of them indeed other than interesting, of a ride to Carmarthen, thro' Rebecca Gates, over steep eminences, thro' a country pleasant tho' ill-cultivated, thro' a population cheerful and innocent of aspect tho' somewhat out at elbows here and there. At Abergwili the Bishop in his wide secluded mansion sat waiting for me; all friendly, all quiet and green: nevertheless, as you predicted, I have to record that the last I have yet seen of *rest* was at Llandough, blessings on its green trees and solitary knolls;—it is the last I am yet like to see of that invaluable quality for some time! The Bishop led me incessantly about in search of the picturesque, on high trotting horses in all weathers, sometimes twenty miles off on one ride; conversation wise but *not* restful going on all day, and prayers in Laud's Chapel, and other solemnities in other places going on from 7 in the morning till midnight. We had the Judge[2] one evening and a shipload of noisy barristers. On friday morning I was not unwilling to embark into the green world again; on the mail coach towards Monmouth, towards Gloucester, towards Worcester, and Liverpool where I now heard that my Brother had arrived and was waiting for me. On Saturday evening I at length reached this house, for welcome pause of a day or two. On the morrow morning we set off,[3] if the weather will hold up for a week's *walking* in North Wales. I go to it as to a duty, with little hope of anything but toil from it; with almost a kind of wish that

TC-CR, 24 July. Addr: Llandough / Cowbridge / S. Wales. MS: NLS Acc. 9294. Pbd: *Central Glamorgan Gazette,* 11 March 1881 (imperfectly); John Howells, "Carlyle's Holidays in Wales," *Red Dragon Magazine* 5 (April 1884): 339; Faulkner 155–56.

1. Morriston is an industrial village, 2 mi. NNE of Swansea, SW Wales.
2. Sir Robert Rolfe.
3. In fact on Wed., 26 July.

the clouds would become electric again, and honourably deliver me from it. But failing this, we shall have to go to the Isle of Man, which will be equally bad. The wicked, it is written, have no rest.[4] In a week, however, I shall be ready here again for the first Steamer into Annandale; and then in my Mother's house I will lie down and sleep again whatever befal!

This, in hurried style (for I am in dreadful hurry), is my travel's history[5] and prophecy. I add to it a cordial remembrance to your good, kind, quiet Mother, whom I shall long remember; and many grateful thanks to you,—and to *Madge Wildfire*[6] and the St. Donat's Sea, which made my stay in your domain so useful and pleasant to me. Right hearty thanks and blessings to all.

Yours most truly, / T. Carlyle

JWC TO TC

[24 July 1843]

Dearest

I have been very busy all morning shifting the books—you who put them up before "with your own hands," can understand feelingly what sort of a dusty tiresome job that has been—and that the sight of a letter *already written* to you returned to me by the Bishop of St Davids,[1] should be under the circumstances not so unwelcome as it would otherwise have been— I do not remember a word that is in it—and if I open it to see; most certainly I should not find it worth the forwarding—so I send it to you unopened—in the humble hope that be it ever so stupid; it will be as good as any other I could have written today—for besides the fatigue of the books I am headachy and dull—*from natural causes*— I have a very good letter from Jeffrey today in

4. Cf. Isa. 48:22.
5. Cf. *Othello* 1.3.
6. Redwood's mare, named after a character in Scott's *The Heart of Midlothian,* "mettlesome & fidgetty" according to Redwood, who wrote to TC, 28 Aug., that he followed TC's "Itinerary with interest, but also not without some jealousy of that Bishop's 'High trotting horses' and the picturesque rides he had to take you, & of his 'wise conversation' withal. It was my hope you would be bored and tired there, and not again be tempted off from us just on beginning to nestle into your crib. . . . My own spider-like life gives me no other chance of catching any lovers of sphere musick— May Yankees or Blue Devils therefore by and bye beset you."

JWC-TC, [24 July]. Addr: Care of Miss J. Welsh / 20 Maryland Street / Liverpool. PM: 24 July 1843. MS: NLS 602.120; longhand copy with TC's notes: Berg. Pbd: A. Carlyle *NLM* 1:124–25 inc. On the envelope TC noted: "24 july 1843 (*incloses* '20 july'). (*in* [some of it]; Masson, Terrot)."

1. The letter of [20 July].

the patriarchal vein—he has been very ill again but is now better—

Robertson brought here last night to tea a youth from Aberdeen of the name of Mason— —A news-paper Editor poor thing, and only twenty!—he is one of your most ardent admirers and immitators[2]— Robertson said "he had come up to town to see the *lions* and so he had brought him to *me*"—("my Brother plays the German flute" &c)— He is a better "speciment" of Aberdeen than I ever saw before—an innocent intelligent modest affectionate-looking creature— I quite took to him—when he went away, which he seemed to do very unwillingly, I said that he must come and see us when he returned to London and I hoped to make up then for his present disappointment by introducing him to you—to which he answered with a cordial grasp of my hand "Eh! What a real shame in ye to say *that*"*!* He told me "if I would come to Aberdeen they would get up a mob for me in the fish-market Place, and give me a grand hurrah—and a paragrap[h][3] *of course!*" I must tell you before I forget When Helen was handing me over some of the books she said—"take care—that ane's the Maister's *sartor* RESART—and a capital thing it is—just *noble* in *my* opinion"!!— She told

2. " 'Robertson' is the blustrous John Robertson, whom Mill had at that time as Sub-editor, or Subaltern gen*lly*, in the *Westr Review* [actually his affiliation ceased in 1840]; and who took absurdish airs on that dignity,—the igno*rt* fellow, not the intrinsically bad, and sure enough the abund*tly* unlucky! Some few years after this, he vanished suddenly as if *underground,* and ever since there continues, tho' still living, and latterly in Engl*d* ag*n*. 'Masson,' whom he introduces, is the now well-known & deservedly distinguished *Professor Masson,*—whose Portrait is recognisable in every feature as given here" (TC's note). David Masson (1822–1907; *DNB*), biographer and ed.; M.A., Aberdeen Univ., 1839; studied for ministry, Edinburgh, 1839–42, but never ordained; ed. of the *Banner,* an Aberdeen weekly, 1842–44; worked, in Edinburgh, for W. & R. Chambers, 1844–47; moved to London, 1847, where he was a magazine contrib. and became friendly with the Carlyles, Thackeray, and other writers; prof. of English lit., Univ. College, London, 1853–65; pbd. *Life of John Milton,* 7 vols. (1859–94); founding ed. of *Macmillan's Magazine,* 1859–67; prof. of rhetoric and English lit., Univ. of Edinburgh, 1865–95. Of this first visit to Cheyne Row, Masson writes: "Robertson took me one afternoon to Chelsea for a call. . . . Carlyle happened not then to be in town. . . . But, though it was a disappointment to me not to see the great man himself, we had the pleasure of a most kind reception by Mrs Carlyle . . . . I shall never forget the first impression made upon me by the appearance of this remarkable lady, . . . so fragile in form, with a delicately cut and rather pained face of dun-pale hue, very dark hair, smoothed on both sides of an unusually broad forehead, and large, soft, and lustrous eyes of a gypsy black. . . . She was . . . one of the most brilliant of witty talkers, full of light *esprit*. . . . Her most characteristic vein was the satirical; within this, the form to which she tended most was the satirical narrative; and the narratives in which she most excelled were stories of things that had recently happened to herself, or within the circle of her acquaintance" (David Masson, *Memories of London in the 'Forties* [1908] 35–37).

3. Letter omitted.

me the other day—that "Bishop Terrot was really a wee *noughty* [insignificant] body as ever she set een upon" I like that word *'noughty'* much—

I have got for reading Fielding's *Amelia!* and *the Vicar of Wakefield*[4]—which I am carrying on simultaneously—I find the first a dreadful bore—one prays to Heaven that the poor woman would but once for all get herself *seduced,* and so let us have done with her alarms and precautions; on any terms! "Upon my honour" I do not see the slightest sense in spending one's whole existence thro out three volumes in taking care of ones *virtue!*—do you?— Love to them all—without kisses since you are not *up to* these— I shall send the Examiner to you today— How happy the Choreleys will be and Mrs Paulet— — Oh bliss! Ever your / J Carlyle

TC TO JWC

Liverpool, Tuesday, 24 [25] july 1843—

Dearest,

Your Letter lay waiting on the table this morning; many thanks to Goody for it, a poor sick Goody! I did not write yesterday, and have hardly a quarter of an hour for that object today: if you add *John* to Liverpool, you will not expect Letters from me at present. Tomorrow we quit but for what *place* becomes again uncertain; out of this place, with Jack appended to me, I must soon go; whitherward is not of much moment: to the air, to the Sea or the grass, all shall be equal to me. We had after some slight but sufficient deliberation settled for a week's *walking* in North Wales, to commence by a sail over to Bangor or the Menai Bridge: by that I think we are likeliest to hold, tho' today all manner of questionabilities, weather and what not have risen; and a sail to the Isle of Man[1] is proposed instead: this latter, as I at once declared my *indifference* as to the whitherward, is likely to be given up again, and Wales to return whatever weather it may be. The whole thing is to last but a week; that I have stipulated for; and then I consider that it will be wise to become a *single* man again, or at all events to go across to Annandale soon, if Jack is to continue with me. I think

4. Henry Fielding, *Amelia* (1751). Oliver Goldsmith, *The Vicar of Wakefield* (1766).

TC-JWC, 24 [25] July. Addr: 5. Cheyne Row, Chelsea / London. MS: NLS 611.137. Pbd: Froude, *Carlyle* 3:315–16 inc.; Bliss, *TC* 177 inc. TC misdates the letter: he writes on Tues., 25 July, in reply to JWC to TC, [24 July].

1. In the Irish Sea, between Liverpool and N Ireland.

he will do better if *I* resolutely take the command. His friendliness is great; but he goes about like a "torch of confusion";[2] an intolerable element of chaos tied to your right hand. Poor Jack, I have many things to ask of him too; and gradually get them out of him by patience. His account of poor Alick is sufficiently distressing on some sides: a tragic history; may that prove the *crisis* of it! My poor Brother, true companion of my young days, which all rise with a strange sad distinctness in my solitary hours at present, will be about arriving on a new shore in these very days. On a new arena to begin a new life; God grant it might be a wiser and more prosperous one!

Yesterday we went to call for the Chorleys:[3] joy to the ridge-tile at sight of us; and a long ethico-philosophical and miscellaneous discourse with the elder Brother the Mother and Daughter; which latter two are just bound for Wales, to the second Brother's house, who has gone to live in Tremadoc in that country: the invitations to bend thitherward were many and pressing,—but waved aside, as was the invitation to a dinner here. The Brother's passionate entreaty to come and bear him company in his silent empty house on our return was much more tempting; nor did I entirely say NO to it. *You* direct your Letters hitherward however; I will leave my trunks and all things here, in little Jeannie's care, who already has taken *wife-like*[4] charge of me (blessings on her), and sent out my things to be washed without plague to me!

This day we went to call for Mrs Paulet;—after a good deal of burbling from Jack, who however paid for the *fly*, we got thither, half an hour before our time: there had been a Note sent about it by Jeannie, and as no answer had come I was not for going at all; but had we waited half an hour (which I found afterwards would have brought us to the time she mentioned) all would have been well, for—Mrs Paulet was gone to Liverpool, and we drove quietly home again! The chances now are, it would appear, twofold: *first,* that she never got Jeannie's Note till her arrival in town this morning; which will do

2. Untraced.

3. Jane Chorley (d. 1851) and her da. Mary Ann (Phoebe) (1805?–63); see 9:328. Also the second brother John Rutter Chorley (1807?–67; *DNB*), poet and previously sec. (see 9:401) and treas. of the Grand Junction Railway, 1841. They all lived at 2 Sandon Terrace, Upper Duke St., Jane and John Rutter being listed there in the 1843 Liverpool directory. TC mistook the age of the brothers, as the oldest was definitely Dr. William Brownsword Chorley (see 9:400–1), now apparently manager of a slate quarry at Tremadoc, N Wales. TC noted in his Journal, 2 Oct., that it was William that he visited at Tremadoc. The youngest brother, Henry, lived in London.

4. Cf. 15:21, 28.

very well: *second,* that she counted herself safe till the hour we had mentioned (or rather *they* had mentioned); which will do rather ill! But Jeannie seems to have no misgiving as to that latter chance; and so, at any rate, it must stand;—and so, at any rate, I am well contented that it stand, for I was in no mood today to encounter the Moral Sublime in female headdress, and liked greatly better to return home in a silent condition.— Passing along near some Catholic Chapel, and noticing a great crowd in a yard there, with flags, white sticks and brass-bands, we stopt of [our?] hackneycoachman; stept forth into the thing,—and found it to be Father Matthew distributing the Temperance Pledge to the lost sheep of this place;[5] thousands strong, of both sexes, a very ragged, lost-looking squadron indeed! Father is a broad solid, most excellent-looking man, with grey hair, mild intelligent grey eyes, massive rather aquiline nose and countenance; in a long black frock-coat and white neckcloth, of aspect like any other excellent clergyman (Kingsley for example beaten down four inches shorter[6]): the very face of him attracts you. His speech, in a strong Cork accent, with the softest mild voice, worn *hoarse* at present by much work, is quiet, clear, rational, and listened to with profound assent by the poor ragged people, about half or more of whom seemed to be Irish. We saw him go thro' one whole act of the business,—"do," as Darwin would say, an entire batch of teetotallers: I almost cried to listen to him; and could not but lift my broadbrim at the end, when he called for God's blessing on the vow these poor wretches had taken, and murmur audibly, "So be it!" He has done about 80,000 in Manchester; already some 60,000 here (as a man told us), and means to continue "all *this* day, plase[7] God, and till tomorrow at sunset,"—which announcement the audience responded to with a low but heartfelt sound, far better than a shout.[8] I have seen nothing *so* religious since I set out on my travels, as the squalid scene of this day; nay nothing properly reli-

5. Theobald Mathew (1790–1856; *DNB*), Irish Franciscan priest, known as the "Apostle of Temperance"; preached against intemperance in Ireland, England, Scotland, and the U.S.; heard by JWC in Aug. For his 1840 campaign, see 12:254.

6. Rev. Charles Kingsley, Sr.

7. In imitation of Father Mathew.

8. The *Examiner,* 29 July, reported: "The Reverend Theobald Mathew, on account of a dispensation from the Pope to move about according to inclination, unrestricted by episcopal interference or control, arrived in Manchester last week. He has occupied upwards of nine hours a day in administering the pledge of total abstinence. Up to Saturday evening [22 July] 18,000 persons took the pledge. On Sunday it was administered to 30,000, and on Monday and Tuesday to 32,000, making in all a total of 80,000 pledged teetotallers in Manchester." In Liverpool he "administered the pledge to upwards of 30,000 persons."

gious at all, tho' I have been in Laud's Chapel, and heard duly, with damnable iteration, of "the means of *graice* and the hope of *dlary*"[9] from that portentous human snipe,—not a bad fellow either, poor devil! But we are in a dreadful mess as to all that; and even a strong Bishop Thirlwall constitutes himself a Macready of Episcopacy as the *best* he can do, and does it uncommonly well;—and is "a strong-minded man, sir," and a right worthy man in his unfortunate kind. As to Cuittikins—O my Goody, what would have become of thee as Mrs Bishop Cuittikins, a "noughty" creature?

On the whole, it seems terribly absurd to run away for a week out of earshot from thee, and hide among foolish Welsh Hills which I do not even wish to see! Write for Saturday hitherward; Jeannie will forward it,—I will tell her how when I have had time to consider. Perhaps I shall return *hither on* Saturday: the one point I have any wish about was to see Snowdon, and that can be done before then. I will write to thee out of Wales: look out, but not with impatience on the *third* post-day after this; the second, I doubt, is not possible.— *Wet* news, but otherwise good from Helensburgh. God bless thee my darling. And so ends, thy unfortunate / T. C.

TC TO JWC

Llanberws (foot of Snowdon)
Wednesday Evg
26 july, 1843—

Dearest,

You got no Letter from me today; but Babie was appointed to inform you what had become of me; and here I am safe in the heart of Carnarvonshire, and in a condition (were the ink a *little* more fluid—which by libations from a punch-jug I have just made it!) to scribble you an authentic word, in hope of falling in with a Post-Office somewhere tomorrow. The Herr Zangbein [Mr. Tongleg],[1] poor fellow, has been of real use to me today; he knows the country and its conveyances, regulations, and peculiarities thoroughly well; he pays all the bills &c for me; and if Carnarvonshire contained in it one tolerable

9. Meaning "glory," imitating the curate's accent; see TC to JWC, 19 July. "We bless thee . . . for the means of grace, and for the hope of glory" (the General Thanksgiving of Morning Prayer, Book of Common Prayer).

TC-JWC, 26 July. Addr: 5. Cheyne Row, Chelsea / London. PM: Caernarvon, 27 July 1843. MS: NLS 611.138. Hitherto unpbd.

1. John Carlyle's nickname, meaning "long legged"; derived from either "tongs" (see 1:296), or from "teeng," "tang," or "tong," a projecting spike, i.e., something long and thin.

tobacco-pipe accessible to me, I should really have cause to declare myself "far better than could be expected." We have had a most quiet grey day,—for I insisted on sitting silent amid the pure green inarticulate Lea and blue Winds; to all waiters, *crimps* of inns, and other fatal-looking persons I merely responded by a silent beckoning towards *Tongleg*, who seemed to take delight in the office of answering. He is now out of doors smoking a cigar in the rain under the porch, and I am very glad to write once more a word to my own poor Goody, the patient recipient of all my twaddle.— Alas here he is again, the cigar done! Nevertheless I continue, having handed him a Newspaper.

We got fairly on board a Steamer called the *Ayrshire Lassie* about eleven o'clock this day; a rainy morning issuing in a grey west-wind day, not unfavourable to the pensive mind that loves withal a moderate temperature. Arbuckle attended us on board: he is going to the equatorial regions again,[2] poor fellow, in about a month—under better auspices this time: a really admirable man in his still way; to whom I wish heartily well. Babie at parting was constituted mistress of all my goods, the keys were left with her; your Letters only being sealed. She is to darn socks for me, to sew on buttons &c &c: I kissed her pretty lips at parting, poor Babie; for she has been the cheerfullest thing I have seen since leaving thee: a really bonny phenomenon; one of the nicest bits of lassies you will find in a summer days riding. It is really sad that she should be left yonder in the reek of cookery and wine-drinking, and stolid dulness;—I wonder what the young men are about that they do not marry her forthwith, and almost steal her away the good little child! Nothing could be kinder or wiser than she has all along shewn herself.

But as for our journey,—it was sea and lime-stone Mountain, bay and promontory; Great Orme's Head, Little Orme's Head, *Pen Maen Maur* (a Mountain not unlike Criffel, washed by the Sea),[3] and then towns, Beaumaris, Bangor, the Strait of Anglesea, and the Menai Bridge, clearly a wonder of the world: altogether a very reasonable day, since you were allowed to sit silent and look at it. In the Mersey River, coming out along with us, were from 3 to 2 hundred ships, the morning's message of that great smoky Monster; and at night we are *here*, in the eternal slate wilderness; one of the dullest Inns I ever sat in, truly almost an enchanted palace, for it is a huge place like a

2. To Brazil.

3. The Great and Little Orme's Heads are promontories on the N coast of Caernarvonshire, ca. 3½ mi. N and NE of Conway. Penmaenmawr is a mountain (1,550 ft.) ca. 4½ mi. SW of Conway, the last of the Snowdon range. Criffel is a mountain range in SE Kirkcudbrightshire (see 13:187).

Castle, and of the best equipment; all kept by a solid Scotch Farmer named Johnstone;—and owing to the badness of trade, there seems to be not a soul in it but our two selves; or the rest at least are all in apartments, and sit remote from the "Coffee-room," thro' which only the Mountains and the Night have the privilege of looking in at the windows. We came in a kind of tub-gig from Bangor, 14 miles; well defended from the rain; already supplied with tea, and possessed of a pipe tho' a scandalously bad one. We have had one temperate glass of brandy, and a walk out to look at "the old tower"; it is now past ten, all quiet, and if I had done scribbling here, I am off to bed.— Tomorrow we propose climbing Snowdon; but the weather alas promises ill. Small matter to me *which* way! I have already seen somewhat; and shall know always where to conceive *Silence* as resident in future. This place is some four miles from the end of a narrow Lake among wild barren gnarly slate hills; or rather it stands at the junction of two Lakes (once one), which gradually contract a little farther eastward (Snowdon crushing himself there very close upon his neighbour *Glyddir*) into a certain Pass of Llanberws, very frightful to see (it would appear); at the old Tower tonight about nine in a drizzly evening, it was the strangest scene I ever looked on: A world all of slate, huge Mountains, stumpy blunt blocks, small fragments and fractions sticking thro' the patches of grass,—slate, slate everywhere. The two Lakes once one [look?]ed earnest as very death, a few intermittent lights glimmered fitfully (not abov[e] three I think) about the foot of the hills; and far up on the mountain sides, there arose ever and anon a rustling among the slate-quarry rubbish, which hangs like a river all down the declivity, and jingles in that way, we are told, all days and all nights of the year, never entirely *done* with jingling at all! It was most strange in the dead solitude. I shall remember Llanberws. By the bye you pronounce it *Lanberries* in Christian speech; and so enough of it now.[4]

Dear Goody how many thousand things deserved better to be said than this Tourist twaddle! Thou hast saved the old Stimabile, saved the young Mudie, thou art a wise *good* Goody!— Babie doubtless told you about the end of the Paulet adventure: well, I have only to add that the Lady somewhat—disappointed me! She is not beautiful entirely; she is not wise entirely; there is no danger at all of falling in love with *her*, I should conjecture! Yet I doubt not I shall like her very

4. The lakes of Llanberis, which TC spells with a "w" instead of an "i," are Llyn Peris and Llyn Padarn. The narrow rocky Llanberis Pass is at 1,169 ft.; Glyder Fawr is 3,279 ft.; the tower was the remains of Dolbadarn Castle, overlooking Llyn Peris.

well; for there is endless animation, good humour, and a dash of *haverilism* [silliness] (I almost think) which will do excellently, and best of all, to dine with;—as I engage to do on our return.

The whole house is to bed but myself, even Jack has just gone; and this Letter has to be "left on the table," and will go tomorrow morning, by some mysterious early conveyance, by some route or other. From the heart of the Mountains I send a blessing and goodnight to my Dearest. Fail not to write! Good Night, & sleep! / T. C.

JWC TO TC

(Chelsea, 26 July 1843

My dear,

Two days and not a line from any of you! Your accustomed punctuality taken into account I find this very myst*e*rous.

When the postman brought me today only a *n*ote from the never failing Geraldine, and a—Newspaper for you, I really turned quite sick with apprehension of I know not what. It is not right to have inflicted such a feeling on me, unless there be some very imperative reason. Meanwhile I cannot write to you— You do not deserve that I should— And I am too uncomfortable for writing, until I know the meaning of your silence.

Ever yours / Jane Carlyle

You would receive *two* Letters from me yesterday morning.[1]

TC TO MARGARET A. CARLYLE

Tremadoc (Carnarvonshire,
N. Wales)
Thursday 27 july, 1843—

My dear Mother,

Jack will not write; therefore I must write to you, one word: I have Jane to write to also, and really not five minutes to do it; so I must be *brief*.

We are well, and are *doing* the thing we proposed to do,—which I hope will be a good thing! We came away from Liverpool yesterday morning by a Steamboat to Bangor. We have been a pretty way into

JWC-TC, 26 July. Longhand copy of MS with TC's notes: Berg. Hitherto unpbd. TC notes at top of the copy: "this must count as another letter; this will really be '80'; call it meanwhile '79*a*.' "

1. Of [20 July] and [24 July].

TC-MAC, 27 July. MS: NLS 521.16. Hitherto unpbd.

the interior of Wales; we have climbed over their highest Mountain (today, in the middle of mist); we have had various adventures, not unpleasant; and are now lodged in the house of a Mr Chorley a friend and admirer of mine, with whom we shall likely stay over tomorrow. A pleasant enough journey then will bring us in contact with the Liverpool Steamers again, and then we shall come across to our old place;—and the only farther tourifying or travelling that will then remain for us will be a voyage over to Annandale in some steamer that is convenient. Probably if all go well, in something like a week hence. But you shall *hear*, dear Mother, when we get to Liverpool, more minutely than now. At present I can add no other word, except a hearty wish that I, for one, were at Scotsbrig beside you at this hour: perhaps it would be better for me!

Good night, dear good Mother; a blessing to you and to all and every of you.

Whether Jack is coming back with me I know not: but should rather apprehend not—as the *sough* [general feeling] of him goes at present. However, one cannot say.

Once more good night, and blessings on you.

Your affectionate son / T. Carlyle

TC TO JWC

Tremadoc (Carnarvon)
27 july, 1843—

Dearest,

We did not perish on the summit of Snowdon today, but only gazed over precipices into whirlpools of mist; got down safe;—and are at present well lodged in the hospitable C[ott]age of the younger Chorley (the squinting one), who lives here "managing a Slate Quarry" for his own behoof; and who received me as he would an *Avatar* of Vishnu![1] A really hospitable excellent little man. He has made me brandy and hot-water ready with toast, pipes &c &c, and inquires most pointedly "how Mrs Carlyle is"; and will drive us tomorrow in tub-car or even pony phaeton to see the sublimities of his Slate Quarry; and otherwise do wonders: in short we are extremely well here;—and shall get back to Liverpool, I hope, about Monday, and *end* this Expedition more handsomely than at one time could have been hoped. I snatch a moment from amid the jingle of glasses, and

TC-JWC, 27 July. Addr: 5. Cheyne Row, Chelsea / London. MS: NLS 611. 139. Hitherto unpbd.

1. Incarnation of the second god of the Hindu triad.

leave John to talk (*ach Gott!*)—and write one word to my poor Goody to this effect. God bless her, poor little bairn; she is too far away from me tonight.

Our expedition over Snowdon was a most laborious walk of 14 miles; Snowdon consists, I think, of some six or seven circular winding ridges of slate precipices, soaring beyond the eagles flight; scraggy sloping on one side, sheer down on the other: the mist met us today about 1000 feet from the top, and one might as well have been in the Thames Tunnel for any sight![2] We had a guide (for the sake of Teangleg's[3] carpetbag;—I carry no luggage but a razor, shavingbrush, shirt and pocket comb): we met at the top of the mountain two other large parties from opposite sides; like *ghosts* of parties escorted by their Charons:[4] it was very strange, almost ghastly; I shall always remember that bitter windy mist on the pinnacle of Britain,—and will *tell* Goody all about it, at some better time.

The Day after tomorrow, however, I mean to get upon the Coach roof; go along the North Coast *till I come in contact with a Liverpool Steamer;* and there embark, and in Heaven's name end these tumblings and tourifyings: I find I do not at bottom care two pence for all the picturesqueness in the world; and really have *done* my picturesque affairs to a very tolerable extent now, I think. Heaven help us!

What Goody is to do; where *she* to go for a little country air? Dearest, there is nothing here I can invite thee to: canst thou contrive aught for thyself? Sussex coast with Macreadys, Suffolk with Bullers; anywhere, anyhow in honesty:—alas, in this endless whirl I cannot get a moment to consider of anything whatever. It does become *too much.* I send thee my love and my prayers. Good be ever with thee Dearest.

I hope to find a Letter in Liverpool: shall I not? No such *Letters* as these of mine were ever written before by any rational man—eheu [alas]!

T C

2. Tunnel under the Thames in London, connecting Wapping on the N bank to Rotherhithe on the S; constructed, 1825–43, originally for foot passengers but later a railway tunnel.

3. Variant of John Carlyle's nickname, Tongleg.

4. Ferryman of the dead over the Styx.

JWC TO TC

Friday [28 July 1843]

Dearest

I write to you *in the vague* as you desired that I would—tho it would have suited my practical spirit better to have waited until you "found a fixed point"—

Well! the most remarkable thing I have to tell you is that I—little I—have been to Tunbridge Wells!! Went and came in the same day!—you may guess then with what *Spirit* of locomotion— —John Sterling came in the beginning of the week—and since then has been I am sure in one thousand on[e][1] hundred cabs and other vehicles to say the least— He was going to Tunbridge to visit M*rs* Prior, and M*rs* Prior—having as I told you conceived a wonderful liking for me he proposed to take me with him—so we left this at seven oclock yesterday morning and were at Tunbridge by half after nine! and at the Wells an hour after that[2]—M*rs* Prior gave us the most animated welcome—an early dinner served on plate—at the most magnificent Hotel imagination ever painted to itself, and drove us back to Tunbridge in her carriage. I should detest *living* at Tunbridge Wells—even in that most magnificent Hotel! but it was charming to look at with all its "curiosities and niceties"[3] for a few hours. and the drive from the Wells to Tunbridge was really as picturesque as the lover of nature (not I) could possibly desire. John is back again today to Ventnor—whither I could not accompany him for plenty of good reasons—first because my chaos is not settled yet—and still more final—"the Maurices" are going to ruralize with him for a month on their own suggestion!— He poor fellow candidly acknowledge[d][4] that he dreaded it as a considerable of a *bore*—

JWC-TC, [28 July]. Addr: Care of Miss J. Welsh / 20 Maryland Street / Liverpool. PM: 28 July 1843. MS: NLS 602.121; longhand copy with TC's notes: Berg. Pbd: A. Carlyle, *NLM* 1:125–28 inc. On the envelope TC noted: "28 july, 1843 / Varnhagen, Horse-buyer, &c (*not,*—or / only *part?.*"

1. Letter omitted.

2. Evidently JWC and Sterling went by rail to Tonbridge, 30 mi. SE of London, and then on another 5 mi. S to Tunbridge Wells.

3. Coterie speech. " 'Curiosities and niceties of a civilised house.'—Old phrase of my father's" (TC's note in Froude, *LM* 3:221).

4. Letter omitted. Anna and F. D. Maurice. Frederick Maurice writes: "Sterling had now settled . . . in the Isle of Wight. . . . [A] change . . . had been taking place in the relations between Sterling and my father. On this subject my father bitterly reproached himself throughout life. Sterling had more and more passed under Mr. Carlyle's influence, and as more and more his opinions and my father's diverged, my father's anxiety and distress at the change in his friend's views of life, drove him again and again into indignant protest, and, as he thought afterwards, into fierceness of expression that he could not excuse. . . . Always his conscience seems to have smitten him for not having been sufficiently gentle, suffi-

A thing almost equal in energy I have to do this very day viz: to *dine* with the Kay Shuttleworths at seven oclock![5]— I am to meet M*rs* Austin[6] who is here for a little while and look forward to the whole thing with a sacred shudder— A dinner is hard enough on me at any time— but on my *own* responsibility—without the Lion to take the responsibility quite off my weak shoulders "terrible is the thought to me"— however the Lady came herself and pressed so hard—and we had used them so scurvily hitherto that I had not force of character enough to say *no*—to mend the matter I have got a stiff shoulder—but I will try the showerbath on it before dinner time— All these Daniels too called again[7] the other day when I was out and left the most magnificent bouquet worthy of the garden of Eden! with many kind messages—so you see I am popular in your absence—

But I must not forget to tell you of another visitor whom I was quite sorry you did not see—a Prussian General officer sent by Varnhagen von Ense[8]— He sent in his card and letter of introducty[9] begging to know when you would return—so recognising Varnhagen's writing I of course invited him in and received him in my choicest mood[10]—a thing not ill to do the man being the very beau ideal of a Prussian Officer—so highbred and intelligent and *brave* looking— He is here buying horses for the army—his faculty of English was not great but happily little Bölte was here at the time, come to have tea with me, and he knew some of her relations in the army, and it was "a

ciently sympathetic, with not having helped instead of having disputed with his friend" (*Life of Frederick Dennison Maurice* [1884] 1:345). Nevertheless, the rift was there; Maurice was to regret TC's biography of Sterling; and, in a letter to Charles Kingsley, he later described his distress at a dinner-party dispute about Emerson among himself, TC, and Sterling, viz., about "the creation of all things and all substances by man's thought" (*Life* 1:346). For Maurice's prickliness, and for this argument, see also 10:245, 252. He defended TC for attacking the clergy, which he thought good "for us": "I cannot find that Carlyle leads us directly to a centre; but I do find that he makes us despair for want of one, and that he expresses the indirect wailings of men in search of it better than all the other writers of the day." At this time, in 1843, after the death of Susannah Sterling (who was Anna Maurice's sister), the Maurices were "more than ever anxious . . . to comfort Sterling . . . and to be of help to the little ones. Great part of the summer was spent with them" (*Life* 1:352, 348, and 347).

5. James Phillips Kay Shuttleworth (1804–77; *DNB*), educationist, and his wife, Janet (d. 1872); see 14:194.

6. Sarah Austin.

7. See JWC to TC, 14 [July].

8. Wilhelm von Willisen (1790–1879), Prussian general and military author; on Blücher's staff, 1815; had been prof. of military history at the Berlin military academy; apptd. to the Fifth Corps at Posen, 1840; major-gen., 1843. Bunsen had invited TC to meet Willisen; see TC to JAC, 13 July.

9. Thus in MS.

10. Coterie speech; see 4:424.

mutual strike" between them— He is a man about fifty I should think and stands some six feet two inches high—"plumb and more than plumb"[11] Considering what I could do for him I could think of nothing better than sending Krasinski—who could *speak* german and is a *gentleman* at least and *idle* to offer him any services in the way of pointing out *sights* &c—but he was only to be two or three days here at present and then for a week after the first of August— Krasinski waited on him immediately on receiving my note[12]—and would show him at least that I wished to be civil if I knew how— He told Miss Bolte that Varnhagen had lent him your *Past & Present* to read on the journey—and that he had left it in the Derby Coach! (strange fate for the book sent to Berlin!—) he "was afraid to go back without it for tho' he had bought another copy here Varnhagen would so regret the loss of the inscription— Could you not write an inscription on a blank page and send it to the General's address for him to paste on[13]—

Another German also sent by Varnhagen came within the same twenty-four hours and left a small book and another letter[14]—but I did not see *him* as he went away when he had handed in his documents—

Besides my own work I have a deal to do in fitting out Juliet Mudie just now with all the necessaries of "a clothed animal"—which are amazingly manifold when one has to commence from the very shift—the poor girl is here helping me to sew—and leaves for Manchester on Saturday week—where I have now very little doubt she will do extremely well—since she came this last time under these new promising circumstances she looks quite a different creature—so active and willing and *happy*—her countenance that was so stern is become quite radiant—and her gratitude for leave to be *a nursery maid* shows by its intensity what misery she must have endured in her late position—there is hopes of the other two children being placed thro Krasinskis friend Mrs Byson[15]—and then the Mother may take a *situation* herself or drown herself if she like for me—

11. Coterie speech.

12. The *Examiner*, 5 Aug., reported: "We noticed very favourably, last year, Count Krasinski's work on the *Reformation in Poland*. It is a book of an admirable spirit—embodying the noblest arguments, and breathing the most ardent hopes, for Polish nationality and independence. We now observe, with singular pleasure, that the King of Prussia has singled out the author for a mark of special favour and approval. We hail it as a good omen for the Polish cause in Prussia."

13. "I well remember all this of the Prussn Officer &c; his loss of the *Past & Present* 'Inscriptn' was ingeniously supplied,—(wrote a new inscriptn, namely, and sent it to the Publishr to be bound with a new Copy!)— The Kay Shuttlth Dinner (whh follows in next Letter) I also remembr well" (TC's note).

14. Unidentified. For the book, *Leitfaden zur Nordischen Alterthumskunde*, see JWC to TC, [13 Aug.].

15. Unidentified.

Bless you—I must not scribble any more at present for several things are awaiting my legislation

Ever your affectionate / Jane Carlyle

TC TO JEANNIE WELSH

Tremadoc, Carnarvonshire,
29 July, 1843.

Dear Cousin Jeannie,—We have got across Snowdon, and proceeded under various auspices, especially under very bad weather, thus far; and now to-morrow morning we are about to turn round for Carnarvon, and after that towards Liverpool; where finally we hope to arrive by the *Ayrshire Lassie* or some other obliging steamer on the evening of Monday. We will come direct to Maryland Street, and the kind little cousin there. Our Doctor, I believe, will go back to his "Feathers,"[1] and I at present seem to feel as if I should rest better in my big room for a pair of days than anywhere else. We shall have to go to the Paulets—could you undertake to appoint Tuesday for that, or Wednesday at latest? I think the Annan steamer sails about Thursday. I am horribly tired of tourifying, and want immensely to be at rest somewhere.

I add not another word this night, but my love to Cousin Jeannie, and all the other cousins, and am always the good Baby's

Most devoted
T. Carlyle

We are in the house of Mr. Chorley here, who sits looking at me while I write.

TC TO JWC

Carnarvon, Uxbridge Arms Inn
Sunday july 30, 1843—

My dear Bairn,

Here we are at last, out of the Hills and the rain-torrents and confusions; quietly waiting for the Welsh Tour's terminating—by a Steamer to Liverpool tomorrow morning. Thank Heaven! Not that all has not

TC-JW, 29 July. Pbd: Elizabeth Garrett Bell. "A 'Not Unblessed Pilgrimage.' The Carlyles' Married Life," *Cornhill Magazine*, n.s. 57 (1924):66.

1. Hotel.

TC-JWC, 30 July. Addr: 5. Cheyne Row, / Chelsea / London. MS: NLS 611. 140. Hitherto unpbd.

been what they call "well"; but "well" in the travelling way is not near good enough for a poor wretch like me. I have been awake at all hours from 3 to 6; I have &c &c: in fine, thank God here I am!

We left Chorley's this morning at seven; the good Chorley accompanying us with smiles and benedictions to the side of the Coach; a Mackintosh Cape too was not the least of his favours. He is the cheeriest, kindliest, [beste?]-humoured little man I have for many a day fallen in with; he quite gained my heart by these qualities,—he had well nigh induced me to take up my autumnal *residence* in a Lodging in his Village, just over the way from him: it was very cheap, room in it for Goody and Ellen;[1] decent people;—cheap, clean, but very *damp*, very distant (for some of the parties): I do not think it is likely *you* will say yea; tho' I did promise to consult you! The region is rocky, picturesque, but barren, weedy; the natives have almost no English, and I doubt extremely little sense;—moreover, it seems and is said to be the dreadfullest place for *wet* that could anywhere be met with; Dumfriesshire a mere Sahara to it. Tremadoc will not do, will it? I was for trying it a week on my own basis; but Jack would not (having the perpetual motion in him), so it is left behind us over the slate hills. The women Chorleys are going thither early next week: does that make you shriek at the idea!— Well, there is something right good in that worthy little Chorley; I shall long remember him as the pleasantest thing I have seen in Wales. Blessed be Heaven however there is a Liverpool Steamer tomorrow morning: perhaps I shall get some sleep in my old bed there;—at all events I shall get to Annandale in the course of the week, and there—! Ah me!—

There will be a Letter from thee tomorrow in Baby's hands;[2] perhaps more than one. I do want much to hear about all thy *outs* and thy *ins*. My poor Goody!— As for myself I will not try to write any farther in these present circumstances, where pen, place, head, hand, paper and ink are all against me. I should like well to hear that the Painting of the House was done, and Goody free for some country or sea-side expedition, where I might be in waiting for her, or join her, or in some way see the face of her again!

I wrote to Jeannie yesterday; heralding our advent: she will get the Letter tomorrow morning.— Here is dinner! Adieu, adieu.

Thine ever / T. Carlyle

1. Helen Mitchell.
2. Jeannie Welsh's.

TC TO MARGARET A. CARLYLE

Maryland Street, Liverpool
Monday Evg 31 july, 1843–

My dear Mother,

Jack and I are safe home from Wales about an hour ago; that is all I *can* find room to say today, as my hand is quite out of order, and the Post is departing. You shall hear more either tomorrow or next day. Jack is gone back to the Inn he lodged at; I am here but have yet seen nobody. They will all be here at dinner.—— I think of getting over to Annandale this week; Jack does not seem certain yet what he will do.

Here *he* is at this moment! I add not a word more, but my love and regards to one and all.

Good day dear Mother.

Ever your affectionate
T. Carlyle

JWC TO TC

Monday night [31 July 1843]

Dearest

The Postman presented me your letter tonight in Cheyne Walk with a bow extraordinary– He is a jewel of a Postman–whenever he has put a letter from *you* into the box he both *knocks* and *rings* that not a moment may be lost in taking possession of it–in acknowledgement whereof I crossed the street one day, when Cuttikins[1] who staid a week and returned twice was with me, and at that moment doing the impossible to be entertaining–for the purpose of saluting his (the postmans) Baby the which he was carrying out for an airing–the rage of Cuttikins at this interruption was considerable–he looked at me as if he could have eaten me raw and remarked with a concentrated spleen–"Well I *must* say never did I see any human being so improved in *amiability* as *you* are!– Every *body*–and every *thing* seems to be honoured with a particular affection from you!" every THING thought I except *you*–but I contented myself with saying "isnt it a darling baby?" Poor Cuttikins his Aunt did not die–so he is gone with the

TC-MAC, 31 July. MS: Berg; longhand copy: NLS 521.17. Hitherto unpbd.

JWC-TC, [31 July]. Addr: Care of Miss Welsh / 20 Maryland Street / Liverpool. MS: NLS 602.122; longhand copy with TC's notes: Berg. Pbd: Froude, *LM* 1:212–15 inc.; Bliss, *JWC* 121 inc. TC noted on the envelope: "Chelsea, 1 Aug*t* 1843 / dinner at the Kay Shuttlw*th's;* Terrot, Sterling &c (hardly?)." Mon. was 31 July.

1. "B*p* Terrot" (TC's note).

prospect of alas—of having to *return* ere long— The last day he came John Sterling exploded him in a way that would have done your heart good to see— John looked at me as much as to say "does he bore you?"— and I gave my shoulders a little shrug in the affirmative—whereupon John jumped to his feet and said in a politely under tone as audible however for the Bishop as for me "Well my good friend if you cannot keep your engagement with me, I must go by myself—I am too late already!"—the cool assurance of this speech was inimitable, for I had no engagement in the world with him!—but Terrot suspecting nothing sprang to *his* feet and was off in a minute with apologies for having *detained* me!

Well I actually accomplished my dinner at the Kay Shuttleworths, M*rs* Austin was the only lady at dinner— Old Miss Rogers[2] and a young wersh[3] looking person with her came in the evening,—it was a very lockedjaw-sort of business—Little Helps was there but even *I* could not animate him; he looked pale and as if he had a pain in his stomach— Little Milnes was there and "affable" enough, but evidently overcome with a feeling that weighed on all of us—the feeling of having dropt into a vacuum—there were various other men, a Sir Charles Lemon, Cornwall Lewis,[4] and some half dozen other such insipidities whose names did not fix themselves in my memory— M*rs* Austin was an insupportable bore—she has lost all her *sweet* look and what remains is highly quest[io]nable[5]—she has surely the air of a *retired* unfortunate female, her neck and arms were naked as if she had never eaten of the tree of the knowledge of good and evil! She reminded me forcibly of the Princess Huncamunca[6] as I once saw her represented in a barn. She eat and drank with a certain voracity— *sneezed* once during the dinner, just like a hale old man—"and altogether" nothing could be more ungraceful—more unfeminine than her whole bearing— She talked a deal about America and her *poverty* with exquisite bad taste— Indeed she was every way a displeasing spectacle to me[7]—

2. Probably Sarah Rogers (1772–1854), Samuel Rogers's sister; see 12:48.
3. "Waterish; an emphatic Scotch word" (TC's note).
4. Sir Charles Lemon (1784–1868), bart., of Carclew, Cornwall; M.P. for West Cornwall, 1832–41, 1842–57; a founder of the Statistical Society, 1834. George Cornewall Lewis (1806–63; *DNB*), politician and author; see 9:52.
5. Letters omitted.
6. King Arthur's da. and Tom Thumb's wife in Fielding, *Tom Thumb the Great* (1731).
7. Sarah Austin had written to a friend, 10 June: "My own wishes, however, point much more to *rest* and a cottage in England, than to new experiments on Society, new ground to take up in life. I . . . am far from sharing my dear part-

Mazzini's visit to Lady Baring (as he calls her)[8] went off wonderfully well. I am afraid my dear this Lady Baring of yours and his and John Mill's and everybody's is an arch coquette—she seems to have played her cards with Mazzini really too well—she talked to him with the highest commendations of George Sand—expressed the utmost longing to read the new edition of Lelia[9]—nay she made him "a mysterious signal with her eyes having first looked two three times towards John Mill and her husband," clearly intimating that she had something to tell him about *Nice*[10] which they were not to hear—and when she could not make him understand she "shook her head impatiently"—"which from a *woman,* especially in your england, was—what shall I say—*confidential* upon MY honour"— I think it was—"John Mill appeared to be *loving* her very much, and taking great pains to show her that his opinions were the right ones" By the way do you know that Mill considers Robespierre "the greatest man that ever lived" his speeches far surpassing Demosthenes's[11]— He begins to be too absurd that John Mill! I heard Milnes saying at the Shuttleworths that "Lord

---

ner's disgust with mankind, odious as many sides of them are. . . . I shall certainly not leave Lucie, and she will probably stay here till the end of July" (Janet Ross, *Three Generations of Englishwomen* [1888] 1:187). She had apparently returned to England with her da., Lucie Duff Gordon, and her grandda., Janet: "I am the most foolish of grandmothers" (1:185). On 25 Oct. she wrote that she had been engaged by Longmans to trans. L. von Ranke, *Deutsche Geschichte im Zeitalter der Reformation,* 5 vols. (Berlin, 1839–43): "I could doubtless gain much more money and fame by lighter work. But you know my dislike to encounter the public in my own person, my distrust of myself, and my liking for steady *respectable* work. . . . I welcome the forced absorption in drudgery as a potent reason against painful meditations. My nouns and adverbs keep me out of myself, and the honest pride of earning is also a resource against the worst pictures of poverty" (J. Ross 1:189).

8. Mazzini told his mother, 8 May, that he had been asked to give private lessons in Italian lit. to Lady Harriet; by 21 May he had decided to accept but was hesitant as he had no evening wear and did not want to go in the wrong clothes lest it be taken as a brash republican gesture. The meeting finally took place, 26 July, in a mutual acquaintance's house (not named), both Lady Harriet and her husband being very friendly. He found her well educated and open-minded, and they joked together, he warning her to be careful since she might suffer in the early stages of a revolution (*Scritti de Mazzini* [Imola, 1916] 24:120, 133, 204).

9. George Sand had pbd. a new and enlarged edn. of *Lélia* (1833) in 1839.

10. Presumably the town in SE France. Froude, *LM,* leaves a blank.

11. Mill had written to TC himself, 2 Feb. 1833, to protest the opinion of many of the contemporaries of the French revolutionist Maximilien Robespierre (1758–94) that he was a mediocre man, declaring that "it was always a puzzle to me how a mediocre man could remain master of the field among so many competitors, until I read some of his speeches and then saw that he was by far the most *skilful* of the combatants in every sense of the word" (Mineka 12:139).

Ashley was the greatest man alive;—he was the only man that Carlyle *praised* in his book—"[12] I dare say he knew I was overhearing him "the little *Tick*"!

I am quite rid of the paint-smell now—but I have the white-washer coming again tomorrow—I could not turn up the low room till the upstairs one was in some sort habitable again—and all the last week nothing could be got on with owing to Pearson's absence—it is surprising how much easier it is to pull down things than to put them up again—

No—certainly your "damp" cottage[13] with "incessent rains" and the female Chorleys for neighbours is anything but inviting— I *do* scream at the idea—never mind *me* dearest—try to get the most good of the country that can be got for yourself— *I* do not care a farthing for the *country* air—and am busier here than I could be anywhere else— Besides I should like to go to Liverpool when my Uncle returns—and perhaps I shall go with old Sterling to Ryde[14] for a few days next week— He is very feeble become and very subdued—I shall be of great comfort to him and he has no longer the strength in him to *bore* anybody— The Maurices make Ventnor[15] out of the question—but I must have the carpets down &c &c before I go anywhere—the rest of my work—the needlework—could lie over a few days without detriment

I must enclose you a touching document which came today in case it admits of any '*appeal*';[16] but I suppose not— Actually—Juliet Mudie is filling all the lower premises with singing!— Will you tell my

12. Anthony Ashley Cooper (1801–85; *DNB*), Lord Ashley; 7th earl of Shaftesbury, 1851; philanthropist and reformer who brought about many improvements in the conditions of coal miners and working children. There is no direct reference to Lord Ashley in *Past and Present,* although there may be veiled allusions to him as one of the protectors of the people against the exploitation of manufacturers. Milnes's own evaluation of *Past and Present* was that TC had written a book "which is, as Mademoiselle Déjazet says of a certain passion, 'toujours la même et toujours naïve [always the same and always naive].' It would be very dangerous if turned into the vernacular and generally read. It is most unjust and insulting to all but the utterly ignorant and helpless, calling Peel 'Sir Jabez Windbag,' and every attempt at legislation or good of any kind a 'Morrison's pill.' It has sold very well; and the author looks a little fatter and better for it" (Reid, *RMM* 1:293). Harriet Martineau expressed similar views to Fanny Wedgwood: "*very* bad, insolent, bitter, one-sided, full of weary repetitions. . . . His injustice to the aristocracy is shameful,—and his conceit . . . . C. will not stop, but say the same things over and over (till he dies,) once a year" (*Harriet Martineau's Letters to Fanny Wedgwood* 56).

13. "Some Lancashire or Welsh Project, I suppose, wh*h* did not take effect, and is forgotten" (TC's note). For the suggested cottage at Tremadoc, see TC to JWC, 30 July.

14. Isle of Wight, a popular watering place.

15. On the Isle of Wight, where John Sterling now lived.

16. An income tax demand.

darling Babbie with truest love that if she will but be patient a very little longer our letter account shall be balanced to her entire satisfaction—and Lord bless me I had so nearly forgot to do what I undertook—that Geerpole Marriotti called here on Saturday forenoon to beg from you an introduction to Nickison[17]—he having written some little thing for the magazine "of course he does not ask you to recommend what you never read, but merely to introduce him—and to request that his paper may be *looked* at—" Pray send him your card with a word on it—I hate the creature but I dare say he is ill enough off—

I shall leave this open till I see if tomorrow brings me anything—but it was surest to write tonight—tomorrow I have to go to the City for some ready-made nightshifts for Juliet—

Tuesday morning

I have your letter—I think I have received them all—the impatient note was written just when you were leaving Liverpool[18]—Your own / J C

17. " 'Have ye ever sich a thing as a gearpoule?' asked eagerly an Irish Emig*t* once at Ecclefechan, to the wonder of his neighbours there.—" (TC's note); cf. JWC to JW, 8 Jan. " 'Mariotti,' had been introduced by Mazzini, who [listened?] with*t* loving him; his real name was *Gallenga,*—a very *fanatic* of vanity and the impatience to be known" (TC's note). Luigi Mariotti, pseud. of Antonio Carlo Napoleone Gallenga (1810–95; *DNB*), Italian educationist, journalist, and politician living in exile in London; see 15:118–19. " 'Nick*n*' was Booksell*r* Fraser's successor" (TC's note). Mariotti had contrib. "The Age We Live In" to *Fraser's*, 24 (July 1841):1–15, before Fraser's death. His next contrib. was "Bull and Nongtongpaw," 30 (Oct. 1844):418–26.

18. "Supr*a* (79a) N*o* 80" (TC's note), referring to JWC to TC, 26 July.